HEAVEN'S WRATH

New Netherland Institute
Exploring America's Dutch Heritage

For more than three decades, the New Netherland Institute (NNI)—an independent, nonprofit organization—has cast light on America's Dutch roots. Through its support of the translation and publication of New Netherland's records and its various educational and public programs, NNI promotes historical scholarship on and popular appreciation of the seventeenth-century Dutch mid-Atlantic colony. More information about NNI can be found at newnetherlandinstitute.org.

HEAVEN'S WRATH

THE PROTESTANT REFORMATION AND THE DUTCH WEST INDIA COMPANY IN THE ATLANTIC WORLD

D. L. NOORLANDER

CORNELL UNIVERSITY PRESS
Ithaca and London

Published in Association with the New Netherland Institute

Open access edition funded by the National Endowment
for the Humanities.

First published 2019 by Cornell University Press

Library of Congress Cataloging-in-Publication Data

Names: Noorlander, D. L., author.
Title: Heaven's wrath : the Protestant Reformation and
    the Dutch West India Company in the Atlantic world /
    D. L. Noorlander.
Description: Ithaca : Cornell University Press, 2019. |
    Series: New Netherland Institute studies | "Published
    in association with the New Netherland Institute." |
    Includes bibliographical references and index.
Identifiers: LCCN 2018060433 (print) | LCCN 2019000906
    (ebook) | ISBN 9781501740329 (ret) |
    ISBN 9781501740336 (pdf) | ISBN 9780801453632
    (cloth : alk. paper)
Subjects: LCSH: Reformed Church—Netherlands—
    History. | Calvinism—Netherlands—History. |
    West-Indische Compagnie (Netherlands)—History. |
    Reformed Church—America—History. | Dutch—
    Africa, West—History. | Netherlands—Colonies—
    America. | Capitalism—Religious aspects—Protestant
    churches.
Classification: LCC BX9474.3 (ebook) | LCC BX9474.3
    .N66 2019 (print) | DDC 284/.2492—dc23
LC record available at https://lccn.loc.gov/2018060433

Cover image: Detail from *Battle of Guararapes* by Victor
Meirelles. Oil on canvas, 1879. Courtesy of the Museu
Nacional de Belas Artes, Rio de Janeiro.

CONTENTS

Acknowledgments

I would like to thank the many people and institutions who made this book possible. My MA adviser at the University of Utah, Eric Hinderaker, introduced me to the field of Atlantic history, and he was the first to suggest that I apply for the PhD program and work with Alison Games at Georgetown University. Because I had studied English as an undergraduate student, it was also with Dr. Hinderaker that I first started thinking seriously about history and about the Dutch place in early America. I owe him a huge debt for getting me started on my current path.

I also owe a debt to Alison Games and the other members of my dissertation committee at Georgetown University: Adam Rothman, Amy Leonard, and (at Clark University) Wim Klooster. Their suggestions, insights, and critiques were invaluable. They offered encouragement and countless other types of support as I moved from proposal to dissertation, from dissertation to book, and from graduate student to professor. During my Georgetown years (and my year of intensive research in the Netherlands) I also enjoyed assistance from the Interlibrary Loan office at Georgetown's Lauinger Library, the Georgetown History Department, the Graduate School of Arts and Sciences, the International Seminar on the History of the Atlantic World at Harvard University, and, most critical for my material needs, the U.S. Fulbright Program and Netherland-America Foundation. I could not have conducted the necessary research without their assistance. Also very helpful were the many archivists and librarians in the Netherlands who put up with my endless questions and requests. Individual archives and libraries are too many to list here, but I should mention the Stadsarchief Amsterdam, the Nationaal Archief in The Hague, and the New York State Archives in Albany as especially important for my research.

I don't know how I would have survived my first months in Holland without Mark and Debby Gunderman. Thank you for the accommodations, rides, food, gifts, friendship, and everything else. Since that time I have also received support of one kind or another from Beloit College, SUNY Oneonta, the National Endowment for the Humanities, and the New Netherland Institute. My colleagues at SUNY Oneonta had the faith to hire me in 2013, and I have received both moral and material support from them for the completion of this book. Just down the road from Oneonta, the New Netherland Institute deserves recognition in probably most good projects on the Dutch in America. In this case, NNI provided support to present aspects of my research at different meetings and conferences through the years, and they recently partnered with Cornell University Press to help fund this and other monographs on the Dutch in the future. I thank them for that decision, and I thank the editors, staff, and anonymous readers from Cornell University Press for all their help and suggestions. Michael McGandy was a font of wisdom and patience as I navigated the many challenges of the long writing and publishing process. If there is anything good in this book, credit belongs partly to him and partly to the many others mentioned here. If there are any errors, they are mine and mine alone.

Finally, I must thank my wife, children, parents, siblings, and friends outside of academia for their love and encouragement. My wife, Kim, and our four children have been shockingly good-natured and accepting of our many scary adventures and endless life of relocation and deprivation. There are no words that could possibly capture my deep gratitude and love for you.

HEAVEN'S WRATH

Introduction

The Role of Reformed Christianity in the Commercial and Colonial Endeavors of the Dutch Golden Age

King Charles X of Sweden thought he knew the culture and character of his European neighbors to the southwest. "Here is your religion," he once said to a Dutch envoy, exhibiting a large silver coin: "You serve only your Idol, which is Commerce."[1] Likewise, the English leader Oliver Cromwell purportedly grumbled that the Dutch loved gold more than God after they rejected an English alliance in 1651.[2] Cromwell's countryman, Governor Thomas Lynch of Jamaica, revealed his own cranky, pithy version of the Dutch worldview when he said that "Jesus Christ was good, but trade was better."[3] Again and again, frustrated and bemused friends and enemies claimed that Dutch devotion centered on profits rather than God, that wealth and commerce always trumped religion in the Netherlands.

If the Dutch disliked these pompous lectures, they rarely said so, maybe because of some precocious, entrepreneurial sense that the customer is always right. In truth, contemporaries distrusted and disapproved of them for reasons that had little to do with faith. Nor is it likely that their hypocritical critics—in this case a monarch, a member of the English gentry, and the complicit governor of an infamous pirate haven—appreciated their own wealth any less. They just acquired it differently. Their disdain might reflect the simple misgiving and distrust that people often harbor for competitors. Or it might reflect a clumsy effort to identify and explain their differences, to understand a Dutch economy and state whose basic characteristics will feel more familiar to today's readers than they did to most Europeans at the time. Together the dispersal of power in the Dutch Republic, its merchant rulers, its social mobility and access to office, and the simplicity of Dutch political culture in general offered a sharp contrast and a subtle challenge to the growing pomp and spectacle of monarchical neighbors.[4]

The Republic was the first hegemonic power in the capitalist world economy, "the first modern economy."[5] Beginning in about 1590 and continuing through the seventeenth century, the Dutch enjoyed high wages and employment rates. Situated at the mouth of major rivers like the Rhine, which carried commerce to and from central Europe, they also traded with nearby England, France, and the Baltic states. Their soil was never the finest quality, but even that worked to Dutch advantage: nobles and ecclesiastical officials in the Middle Ages had taken less interest in the Low Countries, giving generous terms to peasant farmers to colonize the newly drained lands. By the early modern period the peasantry owned much of the land outright and people could buy and sell property with relative ease. Regular imports and a fluid land market, unencumbered by the commons, allowed them to specialize in single commodities, for they could now buy the grain and other needs that farmers elsewhere had to grow or make for themselves.[6]

Agricultural specialization and urbanization mirrored the rise of various industries, including dairy, textiles, soap, beer, pipes, munitions, paper, books, and shipbuilding. Dutch merchants brought gold and ivory from West Africa, silver from Spanish America and Japan, and tobacco, sugar, and other new goods to the Netherlands, then reexported them alongside Dutch manufactures throughout Europe. As the continent's leading trade entrepôt, Amsterdam became a financial center as well, offering marine insurance and other products that diversified risk and lowered costs. At one of the world's first stock exchanges, one could bet on the outcome of almost any event and buy shares in corporations like the Dutch East India Company (VOC) and the Dutch West India Company (WIC).[7] The city's exchange bank facilitated payments and issued the most dependable money in Europe. The Dutch commanded high prices for quality goods, but technological efficiency and cheap credit resulted in low freight rates. When they chose to do so, they could flood a market with reduced merchandise and undercut rivals who simply couldn't compete at the same level.

Given these economic developments and advantages, is it any wonder that even their allies regarded the Dutch with envy and scorn, that contemporaries like Oliver Cromwell and King Charles X questioned the Dutch commitment to everything but the almighty guilder? When former allies became enemies on the battlefield, the rhetoric could reach whole new extremes. Then the lectures about Dutch greed and false worship became unambiguous expressions of enmity, even more prejudiced and imaginative than before. During the First Anglo-Dutch War (1652–1654), one anonymous Englishman took great delight in describing his theory that the Dutch were "descended from a horse-turd, which was enclosed in a butter-box." The diarist Samuel Pepys wrote more bluntly during the second war (1665–1667) that "the Devil shits Dutchmen."[8]

The relationship between faith, worship, and the emerging capitalist economy is no less puzzling today, more than four hundred years after their fellow Europeans first accused Dutch merchants of misplaced devotion.[9] This book is about Dutch expansion in the seventeenth-century Atlantic world, not capitalism or modernity per se. But the projection of Dutch power to Africa and America under the West India Company fostered economic development, and the company is an obvious potential subject in any discussion about religion and affluence, especially because—whatever the Swedes and English believed—many Dutch did in fact promote a cultural, religious mission overseas. They could do so because their joint-stock companies, while certainly "modern," were not the simple entities that word might imply. They were not just producers or trading mechanisms, nor were they strictly private. Early modern joint-stock companies employed thousands of sailors and soldiers, waged war on competitors and enemies, established colonial settlements, collected taxes, and wrestled with questions of political, legal, and religious authority. Within their spheres of influence, they bore the same powers and responsibilities as the state. To steal a useful term from the British world, the WIC was "a company-state."[10]

Understanding the role of religion in the commercial and colonial endeavors of the Dutch Golden Age begins with an acknowledgment of the manifold goals and powers of these joint-stock companies. Because the WIC was an extension of the state that created it, it necessarily partnered with the Dutch Reformed Church, which enjoyed a monopoly on public worship in the Netherlands and its colonies. But the church-company relationship wasn't just a thoughtless by-product of corporate organization. Far more than that, the union was strong in this case because of the martial, politically charged times in which the company was born and the Calvinist loyalties of many investors and directors. That context and those influences magnified whatever religious element would have existed in the company anyway, creating religious opportunities and an intense sense of mission for Calvinists in the early Dutch Atlantic. Before expanding on that argument and explaining some of the long-term impacts of the church-company union, I will review a few related theories and alternative points of view.

The historiography on religion and economic development is an old one. Most famously, the sociologist Max Weber argued in *The Protestant Ethic and the Spirit of Capitalism* (1905) that Calvinist doctrines produced the mental conditions or frame of mind amenable to the new economic age, that a belief in predestination encouraged people to work hard and save money as they searched for signs of God's favor in their earthly, secular callings.[11] Though the Weber theory has had a long, controversial life in the English-speaking world, Dutch scholars have never shown much interest in it. In a smattering of articles and chapters over the years they dismiss it because, for example, Weber confused later Protestant beliefs with early Calvinism. They also maintain that Dutch theologians didn't teach or write much about seeking heavenly signs, which is critical for the psychological component of Weber's argument. Perhaps most damning, the Reformed Church opposed lending, usury, and other practices that drove capitalist growth. And some Calvinist ministers expressed discomfort with wealth. Similar to the English and Swedish critics cited above, they taught that riches were potential spiritual dangers and threats to genuine godliness. According to the current consensus, the Dutch flourished *despite* the public church, not because of it.[12]

In the only book-length treatment of the subject in a Dutch context, the influential *Religious Factors in Early Dutch Capitalism* (1967), Jelle Riemersma went beyond a simple discomfort with trade and identified a gradual separation of religion and business between about 1550 and 1650, as if the Dutch came to see business in neutral terms.[13] On the topic of global expansion, Riemersma wrote that "commercial enterprise was no longer seen in relation to an ultimately religious purpose." Modernity meant a "divorce between the pursuit of commerce and that of wider political and religious aims." He contrasted state-sponsored Spanish and Portuguese expansion with the independence of joint-stock companies, whose concerns were "strictly commercial."[14] Similarly, one sometimes reads that the WIC "was organized strictly as a trading and commercial endeavor," that the VOC was a "secular" institution "with no ecclesiastical ties or obligations." Freed from so many burdens, the Dutch could make pragmatic, rational choices in the name of profit. Instead of losing money to "ecclesiastical or empirical purposes, as was often the case with the Spanish," the Dutch could reinvest their earnings.[15]

The longtime focus on trade tends to foster an essentialist imperial identity that strips Dutch expansion of other elements and leaves the Dutch without any meaningful ideologies, religious or otherwise. After all, they were an "alongshore folk" and theirs was a "commercial empire."[16] The reality behind these statements is that, because the Republic was small and prosperous, Dutch colonies struggled to attract sufficient numbers of people. The WIC's late arrival in the Atlantic world, its years of privateering, and the hostile, un-healthy climates it encountered in some regions also played a part in reduc-ing the Dutch influence and Dutch presence in the long term. However, as I demonstrate below, at different times and places the Dutch engaged in activi-ties and shared and borrowed ideas that are sloppily labeled English, Span-ish, and French in other contexts. No one had a monopoly on any one plan or practice. Expansion was experimental and diverse. The experience itself could either create differences among Europeans or act as an equalizer, de-pending on the specific conditions in each locale.[17]

Related to Riemersma's argument about a "divorce" between religion and business in the Netherlands, the following are five of the most persistent claims about Dutch expansion: First, WIC directors and merchants were indifferent to religious questions and, in the interest of profit, they neglected ecclesiasti-cal needs abroad. Second, Dutch colonies, such as they were, lacked European institutions. Under company government, they were mostly glorified trading posts.[18] Third, to cut costs and find submissive, pliant clergy, both companies hired incompetent men: uneducated, inefficient, and lazy. Fourth, the clergy's main purpose was to serve company employees in *handelskerken* ("trade churches") in Dutch forts and ships.[19] And in the same vein, fifth, the Dutch showed no interest in the souls of indigenous people. Detached from the af-fairs of church and state in quasi-private institutions, they could ignore other distractions and concentrate on trade. Often compared with pious neighbors like Portuguese Jesuits in Asia and, for so long in the colonial American con-text, New England Puritans, the "businesslike Dutchmen" begin to seem rather single-minded. They did not allegedly care about dogmatic differences nor spread their religion; they found the union of mission and commerce "entirely strange."[20]

W. J. van Hoboken created a counternarrative in a widely read essay in the 1960s, arguing that the WIC was a Calvinist institution, a company with sig-nificant religious and political aims because so many of its directors were migrants from the southern Netherlands and refugees of war.[21] But Van Hoboken did not explore the implications of his thesis afterward, and he was ignored or criticized for decades for reasons I have already described. Com-pany directors were only concerned with profit, wrote his first critic, J. G. van Dillen: "Their deeds testify more of greed than of a Calvinist philosophy of life." Van Dillen explained that every director loved silver, but they expended little effort on missionary work and most of them didn't care about religious dogma.[22] A related argument (and a sixth major theme in the literature on Dutch expansion) is that the directors, like the Dutch in general, were too tolerant to be strict Calvinists. They purportedly winked or connived at nonconformity in their colonies whenever it suited their interests. Siding explicitly with Van Dillen, the historian George Smith divided his 1973 book on New Netherland between "The Church's Point of View" and "The Merchants' Point of View," and he claimed that WIC directors tolerated illicit worship because the colony was "first and foremost a commercial enterprise to which the Reformed faith was appended as a godly afterthought."[23]

Despite their positive contributions and strengths, I read historians like Riemersma, Van Dillen, and Smith and feel that they draw the lines a bit too stark, that the church's concerns about trade and wealth, the fervent pursuit of riches by Dutch merchants, and the independence of joint-stock companies don't merit an interpretation that always seems to diminish religion as a consequential force in the Dutch world. Themes like indifference, neglect, and tolerance, when the latter is just the fruit of self-interest, suggest an *absence* of religion among the seventeenth-century Dutch.[24]

Recognizing and studying the West India Company's social responsibilities and civic agenda became more common in the 1980s and 1990s, in part because of the invaluable Dutch-to-English translations of the New Netherland Project, based at the New York State Library in Albany.[25] Yet the best recent scholarship still tends to come from people who utilize original Dutch sources: Jaap Jacobs, Janny Venema, and Willem Frijhoff (to name a few). Jacobs and Venema don't write strictly about religion, but it occupies a central place in their work because of their interest in colonial society. They deal with Dutch government, politics and social status, the Reformed Church, and related matters, emphasizing the successful plantation and growth of Dutch institutions in New Netherland.[26] Frijhoff argues that, too often, "commercial interest" and "religious concern" are portrayed as polar opposites. In his biography of Everardus Bogardus, who worked as a minister for the WIC in West Africa and New Netherland, Frijhoff provides a fine example of the opportunities available to those who are willing to look at Dutch expansion in fresh ways. He takes a former nobody, the "evidence" for the inferiority of Dutch clergy in New Netherland, and writes nine hundred pages on Bogardus's life and thought, starting with his days as a visionary orphan in Holland.[27]

Looking beyond New Netherland, the only monograph on a religious topic for any other WIC colony is Frans Schalkwijk's book on the Reformed Church in Dutch Brazil, which I use extensively in chapter 5.[28] I also make use of a growing number of regional, oceanic, and global histories that address social questions in the Dutch world more generally. To take just one notable example, in his book *Innocence Abroad* (2001), Benjamin Schmidt shows how the Dutch exploited the image of the tyrannized Native American to foster a sense of "nation-ness" in the young Republic during the war with Spain. Schmidt poses a challenge to the pervasive reputation of indifferent Dutch traders. He argues that they took their imagined responsibilities toward Native Americans quite seriously, believing that in places like Peru and Chile, which they tried on different occasions to conquer, oppressed Indians would flock to their banner, convert to Protestantism, and join the invaders in overthrowing the Spanish. In short, "the Dutch Republic showed itself willing to put its money where its rhetorical mouth was . . . by investing substantial funds and effort into forging an 'alliance' with its American 'brethren.'"[29]

While religion was just one component of the Dutch cultural, imperial mission, in this project I decided to favor the topic because it offers a real contrast and an effective tool for challenging the persistent infatuation with the "commercial character" of Dutch expansion. I chose the framework of Atlantic history in order to set bounds on an otherwise massive undertaking, but more importantly because the western hemisphere is the more neglected of the two in Dutch historiography.[30] Atlantic history also discourages the tendency to generalize about a people based on their lives and work in one region. A broad, comparative analysis will have wider appeal and, I hope, rescue the WIC from New Netherland, whose place in the Dutch world doesn't justify its profound influence on nineteenth- and twentieth-century views of the company.[31]

On the question of whether there was an "Atlantic world," whether that term is an artificial category that works, at most, for the British and Iberians, the Dutch case offers much food for thought.[32] Certainly there are potential problems and pitfalls whenever one employs names or borders that didn't exist at the time of one's study, and in this book I try to deal candidly with matters of international concern. For instance, I show that the Reformed Church saw the companies as similar institutions and participants in a kind of global mission. Some clergy moved from one hemisphere to another, working intermittently for the WIC and VOC over the course of their careers. And various ministers, company directors, merchants, and other personnel were born in foreign countries and continued to have family and business ties in non-Dutch lands. For these reasons, even the word "Dutch" starts to seem inadequate, never mind the controversial "Dutch Atlantic."[33]

More than anything else, however, the Republic's division of the globe between a WIC and VOC demonstrates that the Atlantic world didn't just spring from the minds of modern scholars. The Dutch could have and did briefly consider combining the companies, but they did not.[34] They referred to Asia as the East Indies and everything else as the West Indies, often meaning the Caribbean or Brazil, but sometimes using the term even for Africa. Likewise, the Reformed Church in the province of Zeeland had an East Indies committee and a separate West Indies committee to oversee religious needs in Africa and America. In one regard the Dutch weren't alone: England and France also founded East India Companies. The fact that they didn't do the same for their territory in the western hemisphere, leaving it open to multiple companies, merchants, and proprietors, is a reminder that they also approached the world in two halves. To make the same division today is no artificial, anachronistic imposition; and nowhere is that more clear than in the Dutch case.

Rejecting the spiritual / secular dichotomy and essentialism of some Dutch history writing, I begin with the modest proposition that religion mattered to seventeenth-century peoples, then ask the following questions: How did Reformed Christianity, the public faith of the Netherlands, influence the Dutch experience abroad? How did the Reformed Church and the West India Company interact in each setting? What effect did the major religious issues and divisions of the period have on the WIC and its directors, merchants, employees, settlers, and indigenous allies? Conversely, what effect did expansion have on Dutch Calvinism? If my institutional approach (meaning the attention I give to church and company) seems somewhat conventional, the book is laying a necessary foundation. Based in Dutch-language sources, including letters, diaries, meeting minutes, naval logs, and other manuscripts and printed materials, this is the first comprehensive study of the WIC and Reformed religion during what Wim Klooster calls "the Dutch Moment," or the middle decades of the seventeenth century, when Dutch power and influence in the Atlantic world were at their greatest.[35]

My argument has a few different layers. Most simply, I want to show the strength and immediacy of the church-company relationship: not Jelle Riemersma's "divorce" or George Smith's religion-as-afterthought, but a clear marriage of religion, trade, and expansion. In that regard this study corresponds with research in the English-speaking world on the compatibility of the Puritan religious order with the market economy and the malleability of Puritan religion when it came to questions of profit and trade.[36] In fact, I have found that the Dutch Reformed Church was far more accepting of trade than the anti-Weber literature allows. And by "the church" I don't just mean the clergy. Torn between their international connections and interests and their concerns about wealth, their feelings about expansion were complex. But by focusing only on clerical views of economic developments in a religious community that explicitly rejected authoritarian clergy and required lay participation even in the most powerful ecclesiastical councils, one brings what might be called a Catholic mind-set to a discussion about Protestantism. The clergy's dependence on joint-stock companies and the merchant voice and influence *inside the church* contributed to a remarkably flexible, accommodating attitude toward trade and secular work in general. Dutch Calvinists, both laymen and clergy, could see God's hand everywhere and interpret any respectable activity and occupation as pious.

Among the religious language and ideas that proved important to the WIC in understanding and explaining its work, three rise above the rest in regularity and ubiquity: anti-Catholicism, reformation, and divine sanctification. The first is problematic because there were still many Catholics in the Netherlands in the seventeenth century, and some of them worked for the WIC. However, I will argue that the Calvinist influence was extra strong in the company, which became, as a result, an anti-Catholic, anti-Spanish, anti-Portuguese tool. Calvinists were quite mindful and loud about the WIC extending the wars and social movements of the Protestant Reformation to Africa and America. They wanted to destroy Catholicism, convert and reform preexisting populations, and establish their own institutions and cultural traditions. The word "reformation" could and did contain all of these possibilities. Finally, with "divine sanctification" I'm referring both to the above-mentioned tendency to sacralize secular pursuits and to the idea that the Dutch were, like the ancient Israelites of the Bible, God's chosen people. The combination of WIC warfare with the notions of divine sanctification and the new chosen people made the Old Testament a particularly critical book of scripture for Calvinists in the Dutch Atlantic.

In conclusion I must acknowledge the disagreement and competition in the West India Company over its policies and purpose. I recognize that it had needs and sometimes harbored ideas that competed with the ones outlined here. Company directors from different Dutch cities disagreed about the relationship between migration and trade; they fought over their monopoly rights, the value of individual colonies, and the costs of social planting. A minority of early directors didn't even sympathize with the strict Calvinists in the Netherlands. Whatever else it was, their company was also a business—a profit-seeking corporation—and their religious activities could affect their profits. Perhaps the best way to describe the company's approach to religious matters isn't "neglect," nor was it on the other hand a purely idealistic, blind commitment or consistent religious radicalism. Rather, the WIC had to weigh its many commitments and, in the end, it settled on a supportive yet cost-conscious approach befitting an early modern company-state.

Yet the WIC was still a haven and tool for Calvinists, and those qualities made a difference in the Dutch Atlantic. The *wrath* of the book's title reflects the final argument that, whatever materialistic pragmatism existed among WIC merchants and directors, however much their history, laws, cosmopolitanism, and the church's pan-European, global connections fostered a tolerant quality among the Dutch, religious fears and a constricting Calvinist dog-matism undermined that tolerant streak and had the greater impact on the company. Calvinists saw the wrath of God in the thunder and lightning; they saw it in disease epidemics, Indian attacks, and lost battles. They feared his an-ger when colonists didn't live by every moral precept or worshipped the wrong gods. Calvinists became the instruments of divine wrath in warring with the hated Spanish and punishing sinners and nonconformers in colonial courts, all of which imposed costs—monetary and otherwise—that the small Republic and its people-strapped colonies couldn't afford. At the same time, the Reformed churches of the Netherlands inadvertently contributed to prob-lems later blamed on the WIC because they kept an iron grip on colonial hires, publications, and organization. I contend that, as much as any commer-cial inclination, the expense of the Calvinist-backed war and the church's me-ticulous, worried management of colonial affairs hampered the mission and reduced the size and import of the Dutch Atlantic world.

CHAPTER 1

The Dutch Reformed Church and the World

The International Concerns of the Calvinist Ministry

Amsterdam was growing up. Born as a small fishing village in the flood-prone Low Countries of northern Europe, by 1595 it was a burgeoning metropolis. After centuries of habitation, even the most skilled engineer couldn't relocate the whole place, but the Dutch could make other improvements, and they were doing so with gusto. Just outside the old eastern border, they had created new islands from the marsh, new harbor space and ground for lumber- and shipyards. They reassigned the old yards for residential construction, then extended and thickened the city's walls to encompass and defend all these additions from their enemies. Unfortunately, the hefty new gates and bastions didn't hinder the wind and cold as easily as they thwarted hostile armies. But at least the updated canal system channeled the water more effectively than ever before. And increased private fortunes allowed residents to replace yesterday's wooden structures with snug homes of stone and brick.[1]

Stepping from the damp streets of Amsterdam into the sprawling edifice known simply as the *Oude Kerk* (Old Church), an attentive visitor would have looked around and discovered a different, more controversial transformation. If he had visited the same building, say, thirty years before, and if his memory was very good, he might now notice something about the decorative work: there wasn't much of it. Where was the grand painting that once filled the space behind the high altar, the picture of a bruised and bloodied Jesus Christ, suffering on the cross? Where, for that matter, was the high altar? Most of the art and statuary that had welcomed the imaginary guest during his last visit were gone. In their place he found only naked, marred walls that hinted at another violent story, much more recent than the Crucifixion.[2]

If the new austerity inside the church seemed incompatible with the growing affluence outside, global commerce still found its way indoors from time to time, and not just because the *Oude Kerk* doubled as an early stock exchange.[3] The sounds of trade and science sometimes echoed among the pillars even during Sunday services, depending on the date and place of local ministers in their preaching rotation. Regular listeners had learned to expect anything when Reverend Petrus Plancius took the pulpit. Speaking in a Flemish accent, wearing a long beard to match his long, dark cassock, Plancius might begin like anyone else, reciting the Christian creation story and the fall of man. Soon he was talking about India, then America and Africa. His sermons ranged from the western hemisphere to the East and back again, even beyond this planet to the stars. As subjects for Christian clergy, heaven and creation were not unusual, of course; but the words assumed extra significance in the age of Copernicus and Galileo, the age of Christopher Columbus and Francis Drake. Those thinkers and mariners had opened new worlds of spiritual material for preachers who were willing to use it.[4]

Reverend Plancius wasn't alone among Dutch clergy in his concern for international affairs and his interest in European expansion. Part minister and theologian, part astronomer and cartographer, he was the human counterpart to the multipurpose edifice in which he worked, a new kind of cleric for Amsterdam's rising prominence and commercial might. Exactly how he acquired his particular skills is unclear, though his interest in all things foreign probably had something to do with his mobility and travels: from his birth and upbringing in Flanders to his theological training in England and Germany, from his return to Flanders and his exodus to Holland—Plancius crossed many borders in his life. He had converted to Reformed Christianity when it was still dangerous, when, in the 1550s and 1560s, it was an illegal, underground faith and the relationship between the Dutch and their Spanish overlords had nearly reached a breaking point. He was ordained in 1576 and spent his early career founding and shepherding fledgling congregations in his native province, then fled north, disguised as a soldier, when a Spanish army captured Brussels in 1585. By December of that year he was serving the Dutch Reformed Church in Amsterdam.

Plancius expressed his global concerns in his sermons and in the work he did outside the church. He was a director of the *Oude Compagnie* (Old

Petrus Plancius teaches lessons in navigation from his pulpit in Amsterdam. Originally printed in *De Vyerighe Colom*, by Jacob Aertsz Colom (1652). Courtesy of the Scheepvaartmuseum, Amsterdam.

Company), which would ultimately merge with other firms to form the East India Company, and some of the first Dutch ships that sailed to Asia in the 1590s used his maps and instructions. For more than two decades he taught lessons in navigation, examined potential captains and other officers, inspected naval equipment, and advised Dutch authorities on all matters related to expansion. For good reason, his biographer described him as "the intellectual center of Holland's expeditions to the East and West."[5]

Plancius was unique among ministers in the extent of his extracurricular activities and the depth of his secular expertise. His general curiosity or interest in the wider world—his cosmopolitan worldview—was far more common, shared by clergy and merchant, shopkeeper and artisan alike. No one in Amsterdam could have missed the relationship between the city's ongoing transformation and the harbor, and only a true recluse could have been apathetic. Many Netherlanders also had personal reasons to pay attention. Never mind the simple, terrible excitement of finding continents and cultures that, until recently, were as distant and unimaginable as heaven itself. They had stories like that of Plancius: newcomers and refugees, they might be worried about family and friends living in other lands or family going abroad to work in one of Europe's growing empires.

Beyond these general interests, clergy claimed a special international charge because they were supposed to interpret and communicate all religious matters, and the major political, imperial developments of the time were saturated with religious meaning. It wasn't enough that Spain threatened to overrun the Dutch and reestablish foreign rule; Protestants cared especially that it was *Catholic* Spain and *Catholic* rule. They didn't just fear that Spain and Portugal, united under the Hapsburg Crown, might conquer Europe and the world. The expansive new empires in America and Asia were odious because they spread the wrong faith. The Protestant Reformation and endless wars created a strong anti-Catholic strain that fed and colored global developments, making it easy, even in a land that still had a large Catholic population, to associate "Catholic" with "enemy." Ministers simply built on the predisposition among contemporaries to see life through a spiritual lens and interpret their religion in light of temporal events.

As the Dutch began their own imperial adventures under the aegis of the East India Company (VOC) and West India Company (WIC), Reformed clergy in the Netherlands learned that managing ecclesiastical growth was challenging, often contentious, because they belonged to a new institution with a newly determined and possibly still vulnerable creed. Equally challenging were the tremendous distances between them and the new congregations they were supposed to help found and supervise. Most clergy never served abroad, but they cared enough about exporting their faith to monitor colonial affairs and quarrel about methods and oversight, usually asserting the authority of the churches and councils of the Netherlands over colonial churches and councils. While their obvious intent was to aid and strengthen the religious mission, they produced at the same time a uniquely subordinate, controlled position for colonial clergy in the Dutch Reformed system, sometimes stifling the creation of colonial councils. Amsterdam offered—if not a front-row seat— one of the best places in Europe both to direct and observe these exciting, divisive changes. Its far-flung commercial and financial connections made it a global religious center, as well. From Amsterdam's crowded docks and warehouses, its cold chapels and hard pews, believers watched and waited for the destruction of Catholic power and the triumph of "the true Reformed religion."[6]

The Reformation in the Netherlands

For as long as anyone could remember, the Dutch had been ruled by outsiders: noble families like the Burgundians in the fourteenth and fifteenth centuries, then the Hapsburgs, based in Spain and Austria. Through war and marriage, the Dutch were always part of someone else's kingdom or empire, never the cohesive people implied in convenient terms like "Dutch." In reality, the Netherlands (or Low Countries) were many different provinces, principalities, and city-states, and they sometimes even made war on each other. Whatever unity the Burgundians and Hapsburgs managed to impose, it was a loose, uncomfortable association that the Dutch eventually resisted with violence. Ironically, real unity and international power was only born in reaction to Hapsburg centralization and the loss of local control. The Dutch would live with this tension between local and national, local and international, for most of their history.[7]

Efforts to increase Hapsburg power in the Low Countries were still new when, in 1517, a German priest named Martin Luther inadvertently started the Protestant Reformation by criticizing the Catholic indulgence system, which undermined the true faith-based message of the Gospel, he said, because it linked salvation with money and personal endeavor. He thought salvation came only through God's gift of grace to those who believed, and he worried that in buying indulgences, drawing on the good works of others to escape penance, Christians might come to see *works* rather than *faith* as the source of salvation. Likewise, the long-dead Christian saints whose righteous lives had created this accessible excess of works, this "store of merit," might replace Jesus Christ. Luther's original plan in sharing these ideas was merely to start a discussion and identify potential areas for ecclesiastical reform. In time he grew further and further apart from the Catholic Church, and his message grew to include a critical reassessment of papal power and church government in general.[8]

The Dutch were receptive to these criticisms because they had heard them before. More urban and literate than much of Europe, the Low Countries had always been a place of religious innovation, beginning with a spiritual, educational movement called the *Devotio Moderna* (Modern Devotion) in the late medieval period, continuing through the Renaissance with the reforming impulses of Christian humanism. Some ideas that people now began calling "Lutheran" were actually just iterations of old concerns within the church. Still, Luther's example and writings inspired a new wave of dissent among the Dutch. Other influences would soon include Huldrych Zwingli, John Calvin, Theodore Beza, John Laski, and more. None of them ever lived in the

Netherlands, but their ideas arrived indirectly through the printed word and other international channels. Dutch priests traveled for ecclesiastical training with some influential reformer, studying at Luther's monastery, for example. Then they returned and shared their learning at home.[9]

Among so many reformers, the Dutch Reformation is hard to characterize with precision. Some dissenters expressed anger about indulgences, others about infant baptism. Some disliked clerical celibacy, others the veneration of Mary and the saints. They saw saintly devotion as just another misguided, blasphemous distraction, similar to indulgences in that, by venerating a saint, one might soon forget about Christ. Above all else, these "heretics," as Hapsburg law described them, wanted the word of God (i.e., the Bible) translated in their own language, and they wanted preachers who preached from the scriptures. They probably couldn't have identified their ideological pedigree with any more precision than historians today. Humanist, Lutheran, Anabaptist, Reformed: they pooled at first into a muddled, eclectic Protestantism that existed very uneasily with the public Catholic Church. In fact, between the 1520s and 1560s, more people were executed for religious beliefs in the Netherlands than anywhere else in Europe. The bloodshed and repression of the Inquisition paralleled efforts to centralize Hapsburg control and reform political, judicial arrangements in general. While the Spanish failed in the religious sphere, never stopping illicit activity altogether, they did succeed in preventing any one Protestant movement from rising above the rest.[10]

Reformed religion (sometimes called Calvinism) was a latecomer to the Reformation in Holland and other northern provinces. The first congregations appeared there in 1566 in the wake of the *beeldenstorm* (Iconoclastic Fury), when mobs descended on Catholic chapels and destroyed their "idolatry," meaning statues, paintings, and other symbols of the old faith. The uprising began in the south and spread rapidly north in the summer and fall of that year. Again, no Reformed Church had existed in Holland before. It would become the public church of the new Dutch state not because it had the most adherents, but because its supporters were the most outspoken, organized, and militant during what soon became a more general revolt against Hapsburg rule. They took advantage of the widespread antagonism toward the Inquisition and, by extension, the Catholic Church. In that sense, the Hapsburg monarchs Charles V and Philip II prepared the ground more than anyone else for the reformation they wanted so desperately to prevent.[11]

When Philip responded to the *beeldenstorm* with a large army, the most active political agitators and religious dissenters fled to foreign cities like London and Emden. The rebels lost their homes and livelihoods, and their churches in the Netherlands dissolved. They quickly regrouped, however, and at the

Synods of Wesel (1568) and Emden (1571) they aligned themselves with John Calvin by adopting his ecclesiastical offices and organizational preferences, modified slightly to meet Dutch needs. Building from the ground up, the reformers intended the new scheme as a remedy to the hierarchy of the Catholic Church and the spiritual tyranny it allegedly engendered. A *kerkeraad* ("church council" or consistory) would lead each congregation, and the consistory would send elders and ministers to a regional classis to meet with representatives of other consistories and select envoys for infrequent provincial synods. Still somewhat hierarchical, it was at least a hierarchy of councils. And the onus of teaching, preaching, charity, and discipline now fell at the regional and local levels (where the rebels preferred everything).

The following year, many exiles returned to the Netherlands and began freeing Dutch towns from Spanish control, expunging Catholic worship as they went. Some towns only opened their gates to these pirates or "Sea Beggars" on the promise that they would leave Catholic institutions alone, and the Dutch nobleman William of Orange, who feared disunity, issued a decree of tolerance. But the Sea Beggars would not forget what the Spanish had done to their lives and property. In revenge they commandeered churches, murdered monks, and sacked cloisters. Under pressure from radicals, Holland outlawed Catholic worship in 1573, and William finally joined the Reformed Church that year. Reformed congregations began to emerge in towns and cities all over the north.

Yet the Calvinist victory was incomplete. Growth was slow, especially in the countryside, and the federalist arrangements of the new Dutch state didn't lend themselves to rapid change. Really just a loose confederation of otherwise independent provinces, each still wary of centralization, the Dutch Republic formally came together in 1579 for the purpose of fighting the war. Every city still had its own council, every province its own legislative body or "States," including the States of Holland, States of Zeeland, and so on. For matters like diplomacy and war, the Dutch utilized a national legislature called the States General and, mostly to lead the army, the provinces appointed a stadtholder (usually from the House of Orange). The States General was a slow-moving, inhibited body because delegates represented their provinces, returning home for instructions whenever new issues arose. And except in the unincorporated borderlands, the States General had little independent taxing power. Authority gravitated toward populous, prosperous Holland, whose influence was so great, its own executive sometimes rivaled the stadtholder as national leader.[12]

On the religious question, many rulers still had reservations. They worried about exchanging the unwanted power of Rome with the equally unwanted

City with WIC chamber

Other town, city, or island

Provinces are in CAPS. All bodies of water are in *italics*.

FRIESLAND

GRONINGEN

DRENTHE

North Sea

Zuiderzee

OVERIJSSEL

HOLLAND

UTRECHT

GELDERLAND

IJssel

Lek

Waal

ZEELAND

Maas

Rhine

BRABANT

FLANDERS

Scheldt

Alkmaar	1	Emden	11	Middelburg	21
Amersfoort	2	Enkhuizen	12	Rotterdam	22
Amsterdam	3	Gouda	13	Texel Island	23
Antwerp	4	Groningen	14	Tholen	24
Arnhem	5	Haarlem	15	Utrecht	25
Brielle	6	The Hague	16	Veere	26
Brussels	7	Hoorn	17	Vlissingen	27
Delft	8	Kampen	18	Walcheren	28
Deventer	9	Leeuwarden	19	Wesel	29
Dordrecht	10	Leiden	20	Zwolle	30

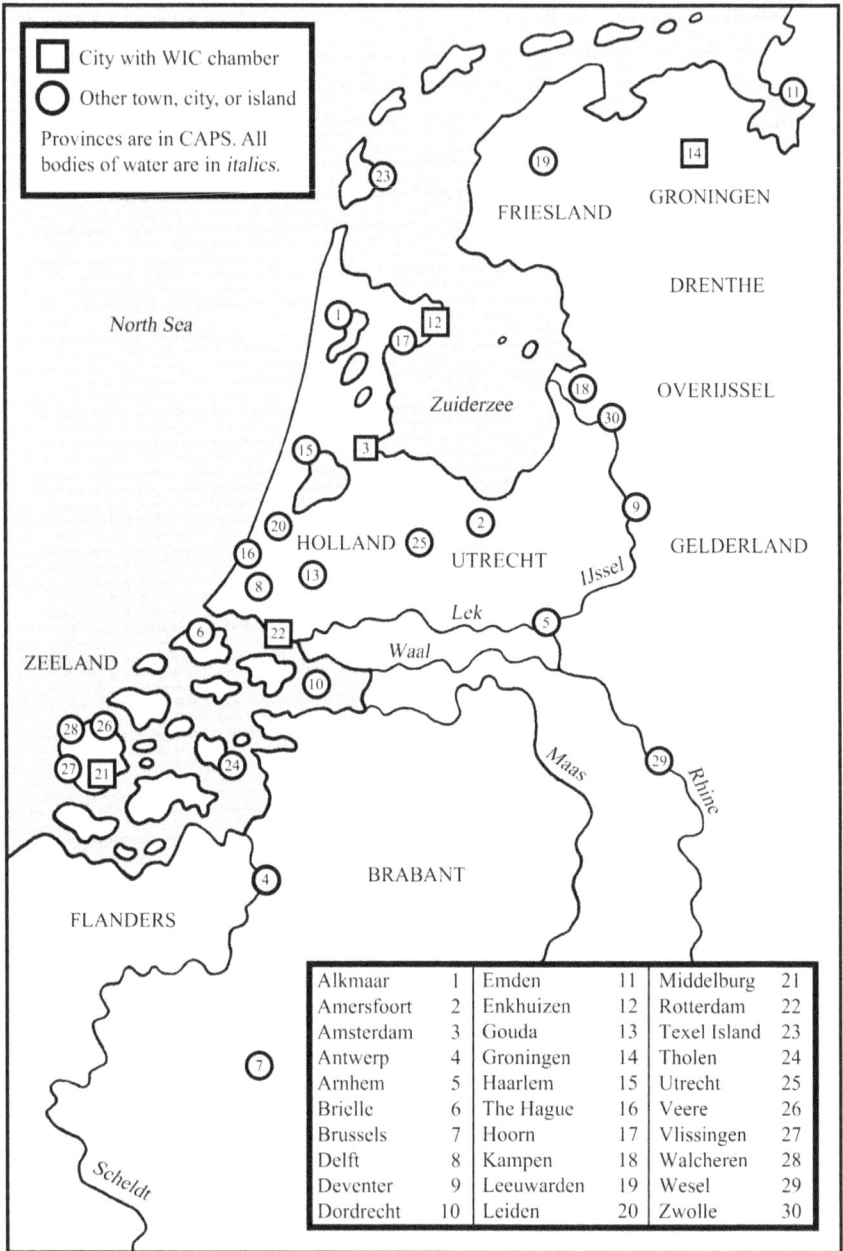

The Dutch Republic in the seventeenth century, with parts of the Spanish Netherlands. Map drawn by author.

oversight of their private lives in powerful, sanctimonious consistories. Some also believed that they, as civil guardians of the church, should have more control over it. They wanted an inclusive state church, with membership and Communion open to everyone in society simply because they were born there. Calvinists tended to oppose these measures, choosing to restrict membership, for example, to men and women who made a public profession of faith and accepted church discipline; and ultimately they got their way on the membership issue. However, the recent history of repression under the Spanish fostered a limited tolerance in the Dutch Republic. The state supported the church by giving it former Catholic property, paying salaries, supplementing clerical education, and including church officers at official functions. But after the initial, bloody days of the Sea Beggars, no one in society faced any threat because of their beliefs. This commitment to what the Dutch called "freedom of conscience" permitted people to worship how they wanted, as long as they did so quietly in their own homes, with their own families. All public worship was reserved for the Dutch Reformed Church.[13]

Bolstered by 100,000 refugees from the southern Netherlands, the number of Reformed members in the north grew over time. In 1587 perhaps 1 in 10 was a member in Holland; by 1600, between 12 and 18 percent, with the Republic as a whole reaching about 37 percent by 1650.[14] Indeed, membership was difficult to come by because the church made it so. These figures don't include people who avoided public examination and discipline but still attended services and married in the chapel, then had their children baptized there. One didn't have to be a member to participate at that level, and many more people were members in the sense that someone today might define the term. The degree to which civic rulers heeded the church's complaints about non-Reformed worship and other unwanted conduct in each town and city depended most on whether rulers there sympathized more with the first or second kind of churchgoer.[15]

Religious divides in this period revealed themselves most dramatically during the Arminian controversy, which began in the Netherlands but quickly drew the attention of other Europeans and, in the long term, inspired a more fastidious management of ecclesiastical affairs in Dutch colonies. The minister who started the controversy, Jacobus Arminius, espoused views on predestination and grace that contradicted the official doctrines of the church and upset colleagues, first in Amsterdam in the 1590s, later at the university in Leiden. Arminius and his followers taught that John Calvin's interpretation of predestination made God the author of sin and destroyed man's freedom. According to Calvin, all are saved or damned from the beginning of time, and there is nothing they can do about it—no way to resist God's grace once he offers it, no way to obtain it if one is numbered among the unlucky damned. The gentler doctrine of the Arminians held instead that God, in his omniscience, *foresaw* that some people would have faith and some would not, and he predestined them accordingly. But his foreknowledge didn't destroy free will. They could reject God's mercy, Christ having died for all, and their choices affected their eternal fate. Unlike Calvinists, Arminians didn't want to impose their doctrines on the church; they just wanted space within it—an inclusive organization where the answers to every mystery weren't inscribed in stone and ministers of both stripes could work side by side. Their objectives were more in keeping with the open state church that so many rulers wanted.[16]

Calvinists had ample secular support of their own, and the disagreement escalated over the course of three decades, taking on more and more political baggage until it nearly exploded in civil war. When the two sides began organizing separate consistories, even a separate church in Amsterdam, the States of Holland decided to skirt the power of the States General and raise an army, supposedly to keep the peace. This provincial army was the fatal development, because Maurits of Nassau, the prince of Orange, then cast his lot with the Calvinist faction and marched his own army to The Hague, where he and his allies in the States General arrested, tried, and beheaded the Arminians' most prominent supporter, Johan van Oldenbarnevelt. More important for resolving the religious dispute, an international synod met in Dordrecht in 1618, and there the Arminians were decisively defeated. They were heard and refuted, their doctrines condemned and banned. Arminian ministers who fled the country soon returned to work illegally alongside other nonconformers, sometimes with the quiet support of local rulers. But Dordrecht was still a critical Calvinist moment. No longer just a faction in the church, Calvinists controlled all public religion in the Netherlands and its nascent colonies.

The Synod of Dordrecht is also a reminder of the international debt and orientation of the Dutch Reformed Church, with or without the VOC and WIC. A movement born in war and influenced by men like John Calvin, who was himself a refugee, could hardly have avoided an international outlook. To Calvin's impact and the foreign envoys at Dordrecht we could add the Republic's many southern immigrants and the importance of foreign cities like Wesel and Emden as sites for major Reformed synods. Along with London, they fostered the Dutch church during its difficult early years, providing a base for the Sea Beggars and a source for alms and illegal printing. They served as a sanctuary for Dutch congregations and clergy who came and went according to the ebb and flow of their fortunes in the Netherlands. Then when their own troubles ended, Dutch cities provided the same support to others: most famously the English Pilgrims, who found a temporary home in Leiden before sailing to America. But the Pilgrims were just one among many foreign congregations, not to mention foreign students and professors at Dutch universities. If international bonds were more European than global at this point—English, German, French—the many outside influences in the church had at least prepared the ground for growth in the future.[17]

Organizing for Colonial Expansion

Far more than its sister organization, the West India Company was born in the shadow of religious controversy and war. The six small merchant firms that merged in 1602 to form the East India Company had to worry about the war with Spain, of course, because it dragged on for many years. And the Arminian issue wasn't settled at that point either. But creating a similar company for the Atlantic sphere—creating the WIC—got caught up in the complex religio-political divides that only escalated during the fifteen years after the VOC's founding. Postponing the WIC until 1621 (for the sake of a temporary truce with Spain) was among the reasons for the bitter partisanship and near-civil war described above. The Orangist, Calvinist victory in that dispute paved the way for a renewal of war and the creation of the new company, dedicated to attacking Dutch enemies in Africa and America.

Together the two joint-stock companies imposed significant strains on the church because it suddenly needed so many clergy abroad. The reformation of the Netherlands was nowhere near complete, yet now the church had to think globally. Moreover, its relative youth and diffuse, presbyterian organization raised controversial questions about colonial oversight, unique to Protestant expansion: How could an organization without permanent national institutions, a church designed to operate first at the local level, supervise a project of widespread interest and scope? Who was in charge and where did they get their authority? The rifts surrounding Arminius and Dordrecht only heightened everyone's sensitivities and motivated the churches at home to establish a system wherein colonial churches and councils functioned somewhat differently and less independently than similar councils in the Netherlands.

The church in Amsterdam first learned about colonial personnel needs from the above-mentioned Petrus Plancius, the sometimes minister, sometimes cartographer of Flemish descent. In addition to his other duties, he now became the VOC's mouthpiece in the consistory.[18] The latter's response in this first instance was later mirrored by other church councils in other Dutch cities when they faced similar issues: they appointed deputies to look into the matter and report back, then they deliberated and gave new instructions to the deputies, who completed the task under the council's direction. "The task" could be finding clergy, writing letters, seeing the companies about salaries or books, and countless other issues. The churches in Amsterdam and Zeeland bore the heaviest colonial burden because the VOC and WIC, mirroring the federalist organization of the church and country at large, were divided into chambers, each based in a different city or region; and the greatest power in both companies resided in the Amsterdam and Zeeland chambers. They had invested the most money and sent the most ships; letting their churches find personnel and supervise religious growth on other continents was the easy, early answer to oversight questions.[19]

Until 1612, most colonial clergy were stationed in Asia, rarely in Africa or the Americas. Some worked in the western hemisphere aboard the ships of the Dutch admiralties or the odd merchant ship, but few ministers worked permanently at one of the short-lived forts or colonies that Dutchmen established on the Amazon River and Wild Coast (northern coast of South America) before 1612. By that point the growing trade to Africa needed protection, so the admiralty of Amsterdam built Fort Nassau on the Gold Coast, creating the first permanent post for Dutch clergy in what would one day be WIC territory. It arranged for ships and supplies, sailors and soldiers, then began searching for "an exhorter or reader"—not an ordained minister, but a lay preacher to read sermons and offer prayers. The admiralty heard of a man from Haarlem who might be interested, Meynert Assuerus, and after the church located and examined him, Plancius issued his instructions. The admiralty told the commander at Fort Nassau, "You will let him teach and exhort the people on water and on land, and respect him in his office."[20]

The church's early experience in the Atlantic world was discouraging. It soon learned, if it didn't already know from its decade in the East, that there were special challenges in managing ecclesiastical affairs on other continents. Assuerus returned from Fort Nassau followed by rumors of immorality, and the Amsterdam consistory then received a letter from his replacement, Jan Arentss, who confirmed Assuerus's gambling, drunkenness, and frivolity.[21] Arentss's successor, Jan Hermanss, was also problematic. The admiralty sent Hermanss to Africa in 1617 on a three-year contract. Yet he returned after a stay of only six weeks, complaining about noise and drinking at sea and an "atheist" captain who wouldn't let him offer prayers. He said his quarters in the fort were inadequate, "above the prison, among the soldiers," with no quiet place for study. He also reported vulgar conversation and singing, which forced him from the barracks; and the commander treated him like a common soldier, he claimed. Having determined that the "peace of the Lord" didn't exist at Fort Nassau, he decided to return. Consistory members were not happy about his short stay, but they did admit that his experience was bad, and they sent delegates to address these issues with the admiralty.[22]

The close relationship between secular and ecclesiastical authorities continued under the WIC. As the company prepared to send its first fleet to Brazil in 1623, the Amsterdam consistory kept an eye on these "West Indies ships" and at least twice sent representatives to ensure that the WIC provided for the religious needs of sailors and soldiers. Company directors said they were doing everything possible, and they thanked the consistory for its concern. Later they announced plans to hire one minister and three *ziekentroosters* ("comforters of the sick"), then the church began looking at candidates. It also made arrangements with the directors for books, and they agreed to pay some salaries early, months before the fleet sailed. The consistory had asked for the extra time and funds to train the new *ziekentroosters* in their responsibilities.[23]

The destination of this first fleet, part of the WIC's first Grand Design in the Atlantic world, was supposed to be secret, known only to company directors and a handful of other well-connected individuals. But in his multivolume *Historisch Verhael* (Historical Story), published in serial form in the 1620s and early 1630s, the former minister and medical doctor Nicolaes van Wassenaer reported a strangely informative visit about the fleet from a self-proclaimed prophet named Philip Ziegler. The question of how Ziegler got his information and whether Van Wassenaer could have known much about Brazil is less important than what it reveals about the religious fervor and apocalyptic visions and rhetoric surrounding the religious wars of which the company was now a part. Ziegler was a German and former Lutheran who had by the 1620s joined a cryptic, mystical sect known as the Rosicrucians. Van Wassenaer prefaced his description of the Ziegler visit to his home in Amsterdam by sharing stories of past prophets and expressing his own belief in the sanctity of the WIC's work and the value of prophecy in their own day. That God would no longer grant the gift of prophecy struck Van Wassenaer as "absurd."[24]

After explaining his former spiritual experiences to Van Wassenaer, Ziegler asked if the doctor was anxious about the recently departed fleet, "which I declared to be the case," Van Wassenaer wrote. Then Ziegler produced a sketch of a bay and castle very much like the ones at Bahia, the capital of Brazil, surrounded by flames and lightning and angry animals. Within the flames and lightning were the words "Mene, Mene, Tekel, Upharsin," which come from the book of Daniel and refer to the fall of a certain Babylonian king. "God hath numbered thy kingdom, and finished it," interprets Daniel. And Ziegler now offered his own interpretation of what was probably his drawing: "This . . . shall

Philip Ziegler's imaginative drawing of the Dutch attack on Bahia. Originally printed in *Historisch verhael*, by Nicolaes van Wassenaer (1622–1635). Courtesy of the Koninklijke Bibliotheek, The Hague.

be the first fall of the Spanish Empire. This shall be the beginning of the destruction of Spain." He also pontificated on Dutch freedom and the reputation the WIC would earn for the Republic among its allies, all of which was "like a thunderclap to my ears," Van Wassenaer wrote, especially when Ziegler went on to describe recent international treaties that weren't yet public knowledge. The prophet finally declared that he had other secrets, but he wouldn't reveal them because even he couldn't comprehend all that God showed him.[25]

The Amsterdam and Zeeland churches were less mystical than Ziegler, but equally excited about the possibilities the WIC offered for destroying the enemy and sending their faith to new lands. Both relied heavily on a regional council called a "classis" (plural: "classes") to deal with expansion. In Zeeland, the classis whose borders corresponded most closely with company borders was the Walcheren classis, which created two permanent committees to deal separately with Asian and Atlantic affairs. By contrast, the Amsterdam classis first delegated all colonial responsibility to the Amsterdam consistory. But the other towns represented in the classis wanted to be involved as well, and by 1636 they had convinced their colleagues to emulate Walcheren in creating not two but one Indies committee to deal with Asia, Africa, and America together. Other minor differences included the size of the committees and the time commitments of each committee member—six years and more in Zeeland, two years in Amsterdam. Organization and responsibilities were otherwise the same in both places. Under the critical eye of the classes, the committees conducted exams and discussed theological questions that arose overseas. They benefited from the first-hand knowledge of ministers who returned to Europe after a few years abroad, then reported to or even joined the Indies committees.[26]

Separated by about one hundred miles, the Amsterdam and Walcheren classes occasionally faced issues of such importance that they communicated and worked together: illicit worship in Dutch colonies, colonial churches creating classes without consent, reports of the WIC meddling in ecclesiastical affairs. Any of these things could inspire contact, especially if they involved Brazil, the focal point of early Dutch interest in the Atlantic world. If the WIC's highest governing body, the Nineteen Lords, was meeting in Amsterdam, the Walcheren classis would write to its counterpart in that city and ask the clergy to visit the company. If the Nineteen Lords were meeting in Zeeland, the Amsterdam classis would ask the same of Walcheren, though both usually found that the other was already aware of the problem and pursuing the same solution, whatever it happened to be. At least twice Walcheren sent envoys to Amsterdam to meet and strategize with the classis there before visiting the company together.[27]

Other Reformed clergy and other church councils, lacking the access of their colleagues in Amsterdam and Zeeland, still tried to insert themselves into decision-making processes and still tried to participate in the colonial project. Some wrote books about the growing Dutch Empire; others simply wrote letters, maybe learning about problems from acquaintances overseas, then sharing their views with the Amsterdam and Walcheren classes, who sometimes responded and passed on colonial correspondence that shed light on the relevant issue or question.[28] Clergy could also learn about foreign developments at their provincial synod, consisting of ministers and elders from every classis within a province and nonvoting representatives from several synods outside it. And the synods could be helpful in advancing whatever agenda the Amsterdam and Walcheren classes had set. For instance, they might help answer theological questions or confirm a decision made by one of the classes; they might send letters or deputies to the WIC to complain about a shortage of ministers. But they met too infrequently—usually once per year in provinces that had them—to be highly involved in Asia and the Atlantic world. They would have been a slow, inefficient alternative to the system that developed informally around Amsterdam and Walcheren.[29]

Sporadic correspondence and annual synodal updates were meager substitutes for direct access, and the clergy left on the outside weren't pleased with the situation, sometimes vehemently against it. They decided that if the dispersion of power in the Dutch Reformed Church didn't accommodate widespread concerns like global expansion, they would create a new, national body, a permanent Indies council with delegates from several synods. The Amsterdam and Walcheren classes had flirted with a similar idea at the WIC's founding, but as insiders they had few reasons to pursue the scheme (and many reasons to oppose it).[30] The Utrecht synod took it up next: delegates discussed colonial religion at the 1624 meeting, resolving in the end that power belonged to all Dutch churches collectively. The following year they asked future WIC minister Cornelis Leoninus to visit the synod of South Holland and promote the new council there.[31]

The Leoninus assignment was the first step in a long, costly campaign. Ultimately it was also a futile campaign, but in its very persistence it reveals the depth of interest in the church for international developments. Activist synods included Utrecht, Overijssel, Gelderland, South Holland, and (belatedly) Friesland. The first four began working together especially well in the 1630s because the charters of both companies were set to expire in the near future, and everyone knew that if there was ever a chance to obtain power, it was during negotiations with the States General to renew the charters. In that decade their protests grew louder and more frequent, their correspondence more regular. They asked for news, they asked for updates, they demanded records from colonial churches. At one time or another they made their case before both companies, as well as the various provincial States and the States General. In a warning that must have had special resonance after the Arminian controversy, they told anyone who would listen that the current arrangement caused confusion and chaos, threatening the doctrines and traditions for which Reformed believers had fought so hard in recent years. Without proper care, they said, impurities would creep back into the church. The only remedy was a national ecclesiastical partnership of the type that they, in their very work on this issue, were already showing possible.[32]

The prominent part played by the Utrecht synod in this dispute probably had something to do with Gisbertus Voetius, a university professor and minister who was just emerging as a major figure on the national scene. No single individual could ever represent such a long-lasting, widespread phenomenon. But his life and career allow us to put a human face on the moment and go beyond motives like "power" and "doctrinal purity." As far as religious representatives go, Voetius is far better than the prophet Philip Ziegler because Ziegler, unlike Voetius, was a radical outsider and transient who never had much impact in the Netherlands—or anywhere else, for that matter. The two men mostly just shared certain international interests. Voetius was especially moved by the interplay between his understanding of Christian missionary obligations and his concerns about the enemy's missions. According to historian J. A. B. Jongeneel, Voetius was the first Protestant thinker to formulate a "comprehensive theology of mission."[33]

Consider the events that took place during Voetius's life (1589–1676) and the history of the city that he called home (Utrecht). In his eighty-seven years he witnessed the founding of the VOC, the rise and fall of the WIC, the spread of Dutch power throughout the world, and the proliferation of Catholic missions under a newly established institution in Rome, the *Sacra Congregatio de Propaganda Fide* (Sacred Congregation for the Propagation of the Faith). For Voetius, the struggle against Catholics in Europe, America, Africa, and Asia was the same: a global religious contest. His definition of mission was broad, having anything to do with "reformation" and the survival and growth of Reformed Christianity. Planting new churches on other continents was a sacred duty. Echoing his synod's position on supervising colonial religion, he once wrote that planting was not the privilege of individuals and secular institutions, but that of the whole church through its councils.[34] Had it materialized, the centralized council the Dutch considered from the 1620s to the 1640s would have been the Protestant answer to the *Propaganda Fide*, which oversaw Catholic expansion even in places where it was illegal, including (most famously in the Netherlands) Utrecht. The city had been a Catholic capital long before the Reformation and war, and it continued to plague reformers like Voetius afterward, probably contributing to his missionary vision. The parallels between local and global politics made local issues that much larger and distant ones more personal.

The Amsterdam and Walcheren classes opposed the national plan in part because it would mean sharing power and sharing the money they received from the VOC and WIC. They didn't talk much about power and charitable resources in their communication with others, though. They focused on pragmatic issues, like the question of costs—who would fund the new council?—

and the hassles and obstacles of a slow, "useless" institution, as the Walcheren classis once described it.[35] Their day-to-day needs were inconsequential, they claimed, and the weighty concerns that did arise from time to time couldn't wait for deputies to correspond with distant churches, even travel home for deliberation and instructions. Company directors in Zeeland inadvertently proved the point in 1640 when they asked the Walcheren classis to choose ministers from Middelburg (and only Middelburg) for the church's West Indies committee. The WIC usually held its own meetings in that city, and the directors said that committee members from other towns lived too far away to be helpful when the company and church needed to work together. If that were true in a single regional classis, surely a council with members from all over the Netherlands would have exacerbated the problem.[36]

Eventually the churches of the Netherlands devised a solution that each synod could accept, though grudgingly in some cases. North and South Holland created the original proposal in the summer of 1642. For a long time the others resisted, persisting in their political efforts. But as the Amersfoort classis wrote in 1645, the campaign required "great costs and difficulties," and they began to wear down. Between 1646 and 1649 they yielded one by one, Utrecht signing on only after North Holland accused the synod of flouting the general will, and after a final flurry of letters failed to change anyone's mind.[37]

The new arrangement wasn't really new. It left the care of foreign churches in the hands of those whose bounds corresponded with company chambers, which effectively meant that the Amsterdam and Walcheren classes retained the influence they had always enjoyed. They promised now to ensure that colonial religion functioned according to the doctrine and customs accepted in the Netherlands since the Synod of Dordrecht. They promised to report yearly and provide excerpts from important colonial records. They agreed to communicate about serious, unusual questions and concerns. Finally, they assured the other churches that they would accept any clergy for company service, no matter his classis or synod.[38] If anything in this arrangement *was* new, reports were now regular and required, where they had been a courtesy before. Dutch churches could learn what happened overseas with greater speed and detail; they knew the names of any clergy hired by the VOC and WIC. They no longer relied on sporadic, reluctant reports or correspondence from acquaintances in better-connected cities. Each synod monitored Reformed progress around the world—and allowed others to do the same—by copying the colonial reports faithfully, year after year, in their own minutes.[39]

The debate that ended in 1649 wasn't just the ecclesiastical equivalent of federalist problems and tensions within the Dutch state, reflecting provincial jealousies. The young church was suffering the growing pains that all

Protestants experienced, struggling toward an understanding of rights and power in a relatively new and loosely organized presbyterian structure, which reformers had not adopted lightly. Their preference for local control, rooted in basic Protestant beliefs about spiritual authority, created unique difficulties in managing expansion. The Catholic Church had its own difficulties, to be sure, but from different conditions: an independent, international, hierarchical institution growing uneasily within several competing empires—as opposed to the locally based Reformed Church, operating in just one empire, but with no central direction and few useful traditions. Happily for the Dutch, they did at least have a history of international awareness and contact to build on, and the Amsterdam and Walcheren classes were eager to do the building. Meeting the needs of colossal companies and dealing with questions from their counterparts in the colonies was a constant concern, at times dominating all other business in two of the most influential Reformed councils in the seventeenth-century Netherlands.

Less happily, by abandoning the national plan and giving control to two regional classes, the Dutch guaranteed awkward questions and relationships in the future, for the colonial churches couldn't grow beyond the level of congregation and consistory without creating a scenario in which the potential new colonial classis or synod reported to—and was subordinate to—not a synod or group of synods at home, but another classis, meaning the Amsterdam or Walcheren classis. Both of them now had motives even to prevent intensive colonial organization in order to avoid the awkward scenarios and justify their continued management role.

Calling and Controlling the Clergy

The passion for foreign affairs in the Dutch Reformed Church often ended at the point where clergy were asked to serve abroad. The ongoing Reformation left many opportunities to engage in the great spiritual struggles of the day without leaving home; and most Protestant ministers had families to consider. Still, the church had to fill foreign vacancies. Though the WIC's ecclesiastical personnel were relatively few—about 360 men between 1621 and 1674—they were some of the most visible people in Dutch forts and colonial societies, with an influence disproportionate to their numbers. Franciscus Plante, who worked eight years as a minister in Brazil, explained what the WIC needed: experience and education were helpful, a good reputation and good life essential. In those "far-flung lands, with a lack of constant and necessary supervision," any unattractive qualities and unruly behavior might grow worse.[40]

The Dutch sometimes fell short of that ideal, but not for lack of effort. Spurred by the same sensitivities and concerns about heterodoxy and impurity that had permeated the church since the Arminian controversy, they worked hard to ensure that those who founded and administered colonial churches were qualified. Then they continued to watch them closely after their appointments, perhaps because, as a group, the WIC's clergy were younger and less experienced, more dependent on lay ministers than the church at home. Only about 120 of the total 360 were ordained; the rest were readers, *ziekentroosters*, and schoolmasters. Yet they were a capable group, if only because of the very thorough vetting process. Church and company both wanted the best people possible, and in the end, despite the fact that so few men would give up comfy posts at home, they found what they needed—a diverse team from all over the Netherlands and Calvinist Europe. In that sense, "Calvinist" and "Reformed" are more fitting than "Dutch Reformed" as labels for WIC clergy. They provide yet another example of the cosmopolitan life and the church's international connections.[41]

Recruitment was one long, ongoing effort. The church employed many modes of communication, including announcements from the pulpit, formal requests for ministers in classes and synods, letter-writing, and simple word of mouth. The WIC's Nineteen Lords learned about interested men and gave their names to local company chambers for follow-up. A consistory received a letter about a wayward child: Would a stint as *ziekentrooster* in the West Indies set him straight?[42] More often, people put their own names forward by writing letters or showing up at the regular consistory and classis meetings. When they requested specific locations, Asia was the most popular destination. In the Atlantic world they asked to go to Brazil, sometimes Africa, and increasingly after 1650, New Netherland. But applicants often didn't care where they went; they just wanted to travel abroad. Usually they appeared in meetings and explained that they hoped to work for the VOC or WIC, and the Indies committee then decided who was best-qualified, only later making individual assignments.[43]

Clergy served for many reasons, some lofty, some not. Fredricus Kesseler considered the WIC's invitation in "fervent prayer" and decided that he had to go to Brazil because the church there had so many grave needs. Vincentius Soler declared that he was moved by "Christian zeal" to plant the kingdom of Christ and bring his own people (the Spanish) to the truth. And Johannes Megapolensis had "a great desire" to work in America, he told his classis. He had prayed about it for a long time and hoped to "spread the Gospel of Jesus Christ among the blind heathens."[44]

Others didn't give exalted, altruistic explanations. Wilhelmus Volckering wrote simply that he wanted to behold "a strange land." As one of about thirty-five WIC ministers who had recently finished school, he could have added that he was also looking for his first job.[45] Similarly, some lay clergy used the company as an alternative when they lost their income or other support: Cornelis Aertss was an orphan from Texel who had grown too old for the orphanage, Pieter Fransen an elderly instrument maker who fell on hard times and agreed to go to West Africa.[46] Of the sixty-five laymen whose former occupations are known, about twenty had worked as a sailor, soldier, surgeon, or one of the lesser WIC officers. Six of them had been *ziekentroosters* with the VOC in Asia and six were schoolmasters in the Netherlands before. The rest were tradesmen and laborers—often shoemakers or tailors, then a range of others, including ribbon, lace, rope, and sailmakers, hatters and furriers, masons and coppersmiths. The only other common thread among them was their membership in the Reformed Church. Perhaps they were seeking better opportunities, perhaps they wanted to serve the Protestant cause or see the world. The church usually didn't record their motives.[47]

At least fifteen WIC clergy were German or came from Dutch communities in Germany. Differences between the two languages weren't very pronounced in the seventeenth century, especially Low German, spoken in the eastern Netherlands and the northern regions of the Holy Roman Empire.[48] Spanning more than half of the WIC's existence, the Thirty Years War (1618–1648) pushed many refugees to the Netherlands, including Reformed ministers; and they didn't usually need much training to communicate in Dutch. Although the company hired its first German as early as 1623, an exiled German prince named Frederick V sparked a kind of German moment for the WIC in 1628 when he made a personal appeal on behalf of these "sad persons" and, as the church put it, "driven brothers."[49] Other refugees found their way to the company after living in the Netherlands first, like Reverend Kesseler, who served the German-speaking congregation in Amsterdam before going to Brazil, or Johannes Polhemus, who preached and taught school for ten years in the eastern Netherlands before war-related "persecution" forced him from home for the second time. Traveling originally to Brazil, later New Netherland, he was the WIC's longest-serving minister.[50]

English- and French-speaking clergy came to the company with similar stories of conflict and exile, if not in their own lives, in the lives of parents and grandparents. Yet they differed from their German colleagues in at least one respect: the company recruited them directly. Dutch possessions in North America and the Caribbean often bordered English and French colonies, with some contact and migratory spillover. To preach to these newcomers, and to preach to the WIC's diverse, polyglot employees and immigrants, the church had to find men who spoke both languages. Among WIC clergy whose stories are known today, about one-third were foreigners. With the Germans came two Spaniards, seven or eight men from Flanders, a few indigenous Brazilians, at least eighteen French and French-speaking Walloons, and fifteen English—some of whom, like the Germans, may not have been English per se; they came from Dutch communities that had been in England since long before the WIC's founding.[51]

Allied military regiments and foreign Reformed churches based in the Netherlands provided the necessary points of contact. Tasked with finding colonial clergy, the Indies committees turned regularly to English- and French-speaking councils, especially the Walloon synod. For the English, they didn't have to look further than their own classes and synods because English consistories were so integrated in the public church structure—"the English-language wing of the Dutch Reformed Church."[52] As for military regiments, Samuel Bachiler provides one example of their place in these relationships. He moved to the Netherlands first as a pastor of English soldiers during the Thirty Years War. He also ministered to English congregations in the Dutch towns of Heusden and Gorinchem and filled in now and then for a Scottish minister in Dordrecht. A staunch Puritan and outspoken enemy of Anglican rites, he angered English authorities by supporting a campaign to change the Anglican service in Delft. When he was summoned home in 1633 to answer for crimes against the Church of England, he recognized that he might live a longer, healthier life if he ignored the order, so he chose to answer the WIC's call for clergy with his particular language abilities. Bachiler was hired and served about twelve years in Brazil, preaching in English and Dutch.[53]

No matter how dire, employment needs didn't automatically qualify men for colonial positions. They first had to leap various hurdles designed to test their character, skills, and knowledge. When anyone came to the Amsterdam classis asking to work for one of the Indies companies, the committee wouldn't examine him unless he showed written testimonials from people who had worked with him before. If he had the testimonials, and if they were adequate, he could proceed to an oral exam. Responsible for comforting the sick, praying, singing, and reading sermons in the absence of an ordained minister, lay ministers like *ziekentroosters* had to prove their knowledge of Protestant doctrines. And they had to know the psalms and tunes associated with them. Ordained clergy needed a more profound knowledge and had to deliver a sound, vigorous sermon.

Despite the WIC's occasional clerical shortages, the Amsterdam classis rejected more than one in four applicants (about 27 percent). Poor reading and

singing were the most common reasons: Karel van Hartsteen, a schoolmaster in Amsterdam, was a "very incapable singer," Indies deputies wrote. They
told him to practice, and between 1639 and 1645 he returned four times, each
time rejected for his voice. After the fifth exam the classis suggested that he
stick with his current occupation. They informed the tailor Dirck Hendrix,
who also appeared more than once, that his singing was "very bad," that he
had an "unpleasant voice." And they told Jan Schoon that he was "naturally
deficient" in musical matters.[54] They rejected other men for shoddy preaching, age, disability, deficient Dutch, reluctant spouses, alcoholism, theft, and
adultery. If they hired someone and then learned of an unconfessed indiscre-
tion in his past, they reversed themselves, not letting him board the ship. If he
managed to go regardless, traveling to America without proper paperwork and
permissions, the classis went to great lengths to hunt him down and remove
him from whatever post he attained.[55]

At least three-fourths of ordained clergy were university educated and most
of the colonial candidates, including lay ministers, didn't have difficulties of
the kind outlined above. After all, no one was eligible for service unless he was
a member of the church, and to become one he would have already professed
his faith and demonstrated an understanding of basic Protestant doctrines. The
few ordained ministers who hadn't studied at a university were hired mostly
in the 1620s and 1630s. Called *idiooten*, which came from the Latin *idiotae*,
meaning "uneducated" or "ignorant," they had been common in the church
even in Holland during the early Reformation; but as universities proliferated,
they disappeared there. The church accepted them now for the Indies companies reluctantly, usually in cases of great need and exceptional talent. The classis agreed to hear one of them, Johannes Backerus, after he explained that he
had "exercised himself . . . two years" in Christian doctrine. He then preached
eight times over the course of a whole year, the deputies telling him at each
visit that he was getting better but not ready. Only on the last visit were they
"greatly pleased." Accepted for Curaçao in 1641, he was one of the WIC's last
idiotae.[56]

Once an applicant had shown his testimonials and passed the exams, he
signed his name to the *formulierboek* and received his written instructions. The
classis used both opportunities to guarantee (yet again) that its colonial agents
were safe, orthodox believers. The *formulierboek* contained the church's three
official statements of doctrine—the Belgic Confession, Heidelberg Catechism,
and Canons of Dordrecht. Then came the handwritten paragraph that each
man had to read and sign, confirming, in short, that the aforementioned works
were in complete harmony with God's word and that he would teach them
faithfully and oppose all "errors," meaning Arminian teachings in particular.

The signatories also promised that if they ever developed feelings contrary to the creed they would not teach or write them, but reveal them to their classis. If any church council demanded to hear their thoughts on any article or point of Reformed doctrine, they would willingly divulge them immediately. Then, just in case someone forgot, the classis reiterated in their instructions that they were to do everything overseas exactly as it was done at home—"according to God's holy word, and in conformity with the Dutch church order, the Confession, Catechism, and synodal acts of Dordrecht."[57]

The less important, less active company chambers were not always as conscientious as Amsterdam and Zeeland in sending their few ecclesiastical personnel. Together the chambers of *Maas* (Rotterdam, Dordrecht, and Delft), *Noorderkwartier* (Enkhuizen and Hoorn), and *Stad en Lande* (based in Groningen) only sent about 10 percent of company clergy, well below the ratio of investment and participation they had agreed to in the WIC's charter. Sent via Amsterdam, the *ziekentrooster* Cornelis Jacobsen once complained about colleagues hired in Groningen and Delft. He claimed that they didn't know which classis had called them or even whether they were Anabaptist or Arminian.[58] Amsterdam could usually rectify the situation by writing to the relevant church and explaining how hiring in that area—however rare—ought to work. Without any centralized power, the Dutch Reformed Church just needed time after the WIC was founded for each part to get on the same page.[59]

In the end, the church satisfied its colonial charge by leaning heavily on those without deep roots and opportunities: foreign clergy, recent graduates, and some uneducated men. Fewer than thirty established clergy gave up their posts at home to work for the WIC, probably because "established," by definition, meant wives and children and other community ties. The ministers who stayed home and issued instructions worried about the relative youth and inexperience of the whole group, and they looked down on the *idiotae*. Reverend Voetius once wrote that *idiotae* were only suitable among "barbarians" in the "uncivilized" corners of the globe.[60] That he and his fellow ministers in the Netherlands would want to manage growth and guard core beliefs isn't unusual or surprising. But the degree of control exercised in this case, even after the ship had (literally) sailed, seemed to violate the Dutch preference for local governance. Inasmuch as the church's interest in the colonies and worries about what happened there also had something to do with foreign hires and the extra potential for doctrinal corruption in foreign lands, where Europeans rubbed elbows with Voetius's "barbarians," its cosmopolitanism was of a limited sort, working at crosscurrents with attitudes and supervisory methods that would one day prove detrimental to its international mission.

But that's getting ahead of the story. Far more important in generating global interest among Dutch clergy in these early years was the general sense that the enemy was on the march, a century and more ahead of the Dutch in winning converts on other continents. The anonymous author of *Levendich Discovrs* (Lively Discourse, 1622) captured it best: the VOC had already begun to trade and make alliances in Asia, teach "blind heathens," and plant the church. Similar opportunities existed in the Americas, he argued. However, the Dutch faced great peril there, mostly from the pope and "the far-reaching State of the mighty King of Spain," working hand in hand. So long was their reach, so inescapable their influence, even "their vulgar, preening whores . . . threaten us with the foul Spanish Pox" (i.e., syphilis). The author warned his readers about a relatively new Catholic missionary order—already feared and hated in Protestant Europe—called the Jesuits. They will "damn us to the depths of Hell, and arouse the whole world against us," he declared. They swarmed over the earth like locusts, spreading the pope's "Spiritual Consistory" wherever Spain planted a flag. What, he asked, could the Dutch do against such a powerful enemy, against these "Poisonous Monsters"? The answer was to support the WIC and trust that "Almighty God" would protect the small republic. God would help them, through the company, do great things.[61]

CHAPTER 2

Faith and Worship in
a Merchant Community

The Directors of the Dutch West India Company

If the Reformed Church had Petrus Plancius, the map-making minister and clerical champion of exploration and trade, the West India Company had Johannes de Laet, an active and influential director for twenty-eight years, a geographer and linguist, and a devoted Calvinist. The two make a wonderful contrast in their complementary roles: Reverend Plancius, the scholarly man of God, and Director de Laet, the godly scholar. In his wide-ranging intellectual and mercantile pursuits and his consistent support for the church, De Laet embodied the same cosmopolitan, Protestant worldview as Plancius. They were both from the southern Netherlands, and both migrated north after the Spanish victories of 1585. Unlike Plancius, who had to travel abroad for his education, De Laet studied at the new university in Leiden. Yet he had comparable foreign connections because of his profession and marital choices. His first wife was from the Dutch community in London, the second was born in Hamburg.[1]

De Laet expressed his religious allegiances first as an elder on Leiden's Reformed consistory. In that capacity he went before the city's magistrates in 1616 to protest the Arminian presence at Communion. When the consistory split the next year, he followed the Calvinist faction, publishing a work on sin, free will, and the "errors" of his spiritual adversaries. In 1618 he was also a delegate to the Synod of Dordrecht, where the Arminians and their doctrines

36

were quashed. There he wrote a history of the controversy, and later, appointed by the States General, De Laet was on the committee that edited and prepared the synod's records for publication. At his provincial synod in 1619 he helped question and depose Arminian clergy who wouldn't subject themselves to the new order, and he was an active participant on similar councils for thirty years. Never losing his Calvinist bent, when he debated the philosopher Hugo Grotius on an unrelated matter in the 1640s, he attacked his opponent for abandoning the true church.[2]

De Laet was a founding director of the WIC and a regular member of its most powerful body, the Nineteen Lords. Leiden never had its own company chamber, but he and other residents invested enough money to earn one permanent seat for their city in the Amsterdam chamber. He took advantage of his position to examine ships' journals and other colonial records, and he used them to write a lengthy history of the company in 1636: a yearly, blow-by-blow account of almost all WIC voyages and battles to that point. Though it is not a theological work in any sense, it does echo beliefs about the WIC that were common among Reformed clergy. He wrote at the start, for example, that the company was established for "the maintenance of the True Religion and the protection of our freedom," later advising readers to give all glory for WIC success to God. And he tried to heed his own advice, thanking God for victories throughout the book, blaming misfortune on sin and divine will. Because most of the battles he described were fought against the Spanish and Portuguese, appropriating and destroying Catholic property were common themes as well.[3]

De Laet wasn't alone among WIC directors in his interests and allegiances. Founded three years after the Synod of Dordrecht and the Calvinist victory in the public church, the company began its work at a particularly auspicious time for men of his religio-political leanings. Maurits of Nassau, the prince of Orange, had just seized power from Johan van Oldenbarnevelt and discarded Oldenbarnevelt's agenda, including a truce with Spain and a prohibition on American trade. Neither policy had been popular with southern merchants because their previous experience in the Iberian Empires (out of Antwerp) left them with many commercial connections and possibilities in America, and to hinder their access hindered their livelihood. Having moved to the Dutch Republic, they gravitated toward the VOC and WIC because the companies allowed them to continue what they knew, perhaps engage in privateering and found colonies of their own. In the words of Eddy Stols, "A cosmopolitan merchant community, a community that relocated easily, received a new nationality." Under the companies, "a seafaring people that knew very few restraints was mobilized for the nation."[4]

Calvinist influence in the WIC was strong in part because the southern in-fluence was strong: thirty-three of forty-six early directors came from south-ern families. Reformed worship wasn't limited to the south, of course, but it had appeared there first during the Reformation; and many converts came to Holland for fear of religious persecution.[5] Is it any surprise that company di-rectors also belonged disproportionately to the Dutch Reformed Church? Most were full members, and as regular participants on ecclesiastical councils they exhibited a serious commitment to Reformed doctrine and politics. If a name like "Calvinist" is ever appropriate for an institution as large and complex as the WIC, it was appropriate for WIC directors in the first half of the seven-teenth century, when they were most active in the church and supported its agenda, when the war with Spain created opportunities for anti-Catholic, anti-Arminian militants.[6]

The point is not that the directors were religious, though like most Euro-peans in the seventeenth century, they were. Far more than that, their religious beliefs and affiliations shaped the company's goals, policies, routines, and rep-utation. Reformed ideas about religious authority allowed them to partici-pate on church councils and influence ecclesiastical discussions and interpretations of imperial activity, practically uniting church and company. In fact, they sat on the same church councils that, with the WIC, oversaw co-lonial religion. Together their faith and their profession—their dispersed commercial relationships—involved the company in the international Protes-tant community. When De Laet wrote that the WIC was established "for the maintenance of the True Religion and the protection of our freedom," he was probably thinking of its capacity to attack Spain in the New World, take its silver and other riches, and strike at the root of Spanish power. Yet the "main-tenance of the True Religion" meant much more to contemporaries. Protes-tants looked to the WIC and its directors for more immediate support, both political and fiscal. Never mind its national charter; it was an ally of all Euro-pean Protestants in that they could cheer its progress against common ene-mies and sometimes share its wealth.

The Religious Life of WIC Directors

The consistory was the most basic level of organization in the Dutch Reformed Church. Made up of ministers, elders, and deacons, it was the nucleus of the Reformed community, with substantial influence in the lives of individual members. Its purpose and theological justification came from a broadly Prot-estant doctrine called "the priesthood of all believers," which held that the people of God were a collective priesthood, living in and through Jesus Christ, the only true priest. Together they were "the body of Christ." The ministry should not be dominated by clergy with special, mysterious powers and access to God, John Calvin and other reformers taught, but shared according to one's gifts of proclaiming the word (pastors or ministers), governing the church (elders), and serving others (deacons). Ideally, all ecclesiastical decisions were corporate, made by ministers and male lay officers from the congregation. The word "presbyterian," usually used to describe this kind of organization, comes from the Greek *presbyteros* (elder), and means to be governed by elders. Meeting in the consistory, ministers, elders, and deacons looked after the Christian community at the local level. In Amsterdam, sitting consistory members chose their own replacements, often giving a vote to anyone who had served in the past. Municipal rulers had to approve their selections.[7]

Many WIC directors served on Reformed consistories: almost half of the directors in Amsterdam (about 45 percent) and considerably more in the province of Zeeland, which was known as a Calvinist stronghold.[8] Amsterdam directors were especially active from 1620 to 1650, reaching peak involvement in 1635, when eleven of them (including past and future directors) were serving at the same time. Three of them served in Haarlem and Leiden, who also sent delegates to the WIC's Amsterdam chamber. The other eight comprised more than a quarter of the lay members in Amsterdam's Dutch-speaking consistory that year. They numbered ten in 1639 and nine in 1636, 1638, 1641, and 1642, with considerable representation at other times. Church activity gradually declined until 1669, when, for the first time, no Amsterdam director was on any consistory anywhere. At least one or two served in each of the next three years, from 1670 to 1672.[9]

Consistory members served two-year terms. Most directors served more than once in their lives, some as many as twelve times (i.e., twenty-four years). Their main duty as deacons was to care for the needy: they collected and dispensed alms and oversaw other fiscal matters, like church rental property and bonds. They met regularly as a body in the *Oude Kerk* or *Nieuwe Kerk* with a minister, apart from the other ministers and elders unless a question of particular importance brought them all together.[10] As elders, the directors also helped examine those who wanted to become members, heard their professions of faith, held disciplinary hearings when someone violated the church's moral conventions, and arbitrated disputes. A few times each year they went with a minister to visit members in their homes and prepare them for Communion. Also called the Lord's Supper, Communion was a crucial moment on the Christian calendar, so they questioned each member on his or her faith and recent conduct. One surviving list of visitation assignments from the 1630s

	WIC facility
	Church or chapel
	Other facility

Area into which the city expanded
in the 1650s and 1660s

Almshouse	1	Noorderkerk	13
Cattle Market	2	Orphanage	14
City Hall	3	Oude Kerk	15
Dam Square	4	Oudezijds Kapel	16
English Church	5	Pig Market	17
Exchange Bank	6	Shipyards	18
Fish Market	7	Stock Exchange	19
Flower Market	8	VOC House	20
French Church	9	Westerkerk	21
Hospital	10	WIC Office	22
Leper House	11	WIC Warehouse	23
Nieuwe Kerk	12	Zuiderkerk	24

Amsterdam in the seventeenth century. Map drawn by author.

shows seven WIC directors working with Dutch Reformed ministers in neighborhoods all over Amsterdam.[11]

In Zeeland, at least one director, Pieter Duvelaer, was a permanent member of his consistory because he was also a Reformed minister. Crossover between church and company in Zeeland was even greater than Amsterdam because the consistory in Middelburg, where many Zeeland directors lived, invested enough money in the WIC to send its own representative to a group of investors and merchants called the *hoofdparticipanten* ("main participants"). They resolved on July 1, 1625, that the local clergy could appoint one person to attend all future gatherings. After all, the clergy had placed the church "in the Company," the other *hoofdparticipanten* wrote, by collectively investing *f* 4,000.[12] The consistory eventually enjoyed even more representation, maybe indicating additional investment. At least two clergy were present at a meeting in 1646, for instance, and three were attending by the 1660s. In July 1662 they all traveled to The Hague to discuss future negotiations with Portugal and urge the States General to watch and protect the company's interests. The *hoofdparticipanten* did not have the same authority as directors, but they helped select new ones.[13]

As consistory members, WIC directors also belonged to church councils that worked with the company on all colonial religious matters, including the consistories themselves, the Amsterdam and Walcheren classes, and the North Holland synod. At least three future directors were at the Synod of Dordrecht in 1618, where the church considered questions from Asia regarding baptism and other ecclesiastical issues they would soon face in their own territories in the Atlantic world. Many were members of their consistories and classes when those councils began working with the company, sometimes acting as directors simultaneously. Eventually the church formed Indies committees, made up solely of ministers. But it didn't create the Amsterdam committee until 1636, the consistory filling the same role before then. And the classis remained involved in colonial affairs afterward, examining all candidates for the foreign ministry and hearing regular reports from committee members. Before 1636 there was never a year when the Amsterdam consistory didn't have at least two WIC directors. Afterward, one or more of them belonged to the classis or synod in twenty-four of the company's remaining thirty-eight years, giving them considerable representation on the ecclesiastical bodies that handled foreign affairs.[14]

Unfortunately the surviving minutes usually don't reveal how individual members of church councils contributed to specific discussions, but the directors would have taken part in weekly or monthly debates about missionary work, the boundaries of the Christian community in diverse colonies, and the responsibilities of their own company. In the Amsterdam consistory they sat at a long wooden table, taking turns to raise business or address issues that someone else had raised. The classis and synod were larger meetings, but they also offered ample opportunity to participate. The classis gathered at 8:30 a.m., each elder sitting next to the minister or ministers from his congregation; then they selected a scribe and offered a prayer. When their turn came to speak, Indies deputies delivered their report and asked for advice.[15] The WIC directors who do appear in the minutes are searching for clergy, for example, or explaining the company's support for clerical education. In general, they acted as liaisons to the company, just as the company had its own committees and assigned the directors who were also elders or deacons to work with the church on some shared concern.[16]

Consistory membership wasn't necessarily evidence of principled, orthodox Calvinism. The Dutch Reformed Church was the public church, and those who served on the consistory enjoyed certain perks. Most basically they had greater status in the Reformed community. The deacons could access church funds, and they determined all other access. In mediating disagreements among church members and holding disciplinary hearings, elders made decisions that had serious impacts on people's lives. In other words, in an age when the church's good opinion mattered, when it was involved in everything from public charity to public education, elders and deacons held real power.

Southerners in particular may have had a similar motive in joining both the consistories and the WIC. Any immigrant or child of an immigrant, anyone not raised as an Amsterdam burgher, was usually barred from holding secular office. The church and the company thus offered a different kind of power—a complementary, parallel system when the government and church were cooperating as intended, an alternative when they were not. And in Amsterdam, the two certainly did *not* get along from the 1620s through at least the 1640s. During the Arminian controversy the city had been a Calvinist haven, a headquarters for believers from all over the country to meet and discuss mutual problems and work out strategies to resist the latest heresies. Then in the 1620s, shortly after the WIC was founded, Calvinists lost the municipal government. Often labeled "Libertine," the new rulers were more tolerant, promoting a flexible, nondogmatic church, with little influence in the public sphere. Libertines were more likely to ignore illegal worship in conventicles and in the city's now famous *schuilkerken* ("hidden churches"), which the Calvinist faction opposed vociferously. The latter also tended to support the noble House of Orange and resisted all attempts to make peace with Spain.[17]

Partisan divides and Calvinist strength are both reflected in the stark segregation of consistory members and municipal office holders in the company's

Amsterdam chamber. Excluding the directors who came from Leiden and other participating cities, men who were not eligible for office in Amsterdam, about 40 percent were on the consistory at some point in their lives. By contrast, only 20 percent held the office of *burgemeester*, *vroedschap* member, or *schepen* (roughly "mayor," "town councilor," and "judge"). Only five directors overlapped, working for church and government both; and four of those five individuals came to power in the city's Calvinist years or were recognized members of the consistorial party afterward. The one exception was *burgemeester* Cornelis Witsen, who served a single term as deacon in the 1650s.[18]

Disentangling the complicated reasons that WIC directors participated on consistories (faith, status, power, the church's support for global interests) is like performing an autopsy and trying to decide whether the dead man's body used to function because of his brain, heart, or lungs. Before they ended up on the autopsy table, the directors probably would have objected to losing any of the above, even if we could pressure them to reflect on the relative importance of each in relation to the rest. Unless they gave a selfish, materialist answer, most modern intellectuals would likely suspect their sincerity anyway. In the very least, the consistory offers something more tangible than words and something to measure their words against. The divide between church and government in Amsterdam makes the consistory a starting point and tentative guide to the preferences and loyalties of wealthy men during the turbulent years after the Libertine takeover.

Equally tangible, the directors threw the weight of their company behind the church and its political agenda at critical moments, first during conflicts with Libertines over the question of Arminian gatherings in 1626 and 1627. When Prince Frederik Hendrik came to Amsterdam to mediate the heated, escalating quarrel, he met with the town council and delegates from the consistory, later with the consistory on its own. Supporting the church at the first meeting, though representing the company in this case, were the directors, possibly also some of the merchants who had elected them (the *hoofdparticipanten*).[19] Afterward they penned a pamphlet in which they boasted that they "mostly" belonged to the Reformed Church. Like Johannes de Laet would argue in his 1636 history, they claimed that the WIC was founded first to honor God. Their purpose in investing their "considerable capital," they wrote, was to promote true religion in the Netherlands and on other continents, and to destroy the enemy. They were doing their part in America; they just wanted the city to do its part by upholding Reformed privileges and preventing "forbidden conventicles" at home.[20] At the prince's request, WIC directors "employed all their people in the service of the Country" during a Spanish invasion a few years later. To do so, explained one Reformed minister, they had to re-direct troops intended for the conquest of Brazil, which was delayed.[21]

Political opponents sometimes questioned whether God and religion were really among the company's chief interests. But in these early years, even they still described it as a southern, Calvinist institution.[22] One also hears hints of the southern voice (and possible southern insecurity) in the directors' constant appeals to patriotism and country, as if these newcomers and outsiders had something to prove. The *hoofdparticipanten* were "all good patriots," they assured the prince. The WIC had benefited and would continue to benefit the Dutch Republic and the city of Amsterdam in countless ways. They highlighted their allegiance to city and state alongside their hatred of Spain and their love for the church in much of what they said and wrote about the company's work.[23]

With limited success, Amsterdam's Libertine rulers tried to grow their party's influence in the WIC after they came to power. The *hoofdparticipanten* may have nominated potential directors, but they, the secular rulers, made the final picks from the triple slate of candidates the *hoofdparticipanten* gave them. Calvinists could and did still maintain their control by offering only their friends: there are no "Hollanders" on this list, rulers complained in 1626. They complained of the same in July 1629 and again in December, when they asked the *hoofdparticipanten* for "half Hollanders and half foreigners."[24] And they sometimes got their way. Known Libertines in the first generation of WIC directors in Amsterdam include Cornelis Bicker and Albert Burgh, perhaps Reynier Reael. Bicker's brother Andries was the longtime head of the Libertine party, and all three men served as watchdogs in the consistory after the city began appointing secular delegates to prevent the election of overly divisive ministers, elders, and deacons.[25]

But no amount of political pressure could eliminate the Calvinist advantage overnight, nor even in one generation. The birthplace requirement was a limited tool because, as long as Calvinism was popular among the *hoofdparticipanten*, they could just meet the Hollander quota by nominating Hollanders who shared their religion and politics. Calvinists also enjoyed the prestige and power of the law because theirs was the public church. Even Libertines had to join if they wanted to be eligible for most major civic positions. The large majority of WIC directors married and baptized their children in the *Oude Kerk* or *Nieuwe Kerk*, sometimes one of Amsterdam's other public facilities; and unless they used pseudonyms, no director ever participated on the Lutheran or Arminian consistories. The consequences were too great, the consistorial party too watchful and loud. Among the Amsterdam directors who didn't originally live in the city, men who represented places like Leiden and

Utrecht, almost two-thirds served on their own consistories. Add to their number the many Zeeland directors who were consistory members in that most strictly orthodox of provinces, and Calvinists clearly had a strong voice in the West India Company.[26]

"I Will Pay My Vows unto the Lord"

A merchant's wealth and religious affiliations came with financial expectations and responsibilities to match the political ones. That the WIC participated in Dutch Reformed charity is not especially remarkable because, as one of the main caregivers in the Netherlands, church deaconries received support from many institutions, including the VOC, whose success allowed greater and more consistent contributions than the WIC could give. Still, the latter's reputation as guardian of the true religion depended in part on assisting the needy. The many migrants and outsiders in the company's upper echelons also may have given aid more often to Protestants in other countries.[27]

The Dutch did not try to hide their fiscal goals and their desire for riches. Far from it: if only because they needed to find investors before the WIC could finance its work, they trumpeted both. They wrote about capital, profits, and wealth in the very same pamphlets, the same passages, the same *sentences* as they did religio-political objectives—as if all goals were the same. "Invest," urged Willem Usselincx, another southern migrant and early supporter of the company. He said that those who loved the true religion would willingly and happily invest more, and he promised "extremely great profits for ourselves individually and for the Fatherland." In a subtle, plucky reference to the Gospel of Luke, Usselincx told his readers that even Jesus Christ recognized the need to make financial plans and calculate costs. The comparison was plucky, maybe pretentious, because in the relevant passage (Luke 14:28) Christ was talking about erecting a tower—but not a literal tower with literal building costs. He was asking his disciples to give up everything they had to follow him. Perceptive readers would equate Christian discipleship and building God's kingdom with buying WIC stock. Less perceptive readers, people who were not as familiar with the Bible, would still get the message because Usselincx said as much in plain words.[28]

Company directors once teamed up with the Reformed consistory and with Frederick V, a German prince, to publish a tract with a similar message— although in this case, their main goal was to scuttle ongoing peace talks, and they explicitly distanced themselves from "greed." They described investment instead as an act of love. To prove the point, they reviewed the company's history: how it had been postponed during the Twelve-Year Truce (1609–1621) and how so many people had come forward to contribute funds when it finally got off the ground. Patriots had waited a long time for the WIC, the directors wrote. Even some poor had invested their capital "in their poverty."[29] In reality, the VOC had more investors, including more small investors. But the money of small and middling investors in the WIC was a greater proportion of the whole (78 percent) than it was in the VOC (54 percent) because the WIC had far fewer *major* investors, meaning men who contributed more than ƒ10,000.[30] Whether they were familiar enough with the statistics in both companies to make exact comparisons, WIC directors must have at least known that the VOC had more wealth at the top because they promoted their company as a champion or representative of the poor. If it did well, if it prospered from African gold and American silver, everyone's investments would grow at the same rate, no matter their other circumstances. It was the seventeenth-century version of the twentieth-century aphorism "a rising tide lifts all boats."

Dutch theologians counseled the directors about the dangers and proper uses of their commercial treasure. Merchants should not spend money on sinful pastimes and pompous display, but live modestly and give liberally to the church and poor. Then "the affairs of this company" will be "the affairs of God," wrote Willem Teellinck, an influential minister based in Zeeland. God had given the Dutch "a whole new world" and asked only for part of it in return. Reverends Dionysium Spranckhuysen and Godefridus Udemans taught that merchants "insured" their goods and "sanctified" trade when they proffered alms. As the title implies, Udemans's *Spiritual Rudder of the Merchant's Ship* (1638) was a kind of religious handbook for the maritime profession, used in the Atlantic world and probably in Dutch Asia, too.[31] All three men expressed common clerical concerns about the connection between money and profligate living—about prostitution and gambling, for example. Yet they were not afraid to celebrate wealth. Ministers and merchants were, in a sense, codependent. Merchants found in their faith an ideology and validation for their way of life; the WIC helped spread the church and maintain it financially at home.[32]

Some directors weren't sufficiently moderate in their dress and other expenditures to satisfy the devout, at least in Amsterdam, where the general public typically ignored—and maybe even came to expect—a certain level of flashy exhibition from the upper class. One of the grandest, most lavish homes of seventeenth-century Amsterdam was owned by WIC director Guillelmo Bartolotti. His entrance hall boasted two large West Indies maps, as well as thirteen paintings and various furnishings. He packed the rest of the house with art and wall hangings, leather chairs and couches, cabinets, Turkish rugs, mirrors, ebony tables and buffets, oak chests, a bird cage, and (still on the inside) a stone fountain. The tax value alone on the tapestries in one room was ƒ900, "about the cost of purchasing an entire house for a small tradesman."[33]

Bartolotti had earned his fortune as a merchant and banker, teaming up with family and professional acquaintances in the Calvinist diaspora to trade throughout Europe and the Mediterranean world—from Hamburg and Emden to Italy and the Levant. If other directors did not have quite the same wealth, they were often still successful, and they too had many valuable possessions. Perhaps their church work and charitable giving assuaged whatever guilt they might otherwise have felt from the more pessimistic fiscal warnings of their clerical counselors. Samuel Godyn, a dealer in American dyewoods and furs, was one of the most active participants in the church. He served three times as elder in the French-speaking consistory and twice at the Walloon synod. He left money to the poor and for the education of new clergy when he died. In his library were Bibles in Dutch and French, John Calvin's *Institutes of the Christian Religion*, an anthology of Calvin's sermons, and Calvin's commentaries on various Bible books.[34] Even Bartolotti, who never served as elder or deacon, "belonged to the more militantly Calvinist group within the city." He was a full member of the Dutch Reformed Church, and outside his opulent home he fastened a plaque inscribed "Religione et Probitate." Beside it, the deacons hung a box where Bartolotti and any visitors could donate to the poor.[35]

The directors gave both as individuals and as a company. Most donations were private, collected by deacons at church or dropped in boxes hanging all over the city: outside member homes and in public places like the orphanage and *wisselbank* ("exchange bank"). A list of boxes from the 1630s and 1640s shows them hanging at the homes of twenty-four WIC directors in Amsterdam. One was also at the company's warehouse on the waterfront and two at the West Indies House, the company's central offices on the west side of town. Employees would pass the first box as they entered the building, then find another hanging suggestively in the accounting office, where they picked up their pay. Deacons emptied all the boxes once per month, collecting funds that varied sometimes drastically from month to month. For example, soon after Admiral Piet Heyn's famous 1628 victory, when he captured a large Spanish silver fleet, they found ƒ1,227 in the boxes at the West Indies House, and the next month they found ƒ496. Money from WIC boxes was more often between ƒ100 and ƒ200 per month, and from the homes of individual directors, between ƒ14 and ƒ130. Deacons could meet the basic needs of a family of five with about ƒ280 per year.[36]

In addition to these anonymous monies, which could have come from employees or directors or visitors to their homes and offices, the directors

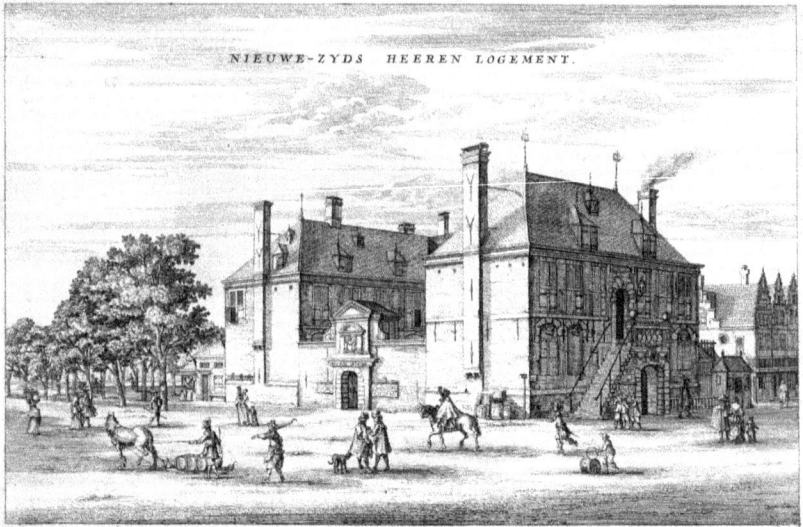

The West Indies House in Amsterdam, later the Nieuwe-Zyds Heeren Logement, engraved by Jacob van Meurs (1663). Courtesy of the Stadsarchief Amsterdam.

sometimes gave more openly. Jacques Specx donated *f* 1,500 at his death. Jan Bartringh, Johan le Thor, and Hendrick Broen all donated *f* 1,000, and others gave lesser amounts. Le Thor also left *f* 3,000 to be divided three ways among the Walloon churches of Amsterdam and Leiden, the third part going to the Swedish town Northoppinghen, where a certain copper company had once selected him to represent its interests in the Netherlands. Other directors gave while they were living, ranging from Jan van Geel's "voluntary gift" of *f* 200 to Charles Loten's donation of *f* 600, tendered shortly after the Heyn victory. Some brought in large amounts on behalf of loved ones. As legacies from their late wives, Loten and Bartringh once handed the deacons *f* 2,000 and *f* 1,000 on the same day. Over one twenty-four-year stretch, these kinds of donations added up to about *f* 23,000, not including money from boxes and other anonymous giving.[37]

The WIC donated to the church in minor, irregular ways. When a visiting minister requested assistance for the construction of a new chapel in his home town, the Zeeland chamber contributed *f* 25, the directors implying when they did so that they and their counterparts in the Amsterdam chamber had acquiesced to such requests before. Somewhat grudgingly, they also once divided an unknown quantity of sugar among the clergy of Middelburg, Vlissingen, and Veere. And in December 1643, they resolved to sell "some old supplies" from the ship *Noord Holland* and give the proceeds to the poor.[38]

More significantly and regularly, the Zeeland and Amsterdam chambers gave one penny per thousand to the deaconries from all goods that arrived in the Netherlands from overseas. In providing these "poor monies," the directors were effectively tithing their own income, since they were compensated from the same imports (one penny per hundred). In Amsterdam they divided the money among Dutch-, French-, and English-speaking churches, sometimes a civil charity called the *aelmoeseniers*. Zeeland directors allocated the same fund to Dutch- and French-speaking churches (probably English-speaking ones, too) in all towns with directors, including Tholen, whose deacons received a one-twelfth part. Any merchants who sailed and sold within the WIC's sphere of influence had to pay, and the company imposed fines on those who were tardy. In January 1634 the Amsterdam directors reported that their poor monies had reached f 6,920. The Dutch consistory's share in that case was f 2,400, which was unusually high. On other occasions it was between f 1,000 and f 1,770.[39] Records are too spotty for any accurate total, but there is evidence that the WIC continued to pay poor monies even after it fell on hard times. Where it had to cut back, it stopped paying interest, for example, on a number of company bonds that someone had donated to the deaconry. The consistory ended up selling the bonds for less than a quarter of their original value and using the money to help fund a new orphanage.[40]

WIC employees sometimes gave to the church against their will. The directors fined them for violating company policies and outright misconduct, like getting drunk on the job, then deducted the fines from their wages and added it to the poor money. More often, employees made the same kinds of open donations as the directors. The deacons would arrive at the West Indies House to empty the collection boxes and someone would hand them an extra f 15. Others would give money before their ship departed, perhaps fearing the dangers of the journey and hoping for a bit of divine "insurance." Or they would return from West Africa and give the deacons raw gold (probably illegally in some cases).[41] At each visit the deacons would also ask about the funds left by employees in their wills, usually collecting between f 100 and f 300 all together from the recent dead. But people weren't always clear about the intended recipient. Deacons from the Walloon church in Middelburg once came to the Zeeland chamber to ask that money left by French speakers be used for the "French poor." Confusion only grew when the colonial population expanded and everyone began to ask if wills should be paid at home or abroad. So diverse was the Netherlands, the directors finally had to tell employees to specify exactly which cities and institutions they wanted to support.[42]

Most salaries were so low that giving to the poor meant giving to one's own peers. The f 8–14 per month earned by sailors and soldiers—even the f 12–18 of corporals and sergeants—was enough to support themselves and maybe one or two others, but not a family of any considerable size. Indeed, the work deacons performed on behalf of poor Reformed members in Africa and America was yet another reason for the close union of church and company. Deacons did more than distribute funds; they sometimes managed an employee's wages when the church was assisting his relatives, like the ƒ24 they once received at the West Indies House for the mother of Dirck Andries, company carpenter, or the ƒ93 they took from the wages of Artus Beck, crediting it to the account of his daughter Helena at the local orphanage.[43] Deacons also sometimes asked the directors to compensate those who had been injured or maimed in the company's service. But unless they could draw funds from whatever wages they still owed the individual in question, the directors paid only hesitantly and at the least possible expense to the WIC.[44]

Their reluctance to treat with disadvantaged employees one-on-one, even when the company was responsible for someone's bad situation, perhaps stemmed from the fact that WIC work was so deadly and dangerous. And they were already contributing to the institutions that dealt with social problems. They tried to maintain a hazy boundary: the WIC was first a business, not a charity, and it was arguably fulfilling its obligations to society on two levels. As they never tired of reminding people, they employed numerous Dutch and immigrant men. They put thousands to work each year in their warehouses and offices at home, aboard their ships, and in their forts and colonies. If the opportunities that they provided paid poorly, so did comparable situations with the Dutch navy and VOC. By giving to the deaconry (and some civic charities) the directors tried to fulfill their duties as prosperous Christian merchants and, at the same time, compensate their employees collectively for the poverty and other difficulties associated with working in the Atlantic world. They sustained the organizations that cared for the company's own sick and injured, its own widows and orphans.[45]

WIC directors were especially well placed to assist needy Protestants in other countries. Their trading and banking, their consistory membership, and their status as "foreigners" (to borrow the *vroedschap*'s word) all enabled the flow of funds across state boundaries. They traded throughout Europe with familial and commercial connections that were at least as old as the late sixteenth-century exodus from the southern Netherlands. With religious wars still raging across the continent, the first half of the seventeenth century saw many more people driven from their homes, pouring into Holland and other stable regions, sometimes just writing or sending envoys to request food and monetary aid. The States General and provincial States had the power to institute widespread collections, yet they didn't grant every request because they

The West India Company warehouse in Amsterdam (n.d.). Courtesy of the Stadsarchief Amsterdam.

feared that the country would be inundated with supplicants; or they worried about the impact of a national collection on Dutch foreign policy. Individual churches and church councils usually collected alms regardless. As *the* major trade entrepôt in Europe, Amsterdam functioned also as a clearinghouse for donations from all over the Netherlands to Protestants in France, Germany, Switzerland, Poland, Hungary, and Italy.[46]

For merchants like Abraham de Bra, supporting these "brethren in Christ" was a sacred endeavor—and quite personal. De Bra's parents had originally left the southern Netherlands not for the Dutch Republic but for Nuremberg, where one branch of the family had remained ever since. A major investor in the WIC and a regular Brazil trader, he only came to Holland permanently in 1633. Both before and after the move he was the primary contact for transferring funds between the two regions, drawing on his credit with banker Abraham Blommaert, whose family was also involved in the WIC. Nuremberg was now home to a whole new generation of refugees, this time from the German Palatinate, and they needed the same help that De Bra's parents had received before.[47]

WIC directors appear regularly in the annals of international charity in the 1620s, 1630s, and beyond. Guillelmo Bartolotti was among the first to notify the Amsterdam consistory about the Nuremberg refugees; Rombout Jacobsen informed the *burgemeesters*.[48] Other active directors included Isaac van Beeck, Frederick van Geel, Hendrick and Marcus Broen, Johan le Thor, Jeronimus Heesters, and Charles Loten. They carried food or remitted alms most often to war-torn lands in Germany, sometimes to duchies where they also had business relationships, like Anhalt: Christian I, prince of Anhalt-Bernburg, was a Calvinist military leader during the Thirty Years War and a major investor in the WIC.[49] Similarly, when the church in Amsterdam learned in 1643 that Catholics in Ireland had risen up against the Protestant, English minority, the classis organized a special day of prayer and gathered a large sum for the English. The collection was "a work of love" for "our brethren in the faith," classis members wrote. They gave the money to fellow elder and WIC director Isaac van Beeck. He purchased grain, cheese, butter, peas, salt, beans, and other supplies, which Charles Loten (director and deacon) carried to London aboard several ships. Both men had family and professional contacts in England or they worked with merchants who came originally from England and sat on Amsterdam's English-speaking consistory.[50]

Whether company directors ever gave enough is a debatable, insoluble question that surely differed from person to person and probably belongs more to theologians and philosophers than historians. In the very least, charity was an important part of the directors' identity and reputation as Calvinist merchants. And their contribution wasn't trivial. Taken together, money from the WIC and its associates totaled hundreds of thousands of guilders over the company's lifetime.

Practicing Piety within the Company

In addition to consistory activity and almsgiving, WIC directors expressed their religious beliefs and observed certain religious rituals in the day-to-day management of colonial affairs. The Zeeland *hoofdparticipanten* once resolved that no one should hold any position of importance within the company unless he first professed "the true Christian Reformed Religion."[51] That probably never became a widespread policy, and some non-Reformed officers did serve the WIC in time. But the Nineteen Lords agreed that they should call the most capable, "god-fearing" men available. They saw victory as a blessing from "God Almighty," who granted success and failure, power and poverty, life and death. When they selected Boudewijn Hendricks to command their fleets in 1624, they asked the clergy in his home town to visit his wife and tell her to "be at peace." "Like everyone in his office," they explained, her husband was "called of God." As they readied ships and arranged for ministers and other needs in the future, they claimed that nothing was "more dear to [their] hearts than Religion."[52]

Compared against the magnitude of daily business, pious expressions in WIC letters and minutes are few and far between. But sugar, gold, fur, tobacco, and other common topics weren't just secular concerns, too profane for God's lofty attention and divorced from his providential arrangements. Perhaps for that reason the directors inscribed company records "in the name of the Lord," dedicated to "the King of Kings, Immortal and Invisible." To "God alone be the wisdom, honor, and glory," they wrote on one occasion: "Praise God Almighty." Borrowing from Psalm 146, they declared that "our help is in . . . the Lord, who created and made the Heaven, Earth, and Sea, with everything in them, Amen."[53] "Everything" necessarily included the commodities they were then taking from the earth and trading with the peoples of the Atlantic world. According to Dutch Reformed ministers Willem Teellinck and Godefridus Udemans, material goods were God's gift to man, helping his children appreciate the wonder of creation and prospering the nation. There was no natural discrepancy in declaring a love of religion on the one hand and pursuing profit on the other.[54]

Just as written minutes began with statements of piety, so meetings at every level began with an invocation—likely just a longer version of the dedication. Generally the scribe didn't record it, except to note that it had taken place. In the minutes of the Nineteen Lords: "the lord Goch read the usual prayer," "the lord Van der Meer called upon the name of the Lord," and commonly, we "call[ed] on God's holy name."[55] Other WIC councils used similar expressions. The Zeeland *hoofdparticipanten* set the prayer as a deadline, forbidding anyone who showed up afterward to vote on new directors. Because at least one of them was always a Reformed minister, he must have offered it for them. In other meetings the president just read the invocation, probably from an orthodox work like the catechism, which contained printed prayers for specific occasions and times of day. In their minutes, in the place where they usually mentioned their own prayer, the Amsterdam *hoofdparticipanten* once wrote that "God will bless [our] consultations and good decisions, amen."[56]

As they took care of business matters during the regular work week, the directors found other small ways to demonstrate their faith and kinship with the church. For sailors and soldiers aboard company ships and yachts that remained in Dutch waters, the directors asked local ministers to come aboard temporarily to preach and offer prayers, even perform a marriage on one occasion.[57] Then they scheduled their Wednesday meetings later than others so they, too, could attend the services that were held that day throughout the Netherlands. Once they offered to carry envoys from the Walcheren classis aboard their yacht to Amsterdam when the classis wanted to see the Nineteen Lords about Portugal's policy toward Dutch Brazil. Echoing the Nineteen Lords' own declaration about love of religion, the Zeeland *hoofdpartici-panten* and directors said that planting the Gospel was one of their "principal objectives." In talks with Portugal, they maintained, the "weightiest matter [for Dutch merchants who visited there] is religion and worship."[58]

Rhetoric about religious intent is easier to accept when it wasn't published with a clear propagandistic purpose, when the directors recorded their views in meeting minutes and other handwritten documents that contemporaries would never see. Setting aside for a moment whether they ever made the Gospel a major priority in their sphere of influence, the directors did seem to believe that by working overseas—even when their work was obviously commercial—they were also spreading Christ's kingdom. To make that case, they didn't even need the more nebulous, metaphysical arguments about the blessings of their profession and the spiritual benefits of material things. After all, they had partnered with the public church, so the church went wherever their ships sailed and the church grew wherever the WIC exercised power.

The directors cared enough about colonial religion to monitor and participate in clerical hires. Despite the fact that some of them already belonged to the consistories and classes that conducted exams, they wanted an official, separate company presence throughout the whole process, sending their own representatives to hear applicants preach, sometimes attending ordinations afterward. When the church's Indies committee introduced them in 1630 to Christianus Wachtelo, who had already delivered his sermon by that point, the directors said they wanted to hear him anyway. A number of them then attended the special meeting set up later that week.[59] "Many" also went to Jan Michielsen's sermon in 1635 and were "often inclined" to do so, the committee reported. In 1640 the directors listened to Johannes Offeringa and Petrus Ongena with "great pleasure." After they asked to hear another candidate's "gift of preaching" in 1643, church deputies actually complained. The WIC should be content, they said, with a simple recommendation. But the directors insisted, and the church arranged another meeting in a chapel called the *Nieuwezijds Kapel*.[60] Only once did they reject a previously accepted minister because of his sermon (more precisely, because of a thick German accent); yet they continued to request and attend the extra services year after year.[61]

For clergy who already held positions at home, the directors also helped secure their release, traveling up to ninety miles by boat, canal, and coach.

When someone already had a calling and wanted to leave it, it wasn't just a matter of walking away. He had to obtain permission from his classis and from municipal or provincial rulers, depending on who paid his salary. He had to go before his classis with the directors and a spokesman from the Amsterdam or Walcheren classis and explain where he was going and why he wanted to serve abroad. If the WIC's call was temporary and the minister hoped to return to his post afterward, church and company had to find a replacement. And if any employee later decided to extend his contract, the directors went through the whole process again, writing and in some cases traveling to his old classis to explain the situation and ask permission for him to remain away from his church.[62] These difficult and costly arrangements help explain the WIC's dependence on younger, less experienced clergy, especially considering spousal issues. The directors had many "tiresome conferences" with Machtelt Steengen, wife of Reverend Megapolensis, before they convinced the two to stay in New Netherland in 1648. She had lived there for about five years and had recently returned to Holland ahead of her husband.[63]

The directors supplemented training and provided other support for future colonial ministers and lay clergy. They paid men half wages for weeks and months before their departure, gave them extra time to learn their trade and refine their Dutch-language skills, and paid for the education of some men at the university. The WIC also considered creating a seminary like one the VOC operated for twelve years. At the behest of various churches and investors, the Nineteen Lords addressed the issue at their earliest meetings, designating a few directors to analyze the VOC's school and report on its operation and costs.[64] In the meantime they helped potential colonial clergy on a case-by-case basis, starting with at least five German refugees, then adding others. In 1630, for example, Anthony Godyn told his fellow directors in Zeeland about a school-master at a nearby Latin school who might be willing to preach overseas. Johannes Loosvelt ended up signing with the company in exchange for ƒ200 per year, which allowed him to study theology at a higher level. In the same period the company funded Franciscus Plante's education in Groningen and the training of a third, unnamed individual. Arrangements seem to have varied from person to person. Some men received straightforward company resources, others drew on their own future salaries.[65]

The seminary never got off the ground because the company saw so few benefits, even from these less costly efforts. Plante served for more than seven years, but other men—other "investments"—didn't serve a single day because they got too ill or died before leaving Europe. And Loosvelt was a major disappointment for different reasons. After supporting him for five years, the directors learned that he didn't want to go anywhere and that he hadn't even been preparing to do so! He had just been living off WIC charity, in a sense, and they demanded repayment.[66] When the Walcheren classis began campaigning again for a seminary in 1638, a director and elder from Rotterdam explained why the company was reluctant now to invest large sums in education. The directors had learned from experience that when they "keep" or "raise" students for "the service of the church and visitation of the sick in the West Indies," neither the WIC nor church benefited much. "When great costs have already been spent on them," he continued, "they are incapable or unwilling to go." The VOC offered a similar explanation in the Amsterdam classis when the latter asked it to reopen its seminary a few years later. VOC directors said that they had enjoyed little "fruit" from their school. But they did offer to subsidize training on a one-on-one basis, like the WIC. Lasting from the 1620s through the 1640s, targeted assistance revealed the supportive-yet-economical, cost-conscious mind-set that characterized all facets of the WIC's religious work.[67]

Subsidizing future clergy was neither fully self-interested nor purely pious and charitable; it was a mixture of all three. It was a pragmatic investment in the sense that good ministers were essential to the smooth operation of colonial affairs, and again, some university students were just drawing on their own future salaries. At the same time, whatever other factors they considered, the long record of religious conflict and migration among the directors could have only heightened their spiritual sentiment and sense of loyalty to Calvinists and Calvinist refugees in particular. Providing aid and opportunities to foreigners via the WIC was just the latest version of an old story among coreligionists in post-Reformation, war-torn Europe. European Calvinists never formed a monolithic clique. But the bonds among them were real, and those bonds often survived national rivalries and disputes. Appreciating the company's foreign roots and connections helps us situate it within the wider community. The WIC was a kind of Netherlands writ small, an extension of Holland's place in Protestant Europe: a refuge for exiles, a second chance when their homes were destroyed, a way to participate overseas in the very conflicts that disrupted their lives in the first place.

One final example of religious devotion and the company's relationship with the Dutch Reformed Church: The merchant Hendrik Haecx lived in Brazil in the early 1640s, serving as deacon on the colonial consistory, sometimes speaking for the church before the government. Upon reaching home he began keeping a diary, and he soon reported rumors that the WIC was going to ask him to return to Brazil. On July 5, 1645, he indeed received notification from the Nineteen Lords. When he met with a small group of them the next day, including Charles Loten, a former Amsterdam deacon, they informed him that they had selected him for Brazil's High Council, one of the most power-ful bodies in the colony. In a message perhaps calculated to resonate with his particular history of service in the church—one deacon speaking to another deacon—they asked him to remember the "planting of God's honor" and "the many widows and orphans" who depended on the company. He was reluc-tant to leave his home and business, he wrote, but after spending an "entire day and night" in "fervent prayer," he decided to accept the assignment. At that point the directors gave him just two instructions: to show no favoritism among the different company chambers and to always seek "the honor of God" in America.[68]

The directors' advice to Haecx resembled their rhetoric about godly goals and pious intent on other occasions. They described WIC success first in spir-itual terms; they tied its fate to the happiness and well-being of people who weren't even on the payroll. His was no simple job offer, they suggested, but a meaningful opportunity to serve God and the poor by working for the com-pany. And in his response, in his hesitation and prayerful consideration, Haecx behaved as a devout merchant was supposed to behave. He downplayed the selfish advantages of accepting the offer, speculated on the potential harm to his business and personal relationships, and turned the decision into a ques-tion about God's will. Having determined that God wanted him to embrace what was clearly also an opportunity for professional advancement and po-litical power, he traveled from Amsterdam to Vlissingen, where he eventually boarded a ship bound for Brazil. Among those who came to see him off were the Zeeland directors and "numerous" Reformed ministers from Middelburg and other places, he wrote, adding that the ship set sail "in God's name." When he met with two ministers on a brief return visit in late 1648, they talked about the church in Amsterdam and Brazil, and they thanked him for his work on their behalf.[69]

The cooperation and codependence of church and company in the Neth-erlands belies the dichotomy implied in that very expression—"church and company"—however necessary and useful it can be. Even if they disagreed from time to time, drawing a stark division between them is especially prob-lematic in this case because of the history and doctrine of the church in ques-tion. With its presbyterian organization and broad, inclusive conception of priesthood, the Dutch Reformed Church was ruled, at least in principle, by elders and deacons. Clergy came to play a dominant role in the church, but lay leaders had a strong voice, and they participated at every level. Company directors were intimately familiar with the major religious issues and prob-lems of the day because they held positions of ecclesiastical authority and worked with Protestants in other countries. As elders they supported the church at home in debates that also took place in their colonies and addressed WIC needs and theological questions in their consistories and other Reformed councils. As deacons they collected money from the company and cared for the widows and orphans of their own employees. Their positions and experience facilitated an endless stream of business between company and church as the two worked literally as one to supervise religious matters in the Dutch Atlantic world.

CHAPTER 3

Baptized by Water and Fire

The Religious Rites of the Company's Early Fleets and Conquests

For all their reputation as a seafaring, commercial people, farm imagery and the language of the soil were surprisingly popular among Dutch writers. Whether it was the WIC colonel who, having participated in the Brazil invasion, compared his exertions to planting seeds and spreading "God's holy name," or the Zeeland merchants who sought God's blessing by planting his word in America, Protestants associated the WIC's work with a figurative harvest: sowing, reaping, extending the boundaries of the Lord's vineyard. More specifically, "planting" was a favorite metaphor in ecclesiastical circles for establishing Reformed Christianity by calling a minister and forming a consistory wherever they didn't exist already.[1]

Unfortunately for the church, the company's early methods did not lend themselves to stable religious life; they did not provide fertile ground for the kind of planting the clergy were called to do, so suddenly and violently did the Dutch Atlantic burst into existence. If the Dutch adopted the language of rustic cultivation from the New Testament, they preferred to filch the crops of other Europeans using the militant tools of the Old. The WIC's original goal was to obtain trade and territory by taking them from the Republic's enemies, and between 1623 and 1643 it made good on its commitments. In addition to hundreds of Spanish ships, the company captured Elmina, Axim, Luanda, and São Tomé in West Africa; and Brazil, Curaçao, and other Caribbean islands in America. In the words of the prophet Joel, the Dutch "beat [their] plowshares into swords, and [their] pruninghooks into spears"; the vine-yard became a battleground, and in place of water, they poured fire, blood, and death on their rivals, impatiently procuring an empire from the most vulnerable parts of the Spanish and Portuguese Empires.[2] Their tactics were inspired in part by religious sentiment—by Calvinist zeal and anti-Catholicism—but in the long run, the regular work of the ministry could not proceed in a war zone, nor flourish in occupied enemy colonies. The many new possessions, so swiftly acquired, also placed unrealistic burdens on those who were supposed to find and support clerical personnel.

If Calvinists recognized the true cause of their challenges, they had no one to blame but themselves. The Dutch Reformed Church was fully committed to the Orangist war party in Europe, and the church's most ardent defenders often worked simultaneously as apologists for the House of Orange and its belligerent foreign policy. They served both camps when, for example, they dismissed the peace process as a secret Catholic, Arminian plot to generate spiritual complacency among Reformed members. According to this theory, when the country was not at war, people forgot Spain's tyranny, religious non-conformers were able to worship with less restraint, Spain recovered from recent military losses and grew strong again, and (as Catholic conspirators al-legedly intended from the start) Spain could then return and reenslave the Dutch. The WIC wouldn't let that happen, supporters believed, because its very existence was tied up in conflict. It was God's instrument for punishing Spanish transgressions and destroying Spain's capacity for violence. Only by continuing their "righteous war" and taking it overseas, only by fighting the enemy globally, could the Dutch suppress nonconformers at home and ob-tain a lasting, uncompromised peace.[3] "Let us plant in America a stem from this ongoing war," wrote one enthusiastic writer. "Let us pillage and plunder the lands of the brutal Spaniards, destroy them with flame and fire, that the cinders rise to heaven. Let us repay them there for all the hardships and cruel-ties that we have suffered in war these fifty-seven years, and make the West Indies," he concluded on a boldly vicious note, "a spectacle of misery."[4]

The Bible was a critical resource for theologians who chose to support this aggressive agenda. In *Spiritual Rudder of the Merchant's Ship* (1638), Godefri-dus Udemans rejected the idea that Christians could not, in good conscience, participate in war. He said that bloodshed was necessary in the face of evil and he pointed out that God himself was sometimes called "warrior."[5] Udemans and his fellow ministers taught a vision of life and time in which God and the Devil used the earth as a cosmic battleground in a primal struggle for the human soul. Like Calvinists everywhere, the Dutch equated their history of conflict and exile with other spiritual epochs, drawing heavily on Old Testament themes and scriptures about the children of Israel and the promised land. They relied on stories about Joshua, who destroyed Jericho, and David, who killed Goliath and expanded the kingdom of Israel by the sword. They quoted Bible passages that seemed to validate conquest: "Thou shalt smite every male," commanded one scripture. Another described "the dead bodies fallen to the earth" and the spoils Israel gathered afterward. In these formulations, the Dutch were the new Israelites. Company officers were Bible heroes; Spain was Egypt and Canaan and other traditional enemies of God's people.[6]

In keeping with the foreign influences in the West India Company, its directors also highlighted the shared, international benefits of their militarism, basically selling their work as a program for global freedom. They said they would draw Spanish attention and Spanish resources away from Europe, alleviating the burden carried by Dutch allies—who did, in fact, sometimes invest in the company. The German prince Frederick V instructed his ambassador in Holland to encourage a warlike organization and agenda for the WIC before it was even founded, probably because he recognized the same potential benefit.[7] In general, WIC aggression was supposed to help free, beleaguered Protestants remain free, and it was supposed to provide breathing room and space for rebellion and conquest for places still under Spanish rule. Those places included the southern Netherlands, where so many WIC directors originated, and America, where oppressed Indians would (the story went) welcome their Dutch saviors with open arms.[8]

Some advocates of Dutch expansion disliked the company's violent methods, doubting their wisdom and profitability. Most famously, Willem Usselincx (1567–1647) promoted immigration, colonization, and trade, not in *place* of war, because he, too, saw war's value; but he was afraid of committing too much energy and too many resources to that end. Conquest, he warned, would be a weak foundation for the Dutch Atlantic empire. He was probably also correct in arguing that his approach would have raised more startup capital for the WIC. Its hawkish rhetoric and clear military aims scared away potential investors, leaving it with less initial wealth than the East India Company (VOC).[9]

In rejecting Usselincx, however, his opponents did not choose profit over piety, as company critics later claimed. Ultimately they all wanted profit, they just differed on how to obtain it most effectively. Usselincx was also a merchant and investor; his plans also centered on trade and wealth. The disagreement was really a question of speed and location, the WIC opting to hurry things along by conquering a lucrative sugar colony immediately. Yet Brazil was still (obviously) a colony; it was still a source for agricultural products and trade. And once established there the company worked closely with Native Americans,

The Dutch Republic and its colonies are in CAPS.

Common regional names are in *italics*.

North Atlanti fishery

North America

NEW NETHERLAND (1609-1664)

New Amsterdam

St. Maarten

The era of WIC privateering lasted roughly 1623 to 1643.

Saba

St. Eustatius

(1630s to the present)

West Indies

Tobago (1628-1678)

Aruba

Bonaire

Curaçao

(1630s to the present)

ESSEQUIBO BERBICE & DEMERARA (1616-1796)

SURINAME (1667-1975)

The Wild Coast (Guiana)

DUTCH BRAZIL (1630-1654)

R

Sal (1624-

South America

The Nassau & Brouwer fleets targeted Peru & Chile in 1623-1626 & 1643.

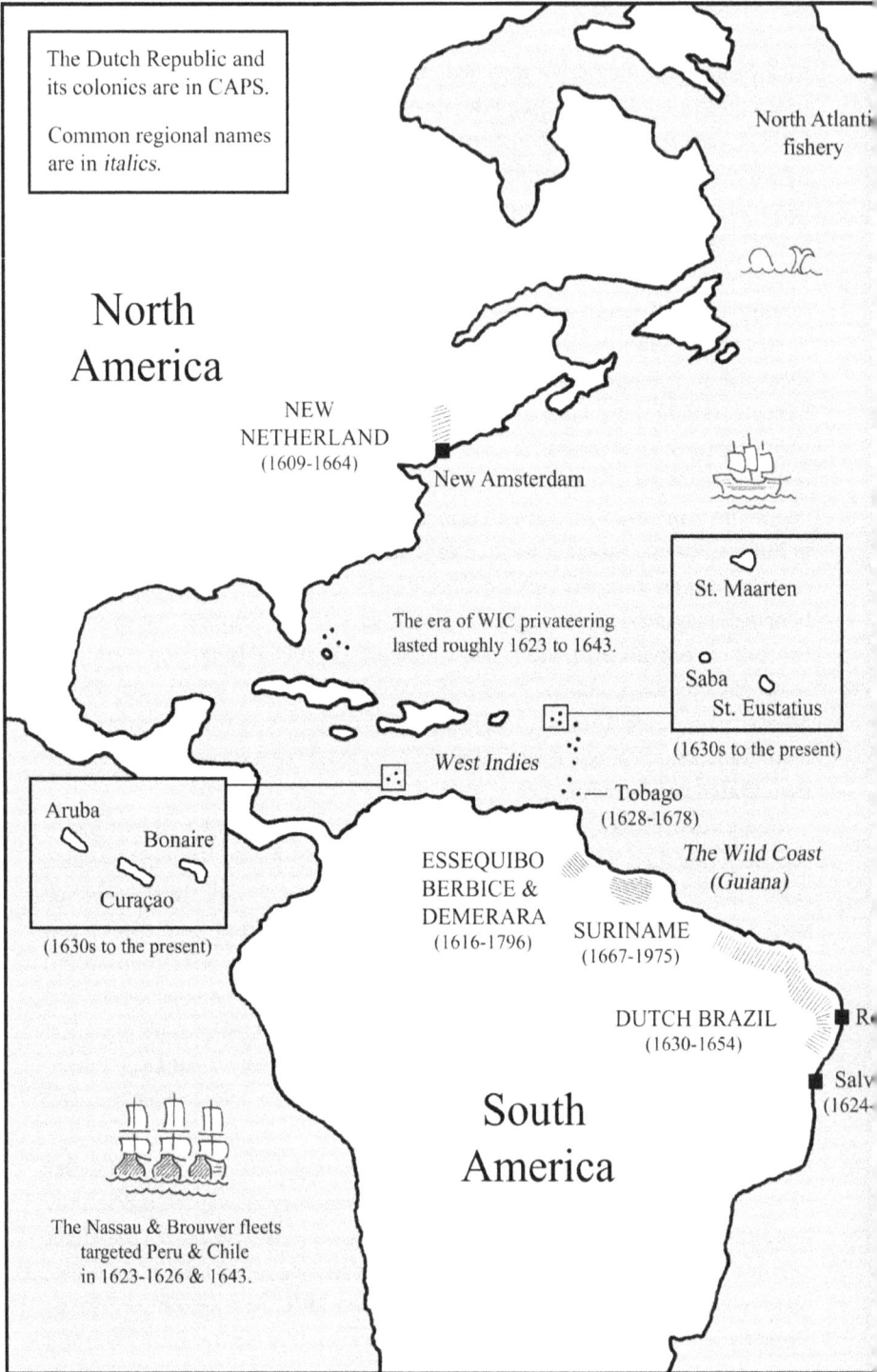

The Dutch Atlantic world. Map drawn by author.

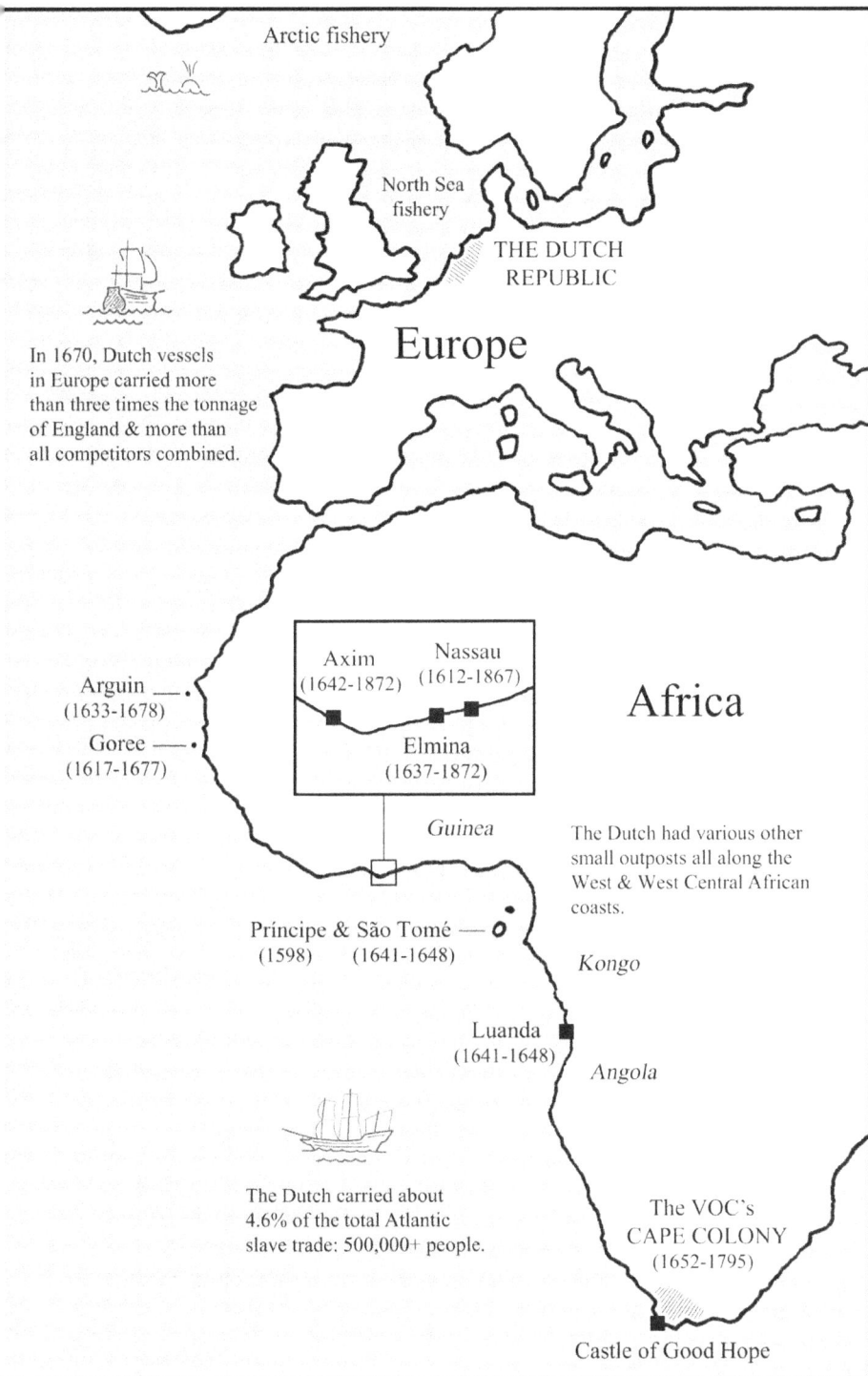

Arctic fishery

North Sea fishery

THE DUTCH REPUBLIC

Europe

In 1670, Dutch vessels in Europe carried more than three times the tonnage of England & more than all competitors combined.

Arguin ___ •
(1633-1678)

Goree —— •
(1617-1677)

Axim
(1642-1872)

Nassau
(1612-1867)

Elmina
(1637-1872)

Africa

Guinea

The Dutch had various other small outposts all along the West & West Central African coasts.

Príncipe & São Tomé — O
(1598)   (1641-1648)

Kongo

Luanda
(1641-1648)

Angola

The Dutch carried about 4.6% of the total Atlantic slave trade: 500,000+ people.

The VOC's
CAPE COLONY
(1652-1795)

Castle of Good Hope

as Usselincx had long proposed. If monopolistic, bellicose practices were, in the long run, detrimental to migration and stable society—and by extension, detrimental to the church—that was not the intent. The directors believed they were serving the church and doing God's work by attacking Catholic Spain and seizing the resources that fed its war chest. Their ideology was a creatively updated version of a concept or philosophy called "Protestant resistance theory," which fellow believers in other European countries had developed over the past century to justify violence against would-be Catholic oppressors. Partnered with the church, the WIC's more active "resistance" would strengthen Protestants at the expense of Catholics and garner massive profits at the same time. Without profit there could be no Protestant strength.[10]

The WIC could claim a religious mission because it continued the wars of the Reformation, extending them across oceans to confront the Spanish and their allies on a scale that religious radicals in England and Germany could only dream about. More intimately, the company shared its spiritual vision in daily and weekly routines that no employee could avoid, regardless of his faith. Reformed clergy consoled the sick and taught them to die as pious, godly men, whether by disease or at the point of a sword. They preached about the WIC's righteous cause, prepared men spiritually for battle, and held regular days of fasting and thanks. From small rituals to grand, global plans and explanations, Reformed religion was the lifeblood of the early Dutch Atlantic empire.

The World in a Small Wooden Shoe

The young *ziekentrooster* Jacob Steendam sailed to Africa aboard the WIC's *Goude Ree* in 1641, about a ten-week voyage. In a poem written by himself and "sung on the Atlantic Sea," he compared the ship to a home, "a house that runs steadily through the flood," never resting, always alive: there people sleep and cook, sing and laugh, work and play. Revealing his wonder and excitement at what was probably his first time leaving Europe, Steendam noted that everything moved and that everything, including the smallest fish, had a name. The ship was not just a means of transport or an instrument of destruction; to those who lived there it was a church, court, and city. In a very Dutch turn of phrase, he called it an entire world "in a small wooden shoe."[11]

Steendam's imaginative description was especially appropriate for sailors. For anyone who intended to fight the enemy on land, then live in Africa or America afterward, a ship still had to fill many functions during the long passage to those terrestrial destinations. Praising the quality and consistency of religious observance under Admiral Piet Heyn during his 1628 voyage,

Reverend Spranckhuysen claimed, like Steendam, that each vessel "appeared to be a church."[12] Most of the company's fleets had a minister, and many individual ships had a lay leader of some kind: a *voorlezer* ("reader") or *ziekentrooster* ("comforters of the sick"). They led the crew in prayers and hymns, and they delivered sermons or read aloud from the Bible and other works approved by the Dutch Reformed Church at home. In the poem cited above, Steendam reminded listeners about the wonders of creation and the brevity of life. To put it in terms they would appreciate, he predicted a spiritual "shipwreck" if they wasted what little time they had. Using his own poetry was unique, maybe even a violation of policies regarding religious literature and church services. But the duty to teach, exhort, and warn against behaviors that might incur God's wrath was the same for all, no matter the medium. It was common enough in naval life that, when ships didn't have clergy, captains appointed men from among the crew to act as temporary readers.[13]

Informal religious observance began with the changing watch at midnight and again at 4:00 a.m. Since at least the sixteenth century, Spanish ships had employed young boys to turn the sandglass every half hour and, as they did, recite a psalm or litany (a call-and-response prayer). The Dutch seem to have ended the tradition—or at least "reformed" it, exchanging the old Catholic litany for songs with heavy religious undertones. As the quartermaster and crew prepared to end the first nocturnal watch, the quartermaster sent two sailors from the upper deck to wake the second watch, one of them singing as they descended: "Here we sail with God exalted / God forgive our sins / Our sins and our misdeeds / God is our comfort, our support." The second sailor then sang, "Quarter, quarter, to the helm, another quarter / Awake. God grant us here / Happiness, and a safe journey for this vessel / Happiness for a safe journey, fine weather." They continued with at least five more stanzas, each like the rest in its focus on forgiveness or protection from the elements and "the infernal, wicked enemy."[14]

More formally, clergy offered prayers each morning and evening. Judging from one collection used in the Dutch Atlantic, it would have taken about five minutes to read them aloud. Typical selections were full of praise for God and his wonders, thanking him for blessings and (again) asking for protection. There were also prayers about false doctrine, the kingdom of Satan, and resisting temptation. The author, Johan Havermans, included one for the traveling man, asking God to make him profitable and bring him safely home again.[15] The choice belonged to the *ziekentrooster*. He could read a prayer from the catechism, which the WIC also used, or in deference to his audience, he might pick Willem Teellinck's prayer for "seafaring Christians" (1622). The latter was a long confession, listing and lamenting common sins and, in true

Calvinist fashion, opining about unworthiness. Teellinck asked God to lead them as he did Israel and to grant such peace and order that the ship could be rechristened with the rather clumsy name "here is the Lord." Beyond thanks and supplication, prayers were clearly also a time for instruction and warning, a daily mini-sermon for a captive audience that needed real reform, according to the church. Officers rarely recorded the prayer in logbooks and journals but did mention it on occasion, usually when something unexpectedly bad happened. Willem Cunyngham once noted an evening prayer because

The poet and *ziekentrooster* Jacob Steendam, by Jan Maurits Quinkhard (1732–1771). Courtesy of the Rijksmuseum, Amsterdam.

the ship caught fire in the middle of it. Nine months later he was "sitting in the prayer" when the wind carried away part of a mast. He may have been tempted to stop praying altogether at that point.[16]

Clergy offered extra, irregular prayers as necessary. Contemporaries tended to believe that, as the creator, God controlled the weather, that he gave good winds and bad, that they could hear his voice—usually his wrath—in the thunder and lightning. Faced with extraordinary storms or shipwreck, even the most irreverent reprobate might find his inner saint. Cunyngham recounted an incident when his ship was driven close to the African shore, and they couldn't bring it out again. Pushed closer and closer to destruction as the hours passed, they finally called on God, he wrote, and God heard them, sending just enough wind to save them. Another officer, Gelein van Stapels, described a Caribbean storm that seemed to shake the earth. Lightning damaged the ship and killed a man, burning all his hair at the same time. The rest got to keep their hair and their lives because, in the end, God heard their prayer too. Van Stapels promised that they would remember his mercy and change their sinful ways.[17]

Deeply rooted in Protestant traditions of communal worship, psalm-singing was another common activity on Dutch ships, sometimes filling the same purpose as a prayer. Remember that Steendam's poem about the wooden shoe was "sung on the Atlantic sea." He also wrote two poems about a storm he experienced on October 17, 1641. He first described the crashing waves and his fears that he might drown. But he knew (he wrote confidently after the fact) that God directed the winds and waters. Evoking the Bible story about the Israelites in the wilderness, he asked God to be the ship's cloud, light, and fire. In the second poem, sung to the tune of Psalm 50, he expressed gratitude for his survival. By assigning it a melody from the psalm book he made it accessible to anyone familiar with Protestant services, including all church members and probably most seasoned sailors, since psalm books appear regularly and in large numbers on WIC book lists.[18] When he saw that pirates were about to attack his vessel off the coast of Spain, the merchant David de Vries and his crew sang the 140th Psalm, which contains King David's plea for protection. Reverend Henricus Selyns reported that his ship didn't neglect religious worship either, but offered prayers and sang psalms every morning and evening. They read "the Holy Gospel" on Sundays and holidays.[19]

Clergy delivered sermons and read scriptures on Sunday and sometimes during the week, as well. According to their instructions, church services were a time to teach, comfort, or rebuke the crew, depending on the ship's needs. Because lay clergy couldn't write their own sermons, the company used large collections like *Huys-boeck*, by Heinrich Bullinger (1582), and Abraham

De Paerrel een Ooftindis Vaerder,   Den Dubbelen Arent een Weftindis Vaerder,

An East Indies ship (*De Paerrel*, left) and a West Indies ship (*Den Dubbelen Arent*, right), by Reinier Nooms (ca. 1652–1654). Courtesy of the Rijksmuseum, Amsterdam.

Schultetus's *Postille* (1621). Both were decidedly Protestant, with sermons on the value of personal scripture study and justification by faith. Especially suitable for sailors, they also contained sermons about respecting one's rulers, and about adultery and the other sins that clergy tried to eradicate.[20] As a group, sailors were not typical churchgoers. Most were believers in some sense, but their actual religious affiliations varied tremendously, and they were never known for being particularly devout. Udemans wrote that they lacked a profound knowledge of God, blaming it on their parents and teachers. They could be controlled, he said, through punishment and exposure to the word of God. Clergy should teach them why they bore the name "Christian" and teach them to behave like true disciples of Jesus Christ.[21]

Of course the quality of preaching would have depended on the skills of each reader. Overall, the whole service probably left something to be desired. The congregation was packed tightly on deck, standing and sitting on hard wooden planks or cannon, maybe sitting on softer objects brought from below for that one purpose. The *ziekentrooster* had to raise his voice above the wind and waves and the screech of birds. More polished, experienced ministers usually only worked on the flag ship (the admiral's ship) in the WIC's large fleets. And they preached at sea as they traveled to their various destinations. Ordained clergy could at least use their own words and improvise when they felt so inspired. All other vessels had the restricted, untrained laymen. Reading for an hour from a heavy book, straining to see the small, tightly packed print while rocking up and down with the ocean on a slanted deck: the job was difficult to do well, and it couldn't have been any less painful for listeners. The alleged superiority of Protestant preachers over Catholic preachers, if there was any difference, must have disappeared at sea.[22]

Clergy offered other services on holidays and special fast and prayer days or days of thanks, designated intermittently by WIC captains and admirals. Because they could only obtain God's blessing "through prayer," Admiral Maarten Thijssen named every Wednesday a "general prayer day" in the fleet. The crew should abstain from any task that wasn't absolutely necessary, he commanded. Admiral Cornelis Jol and others did the same, hoping that "God almighty" would grant them a "prosperous journey and a good wind."[23] Fast and prayer days took the place of saints' days and other Catholic holidays that Protestants had abandoned during the Reformation. On the holidays they kept, days like Pentecost and Easter, they worshipped wherever they could, sometimes even on land. Exploring an island in the Caribbean for fresh supplies in 1626, one crew decided to stay and celebrate Easter because they found a flock of sheep there. These occasions injected a bit of comfort in an otherwise arduous existence, something to look forward to while pulling an oar in the hot sun or climbing the rigging on a cold, stormy night. Whether sailors appreciated the sermon as much as they did the mutton and extra rest depended on their personal religious affiliations and momentary spiritual needs.[24]

Finally, *ziekentroosters* fulfilled the duty for which they were originally named: instructing and consoling the sick. Their handbooks contained short lessons about death and related topics to teach the unfortunate person in need of their expertise. Reading the lessons now, they seem calculated to propagate the image of the stern Calvinist, because they weren't very cheerful. They taught the depravity and misery of man since the Fall of Adam and the need to submit to God's will, allowing him to inflict punishment as he saw fit. More comforting, they also taught about resurrection and eternal life in Christ. *Ziekentroosters* told the sick to desire death because it would free them from earthly trouble, and they reminded them to avoid behavior that may or may not have had anything to do with their illness, like drunkenness and sexual sin. In their sorry condition they should not lose faith, but strive patiently against the Devil until the final hour. *Ziekentroosters* were also encouraged to read comforting passages from the Bible, especially the book of Psalms, and sing and pray with their charges. Prayers for the sick in Reformed literature asked for forgiveness and sometimes taught that one's illness was a direct consequence of his transgressions. According to the catechism, he deserved much worse than he was then suffering.[25]

Traveling with Joost Banckert's fleet in 1647, Hendrik Haecx recorded a rare firsthand account of deathbed instruction and consolation. When the admiral came down with a fever, Haecx sent for a surgeon to bleed him. Then, as Banckert's life trickled from his body, Haecx sat beside his bunk and began to ask questions: Was he at peace? Did he trust that he would find a merciful God when he died? The admiral answered in the affirmative, but he worried that he wasn't sufficiently sorry about his shortcomings, "for I am a great sinner." Haecx wrote in his diary, "I comforted him according to my ability from God's word." Afterward he went on deck for the morning prayer, promising as he left that he would ask "God the Lord Jesus" to restore Banckert's health. Unfortunately, when Haecx returned he found that the admiral's condition had only grown worse, and the man died a few hours later.[26]

During all religious services, sailors had to sit quietly and pay attention. An officer called a *provoost* ("sergeant") kept an eye on them and intervened if anyone laughed or clapped or interrupted in some other way. The *provoost* was responsible for dispensing justice and maintaining order. Among his many other duties, he saw that no one taunted the minister nor hindered him in the execution of his office. For sailors who missed prayers and sermons, he stopped their alcohol ration the first time, then imposed a small fine and whipped them for subsequent unexcused absences. According to the laws or articles used aboard WIC ships, men who raised questions and started "religious disputes" were confined in the hold for three days on bread and water. If their questions led to violence, the *provoost* was supposed to inflict a harsher punishment. Cursing and blasphemy were also illegal, fined ten *stuivers* ("pennies"). Everyone began their employment by taking an oath to abide by the articles, and the *provoost* read them aloud at the start of the voyage and again every four to six weeks for as long as it lasted. He hung them from the mast and in other conspicuous places so "the People" would remember them.[27]

The WIC instructed officers and clergy to respect each other. After all, their appointments were, in a sense, divine: captains commanded their vessels "with God"; admirals were called of God, "like everyone in his office."[28] Clergy were not supposed to reprimand officers in public, never single them out by name during the sermon, which might diminish them in the eyes of the crew and, in such a "rough" crowd, convey the wrong idea about the purpose of church services. As leaders and examples, officers must live especially good lives, the company maintained. If they violated the moral code, reproof should happen quietly and privately. For the same reason, captains were told to be discreet if they felt the need to reproach the minister or *ziekentrooster*. They should support the clergy in their duties, provide a quiet place for study and meditation, and reserve a spot for them at the officers' table. The WIC even devised a seating arrangement, with the minister in the fourth position, after the captain, skipper, and merchant.[29]

Harmony and the nature of worship on any ship depended less on laws and instructions and more on the dispositions and personalities of those who had to enforce them. According to Charles Boxer, some of the greatest WIC admirals were "earnest and God-fearing Calvinists whose favourite reading was the Bible." Even if he is right, no one person—not even the admiral—could preclude problems on every ship in the fleet; and many ships didn't belong to a fleet and didn't have an admiral.[30] The church at home had to intervene, for example, when it learned that some captains were keeping *ziekentroosters* from the officers' cabin, perhaps not recognizing them as ministers or resenting them for their lowly beginnings. Simon Claesz complained in 1628 that when he tried to chastise unnamed "abuses" on his ship, the captain prevented him, then stopped the morning and evening prayers altogether. Company directors sometimes had to adjudicate these disputes, and they didn't automatically side with their captains. They once overturned Michiel van Lunenburch's sentence against the *ziekentrooster* Jacobus Dincklagen, who had gotten drunk during the voyage. They reproached Dincklagen but restored his pay and censured Van Lunenburch for acting alone in incriminating a fellow officer.[31]

Performing the Spectacle of Misery

As WIC vessels searched for prey, hugging the coastline to find Spanish and Portuguese settlements, the Dutch were reminded again and again that their enemy was Catholic. They came across churches and monasteries sometimes even in places with few Europeans, with towers and steeples visible from the sea before anything else. In sketching pictures and describing targets for future voyages, they found that churches were convenient landmarks for logging a particular place. The enemy accidentally assisted their endeavors by planting crosses atop hills and at the mouths of rivers and bays. Trying to navigate the tricky, treacherous approach to Curaçao the first time—trying not to wreck and founder—the Dutch only identified the proper entrance because it was marked with a gigantic cross. But it wasn't just a navigational tool. For militant Calvinists, churches and crosses were also symbols of the ancient adversary, the righteous war, and the conquest and transformation of a Catholic landscape into a Protestant one.[32]

In the rituals they performed before and after battles, in the letters and books they wrote to describe and celebrate them, the Dutch expressed confidence that their fight was moral, that God was with them. Reverend Dionysium Spranckhuysen exemplified this sanctimonious attitude when he described Admiral Heyn's assault on the Spanish fleet at Cuba in 1628. Though he wasn't actually there, Spranckhuysen claimed that Heyn repeatedly called "Good War!" throughout the brief encounter. Theirs was indeed a good war, a "Glorious, Holy work," wrote the minister. Johan Maurits, governor of Brazil, likewise described his military operations as "God's work," and on another occasion, following a battle, he proclaimed that "the victory comes from God."³³ Scattered throughout Dutch texts, this kind of language was sometimes meaningless boilerplate, used in passing without much thought. More often it communicated a vision or message about the company's godly purposes and a desire for divine assistance. And words *became* meaningful as the Dutch used them in ceremonies that were an integral part of life at war for everyone under the WIC. As clergy prepared men mentally and spiritually to fight, they tried to change them, tried to turn them from their sins via warning and exhortation. Though they never achieved a widespread reformation, which isn't surprising, given the army's diversity, some Protestants appreciated the effort. Reformed teachings about proper behavior, sin, God's wrath, and just warfare provided an intellectual basis for the company's bellicose activities, a way for participants to make sense of their work and find significance in suffering.

To encourage the soldiers and teach them to "trust God and our righteous war," the Nineteen Lords commanded ministers and *ziekentroosters* to offer a "fervent, thoughtful, and penetrating prayer" before going into battle. If they had enough time, officers might designate a whole day of rest and worship, then gather the crew prior to attack and ask the minister to pray once more. In large fleets the admiral coordinated widespread prayers with flag signals; or sometimes they waited until everyone had gone ashore. At the Portuguese town of Benguela in West Central Africa they first landed the men and cannon, and then, "having gotten everything in order, we called upon God and so advanced along the beach." When the Dutch later took Luanda, about 300 miles north of Benguela, they also first placed the men and guns before Reverend Fredericus Vittaeus prayed. At least once in Brazil they did so "within earshot of the enemy."³⁴ Geared specifically toward war, these prayers varied only slightly from the regular prayers. The Dutch asked God for a blessing on their weapons; they asked him to fight with them as he did with ancient Israel, to forgive their sins and direct and protect them.³⁵

Religious rituals and discourse gave hope to sailors and soldiers who lived with the relentless, terrifying expectation of pain and death. The colonel in Brazil who offered a prayer so near the enemy's lines had spent the previous few evenings visiting his troops to bolster their anxious spirits. No one today knows exactly what he said, but in the prayers he requested more than once during that campaign, he must have intended to instill in them a measure of spiritual confidence.[36] Captain Pieter Constant of the *Princesse Aemilia* did the same. When he spied sails in the distance and realized that they belonged to the enemy, he assembled the crew for an impromptu speech. Borrowing from the Old Testament story of Elisha, who was once encircled by a large Syrian army, he told them that, though their enemies were many, "God is more than all of them." He promised that they would not lose one hair unless the Lord willed it, and he reminded them of biblical warriors and Dutch heroes like the "pious" Captain Groenveldt, who had helped defend England against the Spanish Armada more than fifty years before. After a "fervent Prayer to God," Constant turned the ship directly into the oncoming privateers, eventually beating them in a long, bloody engagement. Victory was proof of God's "Fatherly care" for his children. And again the Old Testament language: "It was JEHOVA who gave us a manly heart to fight courageously," Jehovah who discouraged the enemy and made him flee.[37]

Gedeon Moris, the author of the Constant account, might have exaggerated the enemy's numbers and embellished other details, as celebratory tracts sometimes did. But the story was lifted from his diary, and its basic elements comport with other accounts and clergy instructions. Udemans taught that soldiers always needed spiritual strength and comfort before battle, that anyone with a troubled conscience should see the minister for direction and reconcile himself with his neighbors and Christ. In a possible reference to the many Catholics and Lutherans in Dutch crews and military companies, Udemans also told soldiers to avoid unorthodox teachers. Then they could face the enemy without fear. Like the sick man working with the *ziekentrooster*, they could die in peace, having lived in the Lord.[38] The main anomaly in the Moris story was that the captain, not the minister, offered spiritual guidance before the fight. The *Princesse* may not have had any clergy, or Constant may have doubted his lay minister's rhetorical skills. The conduct of the colonel in Brazil also suggests that military and naval leaders liked to encourage their men themselves, fusing secular and spiritual duties by adopting the mantle of religious instructor, which was supposed to be reserved for the ministry.

Clergy offered private, one-on-one counsel to individual soldiers and officers. In his book *Olinda*, Johannes Baers described his consultations with Colonel Diederick van Waerdenburch before the 1630 Brazil invasion. Baers recorded the usual religious traditions throughout the voyage, as well as one uncommon decision that reveals the colonel's mind-set and personal religious commitment. To "prepare like Christians for the fight," Baers wrote, Waerdenburch announced that they (presumably all Reformed church members) would celebrate the Lord's Supper, one of only two sacraments Calvinists had retained during the Reformation. Baers loaned the colonel a book about the sacrament written by his father, Paschasius Baers, and they discussed other works of theology, politics, and history with officers at dinner. Baers said that before each sermon, Waerdenburch encouraged everyone to listen attentively. Like pious and godly military leaders before, the minister continued, Waerdenburch conversed frequently with him about his fear of failure in the fight to come. Baers's own quarters were just below the colonel's, and with such low ceilings and a thin wooden barrier between them, he heard him pray on several occasions, usually in the morning and evening and sometimes with servants.[39]

On the day before the attack, Baers preached about Moses and the Israelite victory over an Arab people called the Amalekites. Then the crew sang Psalm 140 and closed with "a penetrating Prayer to God." That evening the colonel asked the minister to come to his cabin, where they took turns praying, talking, and praying again. Baers felt that Waerdenburch was preparing his conscience for the task ahead. When Baers went to his own cabin to sleep, he could hear the colonel still moving about, so he returned, and again they kneeled and prayed. Not for the first time, Baers described the qualities of the holy warrior. He said that Waerdenburch should keep God in his heart and a prayer

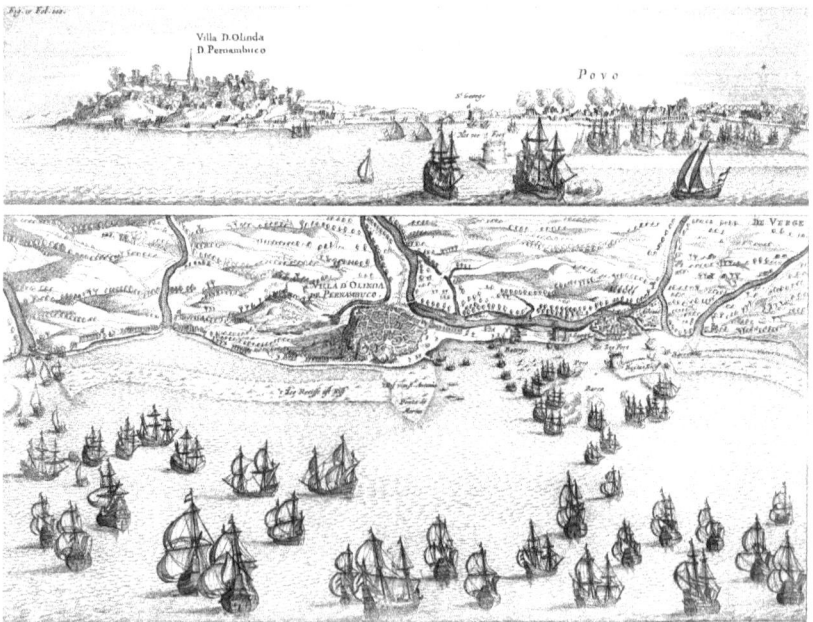

A West India Company fleet conquers Olinda in Brazil, 1630 (anon., ca. 1651–1652). Courtesy of the Rijksmuseum, Amsterdam.

on his lips as he fought; he should take up his weapons in the name of the Lord and slay the enemy, trusting that Jehovah would strengthen him and go before him with "a bare sword."[40]

The Dutch often listed piety alongside military values like courage and manliness. Waerdenburch assured his soldiers on the morning of the battle that he might fall, but he would never run away. They must fight with him or die with shame in the sea. He reminded them of Moses, David, and the prince of Orange and asked them to behave the same: "If you want to be known by all the world as pious and faithful soldiers, act manfully and follow me."[41] In his history of the early WIC, written when the company was at the height of its aggression, Johannes de Laet singled out particular officers as devout men, including Commander Jan Lichthart, Captain Philbert du Busson, and Admiral Adriaen Pater, whose death was especially lamented, De Laet said, because of his piety and "manly courage."[42] When De Laet first introduced Lichthart, he promised readers that they would learn more about his "pious deeds" throughout the book. De Laet then related numerous military stories. Almost two hundred pages after the initial promise, he finally described something we usually associate with piety when Lichthart ordered a prayer before battle and sermons in several languages afterward. Lichthart's death at the hands of the enemy might suggest that death was enough to confer a certain martyr status on the victim: Du Busson (the third pious officer) was killed in battle too. But Lichthart didn't die until two years after De Laet published his book. Dutch authors used the word "piety" as if the act of war itself—fighting or dying in a righteous cause—was its own kind of godliness.[43]

Admiral Pater's death is worth a closer look for how it was celebrated and commemorated later. Sent in response to the WIC invasion, a joint Portuguese-Spanish fleet of twenty ships met Pater's fleet of just sixteen ships on September 12, 1631, near Brazil's capital (Bahia). Most potential participants on both sides held back, leaving a handful of vessels, including the two flagships, to pummel each other in "a homeric duel" (to borrow Boxer's words).[44] Unfortunately for the Dutch, Pater's *Prins Willem* burned to the waterline and he drowned with many others. Or as one anonymous writer described the outcome, Pater gave himself and his ship as "a burnt offering" and "sent his soul to heaven, to Him from whom he had obtained such a courageous heart and respectable victory." Whether the battle was really a victory is, of course, debatable. But from a theological perspective, the metaphor of animal sacrifice—Pater as "burnt offering"—is far more interesting than the question of accurate interpretation. The term refers to the sacrifices made daily at the Jewish temple in Jerusalem during the Old Testament era. In this case the author mixed two biblical themes, one from the Old Testament and one from the New, when he addressed Pater directly. Suggesting that the admiral's death was a kind of baptism, he mourned, "the water must hide you, the flames devour your fire." Pater took Christ's directive to undergo baptism by water *and* fire, meaning baptism by the spirit, too literally.[45]

The WIC *ziekentrooster* and poet Jacob Steendam felt that one didn't have to go as far as Pater, one didn't have to die, to earn the same sacralizing treatment in print. One only had to succeed in whatever task the WIC assigned him. Upon his arrival in Africa, Steendam witnessed General Jacob Ruychaver's attack on the Portuguese and their African allies at Fort Axim, again writing a poem that the crew sang "as [they] prepared to fight." In another poem he described the battle and the "Brave Soldiers" who scaled the walls and burned the village. Yet he reserved his greatest praise for the "Noble, Manly" Ruychaver, situating his deeds in a long chain of scriptural history and spiritual conflict between God, the Devil, and their intermediaries on earth. God's people would have no place in the world without "Manly Sons," Steendam observed. First offering a prayer, the general purportedly led the soldiers into enemy fire without fear. Steendam then made a safe prophecy about him, as far as prophecies go, for he knew that he himself had the talents and position to fulfill it immediately. He said that, just as believers sang songs about the biblical King David, so they would now sing about Ruychaver and the great, holy work he accomplished at Fort Axim.[46]

Epic depictions of WIC officers, written by others, tell us less about the officers' religious beliefs and habits than about the heroic type they were supposed to emulate. Waerdenburch and Ruychaver did at least maintain good reputations in ecclesiastical circles in the long run. Waerdenburch confirmed his religious fervor and enthusiasm in his letters home, and later, as a political figure in Brazil, he was an active elder in the local consistory. During his tenure in West Africa, Ruychaver supported the church's effort to found a school and helped build a Reformed community among employees.[47] Most (if not all) high-ranking officers belonged to the Reformed Church, and if they wanted a place in the growing corpus of national legend, they had to embody the values that writers like Steendam celebrated. They had to avoid public scandal, maintain the usual religious rituals in the fleets and military companies under their command, and display "manly courage" in battle. Again, victory didn't hurt their reputation either, just as WIC success was evidence that the Dutch, like the ancient Israelites, were God's people.[48]

If they excelled at turning their ships into churches, the Dutch transformed more traditional sacred space into a bloody combat zone. The Nineteen Lords ordered their officers to plan attacks for Sundays and Catholic holidays, when they would have the most effect: "when the people from the ships are mostly ashore for Mass." No one could make such precise arrangements at sea, when a fleet's arrival depended on favorable winds and other unpredictable circumstances, but they could do so on land. Four companies under Lieutenant Balthasar van Bijma once captured the Brazilian village of Moriwere "unforeseen" because its residents were "mostly at Mass."[49] As the most substantial edifice in Spanish and Portuguese settlements, a church or monastery was also a potential fort, which is one reason the Dutch took such an interest in them as they sailed the Atlantic coastline. With enough warning the enemy could gather supplies there and fire on the Dutch from behind stone walls. In most of the towns they captured in America, they fortified the churches immediately. Like Protestants everywhere, they destroyed Catholic images and décor "underfoot." They burnt trees and buildings around the church that might provide shelter for attackers, dug trenches, and used churches and monasteries to gather loot and secure prisoners.[50]

The militarization of sacred space is best illustrated in the capture and loss of Porto Calvo, Brazil, in 1635. Ordered to subject its "rebellious" inhabitants by force, Commander Lichthart had difficulty at first because the Portuguese made a stand in one of Porto Calvo's two churches. After the Dutch drove them out, they found bullets and powder inside. Then they secured the building with their own guns and raised their own flag. Left in the hands of Major Alexander Picard, Porto Calvo was soon attacked again. The Dutch had improved the defenses around both houses of worship, but when Picard went to inspect the enemy's position, he was cut off, leaving the biggest church weakly defended. The Portuguese attacked, tore down the palisades, scaled the moat, and entered, allegedly slaughtering those who secured themselves in the magazine and hid under the bunks. The remaining Dutch troops took refuge in a large home and the second church. Both sides brought their cannon to bear, and together they destroyed the town and chapels before the Dutch surrendered, days after the fight began.[51]

WIC officers tried to stop indiscriminate plunder and the unnecessary abuse of Portuguese colonists, probably because they knew that they had to live together in the future.[52] They liked to imagine more virtuous motives, as if their faith and holy purpose affected even their manner of fighting. When they addressed enemy armies, they insisted that they didn't love violence nor enjoy what they were doing. They had "compassion" for them and invited them to be friends: the Portuguese just needed to surrender. The Dutch felt love for "fellow Christians" and did not want to shed "Christian blood," they asserted. The Portuguese had to accept that it was God who made the Dutch mighty and submit to his will.[53] And in peace agreements, the company usually did show some restraint, even allowing priests to carry away church décor and images.[54] Containing the passions of war was yet another skill of the pious officer. When Spranckhuysen described Admiral Heyn, whom he labeled "a Christian captain," he honored him for his purported moderation and tenderness; he celebrated Heyn's pity for the enemy, just as God tempers the sword of justice with the oil of mercy. Victims of WIC aggression in towns like Porto Calvo probably would have wondered at Spranckhuysen's claim that Reformed religion prevented the usual atrocities of war.[55]

In stark contrast to their heroic depictions of high-ranking officers, the Dutch (especially clergy) condemned sailors and soldiers as great sinners and unstable, fickle employees. Religion was part of the problem because many were Catholic, and Protestants suspected their allegiances. WIC rulers at Curaçao and Brazil asked the directors to stop hiring French soldiers altogether. Curaçao's governor, Johannes van Walbeeck, explained that the diversity of religions among his men increased the likelihood of mutiny. And he did have reason to fear, for the French in both places sometimes defected to the enemy. In Brazil the Portuguese sowed division among them with leaflets, "recognising them as fellow members of their church." After the WIC executed a number of soldiers as conspirators, Reverend Vincentius Soler wrote that, "God willing," no "French Papist" would ever set foot on Brazilian soil again.[56] Clergy also criticized blasphemy, disobedience, Sabbath-breaking, drunkenness, fighting, and prostitution—all of which invited God's displeasure and punishment. So they pled for forgiveness before battle and, if they lost, blamed it on their "multitudinous sins." But notions of cause and effect were conveniently flexible. Though success was a blessing from God and evidence of their special standing before him, failure had limited connotations. God allowed an occasional loss to remind them of their unworthiness and reprove them. It was a corrective measure specific to that moment or incident, apparently never hinting that maybe they weren't God's people after all.[57]

For the first twenty years of WIC activity in the Atlantic world, victory was a fairly common experience in war, and the company celebrated with the same rituals that preceded attack, now to give thanks. If they had bombarded the enemy from their ships, they would go ashore following the surrender and, after the usual negotiations and treaties, ask the minister to pray and preach, sometimes more than once in different languages. A colonel in Brazil once dealt with the wounded and buried the dead, then formed his troops into battalions and had them kneel together in "thanksgiving."[58] For major victories the Dutch held days of gratitude, similar to the days of prayer before. After defeating a Spanish fleet in 1639, they thanked the Lord for protecting them, despite their sins. The Brazil council declared that God's "destroying angel" had visited the Spanish, making them sick prior to the fight and cutting down "not just a few hundred, but a few thousand of the same." The council instructed everyone to ask for a continued blessing on Dutch weapons so that the WIC could dismantle the kingdom of Satan and build God's kingdom in its place.[59]

Dutch Visionaries in Chile and Peru

Nothing illustrates the magnitude of the Dutch imperial project like the various Dutch voyages to America's west coast and their hapless efforts to seize Spanish colonies there. They launched two major undertakings for that purpose: the Nassau Fleet (1623–1626) and Brouwer Fleet (1643). Both enjoyed the backing of the Dutch States General and at least one trading company; both tried to acquire the silver and gold mines that funded Spain's European wars. Theirs was a dual religio-economic mission to get wealthy and change the course of the war by taking Catholic funds at their source. They invested a lot of time and resources in the belief that, with only minor encouragement, American Indians, African slaves, and even colonists would rebel against Spanish rule and join the Dutch in overthrowing their mutual enemy and oppressor. Then they would all enjoy the blessings of Protestantism together.

The godfather and prophet of Dutch belligerence in Latin America was the radical, mystical merchant and sugar planter Joan Aventroot. Born in Germany of Flemish parents in about 1559, he had spent his youth and early career in Spain's Canary Islands. There he was open enough about his Protestant upbringing that he had to stand trial before the Inquisition. Though condemned, he got off with only a fine, possibly because foreigners were highly valued in the Canaries, possibly because he bribed the judge.[60] In any case, Aventroot only became stridently vocal after he moved to Holland in 1610. Then he began hurling missives directly at Philip III, king of Spain, accusing him of tyranny and explaining in ponderous scriptural and historical detail the truth and advantages of the Calvinist way. The king was too busy just then to answer his Flemish hate mail, so Aventroot published his thoughts both in Dutch and Spanish and sent thousands of copies to Spain and Portugal with a nephew, Jan Coots. Like his uncle before him, Coots ended up before the Inquisition, but he was less fortunate. He was sentenced to six years as a galley slave.[61]

Aventroot experienced his first-known wonders in 1622, on the eve of the Nassau Fleet. Studying post-Reformation, European history alongside the book of Revelation, he had already done the math and determined that he was

living at the end of times. And he believed that Peru was ripe for the apocalyptic wars that the Dutch had participated in for decades. As he explained to
the States General, he was worried that, through Satan's influence, the Nassau Fleet would be postponed again. But happily, God gave him three witnesses
to the contrary. The first, he wrote, came through prayer: a simple assurance
from the Holy Spirit that the fleet would finally leave. The second came on a
national day of prayer, designated by the States General to petition heaven (in
Aventroot's words) "for the redemption of Christ's Church from Spanish tyranny." On that day he contemplated his concerns regarding the fleet and the
potential for "corruption" if it delayed any longer. Then he drew lots of some
kind and received the same answer or result as he had in the first instance. Lest
any cantankerous reader object to his use of lots, he cited a Bible story to prove
that "God has ordained the lottery not only for Worldly matters, but through
the sanctification of prayer, for Spiritual matters."[62]

Continuing this marriage of worldly and spiritual affairs, the third and most
wondrous witness appeared in one of Aventroot's account books, of all places.
His own description of the incident reveals that some members of the States
General were uncomfortable with his contributions to the impending invasion.
Certain of them were "unjustly" upset with him, he grumbled. They rejected
some of his best proposals and muddied his instructions with "useless advice."
Also distressing to Aventroot, the States General refused to appoint him as general of the Nassau Fleet. Instead they took advantage of the skills and experience he did have, receiving and managing supplies and equipment. And that's
where God got involved. Checking recent payments on September 18, 1622,
just one week after God spoke to him in the lottery, Aventroot found two drops
of "pure red blood" that "divided miraculously" when he opened his account
book—though the blood remained more on the left side than the right, he
added in an honest digression. Not thinking much of it at first, he went to remove the blood so he could see the figures beneath. But then "I came to my-
self," he wrote, and suddenly recognizing this as a sign, "I stood up from the
table and worshiped the Lord." Later he referred to the episode as "the sign
of blood," and he drew parallels between the blood in his financial records,
the blood of Christ, and the blood of Protestants who had died for the cause.[63]

Backed by the States General, VOC, and prince of Orange, the Nassau Fleet
launched in 1623 under the leadership of Jacque L'Hermite—yet another colonial figure who came originally from the southern Netherlands. The WIC
had a chance to participate but chose not to do so because the first plans were
made before the company was founded; and the WIC's new directors were
more interested in taking Brazil. I chose to include the story anyway because
the same ideas and impulses that justified the WIC's wars in the Atlantic

basin underlay the Nassau Fleet. And the latter was inseparable from later endeavors on Latin America's west coast that the WIC *would* endorse. Again, the fleet's main goal was to instigate and support rebellion in Spanish colonies and commandeer them for their precious metals. It carried letters of alliance for Native Americans and written instructions from Joan Aventroot. In its own separate instructions, the States General asked L'Hermite to "pay special regard" to Aventroot's instructions.[64]

Worship aboard the vessels of the Nassau Fleet was generally the same as other Dutch ships and fleets. The flagship *Amsterdam* was the only one with a minister; the other ten had *ziekentroosters* and readers.[65] Surviving records mention prayers and sermons only a few times, always during or after particularly troubled events. For instance, when the fleet ran short of supplies and failed after several attempts to reach Annobón (an island near São Tomé in West Africa), L'Hermite enjoined the unnamed minister to preach a sermon about their situation, petitioning the crew to pray for divine aid and better health. When they did in fact reach Annobón six days later, despite the still-uncooperative winds, the scribe expressed wonder. He wrote in the logbook, "God the Lord wanted to lead us to that place as with his own hand, to free and save the fleet . . . from the looming peril."[66]

Only once do the logbooks afford a glimpse below decks, a possible hint about how non-Reformed sailors and soldiers grappled with a public faith that wasn't their own. Witchcraft, popular religion, and fears and misgivings about Catholic employees all came together in the story of the surgeon Jacob Vegeer. Suspected of killing his patients during the same troubled times that inspired the sermon, he confessed his Spanish parentage and alleged murders under torture. His interlocutors also claimed to find hidden beneath his shirt, protecting him from their torments, a small pouch with a snake's tongue and snakeskin—the "devilish arts," they called it. He had supposedly tried to make a pact with the Devil and killed his patients because they were too burdensome; and he had a plan to kill L'Hermite and other high-ranking officers. So the *provoost* removed his head with an axe.[67] A different account by a Lutheran witness suggests that the admiral had already decided that Vegeer was Catholic before his arrest: L'Hermite was maybe looking for a scapegoat for the fleet's bad beginning, for its slow progress and rampant illness and death. And Vegeer was an easy target because the whole crew had a "premonition" or "bad feeling" about him already. Together the execution and sermon, occurring within days of each other, sent a powerful message about the sources of good and ill and the supernatural forces behind the Dutch war.[68]

Whether Vegeer was really Catholic, whether the surgeon's snakeskin was part of some folk remedy—or if he really fancied himself a witch—he was

clearly a victim of the widespread belief that the fleet represented a specifically Protestant interest and cause. These religious antagonisms reached their
zenith when the fleet finally arrived at Lima, the capital of Peru, in May 1624.
Having missed the silver ships by just five days, L'Hermite decided to attack
the city and incite the uprising that people like Aventroot had long predicted.
But the first direct assault failed, and L'Hermite soon died of an illness that
had plagued him most of the voyage. So the Dutch resorted to a simple block-
ade with only minor probes and clashes over the next months. When the
Spanish governor refused a prisoner exchange, threatening to kill anyone who
approached him again under a white flag, the Dutch marched seventeen captives on deck and executed them.[69] According to the Spanish, fifteen were
bound together and drowned in the sea, and two received special treatment:
the skipper was hanged and "a monk" impaled on a sword. In their brazenly
superior message to the governor, the Dutch blamed *him* for the executions
and for whatever misery followed. They were there, they declared, to get revenge for "the atrocious murders and cruelties committed by the Spaniards in
the Netherlands" and to draw Spanish arms away from the Dutch homeland.
They promised to harass the Spanish wherever Spain spread its "pretended
monarchy" around the globe.[70]

In this instance the harassment remained in the realm of simple, fruitless
harassment. The Nassau Fleet finally abandoned the too-well-defended Lima
and sailed instead for Mexico, where the situation did not improve. They did
burn a village and raze a church, but the Dutch missed the Manila galleons,
and even when they stopped for fresh water, their efforts ended in desertions
and bloodshed. They spent some time in Asia after an exhausting, deadly
Pacific crossing, then straggled home in July 1626 without the promised silver and without presumably distributing their letters of alliance or inspiring
any revolts.[71]

Aventroot managed to find a metaphorical (but unprofitable) silver lining
in the dark cloud that hovered over the Netherlands after the fleet's return.
He blamed its misfortunes on three "hidden faults" or three counterparts to
the three members of the Christian godhead and three divine signs he had
received before: First, Admiral L'Hermite did not carry the Reformed catechism, which taught the true doctrine of the godhead. Second, despite Aventroot's earlier hand-wringing about late departures, the fleet had actually left
four years too early, he now maintained. And third, it placed too much trust
in man—what he called "the fleshly arm." On the question of timing, Aventroot recalculated and discovered that his mercantile training had not prepared
him for the spiritual math required of prophets. In other words, he had made

a few oversights in his original calculations regarding the proper date for the invasion. Only now did he incorporate his own experiences, adding time for the weeks between his first and second signs, then more time for the days before the third sign (the sign of blood). Only now did he know that the true date was 1628, two years hence.[72]

However much he scared some delegates, the States General placed enough trust in Aventroot to support him in a different but related endeavor between the Nassau and Brouwer fleets. Because the fleshly arm had failed, he decided to try the spiritual arm, meaning the written word and nothing else. As Aventroot explained, he pled with the States General not to lose faith; and indeed, on January 24, 1628, a single ship left the Netherlands for Buenos Aires. With the blessing and backing of the States General and WIC, it carried 3,000 copies of a letter to the inhabitants of Peru, written by Aventroot, as well as the States General's promised alliance. Presumably Aventroot intended the letter to make its way from Buenos Aires overland to Chile and Peru. He claimed leadership of the recent invasion, and he outlined all that was wrong with Catholic belief and practice, basically providing a primer on the ideas of the Protestant Reformation. The States General's missive covered similar ground, then it asked readers to reject their king and work with the Dutch to cleanse America's churches and obtain "Christian freedom."[73] The head of this new mission, probably a smuggler of other items, as well, only managed to sneak seventy-five copies ashore. But Aventroot held out hope that, with the proper follow-up, they would be sufficient.

As it happened, the WIC's Brouwer Fleet wasn't much help because it didn't leave for fifteen years, and it targeted Chile instead of Peru. The goal had changed because of L'Hermite's failure at Lima and because, according to historian Benjamin Schmidt, the Dutch felt that Chile offered the same possibilities: many writers praised its beauty and riches, its freedom-loving native people, who resisted the Spanish and continued to fight them in the 1640s, a century after the original invasion. If the mines of that region were less developed than the mines in Peru, it was only because of the ongoing conflict, the Dutch knew. There were plenty of precious metals there. And the "fierce Chileans" (as admirers called them) seemed the perfect partners for whatever conquests the Dutch still wanted to try. Sailing past Chile on his way to Peru, even L'Hermite had opined about the advantages of attacking the colony. His instructions just hadn't allowed it.[74]

Ultimately the Brouwer Fleet fared as poorly as the Nassau Fleet. No mere WIC admiral, Hendrick Brouwer was a recently elected WIC director, and his five ships wreaked havoc on Spanish settlements on the Chilean coast in the summer of 1643.[75] After his death in August, his successor, Elias Herckmans, transported hundreds of Chileans from one location to another and held several meetings with indigenous leaders at the second, safer site (Baldivia). Herckmans delivered a speech about Dutch intentions, gave the natives letters and gifts from the prince of Orange, and watched, delighted, as they laughed and kissed the letters. Like elderly veterans of the same war, the two sides allegedly swapped stories about Spain's transgressions. All was proceeding as predicted, and the Dutch began building a fort and making other long-term plans, but then their expectations crashed headlong into the rigid wall of reality. Given their unpleasant experience with Spanish mining, the Indians were uncomfortable with the Dutch quest for gold, even with Dutch assurances that they were different, that they eschewed force and paid for everything they took. When Herckmans saw that he wouldn't collect sufficient gold or supplies to maintain the expensive undertaking, he departed, returning to Brazil. If he had held out for a few more months, he would have received reinforcements from the WIC there.[76]

Joan Aventroot didn't mourn this latest defeat because he was dead, killed as an eager martyr just a few years after the Buenos Aires incident. Fearing that he wouldn't live to see the great events he had prophesied, perhaps also feeling guilty about his nephew's fate so many years before, at the age of seventy-two he traveled to Madrid to seek an audience with Philip IV, son of the monarch who had ignored his first critical treatises. "Unsurprisingly," writes Thomas Weller, "this ended rather badly." Instead of the king he found himself before the Inquisition, the same court in Toledo that had condemned his nephew. During his trial he confessed that he belonged to "the sect of Calvin" all his life. "In my opinion this is a heretical dog who wants to die as a martyr in his religion," said one participant. The Spaniard continued, "and I really would make his wish come true." Accordingly, Aventroot was burned at the stake.[77]

It's easy to dismiss Aventroot as a fringe figure because there's no doubt he was radical. Few contemporaries claimed the personal, ongoing connection with heaven that he did. But enough people took him seriously, even in the halls of power, that he was able to influence some of the biggest international endeavors of the Dutch golden age. And he didn't deviate much from the WIC's own decades-long martial projects, neither in purpose nor ideology. Those who were interested in foreign developments in the seventeenth-century Netherlands didn't have to choose between war, colonization, and their faith, God or conquest. Depending on how one characterized his work and his favorite mode of expansion, all possibilities were ideologically compatible with the pious life. The merchant and soldier could also be holy warriors, the lover of profits a modern prophet. In this case, because of the recent Reformation and continued religious conflict in Europe, the essential impetus and energy for expansion came from a potent blend of Protestant history and thought, Protestant ritual, and anti-Catholicism. If they accepted the official explanation of the WIC's work, participants could act confidently in the belief that they were building on the progress of the Protestant Reformation, planting the true religion in America at the point of a sword.

CHAPTER 4

Planting the Lord's Vineyard in Foreign Soil

Public Worship in Early Dutch Forts and Settlements

On November 14, 1624, the Amsterdam consistory gathered around a large table in the *Oude Kerk* to discuss religious affairs at home and in the growing territories of the East and West India Companies. At some point during the meeting they were surprised by a visit from Bastiaen Jansz Krol, whom they had sent as *ziekentrooster* to "Virginia" (New Netherland) ten months before. Why had he returned so soon? Krol explained that the colonists "demand[ed] a minister." There were "pregnant women" among them, he said, and they wanted their children baptized. As an unordained lay preacher, he did not have the authority to perform the sacrament. Consistory members recognized the problem, but they also knew that "there are few households there," perhaps too few to justify a minister at a time when qualified clergy were in such great demand. After considering the issue for a week, the consistory decided to give Krol permission to baptize, sending a second *ziekentrooster* to assist him in 1626.[1]

New Netherland was one of many places that fit uncomfortably in the WIC's Grand Designs against the Spanish and Portuguese in the South Atlantic. If Krol's request caught the consistory off guard, it was because most people who paid attention to what was happening in America at the moment had their eyes on the WIC's major fleets and conquests, as they would for some time.[2] However, warfare wasn't the only way to grow Dutch power and influence, nor were Brazil and Chile the only areas of interest. The company was actually a bit of a latecomer to the imperial contest, and as such, it inherited certain preexisting Dutch claims and possessions at its founding. In addition to New Netherland, the Dutch already had a presence in West Africa and a number of small, struggling outposts in South America, mostly on the Amazon River and the so-called Wild Coast (the Guyanas). To these the company quickly added islands like Curaçao and Bonaire: both technically conquests; but they were still very like New Netherland and the other inherited possessions in the sense that they had little-to-no conquered population. Should the Dutch decide to do much *new* planting, they had to plant and build almost from scratch. It was now the WIC's right to make those decisions and strike the proper balance between warfare, trade, and colonization.

In the end the company did promote some immigration, and the church and its representatives—especially lay clergy like Krol—tried to provide pastoral care and re-create Dutch religious institutions in frontier settings that weren't especially suited to the effort. No one at the time doubted the WIC's right to support colonists and build new societies because the charter was clear: "[The company] may advance the population of fruitful and uninhabited regions."[3] Dutch writers and WIC supporters recognized that colonization had ancient roots among the Old Testament Jews and in the classical Greek and Roman Empires, and some writers were enthusiastic about the opportunities now. Even when their main interest or subject was warfare, they also wrote about America's fertile, "empty" lands and the need to send Europeans to establish and grow colonies.[4]

Insofar as they grew rather slowly, Dutch colonies were victims of Dutch success at home, for stability and prosperity tended to attract people to the Republic, not push them away. The church also struggled in many places because of conditions beyond anyone's control, including disease and death, inhospitable climates, and indigenous peoples who could not be supplanted and did not want to change. The WIC founded colonies that quickly disappeared. Some survived as mere outposts, the Dutch presence marked by a fort and perhaps a few huts and other slovenly, primitive facilities. Early colonial populations were disproportionately male: sailors and soldiers with a greater propensity to revolt than to settle or farm. One could (and some did) blame the company for sluggish growth because it feared competition. But its most stiflingly monopolistic policies didn't last beyond the 1630s. Warfare and the adverse physical conditions found in many locations were usually the true culprits behind the sorry state of affairs. According to Reformed thought, the church wasn't officially established before calling a minister and organizing a consistory; yet the sickly, transient population contained too few church members and too few potential elders and deacons. Lay ministers in these settings didn't have the authority to create a consistory anyway.[5]

Early Dutch colonial religion was a cross between the limits and frustrations of public religion in the Netherlands during the Protestant Reformation and the stunted possibilities of shipboard worship in the Dutch maritime world. Where the Dutch at home had depended a lot on former Catholic priests and untrained clergy before they could develop a professional Protestant clerical pool, the Dutch of later generations in Africa and America depended heavily on *ziekentroosters* and other laymen whose pioneering work and place in the Dutch religious, imperial system is often overlooked. Likewise, where shipboard worship lacked many features of the full religious life—church discipline, charity, the Lord's Supper, etc.—early Dutch forts and colonies lacked the same things. Clergy could at least uphold WIC authority through regular exhortation and the condemnation of disobedience and sin. And as much as their environment and positions allowed, they provided the religious services and teachings that Calvinist believers expected and valued. Those familiar services may have meant even more in an otherwise alien colonial setting.[6]

Pilgrims in the Greater Caribbean

Dutch ships had been traveling to the Caribbean for decades before there was any West India Company.[7] They first appeared there in significant numbers in the 1590s, spurred by the Spanish embargoes on salt and other essential products that they used to acquire in European ports that were now closed to them because of the war. In the Caribbean they also found tobacco, sugar, cocoa, pearls, animal hides, dyewood, and potential victims for their piratical, privateering schemes. They acquired some of these products by trade, others by force. More than any other Dutch province, Zeeland took an early interest in the Caribbean, and more than any other Zeeland merchant or merchant firm, a man named Balthazar de Moucheren organized the earliest expeditions to Africa and the Americas. He was a refugee from the southern Netherlands and "a fervent Calvinist."[8]

The Dutch made many false starts on the Wild Coast. After first founding a fort on the Essequibo River in 1596—then quickly losing it to the Spanish—they launched an unknown number of colonial projects in the region.[9] Some were just outposts or "factories," meant to facilitate trade and little else; others were more strictly colonial in nature, reflecting an interest in immigration and social planting. A 1603 request for support from the States General demonstrates that at least some Dutch recognized a connection between immigration and other possible endeavors. In their "Memorial" on colonization they affirmed the beauty and fertility of Guyana, the opportunities for agriculture, trade, and mining. But there could be no riches, they wrote, "until the land is colonized and strengthened with good strong towns and forts." They called theirs a "Christian project . . . for the glory of God and the propagations of His holy word," and they said that Guyana would be a refuge for the destitute and for the exiles of war-ravaged Europe. They lamented the fact that exiles sometimes returned to Catholic countries after living in the Netherlands, then asked, "Who knows but some would have preferred to go to the uttermost bounds of the earth, in freedom of their faith and conscience, rather than return to popery like a dog to his vomit?"[10]

By the time the WIC took control of existing Dutch Atlantic possessions in the 1620s, one small colony had finally emerged on the Essequibo River, and the WIC (usually the Zeeland chamber) continued to promote projects in that region in the future.[11] One of the first attempts under the company was with a group of Walloons and Huguenots who did, in fact, fulfill the basic predictions of the 1603 Memorial: like Balthazar de Moucheren and so many company directors and clergy, the Walloons were newcomers and foreigners in the Dutch Republic, and they looked to America as a possible final destination in their wanderings. They would find, however, that Guyana was a cruel, inhospitable place to those who did not know it well. To most Europeans it was indeed a "Wild Coast."[12]

Walloons and Huguenots sometimes worked together because both spoke French. The former came from the mainly French-speaking regions of the southern Netherlands (the provinces that remained under the Spanish after the Revolt) and the latter were Protestants from France itself. A common gathering place was the city of Leiden, where the Huguenot merchant Jesse de Forest established himself at about the same time as a group of English Separatists known today as the Pilgrims. As members of Leiden's diverse Reformed community, De Forest and his friends would have witnessed English preparations to travel to America, and they were perhaps inspired by them to organize a similar undertaking. Just one year after the *Mayflower* set sail, De Forest had enlisted between fifty and sixty Walloon and French families, about 230 people. Like the Pilgrims they decided first to approach the Virginia Company in England, but the company only agreed to sponsor them on the condition that they disperse among a number of different towns when they arrived. So De Forest turned instead to the Dutch West India Company, which had not existed when he first made his plans. The WIC was happy to have them because, as the company later explained, native-born Dutch with ample work and "enough to eat" had no reason to go abroad.[13] Interestingly, the English had also flirted briefly with Dutch sponsorship. If things had gone a bit differently, the two might have traded places, with the Pilgrims settled on the Essequibo and Hudson Rivers and the Walloons in Virginia or New England.

De Forest sent two possible messages when, in his original petition to the Virginia Company, he wrote that his people were "all of the Reformed religion." First, he was making a simple statement about the faith at the core of the Walloon-Huguenot experience and identity. At the same time he signaled his understanding that England was by that point a Protestant state, and English colonial planners might wonder about the religio-political affiliations of French-speaking Europeans. By declaring their religion up front, the Walloons clarified their allegiances in the major struggles of the times.[14] But the difficult conditions they faced when they first arrived in America didn't usually permit the full, developed practice they had enjoyed in Holland. After coming to an agreement with the WIC they split into two groups, some of them going to the Wild Coast, the rest later to New Netherland. The Wild Coast contingent sent an advance party of ten to twelve men under De Forest to find a suitable location in July 1623. Going ashore a few months later in the region of today's northern Brazil and French Guyana, they offered "many prayers." Then they wandered from place to place, finding occasional European settlers, trading with different indigenous groups, scouting meadows and other potential farmland. In late December they finally agreed on a site for their colony and purchased a field for tobacco.[15]

The experiment only lasted about a year. At one point the Walloons joined with their Native American allies to slaughter (by their own count) 120 indigenous enemies. But they were no match for the local insect population. As the anonymous author of their journal described it, they were "very much inconvenienced by mosquitoes." After coming down with a "severe fever," De Forest died in October 1624, and by December of that year the rest were almost out of stores. Seeing that "we should be obliged to force the Indians to give us food," they chose to quit their adventure, returning to Holland aboard a newly arrived company ship.[16]

In the 1620s and 1630s the WIC's Caribbean possessions and population increased, sometimes immediately by conquest, sometimes sluggishly through the failures and small successes of colonizers after the Walloons. Founded in 1627 by another Zeeland merchant, Abraham van Pere, Berbice joined Essequibo as the only Wild Coast colonies of the era. That they remained "colonies" (plural) instead of becoming one colony is a reminder that the WIC was quite splintered, allocating ownership and control among various chambers and individuals. The continued partition of Essequibo and Berbice is also a testament to their small size: although they were only seventy-five miles apart, both grew mostly along their namesake rivers and never had a reason to merge.[17] As for island settlements, over the fifteen years after Berbice the WIC acquired Curaçao, Aruba, Bonaire, St. Eustatius, and Saba, all of which faced outside threats but generally remained in Dutch hands after their conquest or founding. Conversely, Tobago and St. Martin had numerous claimants and saw endless bloodshed as Spanish, English, French, Dutch, and even Courlandian colonists (from modern-day Latvia) competed for their harbors and soil. Only the southern half of St. Martin joined the other five islands as a long-term Dutch possession.[18]

The religious laws that Abraham van Pere and the WIC issued for Berbice in 1627 were typical for Dutch colonies. In the public sphere they forbade all religion except the Reformed religion, and they required (rather naïvely) that no one deviate from the doctrines and traditions of the church in the Netherlands. Blasphemers would be punished, but otherwise settlers would not suffer for their private religion and private beliefs.[19] When the company formally created the patroonship system the following year, encouraging colonization by allowing wealthy "patroons" (patrons) to start their own settlements in WIC territory, the religious laws didn't change. In other words, the patroons' broad legal powers didn't include complete religious freedom. They had to send and support Calvinist clerical personnel, beginning with *ziekentroosters*, extending later to ministers and teachers when patroonships matured. Their charters reveal a clear expectation that *ziekentroosters* would have a pioneering role in the Dutch Atlantic.[20]

Early descriptions of Berbice and Essequibo also reveal the tremendous obstacles the original colonists faced and the impossibility of employing anything but the most rudimentary worship services. In his 1629 journal, WIC captain Gelein van Stapels wrote that by that date, two years after arriving in Berbice, Lord Cornelis van Pere and his eighty underlings were scattered up and down the river. They had built one large house of logs and tiles, defended with six cannon; but only four people lived there. The rest had given up trying to grow tobacco and other provisions as a group, instead dividing into smaller groups and living among the local Arawak Indians. To gather all the Europeans in one place would take at least eight days, Van Stapels said. And most of them were afflicted for months at a time with debilitating diseases and parasitic bugs and worms in their toenails and feet.[21] Moving northwest along the coast, Van Stapels reported a similar situation at Essequibo, where colonists were also "pretty bad afflicted by the pox." But he did find better

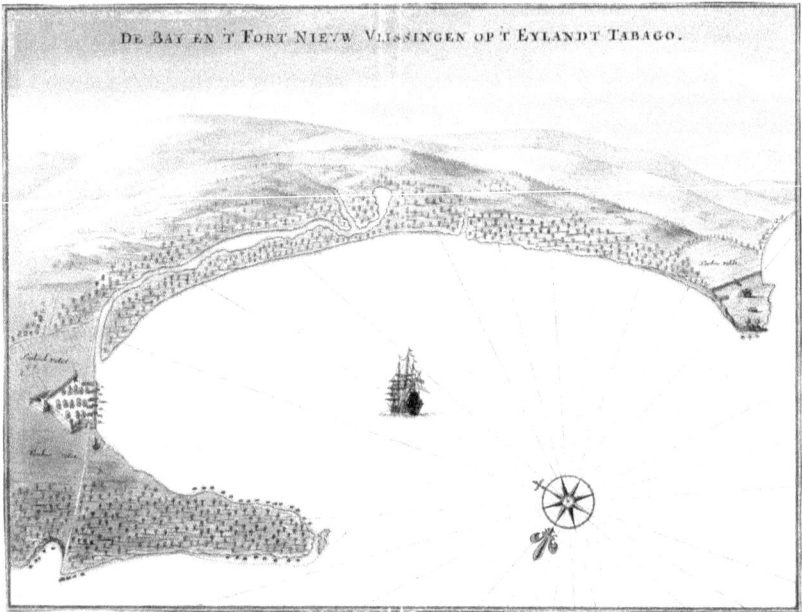

Fort New Vlissingen on the island of Tobago, by Johannes Vingboons (1665). Tobacco fields surround the fort. Courtesy of the Nationaal Archief, The Hague.

conditions in the islands. After one year in their new home, the sixty Tobago setters were mostly healthy, and they already had tobacco fields, huts, three larger houses for officers and storage needs, and a small fort. According to Van Stapels, the lieutenant's house doubled as a makeshift church: "They also say their prayers there."[22]

The Dutch could have begun with a small, preexisting population at Curaçao after taking the island from the Spanish in 1634. But the conquerors feared the inhabitants for their Catholicism, and after the destruction of the invasion, they worried that they would not be able to feed so many mouths. So they deported more than 400 people to the mainland. Curaçao's first governor, Johannes van Walbeeck, explained to his superiors in Europe that the old populace was "entirely papist" and "untrustworthy." As a member of the Reformed Church, sometimes an elder in its consistories, he wanted to promote his own faith and felt that religious uniformity was best, even for Native Americans and African slaves.[23]

Making Curaçao a Protestant island would be difficult, of course, without clergy, and at first the Dutch had no one, not even a *ziekentrooster* or other lay minister. The colony is unique among these early Caribbean endeavors in that its early clerical history is clear from the start. The records of the rest might mention an occasional prayer, a provisional chapel, or an unnamed minister. Only later do they reveal specific identities and stories. In this case Van Walbeeck complained that none of his three ships had carried a *ziekentrooster* or reader—"although in many circumstances we have had great need of one." He therefore appointed the most capable men available, and they did "the prayers and other edifying exercises" to the best of their ability. By "edifying exercises" he probably meant that the officers and soldiers were singing and reading scriptures together, for Van Walbeeck knew that without an ordained minister, the church at home would frown on anything more. He now requested someone who could "lead us from all sin," someone who could teach the men and exhort them to live better lives.[24]

Van Walbeeck's campaign for a minister became a widespread priority when the church learned just a few months after the conquest that the WIC was sending a group of about twenty colonists to Curaçao, both men and women. Among them were Dutch, Walloon, and English names: Thomas Fletcher, Jacob Jacobsen van Domburgh, Laurens Pietersen, and so on. Fletcher may have been a De Forest-like figure, a member of a faction of disgruntled Puritans who had just lost a years-long battle to appoint their preferred candidate to the English pulpit in Amsterdam. Whether the Curaçao Fletcher was the same man, he was undoubtedly the leader of these particular immigrants because he was the first to appear before the WIC with their request to settle in America, and the company later referred to them as "the colonists of Thomas Flitchert."[25] To accompany them as the island's new spiritual shepherd the church selected Fredericus Vittaeus, a young man who had by that point already worked for the WIC in some capacity. Van Walbeeck was especially happy to see him because, he wrote, "I knew him before this in [Brazil] as a person of very sound doctrine and life."[26]

By late 1635, little more than a year after the Dutch seized Curaçao, the island boasted 412 Europeans, most of whom were soldiers, sailors, and other WIC employees. Van Walbeeck complained in his letters and reports of runaways and mutineers, enemy Indians and agricultural problems. In that regard the colony was no different from the American projects that preceded and succeeded it. Yet it had at least survived and grown, which so many others in that time and region failed to do. Curaçao also had fortifications and some few freemen and planter families, and they already had a minister and a few lay clergy. Also encouraging were the minor successes and survival of colonial neighbors like Essequibo and Berbice. As small and uncertain as it still was in the 1630s, a Dutch Caribbean was starting to emerge.

A Seed Sprouts on "the Manhattes"

The *ziekentrooster* Bastiaen Jansz Krol, one of the best-known figures from early New Netherland history, only ended up in that colony because of a bug. Probably born to a Mennonite family in the province of Friesland, he didn't join the Dutch Reformed Church until he reached adulthood. Historians once interpreted the conversion as opportunistic and questioned Krol's commitment and faith, partly because he accepted secular positions after his church service. But as the term "lay clergy" suggests, secular work was both common and necessary. It was also consistent with Protestant understandings of priesthood and religious authority. A recently discovered pamphlet, published in 1623, demonstrates the depth of Krol's anti-Catholic, anti-Spanish, "pro-Dutch Calvinism."[27] The church in Amsterdam first selected him as *ziekentrooster* for the WIC's Brazil fleet in December of that year. However, a last-minute illness prevented his departure, and he recovered just in time for the New Netherland opening a few weeks later.[28]

The people Krol served as *ziekentrooster*—the WIC's first North American colonists—traveled aboard the *Eendracht* and the *Nieu Nederlandt* in January and March of 1624. Krol left with the first group. The second consisted of roughly thirty Walloon and French families from the ongoing Jesse de Forest experiment. Before they set sail they assembled on the docks in Amsterdam, where two magistrates read the WIC's terms and conditions aloud: "They shall within their territory practice no other form of divine worship than that of the Reformed religion," the second article read. The company also required the Dutch language for all political, military, and judicial business, revealing at least a half-hearted hope that the already diverse undertaking would be Dutch in more than just name.[29] Company directors didn't stipulate the language of church services, too, but for the sake of their officers they probably had similar expectations. Regardless, the Walloons may have enjoyed some kind of service in French. Historian Willem Frijhoff believes that Krol spoke the language, and they could have received instruction from one of their own: their original petition to the Virginia Company listed a "theology student" named P. Gantois.[30]

Even if Gantois was among those who traveled to New Netherland, he and Krol would have had a hard time ministering to everyone in the colony because the settlers were immediately divided and established at four locations stretching from the Delaware to the Hudson and Connecticut Rivers. Krol himself ended up at Fort Orange on the upper Hudson. Like the Berbice colonists who needed eight days to gather, he and his flock knew that any large meeting and frequent visits were very unlikely. The dispersal must have been especially frustrating to the Walloons because they had rejected the Virginia Company in part because the English wanted them to live in different towns in America. In this case the WIC was trying to thwart competing European claims by creating the biggest possible footprint with a small number of people.[31]

But the migrations of 1624 to 1626 weren't just about planting a flag and establishing a legal right on the international stage. While the company was certainly divided over questions of colonization and concerned about the potential threat to its fur monopoly, similar movements to Guyana and the Caribbean in the same period—usually in groups of twenty to eighty people—contextualize the New Netherland situation and demonstrate a widespread pattern of colonizing activity in the early WIC. The directors clearly expected their North American colony to grow, for in the two years after the Walloons they sent at least seven additional ships with everything that they believed was necessary to start a new life in an unfamiliar land: farm families, ploughs and tools for dairy production, hundreds of horses, cattle, hogs, and sheep, plus trees, grapevines, unnamed seeds, and experimental spices like anise and cumin, both of which were native to Asia and the Mediterranean. They told their new commander, Willem Verhulst, to identify streams and rivers for sawmills. They asked him to find arable land and look for "other suitable places for future settlers."[32]

The directors also showed that they expected the colony to grow in their orders regarding public institutions like the church. "First," they wrote, Verhulst "shall take care that divine service be held at the proper times . . . [and] enable the comforter of the sick, Sebastiaen Jansz Crol, to perform his duties in conformity with the authorization and instructions given him by the Consistory." Verhulst was supposed to respect Krol, which meant, in part, giving him a seat at the governor's table, providing him with a farm, and building him a home. The directors mentioned the baptismal authority Krol had recently attained during his brief return to the Netherlands. But if that development gave them any ideas about trying to get by forever using the cheaper lay clergy, they must have rejected the option, because in their instructions they designated property for "each succeeding pastor" (*predikant*). In fact they looked forward to the day that New Netherland would have a pastor and *ziekentroosters* (plural).[33] Finally, within the fort the directors wanted Verhulst to build a large facility with a school on one end, a hospital on the other, and the public church in the center. "And when the population shall increase," they concluded, "the school and hospital can be removed to make more room for the church."[34]

Ultimately the company's plans were too grandiose and expensive for the distant American frontier, especially given the many other Dutch endeavors in the South Atlantic at that time. Manhattan Island wasn't even the original target, but a secondary location selected by Verhulst or his successor, Peter Minuit, who were supposed to establish their council on the Delaware River. Verhulst probably chose the island and used it to pasture WIC livestock in 1625; Minuit purchased the land from Native Americans in 1626. The town that gradually emerged there was very different from the one outlined in Verhulst's instructions.[35]

The famous letter reporting the "Manhattes" purchase mentions the same pregnancies and childbirth that required Krol's baptismal authority. And it provides the first glimpse of what the nascent colony was like at a time when the settlers were abandoning their original settlement assignments and gathering at the mouth of the Hudson River: "Our people are in good spirit and live in peace," the author described. "They had all their grain sowed by the middle of May, and reaped by the middle of August."[36] Another source from the same year puts about 270 people in the colony then, and, on Manhattan Island, a stone counting house, thirty homes of "bark," and the beginnings of a smaller fort than WIC directors originally wanted. It was supposed to enclose the whole town, but colonists were living outside it, and the new, improvised version couldn't have contained them all anyway. The same source describes Krol's efforts—still at Fort Orange—and the efforts of a second *ziekentrooster* on

An imaginative depiction of Fort New Amsterdam on Manhattan Island. Originally printed in *Beschrijvinghe van Virginia*, by Joost Hartgers (1651). Courtesy of the John Carter Brown Library, Providence, Rhode Island.

Manhattan, Jan Huygen, to administer the stunted church services of their profession. "Whilst awaiting a clergyman," Krol and Huygen "read to the commonality there, on Sundays, texts of Scripture and the commentaries," meaning the explanatory aids written by Protestant authorities like John Calvin. The settlers did not yet have a chapel, and they wouldn't for some time. However, the WIC was then building a mill "over which shall be constructed a spacious room sufficient to accommodate a large congregation."[37]

The new names and faces, Peter Minuit and Jan Huygen, had enough foreign blood and foreign experience to prepare them for their leadership roles in the diverse young colony. Governor Minuit is a difficult man to peg: a French-speaking, Germano-Dutch Walloon (to coin an awkward term). His father had fled the southern Netherlands along with many other Protestants during the Spanish troubles of the 1580s, eventually settling in Wesel, Germany, which was a haven for religious exiles from England and France, as well. The younger Minuit was born and raised in that environment, moving to the Dutch Republic and working as a diamond cutter before joining the WIC.[38] Huygen was his brother-in-law, and Huygen also lived in Wesel for a time. Religious antagonism and exile were, for both men, a personal, familiar reality, not just because Wesel was home to so many refugees, but because Spanish armies attacked and occupied the city often in the 1610s and 1620s, agitating existing antagonisms and creating new stories. Both also served their consistories as elders and deacons—Minuit probably as a member of the Walloon-Huguenot consistory in Wesel, Huygen with the Dutch-speaking consistories in Wesel and Kleve. The church appointed Huygen as *ziekentrooster* because of his ecclesiastical experience and relationship with Minuit.[39]

New Netherland couldn't and didn't have its own consistory until Reverend Jonas Michaelius arrived in 1628. He was clearly a Dutchman, born in Holland to a Protestant minister father. He had traveled just as much (if not more) than Minuit and Huygen, and he too knew the war firsthand. After his studies at Leiden University he received additional training in Germany, then took up his first post in what is sometimes called a *kruisgemeente*—literally a "cross community," or a church *under* the cross, meaning a hostile, dangerous environment. For Michaelius that meant serving in the unincorporated province of Brabant in the Dutch-Spanish borderlands. Next he returned to Holland, where he worked in two different towns over a period of about twelve years. Like Krol, he was supposed to serve the WIC in Brazil. But an enemy army—not, in his case, a bug—foiled his plans and drove him briefly to Africa, then back to Holland and on to New Netherland. Eventually the mobile minister would even work in England.[40]

In 1628 he didn't know about England yet, of course; he only knew that a colonial post could be just as dangerous and burdensome as any *kruisgemeente* in Europe. His troubles began with an "ungodly" cook and an indifferent captain during the Atlantic crossing. The captain was a "petty tyrant" with the manners of a "big buffalo," Michaelius complained. And the man didn't attend church services when they arrived in America.[41] Far more upsetting to Michaelius was the fact that his wife of sixteen years (fifty years old and pregnant) got sick and died just a few weeks later, leaving him with two small children. His communications with friends in Europe about her death touch on everything from faith and grief to the relationship between women, religion, and colonization. He was clearly devastated by the loss. But for his friends he opined about the will of God and bearing his cross with patience. Courage and patience were especially critical in America, he claimed; and one friend, Johannes van Foreest, agreed, suggesting in return that Michaelius's "learning" (i.e., his education and polish) made frontier life that much harder to bear. Van Foreest mourned Mrs. Michaelius's passing because of her pregnancy and how it would have increased the Dutch, Christian presence in the New World. Happily, he concluded, the year was still remarkable for "the fertility of the women" in general. Michaelius also took comfort in news from Protestant Europe and Dutch Asia, requesting as much information as Van Foreest would send. He found that interesting news, like patience, was especially necessary in a "wild country" without a clerical or marital companion.[42]

Unfairly labeled "the moodiest, bitchiest resident of New Amsterdam" in one recent history of the colony, Michaelius was (it's true) a bit schizophrenic in his feelings about America.[43] Given his family tragedy, and given the value of his descriptions when there are so few other accounts from his era, perhaps we can forgive him. On the one hand the people were "rough and unrestrained," some of them lazy. And the colony was still too sparsely populated, he complained. On the other, Michaelius was obviously happy about how the settlers welcomed him. "I find in most all of them both love and respect toward me," he wrote. The land was fertile yet overgrown, the climate healthy yet (in the winters) too cold. Butter and milk were scarce and livestock too few; but the sheep and pigs were growing in number, and he reported that the 1628 harvest was a good one: "larger than ever before." Despite signs of activity and social, economic development, including a second mill and homes to replace the hovels, Michaelius grumbled that they still lived sober, difficult lives, "like poor people."[44]

Whatever the circumstances of the colonists' physical existence, their spiritual life under Reverend Michaelius changed dramatically, approaching near— though still not replicating exactly—the religious services and institutions of the Dutch Republic. Simple scripture readings and published commentaries now became moments of spontaneous instruction; sermons became more personal, relevant, and lively, no longer regurgitated from a book. Most importantly, lay clergy had not had the training or authority to administer the Lord's Supper and organize a consistory. Full Protestant worship and governance weren't possible without both traditions, and both only arrived in New Netherland with Michaelius. In reporting to Van Foreest that "we have begun to found a Christian church here," he wasn't forgetting or disparaging the ecclesiastical work that Krol and Huygen had been doing for years by that point.[45] His remark might sound like just another elitist snub, akin to the sentiments scattered throughout his correspondence about the extra burdens of learned men and the rough character of poor settlers. Michaelius did sometimes betray a superior, class-conscious mind. But in this instance he was technically correct in suggesting that the church hadn't been established until then.

In another case Michaelius wrote that he had only established "the form of a church," probably because the small colonial population and the distances between forts and settlements prevented the immediate implementation of certain Reformed offices and councils. His first consistory, for example, had just four people: himself, Governor Minuit, Jan Huygen, and Bastiaen Jansz Krol. To govern the church in New Amsterdam Michaelius would have interacted on a regular basis with Minuit and Huygen. Both were elders and both, he said, were "persons of very good character." He probably would have thought well of Krol, too, but again, Krol lived and worked at Fort Orange, rarely making the 150-mile journey downriver to meet with the other consistory members. And none of them were deacons, who typically handled poor relief. Unless frontier conditions really did have the leveling effect that Michaelius suggested, making *everyone* poor, he and his two elders dealt with welfare needs themselves. The consistory could also organize church disciplinary procedures against wayward members and arrange critical religious events like the Lord's Supper. Except insofar as the churches of the Netherlands acted in the same capacity, the New Netherland consistory didn't have the advice and other support that it would have enjoyed as part of a regional classis and synod. The colony had too few people and congregations to justify that type of organization.[46]

Historian Diarmaid MacCulloch describes the Lord's Supper as a religious celebration and "a high festival of community life."[47] It was one of the few sacraments Protestants retained during the Reformation, although they interpreted it differently and held it less often than the Catholic Mass. Frequency among European Calvinists ranged from just once or twice per year in Scotland to four times per year in Holland: once each at Easter, Pentecost, sometime in the fall, and again before Christmas. Amsterdam was the exception, celebrating the Lord's Supper six times per year at the start of every second month. Dutch churches preceded the event with a period of censure and examination, beginning in the consistory and extending from there through visitations to individual member homes. Usually a minister delivered a preparatory sermon the Saturday before the rite. Then everyone gathered again the next day at the church, where they sat at long tables and listened to the minister read about Jesus Christ's sacrifice. When he finished the printed service, the minister read Bible passages as one of his colleagues distributed bread and wine and the congregation ate and drank from tin plates and goblets. They organized other meals and events outside the church where the Lord's Supper was less common and people had to travel farther.[48]

As a young, scattered colony, New Netherland fell into this category. The first sacramental rite under Michaelius was "a great joy and comfort to many," he claimed. He had about fifty participants, both Walloon and Dutch, and he would have had more if so many officers and soldiers weren't still living on the Connecticut and Delaware Rivers (and at Fort Orange). Another problem arose because some members didn't have the paperwork they usually showed prior to the Lord's Supper to prove their standing in the church: some had forgotten it, others had not known it would be necessary in America, and others had lost their certificates in a recent fire. So Michaelius had to improvise, admitting people to the Communion table on the testimony of fellow colonists. He wrote that "we cannot observe strictly all the usual formalities in making a beginning under such circumstances," and he hoped that his superiors in Europe wouldn't think poorly of him for the changes he made. He also broke with Dutch tradition in holding the sacrament three times per year instead of four, at least until the population grew. He didn't create a regular Sunday service in French because most Walloons also spoke Dutch, and some lived too far away to come to New Amsterdam in bad weather. But he did read them a sermon in French before the Lord's Supper, and he read the sacramental service in French too.[49]

What happened to *ziekentroosters* and other lay clergy when an ordained minister took charge? Depending on the length of their contracts, they might continue in their positions, supporting the minister and sometimes working secular jobs as well. The minister still needed someone to read scriptures during church services, someone to lead the congregation in song, and someone to help him visit and comfort the sick. And *ziekentroosters* still delivered sermons at distant outposts like Fort Orange. In a church with a corporate priesthood, a church where governing authority was shared among male congregants, the division between lay clergy, elders, deacons, and other officers could be quite thin. Krol and Huygen both became elders in 1628, even though Krol's *ziekentrooster* contract had expired and Huygen's had one more year. Huygen was also the WIC's storekeeper in New Amsterdam, and Krol became a fur trader and commander at Fort Orange. After Minuit's tenure, Krol even became provisional governor of New Netherland. Their willingness to work these jobs wasn't so different from the merchant or magistrate who served at the same time as elder or deacon.[50]

Two years after his arrival, Reverend Michaelius reported that the colonial church was growing both in numbers and piety. He told Van Foreest, "I had a pretty large congregation in proportion to the place and the population." But he had already had a falling out with one of his elders, Governor Minuit, for reasons that aren't clear today. Michaelius had complained from the beginning that some colonists were trading with Native Americans, possibly violating WIC regulations and rights. Though he wasn't sure at first, and though he originally said he intended to avoid secular, political concerns, by 1630 he couldn't help himself any longer. He now told anyone who would listen, including the directors, that Minuit was an oppressive, fraudulent, fornicating swindler.[51] In an era when the recently implemented patroonship plan was dividing the company into trade and settlement factions, pitting colonist and patroon interests against WIC interests, the minister exerted his moral authority in the political sphere, maybe positioning himself as a company man for his own benefit. Whatever his intent, the directors addressed the conflict by recalling him *and* Minuit to the Netherlands in 1631.[52]

New Netherland and the Reformed Church continued to grow, though slowly, throughout the 1630s. In that decade the former WIC director Kiliaen van Rensselaer founded the only successful, lasting patroonship in the colony on the upper Hudson, near Fort Orange. He sent various small groups of settlers to the area, mostly men and farmers, including some Dutch and some Scandinavians. At first the population wasn't large enough for a minister, though, so Van Rensselaer authorized the farmer Brandt Peelen van der Niekerck to "read aloud some chapters from the Holy Scriptures" on Sundays and holidays. The patroon also ordered his political council to pray at all their meetings.[53]

As the colonial capital, New Amsterdam still had the only minister of the 1630s. And the town got the colony's first chapel and first school in the same period. For the ten months or so between Michaelius's departure and the arrival of his replacement, Everardus Bogardus, the Reformed congregation reverted to the simple services that were so common in the early Dutch Atlantic. Bogardus was a *ziekentrooster*-turned-minister who had already served the WIC in Africa before his North American appointment. When he arrived at Manhattan in 1632 the consistory and congregation were still meeting in the attic of a large stone mill. But Wouter van Twiller, the new governor, built a wooden chapel and parsonage for Bogardus on Pearl Street the next year.[54] Lest he or anyone else in this quaint setting start to feel too disconnected from the more bloody company wars still raging in the South Atlantic, the bells and chimes that called them to church each week reminded them that they were part of something bigger, for the bells had come originally from San Juan de Puerto Rico. The WIC had commandeered them and shipped them to New Amsterdam after sacking the Spanish settlement a few years before.[55]

Under Governor van Twiller and Reverend Bogardus, Manhattan still had none of Spanish America's grand cathedrals and New England's crowded townships. Dutch prosperity at home, the Republic's small population base, and WIC interests and commitments elsewhere conspired to keep the Dutch footprint in North America relatively small. Manhattan in the 1630s was also different because it *wasn't* Spanish and it *wasn't* English; it was now a Dutch island, and the Dutch had to develop a colonial approach that matched their own unique history and their own needs and circumstances. For colonists they could count on some of the many Protestant exiles and foreigners in the Netherlands. And the religious system that had emerged there during the Protestant Reformation provided a model for colonial pastoral care, not because the system was easily re-created, but because lay clergy were, by design, an abundant, flexible group, which made them useful as pioneers and clerical assistants in moments of social change (e.g., the Reformation) and new social development in places like America.

Weeds and Worms in West Africa

Of all the lay positions in the Calvinist tradition, the office of *ziekentrooster* seemed ready-made for Africa. After the early, contested decades of expansion the Dutch consolidated their territory in America. Colonial populations always remained comparatively small, but they did grow, and the church grew accordingly. In Africa the situation was different. There the Dutch didn't face America's weakened indigenous people, terribly susceptible to Old World diseases, sometimes already subjugated or destroyed by prior waves of Spanish or Portuguese. In Africa the Dutch had to cope with powerful, organized states, and the disease/power dynamic was reversed. Now it was the newcomers who suffered terrible mortality rates in Africa's tropical climates. Dangerous pathogens and African power limited Europeans to a skeletal, male, commercial presence on the west coast. Who better to direct the spiritual needs of this

sickly crew than a *ziekentrooster*—a comforter of the sick—whose clerical limitations shouldn't have mattered there?[56]

Yet the limitations did matter to the Dutch in Africa. Ultimately (and in a
few cases briefly) the WIC claimed forts and trading posts from as far north
as modern-day Senegal southward to the so-called Gold Coast, from the Slave
Coast to São Tomé, the Kingdom of Kongo, and Luanda. Stationed at Fort
Nassau on the Gold Coast, the first two Reformed clergy in Africa were both
ziekentroosters: Meynaert Assuerus and Jan Hermanss. The WIC toyed with
the idea of always using *ziekentroosters* there, but after Assuerus and Hermanss
the church insisted on calling at least one ordained minister to what was
then the company's principal fort in the region. And many WIC officers expressed a similar preference.[57] Surprisingly, Dutch ministers in Africa carried
instructions that didn't differ much from the instructions of American colleagues. They were supposed to organize the church and plant the Gospel.
They could preach, administer the sacraments, call elders and deacons, and
hold church disciplinary procedures in the consistory.[58] Their presence and
ecclesiastical powers may have meant that the Dutch didn't yet understand
the limited possibilities for establishing European institutions in Africa. More
likely, Calvinists in the company valued their religious services enough to
employ the more expensive minister even when they knew he would rarely
be able to exercise all his authority.

Lay clergy continued to live and work at most African forts, observing the
same traditions there that they did at sea: daily prayers and psalm-singing,
twice-weekly sermons, and occasional days of supplication and thanks. After
the WIC took it from the Portuguese in 1637, Elmina replaced Fort Nassau as
the company's headquarters in West Africa. More a castle than a fort, it was
home to the local commander and the region's only ordained minister, and
employees sometimes traveled from nearby forts to worship with them.[59]
Elmina also boasted one of the few chapels in Dutch West Africa, built by the
Portuguese inside the castle walls. But the company used the chapel "for buying and trading." A Lutheran soldier and goldsmith named Michael Hemmersam, who worked at Elmina off and on from 1639 to 1645, wrote that
"we held our Sunday with prayer, reading and singing in the great hall of the
general's quarters, which was hung with pikes, muskets, and similar weapons
and was more like an arsenal than a church." At other forts they met wherever they could find space, including the "Commander's hall" and maybe outdoors when the weather allowed it.[60]

Hemmersam's comment about Sunday services is a reminder that many
WIC employees were not Calvinists, nor even Dutch. Still, the company required everyone's presence and participation, and clergy had to choose from

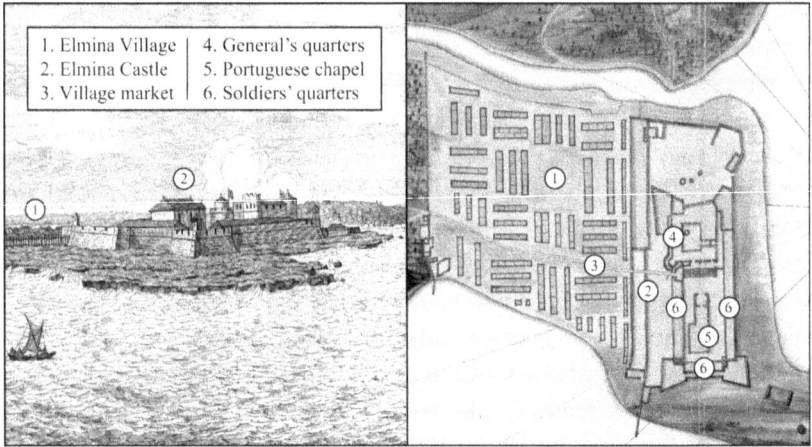

1. Elmina Village	4. General's quarters
2. Elmina Castle	5. Portuguese chapel
3. Village market	6. Soldiers' quarters

Elmina Castle on the Gold Coast of Africa (modern-day Ghana). The image on the left is by Jan van Brosterhuyzen (ca. 1636–1644). Courtesy of the Rijksmuseum, Amsterdam. The image on the right is by Johannes Vingboons (1665). Courtesy of the Nationaal Archief, The Hague.

among this mixed group to appoint elders and organize the Lord's Supper. In doing so they divided the European population. Hemmersam claimed that missing the Lord's Supper was "the greatest loss and cause of regret for me and others attached to the Evangelical [i.e., Lutheran] religion." He also said the clergy "knew quite well what each man's religious affiliation was."[61] Of the 200 to 300 men the company usually kept on the Gold Coast, the number of church members fluctuated drastically. Reverend Meindert Hendricks, who lived at Elmina in the same years as Hemmersam, reported just thirty members.[62] At other times membership reached as low as twelve and, when employees were willing to profess a new faith, as high as seventy. Reverend Bartholomeus IJsebout won over so many Catholics and Lutherans in his weekly, voluntary catechization meetings, he was able to organize a consistory and convince Calvinists in nearby Danish and English forts to celebrate the Lord's Supper with him at Elmina. The church had never "bloomed and flowered" as it did under his supervision, he boasted.[63]

The personalities and enthusiasm of individual ministers like IJsebout probably help explain the fluctuating number of members in Africa. Instability had more to do with disease and mobility, though. Few employees remained in one place; most transferred among WIC outposts or just returned to the Netherlands at intervals. Many also died, including ministers and *ziekentroosters*, struck down by malaria and yellow fever, immobilized by the infamous "Guinea worm," which entered the body in contaminated drinking water and grew to about a meter, usually emerging through the skin of the legs and feet.[64] So common was the specter of death among European employees that Cornelis Jacobsen could write, with only some exaggeration, that *ziekentroosters* were more useful than ships in Africa. He was the schoolmaster at Fort Nassau during the tenure of a minister who was so worried about "land sickness" (malaria) that he, the minister, spent most of his time aboard one of the local, coastal vessels, neglecting his duties at the fort for weeks on end. In general, disease discouraged ministers from working in Africa, thinned congregations, and killed members.[65]

Reverend Benderius, the absentee minister mentioned above, could at least claim that he was a better example than Adriaen Louwerens, a *ziekentrooster* at Elmina who, ironically, got sick and killed himself. It was during Louwerens's third ailment in just seven months that General Jacob van der Wel reported the grisly scene:

This afternoon at two o'clock the *fiscaal* came to me and informed me that the *ziekentrooster*, Adrian Lourens . . . had shut himself in his room and that various people had knocked, and tried to speak to him, fearing that some mishap had occurred. But he did not respond and would not open the door. Therefore the *fiscaal* asked if we might open it one way or another. I went with him, and having forced the door a bit, I saw that the *ziekentrooster* lay dead before it. After opening the window, we witnessed a sad and horrible spectacle, he having strangled himself on the door, wrapping his garter around his neck.[66]

Van der Wel wrote that the suicide came as a shock to everyone, for Louwerens had always behaved himself (the general continued) as a good Christian, ready with godly, comforting words for others, never showing the least sign of despair or weakness. Now an unsympathetic Van der Wel prayed that God would "cast such men from us in the future."[67]

However valuable their instructional role with the sick, clergy were mostly supposed to ignore the dead. Protestants and Catholics had disagreed vehemently on this issue during the Reformation, perhaps more than any other. Protestants had done away with last rites, burial rituals involving candles and crosses, funeral sermons, prayers to saints, and Masses for deceased loved ones because, they believed, no one on either side of the mortal divide could do anything for anyone on the other, and they felt that Catholic traditions smacked of superstition and idolatry. Under public pressure the Dutch brought back the occasional funeral sermon, but their funerals were still a shell of the pre-Reformation variety.[68] If WIC officials in West Africa felt any similar pressure from the Catholic population to hold more extravagant affairs there, extant sources don't show it. At Elmina they buried the dead beside the chapel on a plot of land that was, like the chapel, used for general work purposes. The service took place in military fashion, with musket and cannon salvos, probably followed by a scripture or a few pious words from any clergy who weren't busy hiding or dying.[69]

Another problem for WIC clergy was the lack of interest and the outright challenge from bored, isolated employees who resented efforts to keep them from their few amusements: gambling, alcohol, and sex with indigenous women in the African homes and towns that surrounded European forts. Certain "pious persons" (probably some of his Calvinist supporters or consistory members) once warned IJsebout about "whoredoms" among the soldiers, and when he went to their quarters to rebuke them, they mocked him. After he complained to the local WIC general, they were punished severely; then, "to scare the others," the general sent the chief agitators to a smaller, even more isolated outpost—probably as much for their treatment of the minister as for their original transgression.[70] Secular officers were in a difficult position. They had to support the clergy, but they also worried about the needs of soldiers and tended to be more forgiving. One general defended his men from a minister's complaints, acknowledging that they led rough lives. They were clearly not church wardens, he joked, but they rarely committed wanton harm. Officers had to strike a balance between piety and popularity, with the clergy usually encouraging them to be more strict. They supported clergy by punishing soldiers for blatant misconduct, which was in their own interest, and by attending prayers and sermons and making their subordinates do the same. Some officers also served on the consistory.[71]

The consistory might have been a good tool for keeping order if more employees had belonged to the church. Only members were subject to church discipline, and the consistory probably, therefore, had little influence in African forts. Most of the time there weren't enough members to justify one in the first place. Represented then by the clergy, "the church" still helped maintain order and sustain WIC authority among the motley crew. There was a fine line between choices the company simply couldn't tolerate—insubordination, dereliction of duty, fighting, murder—and behaviors that were sometimes connected to them, like drunkenness and sexual sin. Either of the latter might lead to the former. Whether an officer tried to end these problems because he was most concerned about sin and the wrath of God or for more practical reasons, his interests and the interests of ecclesiastical leaders were often the same.[72]

Faith, power, and justice worked hand in hand. WIC punishments ranged from monetary fines and loss of alcohol for minor infractions, like missing the prayer, to harsh physical penalties for drunkenness and fighting. Lashings were common, and some troublemakers were confined in a dark pit with little or no food and water. The WIC also utilized the infamous wooden horse in West Africa. When Thymen Jansz quarreled with and injured another soldier at Fort Nassau, he had to straddle "the horse"—a narrow, raised wooden plank—for two hours per day for two days, his hands bound and twenty-five-pound weights strapped to each foot. It was a cruel punishment because it could injure the genitals and dislocate the joints of the thighs and legs.[73] Like religious services, these punishments were public affairs, a warning to everyone to avoid trouble and do their duty. Regular prayers and sermons were a convenient time to remind soldiers about God's anger and their oaths to the company. Following the prayer an officer extracted promises from the whole assemblage to behave themselves that day and, after the sermon, he questioned anyone accused of misconduct. Similarly, the minister preached a sermon whenever one WIC commander replaced another, suggesting the divine origins of secular authority. "Suggesting" is perhaps the wrong word here because Reformed theologians never tried to hide their views on church-state relations and the duties of godly rulers.[74]

Fornication and adultery were among the clergy's biggest dilemmas because neither usually interfered with company business, which made them more difficult targets. Also complicating the situation, soldiers and officers both sometimes violated this particular stricture. Most men, including the most powerful, didn't have European wives in Africa. Occasionally they celebrated a marriage at Elmina, but weddings were just as rare as funerals were common. Some of the few marriages mentioned in the fort's journals were between soldiers and indigenous women and mulatto women of Portuguese-African descent. All other relations were forbidden. Given the mobile, transitory experience of most outsiders in Africa, even the sanctioned relationships probably didn't last.[75] IJsebout tried to end the "abominable sins of this place," as he put it, by asking the directors to send the wives of married men and single, marriageable women for everyone else. Though his commander supported his campaign, nothing came of it. His successor, Abraham Oudewater, confirmed IJsebout's assessment and complained that even some church members had "close friendships and peculiar associations" with African women.[76]

The story of Maritgen Jans (also known as David Jansz) highlights the lack of Christian marriage and western society in general in Africa. According to the seventeenth-century doctor and historian Nicolaes van Wassenaer, at the age of seventeen Jans donned men's clothing, cut her hair, and adopted the name "David" because she saw no other way to make a living. Then she signed on with the WIC and sailed to Fort Nassau. Well-liked and helpful, particularly with the sick, she avoided detection, Van Wassenaer wrote, by bribing her bunkmate and hiding her body. When the soldiers went to the river to bathe, she told them that she couldn't swim, and she washed near the shore in her clothes. Van Wassenaer believed that her heavy drinking and regular visits to "a beautiful black woman" were part of the ruse, an effort to blend in with the other soldiers. Another possible explanation is that Maritgen Jans preferred both liquor and women.[77]

Her work with the sick betrayed her in the end, destroying the disguise and forcing her eventually to leave Africa. When Jans fell ill two months after her arrival, she ended up in the infirmary with all the other patients. She still avoided exposure for a time by refusing to change her clothes. But she was too weak to do it herself in the dark of night, and when others finally insisted, she had no choice. Van Wassenaer wrote in his dry, clinical style that "she revealed her Breasts, over which everyone stood wondering, finding beyond a doubt a Young Maid in their presence." Word of the incident spread quickly through the fort, and when someone told Adriaen Cornelisz, the local commander, that "David Jansz was found to be a woman," he immediately assumed the role of the concerned father. He arranged private quarters for Maritgen and, not knowing what else to do with her, began making plans for a wedding with a still-to-be-determined husband. He gave her dresses, a gold necklace, and other gifts "to show her off, so that someone might get the urge to marry her." Before she was fully recovered he allowed "the most pious" suitors to visit and converse with her at her bedside. "Wherever there is only one white Woman," Cornelisz purportedly declared, "there one finds no ugly or bad white Women."[78]

The wedding of Maritgen Jans and Jacques le Fievre, WIC *fiscaal*, was better attended and more grand than they could have hoped, had they met and married in Europe. In accordance with Dutch law, the couple announced their wedding banns three successive Sundays before the ceremony. On the third Sunday the officers, merchants, soldiers, and sailors gathered from all around to watch the *ziekentrooster* Johannes Mercator perform the marriage rite. Everyone "took great pleasure" in the affair, Van Wassenaer claimed, "for such a thing had never happened there before, and it would possibly never happen there again." The group feasted and socialized for three days, celebrating "as if they were at a King's Wedding." But the merriment didn't last, and not just because General Cornelisz finally made them get back to work. He also made Jans return to Holland when her new husband died of an unspecified illness a few months later.[79]

Africa was only like America in that the WIC had claims, interests, and personnel in both places. Beyond those broad generalities, the parallels and colonial possibilities diminished rapidly. Neither the Dutch, English, or French had any serious missions and ecclesiastical presence in West Africa in the period, nor would Europeans obtain one until the Industrial Revolution gave them the medicines and tools to exercise greater control. The *ziekentrooster* and poet Jacob Steendam, who lived in Africa for most of the 1640s, wrote that in "wormy old Guinea," Europeans were like Israel in Egypt, "many hundreds of miles from home." Steendam described himself as an exile, a traveler in a "Strange land," a shepherd wandering far from his own field. Africa was a place for Dutch "Strongholds and Castles," not Dutch cities, a place where God had planted "Our Trade," not society.[80] At times he hoped that it could be more, writing that Africa was a corner of "God's Vineyard." But he decided that it was a lousy vineyard for his purposes. The poisons of disease and sin ruined the soil. The first rotted the body, the second corrupted the soul. Africa was "contrary to our nature," he insisted. "There Christ's true church / Has neither place nor bed," meaning flowerbed.[81]

Using the same metaphor, Reverend Hendricks claimed that among the few fruits of his labor—the "fruits of Guinea"—was the worm sprouting in his foot as he prepared to leave. IJsebout also wrote about the worms that were "gnawing and eating [his] living body," concluding that he would never thrive in Africa: "I am as meager as a stick."[82] If the clergy could not thrive, if they died and even took their own lives, their church could not take root either. In Dutch forts it never grew beyond the limited, half-formed customs of WIC ships and military companies. The number of church members rose and fell, sometimes celebrating the Lord's Supper and forming consistories, always passing or scattering and forcing ministers to start the planting anew.

Chapter 5

Reformers in the Land of the Holy Cross

The Calvinist Mission in Brazil before
the Portuguese Revolt

By 1635, Brazil was in a sorry state. More than
a decade of warfare had damaged its productive capacity. The Dutch were
struggling against a Portuguese enemy whose knowledge of the local terrain
and guerilla tactics created huge problems for the WIC's more traditionally
organized armies. To make matters worse, no one seemed to be in charge.
Company directors had divided power among five members of a High Council, each with different responsibilities, and the council didn't meet often
enough and didn't agree on the best strategy for the future. As the need for
change became more and more apparent, rumors began to spread in Holland
about problems in the colonial church, as well: some clergy lacked the tem-
perament and sobriety required in their profession; some had received their
positions unlawfully. Secular and ecclesiastical authorities on both sides of the
ocean began to call for a reformation of the church and of Brazil generally.
The directors responded in 1636 by reorganizing the colonial government and
appointing the German nobleman Johan Maurits van Nassau-Siegen to the
new, powerful position of governor-general. During his seven-year tenure he
put an end to the chaos of the previous period, spreading Dutch control in
the northeast and overseeing WIC conquests in West Africa.[1]

The word "reformation" resonated with special force among committed
Protestants, evoking the memory of their struggles with the Catholic Church
over a century and more, then their attempts to change the beliefs and behavior

of people in cities like Geneva, most famously, after they created churches of their own. In the Dutch context this impulse lived in an influential religious movement called the *Nadere Reformatie*, usually translated as "Further Reformation." As the name suggests, Dutch reformers weren't content with their early institutional successes. Replacing the old church liturgy and organization with Calvinist variations was a critical first step, but reformers demanded deeper, more meaningful change. They wanted the hearts and minds of their contemporaries. By flooding Dutch churches and homes with God's word, spreading Reformed teachings as far as possible, they hoped to increase individual faith and holiness and expunge sin in a way that their Catholic forebears had failed to do.[2]

Now these same reform movements came to Brazil. Protestants had always intended to extend the Reformation there, but the violence and uncertainty of war overshadowed and dampened all religious work before 1636. With the stability of victory and the administrative changes enacted that year, the church finally received the attention clergy needed, and the reformation of Brazil could begin in earnest. In truth, secular and religious projects went hand in hand. However much they wanted Brazil for its agricultural potential, the Dutch also believed that it couldn't really be subjected without a new religious order. In an age when all western states had a public church, when Europeans were killing each other over differences of faith, few people could imagine, let alone promote, an alternative. The Dutch were different in at least one regard: because of their experience with Spain, they had decided long ago that people should be free to believe what they wanted without threat to life or property. But this "freedom of conscience" operated mainly in private, rarely in the public sphere, where the Dutch Reformed Church still reigned supreme. The illicit alternatives that arose from time to time in cities like Amsterdam were still young and untested; and they had to compete with the entrenched belief that religious diversity was a *bad* thing, not something to which a state or culture should aspire. According to this view, religious uniformity ensured harmony and loyalty; spiritual differences led to discord and conflict.[3]

If diversity was the problem, reforming Brazil would not be an easy task. Ruled by the Portuguese for more than a century before the conquest, to outsiders it was a strange, daunting place—a legitimate military target because Spain and Portugal were then united. About 60,000 colonists lived there in the 1630s, almost half of them in territory taken by the WIC. The colony was also home to countless Native Americans and African slaves, all with their own religious traditions. At its peak, the zone of Dutch control stretched 900 miles along the coast, incorporating parts of seven provinces and many Catholic towns and villages.[4]

1. Corpus Christi Church
2. High Council building
3. Fort Ernestus and
   the St. Francis Cloister
4. Johan Maurits's first
   home; later the court
5. The French Church
6. Johan Maurits's Boa
   Vista Palace*
7. WIC warehouses and
   bakery and shipyards
8. Fort Frederik Hendrik

Mauritsstad

Recife

* Johan Maurits's more famous
palace (Vrijburgh Palace) was located
a short distance to the north of Fort Ernestus.

Amazon
River

São Luís

MARANHÃO

Fort Schoonenborch

CEARA

Frederickstad
& Fort Margarita

RIO GRANDE

Fort Keulen
(Natal)

Mauritia
(aldeia)

PARAÍBA

PERNAMBUCO

Recife

Goiana

Itamaracá

San Francisco River

Igaraçu

Fort
Maurits

Olinda
Recife

Santo Antônio
de Cabo

Fort Cabo
de Santo Agostinho

Salvador de Bahia

Sirinhaém

Porto
Calvo

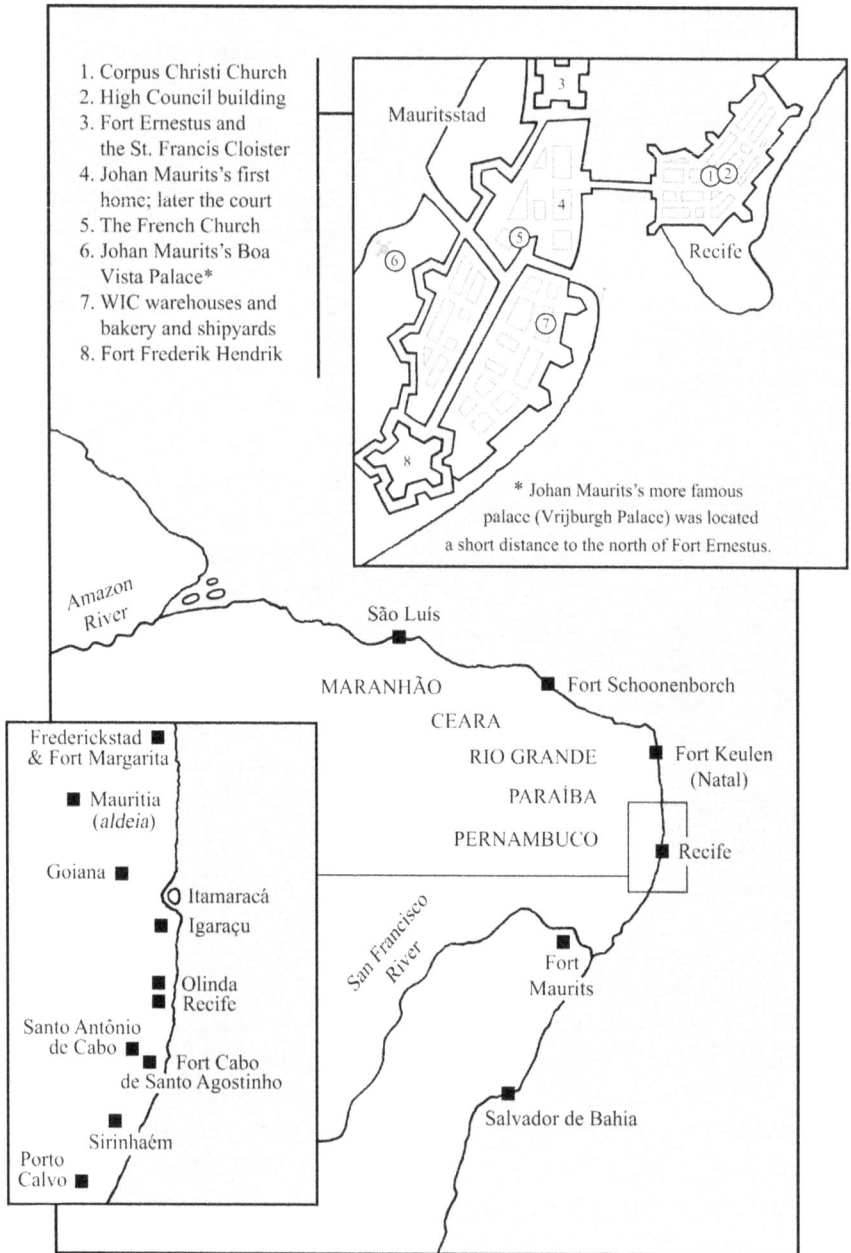

Map of Dutch Brazil with Recife/Mauritsstad inset. Map drawn by author.

Unfortunately Holland's own Catholic past and recent religious alteration provided a weak, unsuitable blueprint for altering Brazil's religious makeup. Despite controlling the church in the Netherlands, ardent Calvinists were a minority even there. The Spanish at least served as a common enemy, casting a stigma on Catholicism. In Brazil the shoe was on the other foot: now the Dutch were the enemy and foreigners trying to impose their faith on a people who, for the most part, didn't want to change. American clergy had to sift through added layers of authority, including local colonial officers, the directors and churches at home, and the municipal, provincial, and national rulers to whom the directors were still subject. Operating in occupied territory also meant that the Dutch had to share the power of the state on some level with prominent Catholics who cared nothing for Calvinist aims and opposed them outright. Warfare and economic stagnation kept the Dutch population relatively low, never more than 7,000 or 8,000 people, about a quarter of Portuguese strength. And some of those few thousand immigrants were Jewish. Appraising the many peoples and religions, clergy complained that their work was unusually challenging. They declared that the Brazilian soil was full of weeds, promising only a "thorny harvest."[5]

Jews and Catholics both enjoyed unique religious privileges in Dutch Brazil: the Jews because of their valuable experience and mercantile connections there, Catholics because they were able to wrest some rights of worship from the Dutch in the peace agreements that the two sides worked out when the numerous Portuguese could have picked up their weapons and continued the fight.[6] Dutch concessions to Catholics sprang from that dangerous time and context, a simple product of war and the best chance for survival and success. No one intended the policy for other colonies; no one proposed a meaningful change regarding non-Calvinist worship in the larger Dutch Atlantic world. Reforming Brazil had always been the WIC's goal, and the reformation remained a priority even after the peace treaties created what can only be described (from the Calvinist point of view) as extra obstacles.

In the end, WIC directors sacrificed the obligatory pragmatism of the war period at the altar of their anti-Catholic, Calvinist God. Relationships between the Dutch and Portuguese would have been rocky regardless of any specific religious policy, just because of the conquest. Calvinist efforts heightened these tensions considerably. As soon as they felt secure in their title to Brazil, the directors made matters worse by trying to undo even the limited rights they had allowed because of the war. Brazil deserves our attention today in part because it commanded remarkable attention in its own day, in part because it was the capital of Dutch interests in the South Atlantic. As the only lasting conquest with a significant, preexisting colonial population, it is also the best measure of Dutch rhetoric, a model for what might have been in Chile, São Tomé, and other Catholic colonies, had the company taken them or held them longer than it did. It finally failed in Brazil, too, but there at least it had enough time to implement plans and show how the company understood its religious responsibilities, how it may have pursued reform elsewhere if the directors' enthusiasm (critics said "greed") hadn't exceeded their resources. And the prognosis is dim: the reformation was a major contributing factor to the Portuguese uprising of 1645 and the loss of the WIC's most prized possession.

From Military Church to Public Church

Before beginning the overwhelming work of turning Catholic Brazil into a Protestant "New Holland," as the colony was sometimes called, the Dutch Reformed Church had to clean house. Some complaints about church personnel were unjust, born in an atmosphere of general discontent. In fact, for every complaint there was at least one positive report in the early period. Political councilor Servatius Carpentier wrote in June 1636 that clergy were then preaching the Gospel among the Dutch, French, and English in "great congregations." They had formed more than one consistory, they practiced church discipline, and they held Communion. Carpentier asserted that, if anything, Brazil needed more ministers.[7] Not counting lay clergy, there were only six at the time. Eight other ministers had served in Brazil since the invasion, but two died unexpectedly, some had gone home with injuries and illnesses, and the rest served just a few years (in keeping with their contracts). Carpentier had nothing but praise for those who remained. One of them, Reverend Jodocus à Stetten, kept good records of his activities, and his journal reveals an active, growing church.[8]

But the bad reports were too widespread to dismiss so easily, sometimes leveled by one minister against another. The colony already had a reputation for dissipation and debauchery, a kind of "anything goes" status that wouldn't change when even the clergy were guilty of levity and drunkenness, or when they left the pulpit to engage in trade. WIC directors gently admonished them twice in the years before the reformation, acknowledging progress, yet suggesting that, when invited to other people's homes, they not drink much. They might inspire imitation, and ministers would then become a "great stumbling block" for Catholics and Native Americans.

If they neglected their main responsibilities, the directors warned, they would lose their authority.[9] The problem was Reverend Daniel Schagen, and the solution was Reverend Fredricus Kesseler. Born in Holland, Schagen seemed like a good choice for a colonial position. He had graduated from Leiden University and served in the small town of Lopik before going to Brazil. In other words, he was educated and experienced. Upon arriving in America, however, he quickly fell from grace, not least by stepping outside approved channels to call three men to the ministry on his own authority.[10] His independence, along with other troubling choices that soon became public, helped convince the churches at home that they must not relinquish their control of colonial religion. In this instance they agreed with the directors that a reformation was needed. So they pulled Kesseler from Amsterdam's German-speaking congregation, which he had served for about a decade, and they called a number of other ministers to Brazil in the same period. To ensure that they would have the support of the new governor, the same churches wrote or sent delegations to Johan Maurits in the months before his departure. They asked him to dismiss bad ministers and watch over the colonial church.[11]

Kesseler was a John Calvin-like figure in Dutch Brazil, and Recife was his Geneva. Located at the mouth of two rivers in the province of Pernambuco, Recife was the WIC's capital and the center of Calvinist efforts to reform the whole colony. And the city grew quickly under the Dutch. They built homes and public buildings, established a fish market, created districts for fighting fire and collecting garbage, laid the streets in stone, erected palisades and forts around the perimeter, planted an orchard on a nearby island, and established Dutch political institutions.[12] Fellow minister and reformer Jacobus Dapper described Recife one year after Kesseler arrived, expressing wonder at all the people and shops. He felt as though he were strolling upon "the Dam" (the main square in Amsterdam). When he preached his first sermon, the chapel was full of families, including women and children, whom he had apparently not expected to find there already. Kesseler's tenure in Brazil was unique because he served all six and a half years in Recife. Other ministers at least took turns working in the army or among the Tupi Indians.[13]

Kesseler made his elevated position known at the very first gathering of the Brazil churches after his arrival. They now constituted a classis, traditionally the most important, powerful council in the Dutch Reformed system. With at least two representatives from each consistory, all classes were responsible for religious matters in the towns and villages within their borders, especially in places without a consistory; and they organized new churches and

Gov. Johan Maurits van Nassau-Siegen (left) and Rev. Fredricus Kesseler (right). Johan Maurits was drawn by Frans Post (ca. 1635–1676) and Kesseler by I. Warnier (ca. 1650). Courtesy of the Rijksmuseum, The Hague, and the Stadsarchief Amsterdam.

consistories when a growing population required it. Whether the issue was poor relief or examinations, callings or excommunications, very little was done in the Dutch Reformed Church without input and oversight from the classis. That it now came to Brazil was a sign of the colony's prominent place in the Dutch Atlantic, for no other colony had one and no other colony would get a classis under the first WIC. In reality, the Brazil classis was doubly unique in that, in the first place, it existed at all; yet it didn't enjoy the autonomy of other classes. It was an ecclesiastical curiosity, a classis by name but still subject to its Amsterdam and Walcheren counterparts. Kesseler enjoyed extra power because they called him and he was their envoy.[14]

Most of Brazil's twelve ministers and a number of elders traveled to Recife in March 1637 to discuss current affairs and begin the work of reform. Before anything else, Kesseler handed over his commission and the classis accepted him. Called to "found and build" the church, he was immediately selected as classis president. Then they read letters from the classes of Amsterdam and Walcheren about the "bad comportment" of certain ministers, with a plea to remedy the situation. After resolving that they would not call clergy locally, leaving that to the churches at home except in "great need," they handed the reins to Kesseler, who examined the church point by point: the state of preaching, Communion, visiting members, consistory meetings, church discipline, keeping accurate records, and the like. In each case the classis resolved to do

better. Then they reread the letters from their superiors and examined individual clergy. In the fervor of reform, they censured almost everyone, including Kesseler's fellow Germans, Jodocus à Stetten and the recently arrived
Johannes Polhemus, who was already quarreling with a WIC officer. They also
discussed how they could prevent common problems like adultery, blasphemy,
and Sabbath-breaking among the colonists.[15]

It quickly became apparent, if it wasn't already clear, that Schagen and the
small group of clergy whom he had called in recent years were the true cause
of Brazil's ecclesiastical difficulties. One of Schagen's appointments had left
before the reformation even began. Another didn't have the skills or knowledge to be minister, and Schagen later admitted to ordaining him with some
discomfort at the behest of a WIC officer. The classis allowed one of his appointments to stay, but they dismissed him when they discovered that he was
involved in an investment scam. As for Schagen, he didn't attend the classis
meeting in March 1637, perhaps sensing that it wouldn't go well for him. The
other clergy accused him of conspiring to prevent the classis in the first place,
and when he finally went on trial in the summer, the great extent of his indis-
cretions came to light. In short, he was a "Worldly Minister" who lorded over
his colleagues, they complained. He wore inappropriately showy apparel, attended parties, witnessed dancing and observed "lighthearted" conversation
without condemnation; and he drank too much, once falling asleep and wet-
ting himself in public. What's more, they said, he neglected his duties in order to work his sugar plantation, even on Sundays. Unable to defend himself,
he lost his post and was expelled from Brazil altogether.[16]

The colonial government kept an eye on these proceedings. Johan Maurits
was away with the army at the time, but his council approved the dismissals
and declared their "great contentment" with the "ardor and diligence" of the
clergy in regulating God's church. Secular support was also necessary to prevent Schagen from returning to Brazil as a private planter. The governor
asked the directors not to allow it, should he try. Johan Maurits described
the changes the church had made and expressed his happiness with the new
ministers.[17]

The clergy were equally pleased with the governor. The son of a zealous
Calvinist prince, Jan VII of Nassau-Siegen, Johan Maurits also belonged to the
Reformed Church. The company appointed him to the governorship because
of his family connections and military experience, possibly also because, as a
German, he could lead the German soldiers better than most.[18] In religious
matters his father's reputation helped as well. Johan Maurits was more moderate than Jan VII, and in time he proved to be quite adept at the political ma-
neuvering and quiet "connivance" that the regents of Amsterdam had made

famous in allowing non-Reformed worship in their sphere of influence. Yet he did so with so much skill that even the ministers tended to like and support him. The otherwise cantankerous Vincentius Soler, after knowing Johan Maurits for a year, wrote that he was "wise, virtuous, strong and religious," an "instrument in the hand of our Lord." Reverend Soler despised the old councilors as "rats without decency." He claimed that they cared more for their own gain than for the WIC.[19]

Though the clergy continued to grumble about religious diversity and other headaches, by the summer of 1637 the first step in the reformation, beginning with Brazil's ecclesiastical and secular rulers, was complete.[20] In gaging the significance of the change, we must take accusations like Soler's with a large grain of salt. Just as some long-standing ministers were caught up in the general atmosphere of discontent, damned more for having served in a period of special difficulty for the WIC and church, harsh feelings about rulers had similar roots. And the clergy could have unrealistic expectations. One of Soler's specific complaints, for example, was that the old councilors—in the few months since his arrival—had not heeded his advice to force 500 Indians and slaves to attend his Portuguese sermons in Recife. His judgment about the WIC's support for the church tended to fluctuate between praise and criticism according to his personal misery meter, which rose and fell in the wake of circumstances that were more economic than religious in nature. Similarly, the praise for new rulers might have originated in their military victories and the sense of direction Johan Maurits brought to Brazil. The expansion of WIC power meant the expansion of the church; greater stability allowed a concerted missionary effort for the first time.[21]

The influx of new personnel in 1636 and 1637 still marked a major turning point for Brazil. Schagen and his clerical cohort had caused serious problems, and some WIC officers were undoubtedly corrupt. Now at least the troublemakers in the church were gone. Ordained clergy gradually grew from nine in 1637 to twenty-one in 1642, even though the church had decided (and announced) that it could get by with a minimum of thirteen men. The ministers were also assisted by twenty-nine *ziekentroosters* and schoolmasters that year, for a total of fifty clergy of one kind or another.[22] Reformed congregations reached a high of twenty-two, twelve of which were independent enough to have their own consistories. So rapidly had the church progressed, in 1642 it created a second classis centered in Paraíba and, for the purpose of regulating religion in Africa and other recent conquests, a colony-wide synod. In five years the church had gone from marginal obscurity, consisting of several scattered military clergy, to the public church of northeastern Brazil and the spiritual fulcrum of the Dutch Atlantic.[23]

"A Rough, Indecent Heap of People"

Having resolved its internal problems, the Dutch Reformed Church set its sights on Protestantization and moral reform. As the public church it was the only one allowed to operate freely and openly in all religious matters, and it was the only church with a legitimate, recognized claim on tax monies and other public resources. The WIC also required that all employees attend Reformed services and all officers respect and support the clergy.[24] Although the church grew and prospered in the ways outlined above, it could never shed its identity as a military church or "church of the conquerors," which hindered the reformation. Expansion spread the ministers too thin, forcing them to oversee an ever-increasing number of towns, forts, and military companies. In Brazil, foreign occupation and religious diversity complicated an undertaking that was difficult enough even for clergy in the Netherlands.[25]

In the competition for souls, the Reformed Church at least enjoyed the prestige and other practical advantages that accompanied official exposure. At the most basic level the company supported the church by including it at all public functions, inviting clergy to offer prayers and deliver sermons at military parades and the festivities surrounding the institution of a new government, for example. When Johan Maurits and his councilors took their place in city hall for the first time, delegates from each major body presented themselves in turn: magistrates or judges called *schepenen*, high-ranking WIC officers, the ministers and elders from Recife, and leading figures from the Jewish community. Everyone except the latter then attended a worship service at the chapel, also sharing a meal provided by the outgoing administration.[26] Secular rulers attended church as a matter of course, if not because they were fervent believers, at least because it was expected of those who held important positions. Likewise, the High Council set an example and lent its authority to the church by sending envoys to the inaugural worship service held in any town still transitioning to the new ecclesiastical system. Regular exposure probably would have drawn some colonists to Protestantism in the long run simply because of the social advantages of belonging to the public church.[27]

Dutch Reformed influence increased when secular officials served on the consistory, which facilitated relations with the WIC and gave the church a voice in government. Merchants, planters, and WIC officers of various ranks became elders and deacons in Brazil: Colonel Diederick van Waerdenburch and political councilors Willem Schotte, Paulus van Serooskercke, Hendrik Haecx, and Mathias Beck (future governor of Curaçao). After the church formed a synod, the colonial council also adopted the controversial but common practice in the Netherlands of sending a secular delegate to the meeting.

Conversely, one representative from the clergy and one elder or deacon often came to the council to deliver their minutes and discuss ecclesiastical needs and concerns.[28]

The governor and his council were generally sympathetic to the church's efforts to reform the city and colony. Among the first orders of business in Recife was creating a good atmosphere for "God's word," preached Sundays and Wednesdays. The Dutch had commandeered the main chapel, but when churchgoers complained about noise in the streets during the sermon, the council agreed to find a solution. Johan Maurits soon issued a placard against all disruptive activity around the church, then appointed an officer to enforce the law and moved the market from the adjacent square to a different location.[29] When clergy claimed that drinking contributed to the chaos, the council also prohibited taverns from serving alcohol during the hours of church service. It imposed fines on all offenders and gave the money to the hospital, run by the deacons. These measures must have had some effect, because the 1638 classis reported that the Sabbath was finally being honored in Recife—though not yet in other places, clergy said. To maintain the necessary quiet for church services, Kesseler and his colleagues visited the council again in coming years to complain about ships firing their cannon in the nearby harbor and the criminal punishments that sometimes took place on Sunday.[30]

Clergy also tried to increase attendance by reminding negligent officers of their responsibility to bring their subordinates to church. According to Dutch law and long-held rights of conscience, the WIC couldn't compel private persons in the same way. But by closing taverns and ending public executions the consistory did at least limit people's options, maybe hoping that, if nothing else, they would come to church because they were bored. For the same reason, it asked the council to prohibit the committees of justice and finance, the militia, and the schepenen from meeting during the poorly attended Wednesday services. In that case the council was less sympathetic, asking the consistory to move the sermon to 7:00 a.m., when magistrates could come without disrupting other critical business.[31]

The Dutch knew the colony would never become Protestant without a serious evangelical effort. Whatever social pressures they brought to bear, they couldn't hope to win many people to the Reformed faith just by making sermons available in Dutch, English, and French. For the longtime inhabitants of Brazil, the many colonists who didn't speak those languages, the church offered services in Portuguese. At the center of its linguistic endeavors was Reverend Soler, a Spaniard and former Catholic priest who preached every week in Portuguese at Recife and Olinda, a few miles up the coast from the

Signatures of Dutch Reformed clergy in Brazil (from the Mulheiser album). Courtesy of the Koninklijke Bibliotheek, The Hague.

capital. Colonists in other towns and provinces would have had a harder time finding a service they could understand, should they choose to attend. The WIC did employ other Portuguese speakers, including some men who learned on the job; and the council encouraged all ministers to study the language. But their few-year contracts and the knowledge that they might soon return to Europe undermined whatever enthusiasm they felt for the project. Reverend Stetten claimed a degree of proficiency. According to Servatius Carpentier, Stetten taught regularly in Portuguese, and his wife Margarita once presented a number of Portuguese children for baptism. In addition to Soler and Stetten, there were at least seven other ministers and various *ziekentroosters* and schoolmasters who spoke the language.[32]

The WIC provided the necessary literature: Bibles, catechisms, psalters, and a pervasive volume listed on company book lists either as *Catholique Reformados* or *Gereformeert Catholicus* (The Reformed Catholic). Frans Schalkwijk argues that they were actually two different books by different authors, united in title and purpose: to attack so-called papist ideas and promote Protestant ideas and rites.[33] At first the directors only sent literature in Spanish, but when the church informed them that the Spanish materials weren't very useful, they arranged for translations and publications in Portuguese. Clergy probably distributed these works among the Catholic population at Portuguese sermons and other public events. They claimed that they weren't having an impact, that the Portuguese despised the newcomers as heretics, shunned Reformed preaching, and refused to send their children to Dutch schools. And indeed, there were few converts. Many Portuguese colonists, if they even accepted the company's anti-Catholic propaganda, may have taken the books home and thrown them in the fire. Yet their priests still worried. They witnessed the proliferation of Protestant teachings and complained that heterodox ideas were growing among their parishioners. With all the advantages they enjoyed, *time* was what the invaders needed most.[34]

Clergy also concerned themselves with cursing, blasphemy, and sexual sins like incest, fornication, adultery, and prostitution. Marriage and sex had become increasingly public concerns for Catholics and Protestants in Europe during the Reformation. Mainstream churches had developed institutions like the consistory and other ecclesiastical courts in part to regulate and punish unlawful sexual conduct.[35] In Brazil the church checked the papers of new arrivals to ascertain their marital status, recorded engagements, and reported all dubious relationships to the authorities. Consistent with Dutch law, impending marriages had to be announced in the church or city hall once per week for three weeks before the ceremony. The consistory told engaged couples to abstain from sex and pressured them to marry quickly to avoid temptation.

If people ignored these strictures, clergy referred their cases to the *schout* (sheriff) for further investigation and prosecution.[36]

In Brazil the church's power in sexual and marital affairs was greater than it was in the Netherlands, which kindled resentment among Catholics and probably others who didn't belong to the Reformed faith. At home, Dutch rulers appointed secular commissioners to oversee the day-to-day minutiae that occupied the church in Brazil. WIC clergy wore two hats, condemning common sins from the pulpit and visiting the High Council when they had clear evidence of misconduct, yet acting for the government, too, by checking papers and recording the names of those who wished to marry, whether they planned to do so in the chapel or before a magistrate. How long they performed the first task is uncertain. At least by 1646 the council was having an officer do it.[37] But they always recorded and kept the lists of betrothed, enabling them to monitor those who planned to marry legally and identify everyone who did not. For the WIC it was just a convenient allocation of authority to a group that cared deeply about the issue anyway. For the ministers it became a nuisance, and they tried to pass it back to the company, arguing that their marital duties were a source of "displeasure" among the "sundry nations" in Brazil. The Nineteen Lords agreed that some secular official should take over, but for one reason or another, the council never made the change.[38]

Calvinists maintained that sexual sin would invite "God's vengeance" or "God's wrath" on the colony, and along with their other reform efforts, they sought vehemently to eradicate it.[39] However, they did not turn immediately to the state. Their first tool was the pulpit and their first responsibility was to errant members of the church. That was one of the consistory's purposes, after all: to hear, judge, and ultimately, by withholding Communion and applying similar pressures, reform the men and women who had willingly joined the community of Christ.

Without consistory records, examples of this disciplinary process are hard to find, but surviving classis minutes provide an occasional glimpse. In the province of Paraíba, about seventy-five miles north of Recife, the local consistory once accused a woman named Elsie Groenewalts of prostitution. Five witnesses testified against her. Because she belonged to the church, the consistory questioned her, trying to obtain a confession for something they clearly already believed. However, she refused to cooperate, and they wanted to excommunicate her. When her case was raised at the classis in Recife, the other classis members decided that she deserved another chance; they would give her six more months, they said. At the next classical gathering the Paraíba delegation reported that, after a great deal of exhortation—and perhaps facing the threat of deportation—Groenewalts had finally confessed her sins and done her penance in the consistory, meaning that she had shown the necessary humility and sorrow. After a period of close observation, they readmitted her to the Communion table.[40]

Members of the High Council also worried that sexual sin would provoke God's wrath. They once told the *schepenen* of Rio Grande to prevent "whoredom" in their province. "Through [prostitution]," they continued, "the Wrath of God falls over the land," and they intended to "root out such sins."[41] If their diverse interests and responsibilities didn't allow them to be as rigid as the ministers, they accommodated the church whenever they could. After the classis complained that some married women didn't live with their husbands, the council created a special garrison for married soldiers and officers, explaining that the WIC also hoped to do away with all impropriety. The clergy's original complaint suggests that their concern wasn't just about employees and their wives, for they objected to women living alone even when their husbands were in fixed locales. The council's solution solved the problem without meddling in the affairs of men and women whose separation probably had more to do with marital discord or economic opportunity than with the kind of misconduct the ministers tended to suspect whenever they encountered single women.[42]

When there were clear violations of the law, the church and WIC could and did act against anyone, no matter their nationality. During the Kesseler-Maurits years, many women were investigated, arrested, and deported for illegal sexual relations. Consistory members watched for possible transgressions and investigated on their own, calling couples before them or the classis to determine whether they were involved in illegal behavior. If it appeared that someone had in fact broken the law, the church went to the High Council, who gave the case to the WIC's *schout* and *fiscaal* for a formal investigation, then the *schepenen* for prosecution.[43] Having a second partner in Europe was a common allegation. The church also investigated "very bad" housekeeping, girls with bad reputations marrying boys from respectable families, men who slept with slaves and servants, and women working in taverns in unambiguous cases of prostitution. The consistory even tried to stop otherwise lawful marriages when they learned that the couple in question lived together before. And ministers were extremely patient. When their suspects were Dutch, they wrote to colleagues in the Netherlands to ask for help in identifying them and determining their marital status, waiting upwards of nine months for the answer before moving forward.[44]

The High Council responded with wary support. Again, it sent women home or to other provinces (more rarely men) when there was sufficient evidence against them.[45] But it had to remind the consistory of that requirement.

In the aforementioned cohabitation case, the council said it couldn't do anything unless the charge was "legally proven true."[46] The church found that its power and influence, however great, couldn't trump the rule of law, and even the power it did have disintegrated into simple, toothless words without the coercive authority of the state. The consistory's extra investigative duties may have been a product of the early years, when Dutch institutions were still taking root; or they may be evidence that secular officials sometimes shirked their duties, reluctant to pursue the placards too rigorously. In the very least, the church suspected lesser officials of undermining reform efforts. About a year after the reformation began, Reverend Kesseler and two other delegates from the consistory complained that the *fiscaal* wasn't conducting an "inquisition" against offenders (a fascinatingly obtuse choice of words, given Holland's history). Two years later Kesseler reported that sin was still commonplace in Brazil. With the connivance of WIC officers, he declared, it was actually growing.[47]

On one occasion the church was bold enough to criticize even the High Council. After the *fiscaal* blamed the council for releasing twelve of seventeen women who had been (until recently) sitting in jail, the church accused the councilors of winking at prostitution and other sexual sins. They, of course, denied the charges, and their subsequent investigation revealed the many administrative layers reformers had to penetrate, the many opportunities for opponents to hinder their efforts. Pieter Bas, it turned out, had approved the release as president of the council of justice. Someone had later changed the date on Bas's written order to make it appear that he had issued it *after* joining the High Council. Having discovered this "abuse," the council then summoned the *schout* Paulo Daems, who once said that he would no longer arrest prostitutes because they weren't punished afterward. As evidence he now reminded everyone of a similar case from a few years before, when Johan Maurits had freed several women at the behest of their creditors. The church had not complained at the time, however, and the *fiscaal* and *schout* testified that the council had never freed anyone else, nor had they ever arrested anyone without a proper investigation, just because the consistory asked. Less than two weeks later the council reported that it had renewed the placards and charged the *fiscaal* to execute them with rigor. The consistory should go directly to him if it learned of any new violations.[48]

The council's reply was an example of protesting too much. Council members did sometimes harbor a more lenient attitude than the ministers, asking them, for instance, to use Christian exhortation before resorting to legal action when unmarried couples lived together: they had the lists of engaged; they could try to change people first with God's word. That the council really practiced connivance is a strong probability. It was a well-known device of moderate rulers in the Dutch Republic, and Johan Maurits described its benefits in his written advice to successors about religion and religious diversity. He must have operated the same way in other matters, especially given the many groups and interests he had to juggle in Brazil.[49]

But connivance was, by its very nature, a hazy nonpolicy, impossible to apply consistently even for the most skilled ruler. The council consisted of men with different temperaments and complex views, including Calvinist views, and reformers often got their way too. Even when there were no clergy present, council members instructed their underlings to prevent prostitution and execute the laws faithfully. And when officials failed to perform their duties, the council threatened to appoint men who would.[50] Clerical criticisms about company officers reveal an extraordinary lack of understanding for an impossible situation. One gets a sense of the council's exasperation in a 1645 letter to the directors, who had obviously been listening to an indignant church. The councilors claimed that most critiques were unjust. They confessed that blasphemy, cursing, Sabbath-breaking, prostitution, and adultery were common in Brazil. They had outlawed them, though, and they were trying to eradicate them. They said that Brazil was inhabited by a "rough, indecent heap of people from every nation." No one could expect them to establish law and order so soon, no matter what they did or how vigorously they did it.[51]

Perhaps clergy should have been more sympathetic. After all, the church had supported the war party and the company's aggressive approach in America. Now they were learning the frustrations of running a military church in an occupied colony. If women sometimes caused scandals by living alone, it was partly because military husbands were so mobile. Mobility also destroyed consistories, with newly called elders suddenly transferred from one province to another, leaving less qualified replacements. Brazil was a "conquered land" with "few devout," one minister lamented. He said that some officers were as rough as their men, that they committed the very sins they were supposed to prevent. From cursing, stealing, and murder to death on the battlefield, from damaged chapels to rapid growth and clerical shortages, the impacts of the invasion and the continued military presence were tremendous.[52] Yet the reformers, once committed to their path, could only lace up their boots and keep marching forward. When religious leaders reproached their secular counterparts and secular leaders grumbled about clergy, the two were behaving like any harried, weary soldier, momentarily easing their shared burden by shifting it from one shoulder to the other. The key word is "shared," for they knew that Brazil would never really be Dutch, they knew they couldn't subject and transform the colony, unless church and state attacked the problem together.

The Failed Reformation and the Revolt

A more serious consequence of conquest was having to live and labor among the conquered. The High Council's "heap of people" included tens of thousands of Portuguese who weren't happy with the regime change, nor with the Protestant and Jewish newcomers who took their churches and property. Even if the council had consisted solely of unbending Calvinist zealots, they never could have imposed their will. Secular and religious power had to be shared on some level or the Dutch wouldn't have lasted more than a few years in Brazil. They banished the hated Jesuits, but they allowed other priests to remain, and Catholics held secular power even in Recife: from lowly orphan masters to powerful *schepenen* who took the clergy's evidence and determined the fate of defendants. Would the *schepenen* support the church's campaign to stop sugar mills from operating on Sunday when most mills were run by Portuguese? Would they rule against Catholic lawbreakers when a Protestant consistory was involved? Portuguese *schepenen* hindered justice at a more basic level by honoring Catholic holidays, regularly immobilizing the court through their absence.[53]

To be clear, Catholic definitions of sin and deviant behavior probably didn't differ much from Calvinist definitions. Problems in Brazil had more to do with sharing power and the natural antagonism of occupation, the coming together of previously separate legal traditions. Reverend Petrus Doornick condemned the system in Paraíba because half of the rulers there were "papists" and the other half were Dutch merchants who had never held office.[54] With his outspoken, combative manner, Doornick won many enemies, including some in the Recife church, which he criticized for wielding too much power in the classis. In his struggles one sees how religion divided the occupier from the occupied and muddied what should have been secular issues in local courts.

The High Council learned that something was amiss in Paraíba when the local *schepenen* wrote to complain that Doornick was "seeking to take their authority." When he came to Recife to defend himself, he blamed everything on them, describing a recent incident in which one of his parishioners had traveled to Frederickstad, the provincial capital, to celebrate Communion. The *schepenen* chose that time, Doornick explained, to seize the man's slave, who was mixed up in some legal dispute. Doornick believed that theirs was no act of convenience, but a calculated plot to "disturb the members of the church" and detract from Reformed services. He said that the same thing didn't happen to Catholics. When they went to "idolatrous Mass," no one molested them. Yet those of the "holy, true religion" suffered abuses that weren't allowed in other lands. He blamed the disapproval of his Dutch critics in Paraíba on the fact that he had rebuked their sins, and he said that some of them were Lutherans and Catholics, suggesting that they were more inclined to take the Portuguese side because they, too, spurned the public church. Unfortunately for Doornick, his quarrel with his colleagues in Recife discouraged them (his most likely defenders) from taking up his case, and he eventually had to return to Holland because of the divisions in Paraíba.[55]

Doornick's interpretation of the Communion incident echoed other complaints about Catholics in the colony. The nature of Catholic worship and Portuguese power differed from place to place, but it caused controversies everywhere. If the Portuguese in one area refused to give up arms unless the WIC guaranteed their religious freedom, the company allowed it. If their compatriots elsewhere neglected to broach the matter during treaty negotiations or had to be subjected by force, their rights were more ambiguous. The result was a patchwork of conflicting policies, with priests free to conduct services in most places but not all. Even where priests functioned legally, the Dutch and Portuguese tended to disagree on the meaning of "religious freedom" and on questions about whether Catholics could worship outside their chapels and perform their own marriages.[56] Originally priests could marry anyone who made the requisite announcements in the Reformed church or city hall beforehand. They sometimes ignored even that law, and they married some Dutch colonists whose unions the Reformed consistory or classis had already refused. Normally Catholics didn't care any less about sexual misconduct, but being out of power, they weren't privy to the same information about individual colonists. Illegal marriage was possibly also a subtle rebellion or expression of contempt for the new regime.[57]

Questions about ecclesiastical property and income caused endless tensions and quarrels. To provide for the Dutch, the High Council usually forced the Portuguese in towns throughout Brazil to give up one of their own buildings. The WIC had destroyed and abandoned Olinda at the start of the occupation, but as the Portuguese rebuilt the old provincial capital and some Dutch settled there, the council asked the Recife clergy to select a chapel for Protestant worship. Because the small Dutch population didn't use it very much, the company eventually gave it back to the Portuguese and the Dutch had to worship in the monastery chapel with the soldiers. The move only led to another dispute two years later over the graves at the first location, and once again, facing a growing Dutch population, the council commanded the unhappy Catholics to hand over the church that they had by then spent a lot of time and resources repairing.[58]

Except on private, rural plantations, the company didn't permit any new Catholic construction, and it seized former Jesuit facilities and lands for its own military and social needs. The High Council rejected a request to build a church on the island of Itamaracà in 1639, stating that "instead of building the Gospel, we would again be introducing the Papacy."[59] It did allow the three Catholic orders that remained in Brazil after the Jesuit expulsion—the Franciscans, the Benedictines, and the Carmelites—to retain most of their property, including nine monasteries. The Franciscans owned little else, living mostly from alms. The Carmelites had rental homes in Olinda, and the Benedictines, the wealthiest of the three, had abundant land and sugar plantations. All other Catholic priests were the individual parish priests who didn't belong to one of the orders: *mispapen* ("mass papists"), the Dutch called them. If these priests didn't have their own farms, they now had to live from whatever money they collected at church and from services like visiting the sick. Needing an income was perhaps another reason they married people illegally. Before the Dutch arrived, each parish received state-sponsored tithes. The priests grew desperate after the old system collapsed and the WIC didn't provide any new means of support.[60]

As a likely source of Portuguese leadership and resistance, Catholic priests were magnets for controversy and disdain. They had to take an oath to the Dutch government and the WIC monitored them as closely as possible. Cut off from the Portuguese bishop in Bahia, they were organized locally under provincial vicars and a vicar general, who lived in Paraíba.[61] The directors in the Netherlands and the High Council in Recife wanted to get rid of them entirely, and the council did consider ejecting the Franciscans, Benedictines, and Carmelites with the Jesuits. But fearing the Portuguese reaction, they decided to wait. The Dutch occasionally deported individual priests for violating laws and plotting with the enemy. They only found a chance for a more serious "cleansing," so to speak, in 1640, when the council obtained evidence that some Benedictines had secretly contacted their superiors in Bahia. In response, Johan Maurits rounded up and deported all three orders, sending sixty men total to the Caribbean. The most feared and hated priests were finally gone, and reformers could seize their property for Dutch use, just as reformers in Europe had done during the Reformation there. Brazilian Catholics only had the poor parish priests from that point onward.[62]

Both before and after the mass deportation of 1640, Catholics pushed at the limited boundaries the Dutch placed around them. Priests used censure and excommunication to intimidate any Portuguese who grew close to the Dutch, and they used similar tactics against French Catholics who served as soldiers in the Dutch army. Reformed clergy blamed the lack of converts on the power of the vicar general and his ability to inspire fear in the Catholic community.[63] In Olinda and Paraíba, where their influence was greatest,

Catholics agitated Calvinists by taking their religion outdoors, marching in processions to venerate saints and celebrate holidays. They also participated in street theater, which was not obviously criminal. Calvinists objected to it because it was usually religious in nature, and they were supposed to control all public religious instruction. They also interpreted physical representations of holy, divine figures as idolatry, and they worried that Catholics were planting their "superstitions" through their performances. Ministers uncovered other supposed Catholic plots in funeral processions and even the weekly Sunday traffic. The High Council summoned strident, provocative offenders and imposed fines, but overall, it tried to find a middle way, once instructing the *schout* in Rio Grande not to allow any obvious aggravations but to give Catholics the benefit of the doubt when they traveled to and from their chapel.[64]

Physical altercations and violence were less common than Calvinist clergy claimed, and they largely ignored their own side's contribution to any conflict that did occur. They first said that Catholics were striking Protestants in 1641, when bystanders in Sirinhaém didn't reverence an "idol" that Catholics carried through the street in one of their processions. The story spread from there to the Recife classis and finally to Holland, where the church complained to company directors. Repeated so often, narrow allegations soon became general truths: Catholics in Brazil *persecute* those who won't participate in false worship. For years the High Council had to defend itself to the Nineteen Lords, explaining that there had only been the one incident and that they had taken steps to prevent it from happening again. Truth be told, they wrote, Dutch "insolence" in the Sirinhaém affair—"and on other occasions"—was "many times as great."[65] Indeed, the council once had to prosecute a Dutchman for murdering a Catholic priest. In a less extreme case it fined a few other Dutch for going by night to Olinda, where they harassed a priest at his home, mimicking and mocking "Papist ceremonies."[66]

If clergy exaggerated Catholic misconduct and even tried to deflect all blame for violence, Reverend Soler proved it with his over-the-top allegations against the vicar general, Gaspar Ferreira, in 1641. On the day before Ferreira traveled to Recife to answer charges of illegal activity, Soler visited the council to ensure that it had the relevant information. To his list of transgressions Soler added that Ferreira was involved in an incestuous relationship and fathered an illegitimate child. The council ought to throw him in prison, Soler declared. The next day when the vicar arrived in the capital Soler ran ahead of him to council chambers to report that Ferreira was causing problems in the street, "intimidating" bystanders who, in Dutch Recife, could not possibly be intimidated by one man and his small entourage. As in Sirinhaém, Protestants were probably the real source of unrest, blaming it on their enemies because it suited their agenda. Only by convincing people that Catholic conduct was beyond the pale could clergy hope to outlaw the Catholic priesthood and Catholic worship. Only then could they hope to effect a serious reformation.[67]

The Portuguese looked at the recent history of deportations, ecclesiastical isolation, lack of funds, and outright animosity on both sides and accused the Dutch of trying to destroy Catholic religion by gradual suffocation. They viewed freedom of conscience—by which the Dutch allowed private worship in one's home—as no freedom at all, and as their processions demonstrate, they weren't content with the greater rights they enjoyed in their churches in most places. More than once they requested full autonomy, including the right to communicate with the bishop in Bahia, appoint new priests, and rebuild their financial base.[68]

Catholics did have reason to fear. At one time or another, the governor, his councilors, the directors of the WIC, and the Dutch clergy all expressed a loathing for the Catholic priesthood and the Catholic faith in general, as well as a desire to expunge them from Brazil. Most Dutch saw it as a question of when it would happen, not if. Zeeland directors spoke of allowing the priesthood to "die out." Johan Maurits said that "in time" he would "erase the memory of the Portuguese language, nation, and religion." When asked to justify his moderate side to unhappy Reformed clergy, he explained that he had to consider the current political reality and what the colony could then bear, implying that he would act differently when circumstances changed.[69] Of course he may have just said what he knew the clergy and his employers wanted to hear. His true opinions and intentions are difficult to ascertain because of his responsibilities. But consider the views of Johan Toner, his secretary, who scoffed at the parish priests who remained in Brazil after the mass deportation. They were old drunks, wrote Toner, and when they died, there was no one to replace them. He claimed that religious freedom was just a tool for drawing Catholics to the WIC for its better security.[70]

The directors were less ambiguous than Johan Maurits. They asked him not to proceed too strictly against Catholics "at first." When he accepted Portuguese demands for revenue, returning two small plantations, the directors expressed their displeasure. They ordered him to take the plantations back, along with all property that still sustained the Catholic priesthood.[71] When the governor recommended that the WIC give Catholics a regular income and allow them to build a chapel in the capital, the directors refused. Then in 1642, in response to growing concerns about Catholic impertinence, they issued orders that they said would even satisfy their critics in the Reformed Church. But Johan Maurits defied them, refusing to make the orders public or show them to the consistory, informing the clergy once more that he would implement only the changes the colony could bear. He told the directors that "the constitution of this state will not yet permit us to practice your orders in full." The company must help the ministers "draw [Catholic] souls away from Papist superstition and reclaim them for Christ," but he believed that "such a great reformation," so soon after the conquest, was reckless. Rather than force new laws on the Portuguese all at once, he continued, the WIC should "gently diminish their religious freedoms from time to time."[72]

So much for tolerance. Even in his farewell advice to his council, when Johan Maurits explained his quiet, shrewd approach to religious matters, he again revealed that it was just a temporary necessity—and that connivance worked both ways. The Dutch should treat the Portuguese with "benevolence and courtesy," he wrote. "Nothing embitters them more" than the "abolition" of their rituals and ceremonies, nor did they like the WIC to meddle with their ecclesiastical personnel. The council should keep an eye on Dutch effrontery and disrespect for Catholic ritual, reproaching offenders not for "an error of religion," but for "discourtesy." When they heard religious complaints, Johan Maurits told his councilors that they should promise to look into the matter and then, for the sake of peace, forget about it. If their zeal for the true religion inspired a more severe approach, they should at least proceed as quietly as possible. He held out the possibility that the situation would change, writing that Reformed religion could "not yet" be implemented everywhere, that heavy interference in Catholic affairs was "premature." Accepting some illicit activity was better than an inquisition *at this time*. To commit itself to full-blown reform, the company would have to deport all Catholic priests, and that would be the "beginning of great unrest and rebellion."[73]

Unless he was just crafting his message for his audience, the governor's advice shows that even he viewed Catholic worship as a necessary but mutable problem. The colony could and would become Reformed, if handled with caution. His recommendation about bridling Protestant passions, echoed by other Dutch writers, suggests that the people who resisted the Catholic procession in Sirinhaém and the men who harassed the priest in Olinda were not unique, that Dutch "insolence" toward Catholic religion really was (in the council's words) "many times as great" as any Portuguese insolence. A loathing for Catholicism doesn't necessarily reflect a corresponding, positive commitment to another tradition. Yet it's difficult to reconcile the aggression exhibited in cases like these with the more common image of the indifferent, business-minded Dutch pragmatist. Johan Maurits was clearly concerned about a strong anti-Catholic element in the Dutch community, fostered by a smaller but loud Calvinist contingent that preferred the direct approach to reformation.

In his advice to his councilors he conceded that they, too, sometimes favored that approach.[74]

Unfortunately for him, WIC directors sided with Calvinists. They originally honored agreements made on the battlefield and they recognized that they had to proceed carefully, but they resisted efforts to expand Catholic freedom even when their own governor believed that doing so was vital to Dutch success. Why did they suddenly adopt stricter measures in 1642 and what did their instructions of that year contain? Portugal's recent revolution and independence from Spain seem to have given the directors the confidence to move forward with plans they had long wanted to implement anyway. No longer bound to Spanish interests, Portugal could seek a separate peace with the Dutch Republic, and the WIC took a keen interest in treaty negotiations between the two countries. The Zeeland chamber sent envoys to the provincial States to ensure that Dutch merchants stationed in Portugal would enjoy some religious rights. The Zeeland *hoofdparticipanten* even proposed that the WIC grant only those freedoms in its colonial possessions that Portugal reciprocated, which would have meant, in effect, that Catholic colonists in Brazil could worship only inside their homes (a "great reformation" indeed). The *hoofdparticipanten* perhaps felt that they could be so bold because, after the Treaty of The Hague (1641), the colony was finally and officially theirs.[75]

The directors didn't go quite so far in their 1642 orders. So concerned was Johan Maurits about the Portuguese reaction, so successful was he at burying the particulars, no copy survived. However, the governor's friend Caspar Barlaeus recorded what appears to be a list of the new restrictions in his history of the colony, published after Johan Maurits left. Some items on the list simply confirmed existing laws, though it would have been disconcerting to learn that the WIC was finally going to crack down on processions, for example, and that all ecclesiastical property belonged to the company. Of particular concern was the restriction on marrying before a Catholic priest. Had the new laws gone into effect, those who did marry with a priest could have been fined ƒ300, deported, and any future children would have lost their inheritance rights. Catholics might have also pointed out that marriage was one of seven sacraments, and that the priest's role in the ceremony had only increased in import during the recent Reformation and Counter-Reformation. Protestants did not consider marriage a sacrament and they already monitored engagements and sex in the colony; yet now they wanted a monopoly on the final rite. No wonder the governor was worried about backlash.[76]

Calvinists may have won the agenda in Brazil, but Johan Maurits was the better prophet. While he probably convinced the directors that it was still unwise to adopt the severe measures they wanted, clergy were aware that something significant had occurred in 1642 because the directors told them: even you will be pleased with our orders.[77] Given their brash, combative style, it's unlikely that the ministers didn't spread what they knew, and the Calvinist political councilors may have provided missing details. Regardless, the council began to adopt a harder line toward Catholics after Johan Maurits departed in 1644. It informed them that the WIC had only granted plantations for the upkeep of their priests provisionally, that the directors wanted the plantations back. The directors had continued to insist that the council take ecclesiastical properties for the company and the council finally did sell them.[78] At the same time, in keeping with the directors' orders to "purify our conquests of them and their kind," it actively sought and deported priests who traveled from Bahia, fearing that they might be spies. But the company's policy on Catholic priests wasn't just about security. The council repeatedly rejected requests for new priests, whether they came from Bahia or anywhere else.[79]

In July 1645 the Portuguese revolted, just as Johan Maurits had predicted. They had countless reasons to resent the Dutch by that point, including (probably most importantly) their growing indebtedness to foreigners and Jews. Religious concerns after the directors' 1642 orders and the governor's 1644 departure were at least responsible for the timing of the uprising, and in fact, the monks from whom the WIC had taken the plantations were among those who traveled the countryside preaching and provoking colonists in the months before. Also relevant to the question of timing, the WIC had recently reduced its military garrisons in Brazil. These different motives and opportunities all converged in the mid-1640s to allow and inspire colonists to pick up their weapons and try to reclaim the control they had lost in the years since the invasion.[80]

The Portuguese called theirs a religious war, a revolt waged "in the name of Godly freedom."[81] In their "Manifest" of 1646, published in Antwerp, they objected to high taxes and abusive rulers, Dutch cruelty and the general atmosphere of distrust. They also wrote about some of the religious changes and cultural threats outlined in this chapter. They said that, according to the peace treaties, they were supposed to enjoy "full freedom and exercise of our Roman Catholic Religion." At first the WIC honored its promises, they continued; "but afterward [the Dutch] took away our Churches, keeping some for themselves." Also, "because of the hate they feel toward our Clergy," the Dutch "banished and exported from the Land all Religious and Spiritual persons."[82] Just before they began their revolt the rebels allegedly poisoned Reverend Cornelis van der Poel and WIC commander Hans Ernst at a dinner at a Portuguese home in Maranhão. A cryptic note about Dutch sins and the judgment bar of God, nailed anonymously to the door of a chapel in Paraíba the next year, captured the tenor of Dutch-Portuguese relations perfectly. The chapel in question used to ring with the readings and recitations of the Catholic Mass. The WIC had seized it and converted it for Protestant worship just as the Dutch were trying to reform the whole colony.[83]

Reverend Kesseler and the Dutch Reformed Church attributed the rebellion to different causes, mostly divine. Never mind Portuguese explanations for their behavior; never mind their fears about the gradual death of their religion and the warnings Johan Maurits had given. Rather, the church taught that an angry God had removed his blessing because the WIC hadn't destroyed Catholicism and didn't eliminate cursing, Sabbath-breaking, and sexual sin. The Recife classis even tried to use the revolt as an opportunity to further the agenda that had already done so much to foment Portuguese antipathy.[84]

Dutch Brazil was by no means finished in 1645 and 1646. But the revolt was the beginning of the end for the WIC in its favorite colony, the critical event of the company's long, drawn-out bankruptcy. The Dutch would fight the rebels for nine more years, beginning in the countryside—which the Portuguese had always dominated anyway—and falling back in an increasingly tight circle around Recife. Both sides enjoyed some support from their respective countries of origin in Europe. The Dutch were, however, at a disadvantage in the 1640s because of internal divisions over the tremendous costs of war and the question of whether the WIC could continue to dedicate so many resources to Brazil. Insofar as anti-Catholicism and sanctimonious rigor highlighted and exacerbated differences between the conquerors and conquered, Calvinists should have shared in the blame and responsibility for the downturn. Their quest to reform Brazil and make it a Protestant New Holland foundered on the very religious antagonisms that validated invasion in the first place.

CHAPTER 6

Turmoil in the Garden of Eden

Dissent and Reform in New Netherland and the Dutch Caribbean

The colonist and poet Jacob Steendam described
New Netherland in 1661 with fervent praise: "a pleasure garden," "the mas-
terpiece of nature's hand," "the promised land," "the noblest of all lands," and
the Garden of Eden. In his earlier writings he had criticized Africa for its heat
and debilitating diseases, its lack of Christian, European institutions. The tem-
perature on the Hudson, by contrast, was warm and pure, and the benefit of
good air, he said, was good health. The Dutch were not "aliens," no longer
Israel in Egypt. In New Netherland they could flourish and attain an "inheritance fore'er." One could build a "house," "community," and "commonwealth," and one's neighbors were freemen and countrymen. While the soil
of Africa was not fertile enough for the true religion, Steendam predicted that
the church would bloom like a lily in New Netherland.[1]

Steendam got carried away, resorting to simple hyperbole, in part because
of his poetic medium, but also because he was trying to attract potential immigrants in a promotional tract. In reality he must have known about New
Netherland's troubled past, including a long, controversial journey from company government to civic government in the capital. And his neighbors were
certainly not all "freemen and countrymen." By 1661 the colony had a small
community of African slaves and former slaves, and New Netherland had
undergone more than one destructive Indian war.[2] As a farm owner and trader,
Steendam also knew that the region was still underdeveloped, which caused

various monetary and other problems. Reformed clergy had constant difficulties obtaining their pay and still complained about the quality and diversity of their flock. Like the clergy of most Christian societies, they believed that New Netherland had some righteous rulers and some bad, some saints and many sinners. Among the sinners they typically included the colony's large non-Reformed population.

In short, what Steendam didn't mention in the 1661 poem was that, from the Calvinist perspective, New Netherland was still a place that needed significant reform, a place where the language of repentance, divine wrath, and reformation reverberated just as loudly as it did in Dutch Brazil. Reformation in the Brazilian context meant transforming a Catholic colony into a Protestant one and, more broadly, turning Brazil into a stable, productive asset. The Dutch didn't originally speak so explicitly about reformation in other milieus. Most WIC outposts and settlements were too raw at first, with no preexisting institutions to capture and change. Nor could one really speak of reform when there were few people to call to repentance and even fewer to fill positions on the consistories and other bodies that would have targeted sinners.

But the wave of change that swept Brazil beginning in 1636 was not restricted to that colony. Within two years New Netherland and its church began a different kind of reformation, born during discussions about the company's larger failures and domination of trade in the Dutch Atlantic. Events in Brazil contributed to changes in New Netherland in the sense that displeasure with the company was general; it made no difference at home where it originated. Military and economic difficulties in Brazil strengthened those who sought change elsewhere. The link between the two is evident in a resolution of 1638, when the States General lectured the WIC about its religious responsibilities in Brazil and the peopling of New Netherland in the very same breath.[3] The directors were a bit sensitive about such things, and for good reason: they had always provided the necessary clergy and, in New Netherland, they had spent ƒ 100,000 on the settlers of 1624–1626. By the early 1640s they were more than ƒ 500,000 in the red for a colony they inherited at the WIC's founding, never part of their original Grand Designs. Religion was only related to these company-wide debates insofar as flourishing societies were necessary for planting Christian churches, and free trade ultimately proved the best route to that end. When Amsterdam merchants and their political allies in New Netherland and Brazil attacked the WIC with religious rhetoric and claims of neglect, they were seizing the moral high ground from Calvinist cousins in the Zeeland chamber who also happened to be the most outspoken defenders of the company's monopolies.[4]

However inadequate its representation of New Netherland and New Netherland's history, the optimism of the Steendam poem is at least understandable in light of the author's unpleasant experience in Africa and the improved colonial conditions he found in America. Furthermore, the time he spent on four continents—Europe, Africa, America, and eventually Asia—affirms the links among those places and the need to pay attention to outside influences when studying any single colony. New Netherland was far more isolated than Brazil, for example; but again, Brazil's shadow did extend to the Hudson River from time to time, and New Netherland developed economic and religious ties with the Dutch Caribbean, as well.[5] The appearance of the Steendam poem in a promotional tract also demonstrates an ongoing Dutch interest in migration and social planting. In Steendam's day New Netherland's population numbered in the thousands. Despite many obstacles and setbacks, Dutch traditions and institutions had survived in the New World. Even the small Dutch Republic could compete with other Europeans for American land and colonies, given the right conditions.[6]

Given the right political and clerical leadership, the Dutch could also match their most pious colonial competitors in righteous zeal. Drawing on the same religious energies that inspired the reformation of Brazil—drawing on the ideology and program of the Protestant Reformation and the *Nadere Reformatie* in the Dutch Republic—Calvinists in North America and the Caribbean took advantage of their elevated position to promote and protect their faith from at least three major threats: unrighteous, uncooperative rulers and a diminished political influence, sinful colonists, and nonconformers in the public sphere. In all three cases, Calvinists tried to foster a godly society by removing the people and practices that didn't conform with their vision of godliness. And they made some positive contributions to colonial life and development. But Calvinists inadvertently damaged the Dutch imperial effort at the same time, just as their fellow believers were doing in Brazil. The divisions, discontent, and population loss that they encouraged took place in the one European empire that could afford the losses less than the rest. That they persisted in their efforts, even as they watched Brazil deteriorate, is a testament to the strength of the Calvinist vision and the widespread fear of heaven's wrath.

Political Strife on the Hudson River

The year 1638 was a watershed in New Netherland and Dutch Atlantic history. Under pressure from the States General, WIC directors finally agreed to address their long-standing differences over immigration and the monopoly by devising a new patroonship plan, opening up the fur and sugar trades, offering low freight rates and transportation costs, and enticing farm families with free land and tax incentives. Hammered out in negotiations with the States General over the next year, these arrangements effectively ended the company's commercial control and made it a simple administrator of Dutch interests in the Atlantic world. Yet the colonists who benefited from the changes of 1638 came to begrudge the WIC even for its few remaining powers.[7]

The company's revised strategy for New Netherland came with a new plan for funding the Dutch Reformed Church. In their Articles and Conditions of 1638 and 1639, the directors declared their continuing concern that "proper arrangement be made for divine worship." Accordingly, they decided that "each householder and inhabitant shall bear such tax and public charge as shall hereafter be considered proper for the maintenance of Clergymen, *Ziekentroosters*, Schoolmasters and such like necessary officers."[8] The company had always expected settlers to contribute to social institutions, but most people were employees or tenant farmers without clear property rights. The taxes or tithes that traditionally supported the church in Europe had not been possible until the company allowed outright land ownership, which again, it only did at this time. In 1638 New Netherland also got a new governor, Willem Kieft, and the colony got its first-known criminal laws and policies designed to create a buffer between visiting sailors and the permanent population. It was no coincidence that the Reformed consistory only started its baptismal register the following year. Something serious had occurred in 1638, and everyone knew it.[9]

The Dutch began to think about new church facilities in the same period. Originally the Reformed congregation in New Amsterdam had met in the attic of a large mill, then in a wooden chapel on Pearl Street. In 1640 Governor Kieft and his council began setting aside certain legal fines for a more lasting house of worship. Despite the colony's reputation today as a Wild West, the WIC couldn't raise the necessary funds just by milking criminals, so in 1642 the merchant David de Vries spoke with Kieft about alternatives, chiding him for building a stone inn to accommodate visitors when the colonists had only a "mean barn" to attend church. All the materials for a better facility were close at hand, he said, including timber, stone, and lime. According to De Vries's own account, he reminded Kieft that the West India Company was supposed to be an instrument for "defending the Reformed Religion against the Tyranny of Spain." When Kieft asked who would support such a project, De Vries replied, "Friends of the Reformed Religion." De Vries was a self-professed Calvinist and Orangist, and at Kieft's urging he pledged *f* 100 to the project. Kieft committed "some thousands of guilders" on behalf of the WIC, then took other subscriptions at a wedding party for Reverend Everardus Bogardus's daughter. Kieft called the colony's first church wardens to oversee the facility and contracted with two English masons from the nearby colony of New Haven to start construction. The building was no Sistine Chapel, but when it was eventually finished, it measured seventy-two by fifty-two feet and, most importantly, it had walls of stone.[10]

In perhaps the surest sign of growth, the patroon and former WIC director Kiliaen van Rensselaer created New Netherland's second permanent clerical seat in 1642. He had recently sent sixty-six new farmers and craftsmen to his own little town of Rensselaerswijck on the upper Hudson. To accommodate the congregation there, he hired Reverend Johannes Megapolensis and issued orders for a small stone church.[11] Van Rensselaer had the confidence to take these steps because the company had lifted its monopoly, giving free rein to an immigration interest that had existed in the Dutch Atlantic from the start. Naturally, people wanted to re-create the institutions they had known in Europe. The Reformed Church had operated in some form for eighteen years in New Netherland, but in the absence of indigenous converts, only a regular influx of Christians could justify multiple ministers and permit the clergy and consistories to pursue their key responsibilities: teaching and preaching, organizing new churches, supervising poor relief, fighting sin, and reforming sinners.

The progress of the New Netherland community and church stalled in the 1640s because of a destructive conflict known as Kieft's War. In an effort to meet construction expenses and pay salaries, Governor Kieft and his council demanded tribute from local indigenous groups, most of whom refused to pay and some of whom reacted to Dutch collection efforts with force. As an example to the rest, Kieft organized a punitive expedition against the nearby Raritans. Dutch troops burned their harvest and slaughtered many of them, sparking years of on-again, off-again bloodshed, not just with the Raritans, but with a growing number of tribes. Kieft's reputation among the settlers declined drastically as Native Americans destroyed colonial property and Kieft tried to impose new taxes to fund the conflict. He also gave the settlers the tools to oppose him when, in desperation, he called together the most prominent men in the capital for support and advice. The councils they formed—called the Twelve Men, later the Eight Men and Nine Men—refused to stay within the boundaries that Kieft set for them, meeting illicitly and expressing grievances to whomever would listen, including the States General in Holland. In short, the war provided the impetus for the bloodied, diminished community to start taking control of its own affairs.[12]

Kieft's War also sparked a holy war of words, a battle for a moral high ground that had once again shifted from beneath the usually sanctimonious West India Company. Adopting the language of the Dutch Revolt, Kieft's enemies labeled him a new duke of Alva, the Spanish governor of the Low Countries who, in the last century, killed thousands of Protestants. Far from defending the true religion against Spanish tyrannies, they claimed, the WIC under Kieft was a sponsor of tyranny and an imitator of the worst Catholic atrocities.[13]

Malcontents found a fiery ally and spokesperson in Reverend Bogardus. A student of the Calvinist *Nadere Reformatie*, he had shown a penchant for public censure and political criticism before Kieft ever stepped foot on American shores.[14] Now the argumentative minister questioned Kieft's authority and defended those whom the governor prosecuted, including an alleged assassin. Bogardus condemned Kieft from the pulpit and in the homes of church members during his visits before the Lord's Supper. Understandably, Kieft stopped attending church, and he encouraged employees to do the same. The quarrel soon bordered on the ludicrous: Kieft ordered his men to beat drums and fire cannon just outside the chapel during services. Finally freed from the obligation to attend, soldiers sometimes harassed colonists who did. Their differences originally had little if anything to do with faith, but church attendance had become a mark of colonial political views. The governor and his friends temporarily remained outside it; his critics gathered around a different authority figure within. At a time when Kieft's War was destroying their homes and livelihoods, causing many to leave and threatening to crush the fragile society before it could grow very strong, opponents found a home in that society's main public institution, the one place where New Netherland looked most like the old Netherlands.[15]

When the war finally ended in 1645, Kieft ordered a colony-wide day of prayer and thanks. In his sermon, however, Reverend Bogardus didn't celebrate the peace, choosing not to honor even the conclusion of something so destructive and divisive. As historian Willem Frijhoff has shown, Bogardus's own contributions to the ongoing strife didn't necessarily make him a bad minister. His meddling and his displays of temper were accepted and expected in the Calvinist tradition, especially where they touched on questions of morality and immorality. Bogardus's primary concern was always about creating a moral, godly community and maintaining the minister as the moral authority within that community. Like other clergy of the same stripe, he reacted strongly to anything that threatened his goals, becoming in those moments the personification of God's wrath.[16] Unfortunately for him and for Governor

Kieft, both men were asked to return to the Netherlands, and both men drowned when a different instrument of God's wrath—a storm—wrecked their ship off the coast of Wales. Their simultaneous demise discouraged partisans on either side from using the tragedy as a divine "I told you so" moment.

The Kieft-Bogardus recall was part of a larger reorganization in which the company decided to remove the management of Curaçao, Aruba, and Bonaire from Brazil's government and placed them under New Netherland's. Fittingly, the new governor, Petrus Stuyvesant, and the new minister, Johannes Backerus, had worked together on Curaçao before. Backerus had not planned on serving the New Amsterdam church but agreed to stay when he stopped there briefly and saw that the town needed him. "Necessity compelled me not to leave the congregation without a pastor," he wrote. Despite his initial assessment that many people were "ignorant in regard to true religion" and "very much given to drink," his Curaçao comparisons demonstrate how far New Netherland had come. While he left only a few church members on Curaçao, here he found hundreds; where Curaçao wasn't growing very much, New Netherland experienced "daily increase."[17]

The war's end and the arrival of new leaders didn't mend all the colony's political rifts, which still ran partly through the church. The company now allowed some popular representation on the council, but the inhabitants of New Amsterdam continued to demand Dutch government, with *burgemeesters* and other municipal functionaries selected from among the foremost colonists. The Nine Men met without consent, addressed the council on matters that Stuyvesant had not approved beforehand, and visited house-to-house to solicit the community's views. Like his predecessor, Reverend Backerus made "common cause" with them against the company when, in 1649, they took their case to the States General. Hoping to avoid the public scandals of the Kieft-Bogardus years, Stuyvesant visited Backerus in his home and ordered him not to read anything of a political nature from the pulpit without authorization. Backerus was only free to speak his mind on ecclesiastical matters, the governor said.[18]

The written complaint that came before the States General in 1649 is a shopping list for any hasty historian who wants to describe the WIC's attitude toward religion without much mental expense. Company directors only cared about their own profits, colonists alleged. Kieft purportedly started the chapel in New Amsterdam because Rensselaerswijck was about to do the same, and he worried about perceptions; he worried about his legacy and reputation if the capital didn't have its own facilities. Besides, they continued, "the people . . . paid for the church."[19] They also complained that the WIC never provided a permanent source of revenue, giving funds to the church only as the need arose. They used a great deal of ink on property in general: officials had collected money for a schoolhouse that was never built, and New Netherland still had no orphanage or hospital. Implying outright theft, the authors of the 1649 remonstrance declared that the company had taken money from the deaconry and never repaid it. They criticized the long-dead monopoly, the high cost of basic provisions, and the recent war. The WIC needed reform and New Netherland needed better rulers.[20]

The directors offered a very different version of events just a few months later. They explained, for example, that the chapel cost more than ƒ 8,000, mostly paid by the company. The people had not given more than ƒ 800, and some who first promised to contribute had never done so. The WIC had designated certain taxes for church property and salaries, but each settler could only pay "according to his means," the directors said, implying that those means were not very great. As for deaconry money, they acknowledged that the governor had borrowed ƒ 900. Yet he did so with the deacons' consent, and he drew up a contract for paying it back with interest. The first payment, according to the agreement, wasn't even due yet. Likewise, they admitted that the schoolhouse wasn't built, but the governor had collected materials and set aside a plot of land, and they had sent more than one schoolmaster to the colony. The schoolmasters "keep school in hired houses, so that the youth are furnished with the means of education, according to the circumstances of the country." If the inhabitants wanted something more, like a Latin school, they could supply the funds themselves. The directors accused the people of ingratitude, of seeking to rid New Netherland of the WIC after it laid a crucial, costly foundation. Privately they grumbled to Stuyvesant about "how much trouble we have had and how dangerous it is to draw upon yourself the wrath of a growing community."[21]

Modern readers doubtless find it easier to sympathize with the colonists over the big, faceless West India Company, especially in light of the terrible Indian war and the understandable quest for civic government in New Amsterdam. But no one today should let their preference for political autonomy blind them to the partisan, self-interested nature of these religious charges. The directors could not mislead the States General very easily on matters like the cost of the church or the governor's business with the deaconry because of the divisions in their own ranks and because one of them (one of the Nineteen Lords) was appointed by the States General. In explaining the difficulty of collecting taxes and building schools, they were just reminding people of the "New" in the colony's name: Amsterdam wasn't built in a day. The WIC had turned wholeheartedly to colonization only ten years before, and half of that time it was fighting an expensive war. Probably deliberately, settlers demanded too much too soon, using religion and other hot-button issues to achieve political ends that profited them no less than the directors allegedly profited from "neglect." In a civic government they would control all civil and criminal suits, taxes and public works, and they would enjoy the prestige and patronage power that accompanied those responsibilities. As the only lawyer in the colony, the leader of the Nine Men and author of the remonstrance, Adriaen van der Donck, could have become a *schepen* and *burgemeester*.[22]

Unluckily for the directors, the Nine Men timed their attack perfectly. The Portuguese colonists of Brazil rose up against the WIC just as the Indian war in New Netherland came to a close, giving the company no respite. When the States General released its findings about New Netherland in 1650, it took sides with the colonists by recommending drastic changes in the colony's government. Stuyvesant's enemies returned triumphant to America and demanded the immediate implementation of the States General plan. When he refused, not having received any direct orders, they continued their vocal, public opposition to his rule as before. Exasperated, Stuyvesant went to the church and removed a pew that the consistory had designated for the Nine Men, accomplishing symbolically what he couldn't do in reality: eliminate those who challenged his authority. The pew was the perfect outlet for his frustrations because, before he removed it, it honored the very men whose status had divided everyone for so long. Once more, because it represented traditional Dutch community, the Reformed Church was a magnet for controversy about status and power within that community.[23]

Recognizing the inevitable, the WIC finally instituted civic government in the capital in 1653.[24] The directors continued to send ministers, Bibles, and other religious materials as they always had, and they still claimed the governorship and other company appointments. But the new municipal court now determined local policy and heard cases that only went to Stuyvesant and his council as a final court of appeals. The new court bore some undefined responsibility for local religious needs as well, and the WIC's old critics—the new rulers—soon found that those needs were a heavier burden than they had imagined. In truth, no one had neglected the public church. If there was no grand house of worship in New Netherland, no stone schoolhouse, if the church didn't enjoy a dedicated income, the real culprits were warfare, return migration, inflation, a lack of specie and basic foodstuffs, and other problems common to new colonies. The WIC's monopoly only stood in the way of growth for fifteen years. And even in those years the directors had flirted with colonization. In other words, they were always willing to let New Netherland become a colony; they just wanted to secure the health of the business by

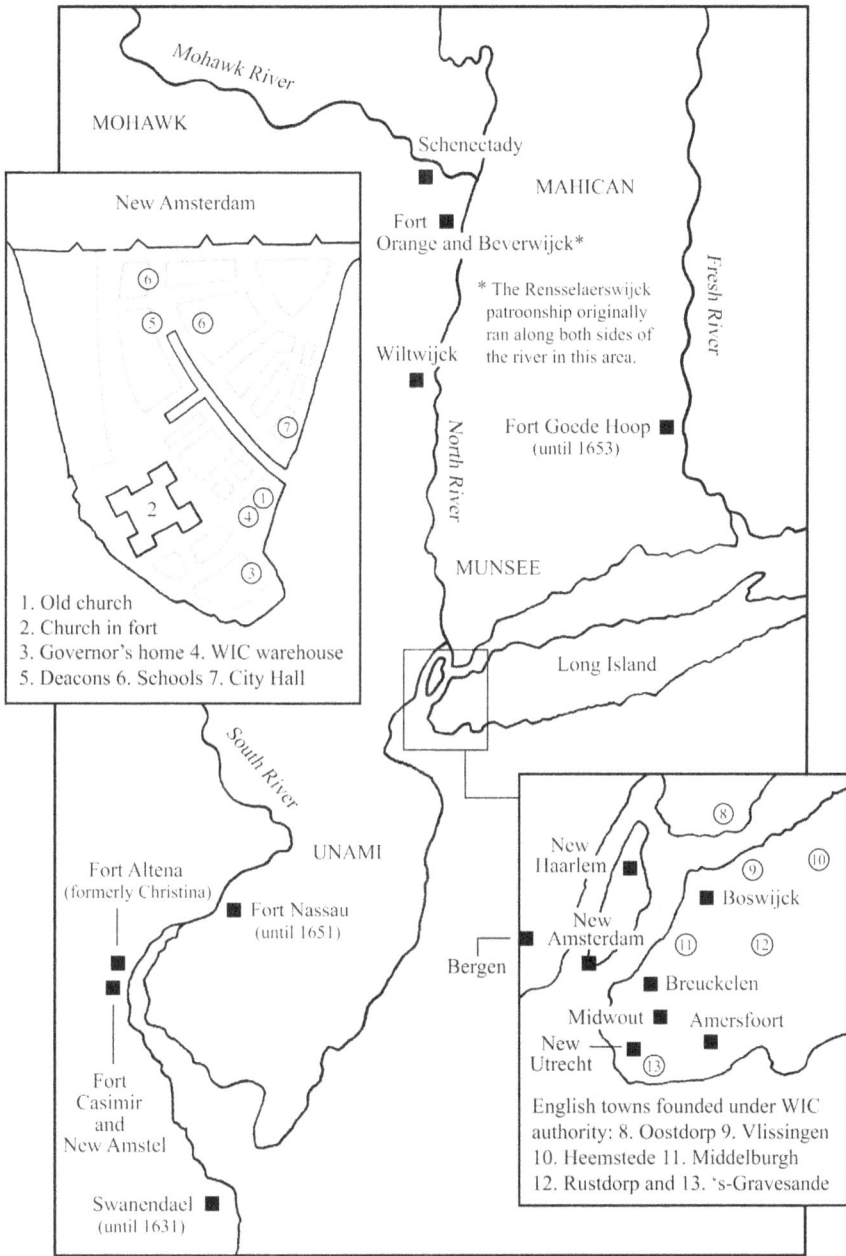

MOHAWK

Mohawk River

Schenectady

MAHICAN

New Amsterdam

Fort Orange and Beverwijck*

Fresh River

* The Rensselaerswijck patroonship originally ran along both sides of the river in this area.

Wiltwijck

Fort Goede Hoop (until 1653)

North River

1. Old church
2. Church in fort
3. Governor's home 4. WIC warehouse
5. Deacons 6. Schools 7. City Hall

MUNSEE

Long Island

South River

UNAMI

Fort Altena (formerly Christina)

Fort Nassau (until 1651)

New Haarlem

Boswijck

New Amsterdam

Bergen

Breuckelen

Midwout   Amersfoort

New Utrecht

Fort Casimir and New Amstel

English towns founded under WIC authority: 8. Oostdorp 9. Vlissingen 10. Heemstede 11. Middelburgh 12. Rustdorp and 13. 's-Gravesande

Swanendael (until 1631)

Map of New Netherland with New Amsterdam inset. Map drawn by author.

retaining some privileges. Ultimately it was a useless endeavor. A relatively small group of merchants and investors with limited resources could never bear all the necessary expenses and still turn a profit. New Netherland could thrive only by opening it to the full force of the Dutch economic machine.[25]

As the colonial population grew to somewhere between 7,000 and 10,000 Europeans, the church grew with it, reaching eleven Reformed congregations in towns along the Hudson and Delaware Rivers (and on Long Island). Assisted by an unknown number of lay clergy and school teachers, ordained ministers eventually numbered six. They were stationed in towns like New Amsterdam, Beverwijck, and Wiltwijck, and they served the small congregations near the capital on an itinerant basis.[26] Though they still bemoaned the shortcomings of communicants, they also reported much progress: education, catechization, new consistories, large groups at weekly services, and regular Communion.[27]

How had the establishment and growth of the church in New Netherland differed from the same developments in Brazil? From the vantage point of Amsterdam, as officials there sent clergy and corresponded about problems in both places, their efforts would have seemed the same—an American project, not limited to one place. Yet the differences are noteworthy. While the Brazil church suffered from internal problems caused by a few troublesome clergy and changed quickly after a widespread outcry from people on both sides of the ocean, New Netherland excited less comment at first. Even more than Brazil's, its religious makeover was incidental to political and economic changes in the colony. No one showed the same concern for New Netherland's church: no visits to the new governor before he left Holland to ask him to monitor its progress, no similar letters from the directors to the colonial consistory, offering advice and recommending improvements in Brazil before anyone else. New Netherland was more isolated. Its growth was gradual because it had to build European institutions and a European population from scratch. Religious complaints came from colonists who sometimes used the issue misleadingly, wielding it as a cudgel to beat the company when their criticism helped achieve other aims, like civil government.

God's Laws and God's Punishments

Curaçao's early ecclesiastical history was surprisingly peaceful compared to New Netherland's, perhaps because no one knew at first if the Dutch would even keep the vulnerable, unfruitful island or whether, if they did keep it, they would try to make it something more than a military outpost.[28] Because its purpose and fate remained unclear for so long, reform movements on

Curaçao tended to be quiet and small. But those reform movements did materialize from time to time. Fearing the divine penalties of inaction, Calvinists rulers in both places utilized the courts and other legal tools to warn colonists and punish them for the many sins and misdeeds that might quash (Calvinists believed) the feeble colonial enterprise.

In 1639 the Dutch Reformed Church in the Netherlands learned from a correspondent at Curaçao that "our Nation here is beginning to increase greatly." Church leaders must have smirked at the writer's definition of "greatly," for he went on to explain that he was talking about just three recent births: two boys and a girl. Having lost their first minister to Brazil, the colonists "earnestly requested the service of baptism and the complete administration of the true religion."[29] When he finally arrived, reports from the new minister, Reverend Jonas Aertss, were generally positive. In August 1640 he wrote, for instance, that the new governor was a good one. Jacob Pietersz Tolck maintained order and, through exhortation and his personal presence, encouraged everyone to attend Reformed services. But Aertss found Curaçao lacking in certain respects. Most importantly, he had not received his books, and he couldn't buy strong alcohol on the island, which actually pleased him because his wife was "much inclined to drink."[30] Reverend Backerus was less sanguine when he arrived in 1643, writing from Fort Amsterdam that he only had ten participants at his first Communion service. He was teaching Protestant doctrines and the church was growing daily, he reported, but with so few members, he couldn't form a consistory and didn't need deacons because he wasn't yet collecting alms at Curaçao.[31]

The reorganization of WIC possessions and the appointment of Petrus Stuyvesant as joint governor of New Netherland and Curaçao in 1647 was a victory for Calvinists everywhere, even if they didn't know it immediately. The son of a Reformed minister, Stuyvesant had married a minister's daughter and subscribed to the orthodox Reformed agenda throughout his life. In fact he may have chosen a career with the WIC because of its reputation as a Calvinist institution. For their part, company directors chose him in 1647 because he had already served a stint as governor of Curaçao, and in that position he had proved himself a loyal company man.[32]

Stuyvesant's decisive, hard-nosed leadership and reform efforts meant far less to Curaçao than New Netherland because he spent most of his time in the latter, issuing edicts and imposing changes that he never could have overseen with the same efficiency in the distant islands. In the secular sphere he improved New Netherland's roads and defenses, clarified property lines, created regulations for fire safety and garbage disposal, and even set a speed limit on carts and wagons in the capital. Among his physical improvements, Stuyvesant

Gov. Petrus Stuyvesant (n.d.). Courtesy of the New York State Library, Manuscripts and Special Collections, Albany, New York. This print was probably made from the Hendrick Couturier painting at the New York Historical Society.

and his council finally completed the chapel, which had languished for years as a mere construction site because of the Indian wars. Similarly, he became an important benefactor to the clergy, personally paying salaries when the WIC at home hadn't yet approved a contract or extension, and paying Reverend Henricus Selyns an extra ƒ 250 per year to hold services at the governor's farm.[33] Stuyvesant also supported the church's campaigns against Sabbath-breaking, excessive drinking, sexual misconduct, and "pagan" holidays and festivities like the Feast of Saint Nicholas and Shrove Tuesday. These things he did, he explained, because of what was happening in Brazil. The difficulties of "our sister state" were a reminder of God's wrath and the consequences of sinful living. "He proceeds no longer by words or writings, but by arrests and stripes," grumbled one colonist. Another said, "Stuyvesant is starting a whole reformation here."[34]

To be clear, the Dutch imported most laws and legal traditions from the Netherlands; their American rulers and clergy couldn't just make things up as they went along, which helped contain the religious ardor of someone like Stuyvesant. His decrees had to be consistent with Dutch-Roman Law, and WIC directors had to approve any novel colonial laws and requirements.[35] Still, a ruler's religious leanings could matter a great deal in the pursuit of trouble-makers and the consistent execution of the law, and Stuyvesant did sometimes test the limits of his leash, both in moral matters and with nonconformers. If his language is any indication, he understood his work in the same cosmic context that so animated Dutch Calvinists at war: God vs. the Devil, the children of Israel vs. the world. He quit the soldier's life for a time after he lost his leg to a Spanish cannonball in the Caribbean. But he found a way to continue the battle in the council chamber and courtroom.

Judging by the tremendous number of laws and complaints about violating them, Sabbath observance and, related to it, drinking on the Sabbath were among the greatest challenges for creating a Calvinist community in New Netherland. One of Stuyvesant's first edicts, issued less than three weeks after his arrival, addressed drinking and fighting "on the Lord's day of rest." Where the old law forbade tavern keepers from serving alcohol only during the hours of the sermon, the new one closed taverns before 4:00 p.m. on Sunday and after 9:00 p.m. every day of the week. Ten months later Stuyvesant said that some people were ignoring the law, so he renewed it, and he created new permissions and regulations for running a tavern in the first place. In consultation with the Reformed minister he also announced a second Sunday sermon—one in the morning, one in the afternoon—and insisted that "all Our Officers, Subjects and Vassals . . . frequent and attend the same."[36] If by "Subjects and Vassals" he intended all colonists, not just his own employees, he was openly flouting long-standing Dutch protections against compulsory church attendance. Over the years he expanded the list of forbidden activities to include any kind of labor, dancing, ball games and card games, parties, and boating during the Sunday sermons.[37]

To try to separate secular and ecclesiastical affairs when we're dealing with a topic like Sabbath laws, which clearly grew from the Judeo-Christian religious

tradition, would be a silly, useless exercise, especially when the Reformed sermon was so often mixed up in Sabbath-breaking cases. In his own descriptions
of the law Stuyvesant ignored whatever precedents existed in the Netherlands
and instead claimed scriptural influences and debts. He wrote about "God's
Holy laws and Ordinances," about observing the Sabbath "in conformity to
God's holy command," and about people who showed contempt for "God's
Holy Word and of our ordinances *deduced therefrom.*"[38] In issuing new laws
he had a tendency to lecture people about debauchery and bad examples; he
reflected on virtue and the invitation of heavenly blessings and curses on
the colony, depending on the choices settlers made. In a reference that Max
Weber would have called Calvinist, not just Christian, the governor decried
drinking and taverns because they distracted people from their occupations—
or translated more literally, their "callings."[39]

The Dutch Reformed Church was also involved in marriage and sexual
cases because, as the only religious institution that could marry people in New
Netherland, it sometimes had to send representatives before the court to testify about broken marriage promises, parental permission, and the like.[40]
Whether the ministers bore the same unusual marital powers and responsibilities as the Brazil clergy isn't as clear in the New Netherland records. But a
1654 case shows that, for a time at least, they did hold the same elevated position. When a dispute arose between the New Amsterdam municipal court and
the colonial council about a certain young merchant and his desire to marry
locally, against his father's wishes in Holland, both sides appealed to religious
authority. Reverend Megapolensis spoke for the governor and the boy's father,
WIC director Isaac van Beeck. The minister had transferred from Rensselaerswijck to New Amsterdam shortly after Stuyvesant arrived in the capital, and
he now objected to the union "in his capacity as high commissioner of matri-
monial affairs." The court, on the other hand, turned to the Bible, specifically
to Paul's writings on marriage and the marriage bed as a legitimate outlet or
escape from sin (i.e., fornication). Yet Stuyvesant would not bend, and the unlucky couple finally had to flee to New England, of all places, in search of
more tolerant authorities. Stuyvesant threatened arrest, sent letters of warning to New England, and finally, having failed to stop the marriage, he called
on "God's holy name" and issued an annulment.[41]

Regulating marriage and sex helped the WIC extend its authority and create the ordered, godly society that Calvinists desired.[42] Linda Biemer has argued that sexual crimes were rare in New Netherland, that women didn't need
to resort to prostitution, for example, because they had greater legal and economic freedoms than women in other colonies. However, Biemer only used
the records of the New Amsterdam court, which was not run by the company

and sometimes clashed with it.[43] Extending the search to include other village courts and (most importantly) the colonial council, led by Stuyvesant, reveals a lot more sexual crime, including vulgarity, exhibition, fornication, adultery, rape, sodomy, and several additional prostitution cases. On the one extreme was the relatively minor but famous and amusing case of the woman who "pulled the shirts of some sailors out of their breeches and in her house measured the male member of three sailors on a broomstick," and the woman who, "in [the] presence of a respectable company . . . hoisted her petticoats up to her back, and shewed them her arse."[44] On the other extreme were five people—two men and three women—who appeared before the colonial council over the same few days in 1658 to answer for their long-standing fornication and adultery. The council condemned them for violating the laws of the Netherlands and the scriptures, then banished all of them.[45]

Banishment was the most drastic consequence of sin. Before people ever got that far, if they were members of the Reformed Church they had to go before an ecclesiastical court—in this case the consistory—for censure or excommunication. Unfortunately, only a few years' worth of consistory records have survived from very late in the colony's history, so historians depend almost solely on secular court records for questions of crime and punishment.[46] In addition to Sabbath-breaking and illicit sex, people were charged most often with theft and disrespecting and slandering rulers. Punishments ranged from small fines and simple warnings to whipping, beating, and branding, from forced labor to banishment and even death. In one case the Rensselaerswijck court skipped all of these options in lieu of a promise from Claes Andriesz that "on the Lord's day of rest" he would "go to hear God's Holy Word instead of going to the tavern."[47]

Given the difficulty of building and maintaining a strong population in America, banishments and executions were most damaging to the Dutch colonial effort. And they happened surprisingly often: more than 110 cases that I have identified in the surviving court and council records, both of which are incomplete. "Minor" and "amusing" were possibly the wrong words for the above-mentioned stories about the broomstick and the woman who exposed herself publicly, because both women were, in the end, banished for their conduct. One of them, Grietjen Reyniers, had clashed with the minister and the consistory in the past.[48] Whether one got off with a warning or met with a more meaningful punishment depended on the severity of the sin and the attitude and history of the sinner. Dutch courts were sometimes willing to give second and third chances, and even banishments "did not always stick," in the words of historian Deborah Hamer. In several of the 110 cases the court either reconsidered its punishment or just didn't carry it out after issuing a judgment.

Describing these fortunate souls, Hamer suggests that the original sentence may have been about the ruler's image and the need to demonstrate his morality and authority to his subjects.[49]

Stuyvesant's council was more concerned with sexual crime and far more likely to impose banishment than the local courts, which could only banish people from the town, not the colony, and did so most often for theft, not sex. More than a jurisdictional issue, these important differences may be additional evidence that Stuyvesant and the company didn't see eye-to-eye with the colonial population and its municipal leaders, in this case on the question of moral deviance and how to deal with it. That said, the company-colonial divide, if there was one, couldn't have been too stark, because some candidates for banishment only got in trouble when watchful neighbors reported on their "immoral," "wicked," "beastly," "dissolute," "whorish," and "Godless lives."[50] Less than a third of the total banishments were women, probably because of their value as wives and mothers. But the council and the courts set aside their population concerns in special cases. When the widow Mary Willems sued one of her lovers for child support, he was able to prove that she had slept with multiple men in the same period, and the council ordered her to "depart from New Netherland," presumably with her child. Similarly, authorities didn't mind banishing pregnant women, and at least in one case, an entire family. Convicted of theft and threatening violence against local rulers, Hendrick Jansen Claarbout was whipped and branded, then shipped to Virginia with his wife and an unspecified number of children.[51]

The Dutch took a biblical view of sodomy, which was the sin or crime in New Netherland's few executions. One of the accused, Harmen Meyndertsz van den Bogaert, accidentally ended his own life when he fell through the frozen Hudson River during an escape attempt.[52] The fate of the other two men shows why he was so afraid: Jan Creoly, a company slave, and Jan Cristhout, a soldier, were strangled, drowned, burned—or some combination of the three—for allegedly forcing themselves on two young boys (in separate cases, years apart). According to the colonial council, theirs was a "heinous and abominable crime," one of the "coursest, foulest, most horrible Sins that mankind would be able to devise." In both cases the council appealed to the story of Sodom and Gomorrah in the Old Testament and warned about a similar fate for New Netherland if they did not act. "The wrath of God" would fall upon the colony, meaning that God would curse it with sickness, war, famine, and other plagues. Homosexuals were "not worthy to associate with mankind," the council continued; their sin "should not be known or named among Christians." The main problem or concern was clearly sodomy, not rape, because even the openly acknowledged victims, the unwilling children, were beaten with rods and, in one case, deported.[53]

Stuyvesant communicated the same concern for sin and the same biblical understanding of the world in his proclamations about fast and prayer days and days of thanks. All the available evidence indicates that he wrote the proclamations himself, possibly in consultation with the Reformed ministers. After he finished the text, he gave it to his secretary and clerks, who made copies and sent it to all the colony's towns, villages, and fortifications. Local rulers would then ring a bell, if they had one, and read the proclamation from the courthouse steps. They also gave it to the highest-ranking ecclesiastical authority in that area to read from the pulpit at the next church service.[54]

Stuyvesant usually began his message with the reasons for each particular prayer day: sometimes to give thanks for some positive development, like the end of the war with Spain or a fruitful harvest. More often he was worried about conflict and natural disasters in Europe, Brazil, the Caribbean, and (primarily) New Netherland.[55] He blamed these problems on the sins that he encountered regularly in the council chamber. "No other conclusion can be drawn," he told colonists, "than that the Holy and Almighty God of Israel, being justly provoked to anger and wrath on account of our sins . . . threatens us with a just retribution of the treasure of anger and just wrath, caused by the spurning of the richness of his Mercy, patience and forbearance, abused by us so as to result in the hardness of heart instead of our reformation."[56] The biblical imagery and allusions to Israel, God's covenant people, were common rhetorical tools for Stuyvesant, as they were for so many Calvinists. But only after a deadly Indian attack in 1656 did the governor begin quoting the Bible directly. In that proclamation he borrowed extensively from the book of Lamentations, which recounts the devouring fire of God's anger in the destruction of Jerusalem and the possibilities for renewal and redemption.[57]

After moralizing about God's recent punishments and blessings, Stuyvesant announced the upcoming day of fasting and prayer, ordered colonists to go to church that day, and asked the Reformed clergy to compose their sermons with the day's special purpose in mind. In particularly trying times he instituted monthly prayer days, usually on the first or second Wednesday of the month. Regardless of the specific events that inspired the decision, the governor's general message was the same: to deflect divine wrath, we must show proper thanks for the good things that happen and we must repent and reform ourselves from all the bad that we do. His message was a community message, not just a Calvinist one, in that Stuyvesant ruled the entirety of New Netherland, and in his proclamations he tried to reach all the colonists. At the same time, as he struggled to understand current events, the proclamations were a tremendous tool for promoting his own interpretations and conclusions, as well as the conclusions of whoever happened to have his ear, like Reverend Megapolensis. And Stuyvesant tried to shepherd people toward public church services on prayer days by banning most of the same labors and activities colonists were supposed to shun on Sunday.[58]

Like the Sabbath laws, the prayer day tradition was imported from the Netherlands. Many colonists were familiar with the formula and language that Stuyvesant used, and most of them probably agreed with him, if not about every interpretation, at least about God's ability to express his will through natural occurrences or through an enemy. But Stuyvesant may have overstepped his bounds when, in 1663, he tried to modify the accepted definition of "Sabbath." Until then one couldn't work on Sunday, but one could engage in drinking and other pastimes after church. Stuyvesant looked down on this custom as a mere "half Sabbath," and in 1663 he tried to align New Netherland's law and "the law of God," as he put it, by expanding the forbidden activities (he added strawberry picking and loud children's games to the list) and expanding the blackout from sunup to sundown. At that point the New Amsterdam court balked, refusing to publicize the new law and even postponing and dismissing Sabbath-breaking cases. When the governor demanded an explanation, the court told him that the law was "too severe, and too much at odds with Dutch freedoms."[59]

Dutch rulers in the Caribbean didn't have to put up with uncooperative courts because in the 1650s and 1660s, their populations still usually weren't large enough for anything more than the governor's council. Not counting Native Americans, Curaçao only reached about 600 people in the period. Local rulers were perfectly capable of pursuing sinners on their own, and they sometimes did so with the same gusto as Stuyvesant, independent of him. Yet they would have also had his reforming example—and possibly his direct encouragement—because of his dual appointment, his rare visits to the islands, and the regular communication and movement of church and WIC officials, merchants, and colonists throughout the Dutch Atlantic.[60] When Stuyvesant needed someone to educate his son and perhaps increase young Balthazar's contacts and opportunities, he sent him to Reverend Wilhelmus Volckering at Curaçao, who later reported that the boy had a "good disposition and well-regulated life." So far, however, Balthazar had not shown much interest in the kind of learning Volckering could provide. One finds similar familial and religious bonds between the two colonies in the island's baptismal register, which lists the names of witnesses like Hillegond Megapolensis, daughter of Reverend Megapolensis in New Netherland, and the absentee witness Jacob Alrichs, Dutch commander on the Delaware River.[61]

Reform-minded clergy generally got what they wanted at Curaçao because the vice-director there during most of the Stuyvesant years, Matthias Beck, was of the same religious stripe as his distant superior. Beck was a former member of the High Council in Brazil and a member of the Reformed consistory in both colonies. The clergy who served under him praised him and claimed a close friendship with him. After what they described as a period of spiritual stagnation and sin, Beck and Reverend Adriaen Beaumont worked closely together to "rebuild the walls of Jerusalem," in Beaumont's words. At the minister's insistence, Beck closed the taverns inside Fort Amsterdam and issued laws against illicit sex, drunkenness, and Sabbath-breaking. The number of church members grew from six to about fifty during Beaumont's short tenure.[62] His successors reported further growth and large congregations at Sunday services because Beck required everyone in the garrison to attend, and they often had visitors from the ships in the harbor. They also added to their numbers with an aggressive catechization campaign. Beck was a "very Devout Gentleman," wrote Philippus Specht. The vice-director did everything in his power "for the reformation and building of God's church."[63]

For his part, Reverend Specht was the main voice and energy behind various sex-related banishments from the struggling, underpopulated island. He believed that when sinners refused to repent of their own accord, the shame of a public prosecution and the fear of deportation helped them change—if not their hearts—at least their outward, public behavior and bad example. Like his Calvinist counterparts in New Netherland, Specht was less worried about the size of the colonial community and more concerned that the colony become the kind of community that invited God's favor.[64]

Spiritual Errors and Horrible Heresies

Ethnically and religiously, Dutch Atlantic colonies were quite diverse. The Dutch constituted barely more than half of the population in New Netherland, and perhaps only half of that group belonged to the Dutch Reformed Church.[65] Adherents of other faiths had to either forego worship services, worship privately with family members in their homes, attend services and rites with which they disagreed, or organize illicit, underground meetings with like-minded colonists. They may have felt more confident about acting illegally in the 1650s and 1660s because in those decades, maybe having learned something from Brazil, the new generation of WIC directors communicated their growing moderation in religious matters. Nonconformers only benefited from the change if their local colonial rulers agreed with the directors and didn't continue to oppose and quash dissent as a threat to the true Reformed religion.

The persistent myth of Dutch tolerance stems from a misunderstanding about the nature of diversity in the colonies and the reception of outcasts like Anne Hutchinson, the famous Puritan from Massachusetts. The diversity that the WIC favored—the cosmopolitanism that I explored at the start of this book—extended mostly to French and English Protestants in European commercial and kin networks. The foreign clergy employed by the WIC were still Calvinists, hired to preach to Calvinist employees and colonists and deliver the Calvinist message to others. Foreign-language needs were especially great in the Caribbean, where the Zeeland chamber sent many Walloons and Huguenots, and in New Netherland, where Puritan neighbors founded settlements on Long Island and elsewhere within the WIC's boundaries. Even in these circumstances the Dutch didn't grant a blanket religious freedom, but "freedom of *their* religion."[66] In other words, they didn't see Puritan and Huguenot beliefs as radically different, as something that had to be either changed or tolerated. Stuyvesant referred to the English as "coreligionists." When Puritans requested permission to settle, he allowed it, explaining that "there is no difference in the fundamental points of the worship of God betwixt these [Dutch churches] and the Churches of New England." Only in "the Ruelinge" or organization of their churches did the two peoples disagree.[67]

Stuyvesant clashed with non-Calvinists and even Puritans when Puritans showed too much independence.[68] In fact, he banished or deported roughly eighteen people for religious activity during his tenure: the third most common cause of banishment in New Netherland. Had Anne Hutchinson lived long enough to organize the same meetings there that she did in Massachusetts, he surely would have banished her, as well. The experience of a different English dissenter, Anna Smith, was not as loud or dramatic, but anyone who is familiar with the Hutchinson story will find similar menacing undertones and suppression in the 1652 Smith case. A variety of radical Protestant called Anabaptist, she allegedly used "slanderous and blasphemous expressions against God's word and his servants." Reverend Megapolensis complained to the colonial council, and Stuyvesant then called an unprecedented joint meeting of council and consistory members at the local schoolhouse, creating a forum where Smith could defend her objections to the minister's teachings before the colony's most powerful secular and ecclesiastical leaders. Unfortunately, if they kept a record of the meeting, it didn't survive, and Smith never appeared before the council again, which means they intimidated her into silence or voluntary exile.[69]

Lutherans, Quakers, and Jews suffered the greatest number of banishments and other repressive punishments under Stuyvesant. He rejected the Lutherans' request for a minister in 1653. After ousting the Swedes from the Delaware River two years later, he let one minister remain, just as the Dutch in Brazil had accepted Catholic priests after the conquest there. Like Calvinists in Brazil, however, the governor tried to minimize the religious consequences of war, deporting two other Lutheran ministers from the Delaware and turning a third minister around when a new group of Swedes arrived the next year.[70] At the same time, to counter a growing number of conventicles, Stuyvesant and his council outlawed the private meetings and immediately began imposing fines and arresting people, even banishing two men on Long Island for "the audacity" of preaching and holding the Lord's Supper in their homes.[71] When the Lutheran church in Amsterdam sent the pastor Johannes Gutwasser to America in 1657, the entire colonial power structure united against him, including secular and ecclesiastical authorities inside the company and out. They forbade him from preaching and ordered him to obey all the new laws. Upon further pressure from the Dutch Reformed clergy, without any evidence of misconduct, Stuyvesant agreed to deport Gutwasser "for the honor of God" and the sake of peace. The ailing minister managed to avoid arrest for a few months by hiding at a supporter's farm on Long Island.[72]

Suppression served two complementary purposes, one of them negative and protective, the other active and evangelical. Authorities intended something like the conventicle law to kill "many dangerous Heresies and Schisms."[73] On the other hand, they were also trying to grow the Dutch Reformed Church. Calvinist clergy objected to Lutheran worship because it would "tend to the injury of our church" and "the diminution of hearers of the Word of God." They knew very well why some colonists attended their meetings: "For as long as no other religion than the Reformed has been publicly allowed, all who wish to engage in public worship come to our service. By this means . . . several [Lutherans] have made a profession of religion, and united with us in the Lord's Supper."[74] Reverend Megapolensis reported that after Gutwasser finally departed for Holland in early 1659, "quietness" was restored: "The Lutherans again go to church, as they were formerly accustomed to do." Even the Lutheran ringleader among the colonists "is now one of the most punctual attendants, and has his pew near to the pulpit," Megapolensis concluded. Reverend Gideon Schaats wrote similarly from Fort Orange the next year that "Lutherans . . . are gradually being led to us." Without competition, "the vineyard of the Lord" would continue to flourish.[75]

So much for tolerance. Like the slow and subtle suffocation of Catholicism in Brazil when more direct evangelical efforts failed, Calvinists hoped to bring Lutherans and other dissenters in New Netherland to the true religion by destroying their other options. It was a gentle (and sometimes not-so-gentle) form of pressure or even force, one could argue—though the Dutch never would have put it that way. Since their own experience with the Inquisition and the revolt against Spain, they had prided themselves in *not* using force in religious matters, in allowing freedom of conscience, meaning the freedom to believe and worship however one wanted with one's own family. By separating public and private they tried to resolve the inherent contradiction between freedom and favoritism: in the name of unity they outlawed every form of public worship but one, promising at the same time not to persecute people for holding different views and not attending services. Their history with Spain and their commitment to conscience rights undoubtedly created a measure of security for anyone who did not belong to the public church, a kind of relative tolerance. However, in playing favorites the Dutch still resorted to other kinds of pressure, for there were many social advantages connected to church activity. And they sometimes used a heavy hand to keep other faiths quiet.

Dutch rulers could also resolve the contradiction by pretending not to notice when dissenters ignored the law. The historian George Smith has argued that this connivance tradition, allegedly adopted by WIC directors, was "the Dutch Colonial Contribution to American Religious Pluralism."[76] Going beyond connivance in the 1650s and 1660s, influential figures in Holland like Johan de Witt and Pieter de la Court promoted a republican political program called "the True Freedom" and openly discussed the advantages of a tolerant society.[77] What this atmosphere meant for the company is difficult to ascertain. De la Court was a WIC *hoofdparticipant* who regularly attended meetings and helped choose new directors.[78] The power of one investor was small, of course, but with or without him, the directors did belong to the new generation. They were less active in church politics and further removed from the war with Spain and the divisive religious contests that marked the previous era. In addition, because of its financial struggles, the WIC sold the Delaware River as a patroonship to the city of Amsterdam in two transactions in 1657 and 1663. The very people who created connivance, the most likely champions of tolerance at home, now controlled the southern half of New Netherland, and decisions about the colony as a whole required their input.[79]

But Smith overstated the use and impact of connivance in New Netherland. The governor during the colony's last seventeen years was opposed to the practice, and even the directors didn't usually embrace it, probably because they disagreed among themselves. In their interactions with the church in

Holland and their instructions to Stuyvesant on religious matters, they gave a range of advice. They claimed to "oppose the plan of the Lutherans," believing that open worship would be "injurious." They feared the "evil consequences" of going down that path. They resolved not to permit a Lutheran minister, encouraged Stuyvesant to draw Lutherans to the Reformed faith, and approved the deportation of Reverend Gutwasser.[80] On the other hand they wished that Stuyvesant had proceeded "less vigorously," and they told him to deal with Lutherans "quietly and leniently." They were not pleased with the law against conventicles and instructed the governor to "let [the Lutherans] have free religious exercises in their houses," leaving open the question of whether people could worship only as families or as nonfamily groups. Lutherans claimed to have the quiet support of some directors, and the Reformed clergy in Amsterdam feared the same, especially when they had to work with the WIC and the Amsterdam regents together on the matter.[81]

Only once did the directors' growing moderation impact religious conditions in New Netherland, and in that case they didn't obtain what they wanted by connivance. It was a fairly trivial matter involving the use of a single word in the baptismal formula: *alhier*. In the midst of all the other controversies, Lutherans began to complain about the moment in the baptismal ceremony when the minister asked the child's parents to affirm that they believed the Christian doctrines taught *alhier* ("here," or "at this place"). Without the word a person of any denomination could answer positively. Including it was a problem for Lutherans because it implied the Reformed Church. The directors urged Stuyvesant to use the old formulary, which didn't include the word, and the colonial clergy even said they were willing to do so, pending advice from Europe. After all, some churches in the Netherlands still used the old formulary.[82] But the ever-sensitive Amsterdam classis disagreed with the decision and "earnestly admonished" the New Netherland clergy, for the sake of uniformity, not to capitulate. Only after years of correspondence, after the directors declared that they would brook no more opposition, after it became clear that they enjoyed the support of some clergy, including the American clergy—then the classis finally gave up the fight.[83]

The directors' arguments during the *alhier* controversy sounded suspiciously like the clergy's reasons for opposing Reverend Gutwasser, suggesting that the directors echoed the clergy deliberately to undermine the classis. They did not advise flexibility because they loved Lutheranism, nor because they were indifferent to religious disagreements. Rather, they said that changing the baptismal ceremony would draw more people to the public church. They asked the governor to utilize "the least offensive" means possible "so that people of other persuasions may not be deterred from the . . . Reformed Church, but in time be induced to listen and finally gained over to it." "Thereby these and other dissenters," they wrote on another occasion, "will be satisfied and kept in the Reformed Church." They even claimed that lenience on the baptismal question would prevent Lutherans from getting their minister. Frequent, contentious disagreements "might result in the permission to conduct a separate divine service there, for the Lutherans would very easily obtain the consent of the authorities here," meaning Amsterdam, and "we would have no means of preventing it." Regardless of the personal religious and political leanings of the directors, the regents of Amsterdam clearly cast a shadow over company decisions after buying the Delaware River.[84]

The best evidence of moderation among WIC directors in the 1650s and 1660s comes not from New Netherland, but the Caribbean, where they conceded generous religious rights to various Jewish settlers. As the situation in Brazil deteriorated and the Portuguese reasserted themselves there, some Jews relocated to other colonies and founded patroonships, both at Curaçao and on the Wild Coast. The directors didn't like or trust Jews in general, and they sometimes expressed their anti-Semitism in their correspondence.[85] Yet they did loosen religious laws for patroons in 1658 and 1659 to allow public worship and instruction in synagogues and schools. A few years later, at the behest of Friedrich Casimir, the Lutheran Count of Hanau-Lichtenberg, the directors chartered a Wild Coast patroonship for "all Religions that believe in God."[86]

The Jews who moved from Brazil to New Netherland in the same period had a very different experience—a more restricted one—because they were needy individuals and outsiders in an established society, not patroons, and their new governor wasn't willing to modify the company's long-standing policies on non-Reformed worship. Nor would any other local leaders, for that matter. Reverend Megapolensis reported "a great deal of complaint and murmuring" in his congregation when the Jews arrived. He called them "godless rascals," and when Stuyvesant agreed to deport them, New Amsterdam's municipal court granted its approbation.[87] The directors then reversed the decision because the Jews owed them an unspecified amount of money. After all their losses in Brazil, giving them another chance in North America was also just a matter of fairness, the directors declared. But the colonists did everything in their power to make the Jews feel unwelcome, maybe even promote a self-deportation: they could not trade on the Delaware River, could not have their own burial ground, could not buy their own real estate, could not serve in the militia, and had to pay extra, inordinate taxes for New Amsterdam's defense. Stuyvesant and the council wrote vaguely and unhelpfully that they imposed these restrictions and requirements "for important reasons." When the Jews complained, the governor told them, "consent is hereby given to them to depart whenever and wherever it may please them."[88]

Stuyvesant showed the same disregard for population needs with the Jews of New Netherland as he did with sinners and other nonconformers. Company directors began to see the harm in these attitudes and policies, and they tried to shorten his leash, overturning his decisions on the burial ground and the Delaware River. They did not go so far as to grant free public worship. They said merely that Jews, like Lutherans, could worship "within their houses, for which end they must without doubt endeavour to build their houses close together in a convenient place on one or the other side of New Amsterdam." These suggestive instructions could have been interpreted liberally to allow conventicles, but that would have required a liberal ruler, which the colony did not have.[89]

The Quakers suffered even more than Lutherans and Jews because, while they did at least profess a belief in Christ, most contemporaries considered them dangerous radicals, unfit for inclusion in the *corpus christianum* because of their novel views on authority and the provocative, disruptive style of their early years.[90] Stuyvesant's reaction to the Quakers was less severe than that of the New England Puritans, who sometimes executed the loud interlopers. And some Quakers did acknowledge the difference, perhaps even gratefully. But he was no friend to the Friends, as they were also called. He decried them as an error-ridden, "abominable Heresy" and a walking, talking disease. In his prayer day proclamations he warned the colonists that Quakers might seduce even "true believers," and in so doing, invite God's punishment on New Netherland.[91] So he tried to deter them with the same conventicle laws and the same harsh punishments he usually reserved for the worst criminals and religious dissenters (sodomists excepted): detention, flogging, hard labor, banishment, and direct deportation. His Quaker policy was "mild" only in the same nuanced sense in which a gunshot to the kneecap is better than a gunshot to the forehead. He inflicted great distress and crippled any potential Quaker growth and contribution to the colony.[92]

New Netherland's Quaker problem lasted from 1657 to 1662. It began with three deportations: Dorothy Waugh, May Witherhead, and Robert Hodgson. The first two got in trouble for preaching and quaking in the streets, scaring the people of New Amsterdam; the third was a question of conventicles, held at Hodgson's home in the English town of Heemstede on Long Island. After arresting him and imprisoning him for several days, the council gave him a choice: pay a hefty fine or "work at the wheelbarrow . . . two years with the negroes." When he refused to work, they whipped him, then whipped him again a few days later and deported him.[93] In the coming months they issued a stricter conventicle law for Quakers and Quaker sympathizers, and they made additional arrests and imposed new fines. In the famous Flushing Remonstrance, about thirty English settlers protested the law on the grounds that they could not, in good conscience, execute it. They even argued for a separation of secular and religious authority. But Stuyvesant shut them down immediately with a series of arrests and trials. Most Flushing magistrates got off on the grounds that they didn't understand what the Dutch meant by the terms "freedom of conscience" and "freedom from molestation," both found in their town charter. And they were quite sorry for their "errors," they now confessed. Their supposed ringleader, the *schout* Tobias Feake, lost his position and paid a fine of ƒ 200.[94]

Quaker controversies flared up again a few years later, ending this time with a slew of banishments and possibly even a small group of self-deporters. Having learned from Calvinist allies among the English on Long Island that Quakers still sometimes held conventicles, Stuyvesant sent various investigators, including on one occasion Reverend Samuel Drisius. On the village of Rustdorp the governor actually imposed three new magistrates and a company of soldiers, billeted in the colonists' homes. The soldiers would remain, he said, until all the men signed a pledge to forego illegal meetings and inform on their neighbors. Only six people refused to sign, and they might have left New Netherland of their own accord when Stuyvesant informed them that they alone would house and feed the soldiers until they changed their minds.[95] Among the six or seven people he banished in this second wave of Quaker troubles, the most famous was John Bowne. Like Hodgson before him, Bowne refused to pay the fine for holding conventicles, so the council kept him imprisoned for months. Then Stuyvesant deported him, not to some other colony, but all the way to Europe, where he made his case before the directors and finally agreed to obey the law.

The Bowne deportation forced the directors to issue their clearest instructions yet on the connivance tradition, along with their concern that Stuyvesant was stifling colonial growth. Regarding Quakers, they wrote in 1663:

We doubt very much, whether we can proceed against them rigorously without diminishing the population and stopping immigration, which must be favored at a so tender stage of the country's existence. You may therefore *shut your eyes*, at least not force people's consciences, but allow every one to have his own belief, as long as he behaves quietly and legally. . . . As the government of [Amsterdam] has always practiced this maxim of moderation and . . . has often had a considerable influx of people, we do not doubt that your Province too would be benefitted by it.[96]

The directors could not have provided better evidence that republicans and Libertines were finally starting to outnumber the Calvinists and Orangists who had dominated the company for so long. However, the Bowne moment was no real victory for religious liberty.[97] The directors told Bowne that he must not hold illicit meetings and made him sign a document to that effect. They also expressed dislike for "sectarians" like him.[98]

Most importantly, the directors' hints and requests for moderation had no discernible effect in New Netherland. Whether they wanted Stuyvesant to allow Lutheran worship or even connived in sending the Lutheran minister, he shipped the latter back to Europe and Lutherans never attained religious freedoms. Whether the directors wanted Stuyvesant to wink at Jewish and Quaker worship, he never did. He and his Calvinist allies in the church and among both Dutch and English colonists often worked together to suppress nonconformers. Then the colony fell to English conquerors just one year after he was ordered to "shut [his] eyes." The Amsterdam classis even expressed its satisfaction with the directors from time to time. After quashing the Lutherans, the classis thanked them for their assistance. Regarding Jews and their "blasphemous religion," the directors "acted . . . in a very Christian manner," the classis reported.[99] Indeed, Calvinists realized their wishes on almost every front. New Amsterdam never adopted the connivingly tolerant traditions of its namesake city on the other side of the Atlantic Ocean. In the face of great religious diversity, the colony remained a laboratory for Dutch reformers and a model of Calvinist governance.

CHAPTER 7

The Harvest Was Great, the Laborers Few

Missionary Work among Africans and Native Americans

Reformed theologians began thinking and writing about missions and conversion long before the creation of the West India Company. As Christianity's loudest champions of predestination, they maybe could have adopted a passive approach to missionary matters, for wouldn't God's elect recognize the truth and come to his kingdom regardless of individual effort, just because God decreed it? But avoiding mission was difficult, if any theologians tried, because the Bible clearly demanded it; and other favorite Calvinist doctrines—covenant theology in particular—functioned as a counterweight to predestination, calling believers to action. Their covenant relationship with God required that they do everything in their power to gather other elect from the nations of the earth and build Christ's church and kingdom. Dutch Calvinists were already discussing the best means and methods for reaching out to Jews, Muslims, and other non-Christians by the early decades of the seventeenth century.[1]

The major trading companies became the best and only means of gathering the elect on most continents. In a very broad sense the companies were evangelical in that they tried to establish and augment Dutch power in traditionally Catholic or pagan lands. Because of the church-company partnership, planting a fort or colony naturally meant planting the church somewhere it had not existed before, thus spreading the Lord's vineyard. Equally vague and broad, the Dutch revealed a missionary mind-set and purpose in their condemnations of Spain and their desire to save Native Americans from tyranny. The implication of their self-appointed savior function—sometimes the direct message—was that Native Americans would embrace all aspects of Dutch civilization.[2]

The companies were supposed to enable missionary activity in a more specific, conventional sense, as well, by supporting the clergy who would preach to Asians, Africans, and Native Americans. Contrary to a fairly common perception among modern writers, no one in the seventeenth century expected clergy to confine their work to employees and merchants in *handelskerken* ("trade churches").[3] Although the WIC's charter didn't mention the topic directly, clergy instructions and early publications about the company show a clear, widespread belief that they would and should work with indigenous peoples. The church in the Netherlands charged its colonial envoys with teaching people who had no knowledge of God and leading them to "the true faith." The WIC's separate clerical instructions were even more direct: "They shall make every effort to instruct the Portuguese, Spanish, and their children, as well as blacks and Indians, in the rudiments of the Christian Religion."[4] If they didn't already know it, churchgoers in the Netherlands learned of these expectations when, with the company's first fleet in 1623, the States General announced a national day of prayer and asked all the churches to pray for "the blind heathens," not just on that one day, but in their public prayers going forward.[5]

Dutch missions in the Atlantic world ultimately floundered and failed for a number of reasons, most of which had nothing to do with Dutch desires or efforts. Never mind the lack of missionary traditions and institutions in the relatively new church; Calvinists began their colonial work at a time when they barely had enough ministers for the ongoing reformation and growth of the church in Europe. Solitary clergy in small, hardscrabble colonies also had too many responsibilities, including their normal work with the congregation, plus sometimes families. Now they had to learn whole new languages and cultures. And the people they were supposed to teach, the Africans and Native Americans, showed little interest in the dry faith of the newcomers, lacking, as it was, in tangible devotional objects and ritual, focused on reading and preaching "the word" in a foreign tongue. Promising beginnings and exceptional missionary successes didn't last long because the WIC overextended itself and lost so many colonies to conquest.[6]

The Dutch Reformed Church could have also blamed itself for its failures. Coming off the recent Arminian controversy and Synod of Dordrecht, the WIC's heyday coincided with an exceptionally worried, controlling, restrictive moment for Calvinists; and the churches of the Netherlands only grew more controlling with the decline and collapse of Dutch Brazil. They never stopped talking about and encouraging missionary work, but they were so afraid of contaminating their hard-won orthodoxies that they inadvertently crippled the missionaries. The church at home imposed near-impossible requirements for potential converts, kept a tight grip on ordinations and employment, denied colonial clergy the flexibility and autonomy of Calvinism's localist impulses, prohibited the teaching and organizational tools that might have made a difference overseas, and forced eager, talented clergy to return to the Netherlands when they showed too much independence. Also relevant were the slave trade and Indian wars. As slavery grew in importance and so few Africans and Native Americans embraced the Calvinist message, sometimes even choosing to fight the Dutch, the old rhetoric about Spanish tyranny and Dutch freedom began to ring hollow. Ironically, the people who first cast themselves as the saviors of so much oppression came to see slavery and subjection as the best possible tools in a much-diminished but ongoing effort to make the world Reformed.

Christianity and the Slave Trade

Something remarkable happened when a slave ship arrived in the Dutch province of Zeeland in 1596: local authorities decided to set the slaves free. A Dutch privateer had taken the Portuguese vessel by force, and the owners wanted to sell the slaves. But the *burgemeesters* of Middelburg and the States of Zeeland refused. They announced in church the following Sunday that they intended to grant the slaves "their natural liberty," then let them live and work in whatever capacity they chose, as long as their employer promised to "nurture them in the fear of God."[7] The reaction was perhaps not so remarkable when we consider that slavery was dead or dying in the Netherlands by the late sixteenth century, as it was throughout northwestern Europe. Because it was limited by that point mostly to the European states of the Mediterranean region, the Dutch had come to see slavery in a negative light and associate it with their Iberian enemies.[8]

If anything, the 1596 episode reveals a hesitation or ambivalence about African slavery, not a firm humanitarian commitment and love of Africans. After all, the privateers wouldn't have brought the slaves to Zeeland in the first place if they had expected to lose their cargo. And there's some evidence that the States of Zeeland only freed the slaves because they were Christians. The Portuguese had instructed and baptized them before leaving the African coast, and the States of Zeeland stressed that fact in their deliberations. In the end, only a handful of the Africans in question remained very long in Zeeland; Melchior van den Kerckhoven, the ship's captain, probably took the rest and sold them in Portugal or the Caribbean.[9] Other Dutchmen were then starting to travel and trade in Africa for gold and ivory, and they usually didn't like what they saw of the local people. They used words like "ugly" and "barbarous," and they began to speculate that Africans and Europeans were fundamentally different, especially in times of great illness and death among white sailors. Decades before the Dutch had to make any decisions about their own involvement in the slave trade, misunderstandings about disease and disease environments inspired conversations about "human nature" and raised questions about whether Africans were, in fact, human.[10]

Very few Dutch merchants carried slaves before the WIC. Some did so on behalf of Lisbon merchants, and some, like Van den Kerckhoven, stumbled onto Portuguese slavers—and then became slavers in their own right—because of their privateering work. The famous Dutch ship that brought the first African slaves to Virginia in 1619 falls into this category, for the WIC still didn't exist at that point. The ship was probably English. The Virginians called it "Dutch" because it obtained its letter of marque in Zeeland, and having officially begun its journey there, it may have had a mixed Dutch and English crew.[11]

WIC directors first took up the question of the slave trade in 1623. Like their predecessors, they exhibited a certain discomfort and ambivalence about trading human beings. An anonymous supporter (probably an investor, if not a director) had just published a tract in which he claimed that the company would not use slave labor at all. They would free preexisting slaves in places like Brazil, he wrote, and employ free Dutchmen and other poor, hard-working Europeans.[12] The directors knew they would have to make a decision because they planned on taking territory from the Portuguese, and the Portuguese had established a link between Africa and Brazil long before. The directors acknowledged the fact by listing it as the sixth item of discussion at their first meeting. A frustratingly brief-yet-vacillating note in the margins of their agenda bears the weight of countless unrecorded, private conversations: "Concerning the Angola trade, that is to say, the trade in blacks, it is not yet possible because we have no place or opportunity to use them in Brazil or elsewhere." "Besides," the note continues, "it appears that this trade is not permissible for Christians." It's not clear whether someone made the note before the meeting or whether it summarizes the views of a special committee the company created to consider the issue more carefully, scribbled later. Committee members included four Reformed elders and deacons and members of the Calvinist political faction in Amsterdam: Kiliaen van Rensselaer, Joris Adriaensz, Guillielmo Bartholotti, and Samuel Blommaert.[13]

The directors' 1624 agenda indicates that they still had not established a firm policy on the slave trade. They vacillated because the necessity and economic benefits of becoming slavers were still uncertain, and some of them clearly didn't feel good about the possibility on moral, religious grounds. Themes like *freedom* and *salvation* were central to their propaganda and emerging self-image. In addition to Native Americans, who were the focus of most of their tyranny/ savior talk, WIC investors claimed at one time or another that, directly and indirectly, they would help free the southern Netherlands from continued Spanish control and lift the yoke from European Protestants who lived under Catholic rulers; they would free black slaves and liberate Portuguese colonists from under the Spanish Crown, which then ruled Spain and Portugal together.[14] When other Dutch tried to participate in this freedom project, going after Peru in the same period, they didn't stop at Native Americans either. They sought the support of "Blacks and Indians" by spreading rumors that they came to set them both free. In a somewhat mixed message, the merchant and visionary Joan Aventroot went so far as to recruit the much-reviled abusers and enslavers of Indians, the Spanish *encomenderos*! He reminded them that the Spanish Crown took one-fifth of their silver and now intended to destroy their land and labor rights altogether. The *encomenderos* were slaves ruling over slaves, Aventroot wrote, and the Dutch would rescue them all.[15]

With the successful conquest and subjugation of northeastern Brazil from 1630 to 1636, support for the sugar industry and concern for its labor needs quickly overwhelmed the few voices that continued to raise questions about the compatibility of Christianity and the slave trade. The Dutch had targeted Brazil in the first place because of its sugar plantations, and after taking them, they decided to utilize the preexisting labor system and even grow and develop it with new slaves from major outposts like Luanda in West Central Africa.[16] Disturbed at these developments, the merchant Jan Pot once went to the Amsterdam classis to ask whether someone in the service of the WIC "may participate in the slave trade with a clear conscience." But classis members didn't seem to appreciate his dilemma. They possibly just felt awkward discussing the subject in that particular setting because some of them were company directors. They told Pot that they found the question "untimely" or "inopportune," then sent him to speak (off the record) with the clergy.[17]

When the company had to explain its decision *on* the record, it did so with a mix of pragmatic and idealistic arguments. Simple necessity was usually the first consideration. The governor of Brazil, Johan Maurits van Nassau-Siegen, said that he still preferred free white labor, but he didn't expect many migrants from Holland and Portugal, so he settled for African slaves. Likewise, Caspar Barlaeus wrote that they had to have slaves for the plantations and sugar mills because Dutch colonists "cannot tolerate this labor."[18] On the idealistic side, they retained their shrinking freedom agenda whenever there was something to cling to. They did liberate the African slaves who ran away and joined them during the invasion. The conquest would have failed without their guidance and military assistance, the High Council wrote, and it refused to return them to their former owners after the peace treaty.[19] The company also justified its new slave policies by claiming that it would be a different kind of slaver, that it would avoid the "barbaric cruelty of the Spanish and Portuguese" by outlawing mutilation and burning.[20]

Godefridus Udemans was the first Reformed minister after the company embraced slavery to address the topic in print. Intended as a "spiritual rudder" for merchants and sailors in the East and West India Companies, his book, published in 1638, outlined in just a few pages most of the ideas that slave-trading Calvinists would use for the next decades, if not centuries. He acknowledged that some Dutch favored slavery and some still opposed it. His own opinion, he said, was "nuanced," because every circumstance was different. Udemans believed that all servitude was unnatural and sinful; but God let his children be slaves, the minister continued, in order to punish them or humble them and teach faith and patience. It was only by God's mercy that some people were born free. Udemans wrote that the lucky, favored Dutch should only purchase slaves if the slaves were originally obtained in a righteous war and sold at a fair price. And the Dutch shouldn't treat them as the Portuguese and Spanish did, but treat them well. The point was to improve their lot, both physical and spiritual, by removing the slaves from heathendom and placing them in a Christian setting. More specifically, Udemans discouraged Dutch traders from selling slaves to Catholics, which he apparently didn't see as an improvement, and he recommended that the Dutch set any Christian converts free after an indefinite period of faithful service.[21]

Udemans undermined his own manumission recommendation when he drew a critical distinction between spiritual and physical slavery. Christ only freed his followers from the former, not the latter, according to Udemans. All pious people were "free" in the sense that mattered most, regardless of their status before the law; all godless people were slaves to their sins, regardless of their comforts and attainments in this life. Udemans probably never paused to ask why, if it really made no difference—if Christ didn't care about physical freedom—any Christian slave owner would choose manumission. WIC directors were already considering how Christianity could make slaves even more useful, for as Christians they might "bear their yoke among us with fervor and patience."[22]

Udemans was no WIC minister, but the company did use his book, and the colonial clergy followed and contributed to these global discussions. Regarding "the souls of the poor people whose bodies we use in our service," the clergy in Brazil talked about how important it was to redeem Africans from "the slavery of Satan," especially considering that all "the learned" agreed: missionary work and conversion were "a necessary requisite for making the trade in black people lawful in God's eyes."[23] And the church would know. When colonial clergy used the expression "our service," they didn't mean the Dutch in general, nor the merchants and planters. As part of their pay, the company provided each of them with their own servant—a person who, in the 1630s, suddenly became an African slave. Reformed clergy appear as purchasers on almost every extant slave list in Brazil between 1636, when the sales records begin, and 1645, when they stop because of the Portuguese revolt. Sometimes clergy in these cases were just picking up WIC slaves according to their contracts, sometimes they bought slaves on their own account, with their own money. In total, they acquired about fifty-seven slaves in those few years, usually priced at between ƒ300 and ƒ500 per slave. WIC clergy bought or acquired at least sixteen other slaves directly from the High Council, for a total of seventy-three church-affiliated slaves.[24]

African slaves and sugar workers in Brazil, by Romeyn de Hooghe (1682–1733). Courtesy of the Rijksmuseum, Amsterdam.

Had anyone still wanted to do so, the church and its spokesmen couldn't very well condemn slavery when the church was so entwined with the company and when the church, too, came to depend on the institution. Although in the long run, clergy in most WIC territories owned slaves, the picture is once again clearest in Brazil. A 1642 "List of persons who have [WIC] negros in their service" shows how some of the slaves were used. On the list were eight Reformed ministers with eleven slaves. Fredericus Kesseler had three slaves "in place of servants"; Johannes Offeringa had one "for service in his house." The council agreed to give Gilbertus de Vaux a second slave when the first "ran away from him."[25] In most cases the church-affiliated slaves did domestic work. The reason some ministers had extra slaves isn't always clear, but someone like Kesseler, who was the leading minister of the time, probably had three because he and his consistory oversaw all the church's disparate social responsibilities. He needed a slave to tend the horses when he sent itinerant clergy to administer the sacraments in places without permanent clergy; he needed slaves for the clergy who still sometimes served the army on a provisional basis.[26] Vincentius Soler once had custody of six slaves because the company was building a special church in Recife, a "French church" for the many French Protestants in its employ. Slaves were building the church both literally and metaphorically.[27]

Finally, the church utilized slaves in the company's hospitals. At least seven of the aforementioned seventy-three slaves were designated for hospital service at the time of their purchase, and other slaves ended up there after working elsewhere first.[28] Managed and funded by the deacons, the hospitals were very much a mixed church-company enterprise. They employed at least one "father and mother," who also sometimes looked after the orphans, as well as a few "wise, godly women," a schoolmaster, a surgeon, a *ziekentrooster*, and again, the African slaves. In Recife the slaves worked "in the kitchen," which probably meant that they had to tend the hospital's cattle and other livestock, too.[29]

If the recent discomfort and ambivalence about the enslavement of Africans still reared its head from time to time, it did so mostly in the publications of clergy who tried to limit slavery's worst abuses, not prohibit it outright. Reverend Johannes de Mey, who worked for the WIC on St. Eustatius in 1643, and Reverend Georgius de Raad created what would have been a controlled, restrained slave system, had anyone decided to follow their blueprint. In both cases it's clear that Calvinists were using the Bible (and particularly the Old Testament) to debate and understand these issues. At the heart of De Mey's and De Raad's analyses was the idea of a single creation, the idea that God created everyone and that everyone was born free. Slave trading was only justified, they believed, under some of the same conditions that Udemans had explained before: everyone's concern should be for the physical and spiritual betterment of the slaves. De Raad was especially adamant that Dutch merchants not sell slaves in Catholic colonies, for Catholics would presumably raise them in the Catholic faith, and in an indirect way, the merchants would be building the kingdom of Antichrist. Both ministers agreed that the Dutch should treat their slaves with mercy and teach them the Gospel—or as De Raad put it, "bring them up in Christian freedom." De Mey explored the laws and traditions of the biblical Jews to find ways that Christian slaves might obtain their physical freedom, as well.[30]

As read and taught by ministers like Udemans, De Mey, and De Raad, the Christian scriptures contained potentially radical ideas: servitude as sin, a single creation for all mankind, humanity's brother-sister relationship, the need for mercy and kindness, and so on. At the same time, everyone could clearly see that God's prophets and chosen people had owned slaves in the distant past, and that the early Christians had lived and participated without much angst in the slave-owning societies of the first century AD.[31] The Bible's chronological breadth and the multiplicity of biblical authors provided a smorgasbord of spiritual options for those who had to confront the Atlantic slave trade. Unfortunately, merchants weren't likely to shun the trade when they could make a great deal of money in an activity that enjoyed (they could argue) so

Rev. Godefridus Udemans (left) and Rev. Johannes de Mey (right). Udemans was produced by J. Sarragon (1635) and De Mey by J. Jongh and Z. Blijhooft (ca. 1640–1678). Courtesy of the Zeeuws Archief, Middelburg.

much historical, ecclesiastical, and heavenly support. Many of them probably didn't care about the theological niceties of Calvinist writers and preachers anyway. Like an eager teenager in search of a parent's permission, they just heard "yes," then absconded without digesting all the tedious, complex qualifications and restrictions. Merchants did, for example, sell slaves in Catholic colonies, and in the long term, Dutch planters were no less cruel than their European competitors.[32]

One of the only seventeenth-century clergy to condemn the slave trade unconditionally was Jacobus Hondius, who reminded his readers that Africans were not "mere Beasts." They were, he said, "People with one and the same natures" as the men who purchased them. But Hondius was the exception to prove the rule, and he never worked overseas. More importantly, he buried his remarks on slavery as the 810th sin in a ponderous list of 1,000 sins that also included things like falling asleep during the prayer and giving sweets and gifts to children on Saint Nicholas Day. It would take a different kind of personality to revive the anti-slavery rhetoric and tendencies that marked the early years of Dutch activity in the Atlantic world.[33]

Recife as a Major Missionary Center

Paradoxically, Dutch missionary endeavors among Africans and Native Americans began in the same period—almost the same year—the company began trading regularly in slaves. In keeping with its other designs, interests, and successes, the WIC's most intensive missionary work occurred in the 1630s and 1640s in the South Atlantic. Centered in Recife and reaching outward from there to other parts of Brazil and Africa, Dutch Calvinists cobbled together an embryonic Protestant missionary program and a Protestant following to suggest that they could one day compete with their Catholic rivals in the Spanish and Portuguese Empires. Missionary successes and failures were not just matters of Dutch commitment and investment, though. Many local conditions and native needs and choices were more important in determining mission outcomes.

The earliest religious encounters between the Dutch and their indigenous allies and trading partners were more superficial and observational than substantive, as if each side was trying to feel out the very foreign other. No matter the continent or culture, the two most common (and contradictory) observations from the Dutch were that, one, Africans and Indians had no religion, and two, they worshipped the Devil. It was not as though the Dutch couldn't and didn't witness indigenous rituals, because they often described them in careful detail. They just didn't seem to believe that a polytheistic, unorganized or noninstitutional religious tradition was in fact a religion. And they interpreted animistic customs as magical and diabolical, sometimes as simple trickery and superstition.[34] WIC directors and officers were at first too inexperienced and naïve about missionary work to foster more meaningful exchanges. They encouraged instruction and conversion from the beginning, but the directors didn't do much more than hire ministers and set them loose, confident in the power of the message and the example their other underlings would set in treating potential converts better than the Spanish had done. A good example and "the good word" were the missionary's first tools.[35]

The Dutch started developing other missionary tools in the 1630s, originally in West Africa, where their social presence was too limited and their power too inhibited to build the kind of educational program they would soon have in South America. Nevertheless, they did found schools on the Gold Coast. When Reverend Laurentius Benderius complained in 1633 that he was making no progress among Africans, he blamed the language gap. His commander said that Benderius was the problem because the minister didn't want to risk his health by leaving the ships to perform his duties. But the directors agreed that communication was critical to the religious mission, and they hired Cornelis Jacobsen to assist Benderius and teach school at Fort Nassau. This first experiment only lasted four months. They organized the school, invited inhabitants from the town of Mouree, and held regular lessons with ten to twelve of the WIC's young slaves. Few of the free families who promised to send their children actually did so, and Jacobsen reported diminishing results and interest as the months passed. So with his commander's permission, he abandoned his teaching duties and became a *ziekentrooster* instead. He felt that the Dutch language and Dutch religion would not grow in Africa until the WIC found a way to separate the school children, some of whom had European fathers, from their "heathen" playmates.[36]

The Tupi people of Brazil were much more responsive to the Protestant message, and for good reason: they had suffered a great deal under the Portuguese. Through disease and slave labor their population had declined drastically in the past century. Under the Jesuits they found some security against mistreatment, but they didn't enjoy much autonomy. In truth, the Tupi seemed to fulfill all the expectations and predictions the Dutch had been making about oppressed Native Americans for decades. And the Dutch knew they needed the Tupi as guides and military allies. The Tupi, for their part, may not have favored Protestantism and Dutch civilization strictly on the merits, as the Dutch wanted to believe. But some Tupi found in the Dutch an opportunity to forge a useful alliance and possibly refashion their circumstances for the better. Each side used the other to pursue different but complementary purposes, and religion was the necessary cultural adhesive of their union.[37]

The Dutch-Tupi alliance and Calvinist mission in Brazil emerged only gradually because of the war—and because the Dutch lacked the experience and tools for such a huge undertaking. After the WIC's first failed invasion, thirteen Tupi traveled to the Netherlands, where they spent five years learning Dutch and providing valuable intelligence about the colony. Some of them were catechized and baptized in the Netherlands, "reared and instructed" at "great cost" to the company, the colonial council later noted.[38] At the start of the second, longer-lasting invasion (1630–1654), the directors told their officers to support the Tupi mission and asked advice on how they, the directors, could help it succeed. Yet some Tupi held back, fearing Portuguese retaliation, many of them even fighting with Portuguese colonists against the Dutch.[39] The clergy only started to report missionary work among the Tupi and among African slaves in the mid-1630s, after the colony was pacified. Reverend Jodocus à Stetten recorded various requests for baptism from "negroes"—probably the runaway slaves who were helping the Dutch—in his 1635 journal, and he did teach and baptize their children. Reverend Daniel Schagen went on the first tour of Tupi villages in the same period. He tried to teach them the Lord's Prayer, along with "other short lessons in our religion." According to the High Council member who accompanied him, the Tupi enjoyed the lessons and requested continued instruction.[40]

The church's first discussions and proposals for a more intensive, long-term mission program involved a mix of translation and education ideas for possible use in Brazil and the Netherlands. Reverend Schagen, the church decided, would begin compiling a "theological Compendium" of basic Protestant principles and doctrines in the Portuguese and Tupi languages.[41] Colonial clergy asked the company to install Dutch teachers and *proponents* (apprentice ministers) in each Tupi village. At the same time, they wanted the company to send twenty or thirty indigenous children to the Netherlands to learn Dutch and be catechized. When they received these proposals, WIC directors expressed their satisfaction and promised to look for qualified men, meaning *proponents* and teachers. The Tupi mission "concerns us deeply," they wrote. They did not, however, agree to support children in Holland. In a possible reference to some of the original thirteen Tupi, they said that young people tended to forget their native tongue when they spent too many years away from home. The directors told the church instead to devise a strategy for achieving the same educational goals in Brazil.[42]

The Reformed mission didn't begin in earnest until the restructuring of secular and religious leadership from 1636 to 1638. Especially crucial was the creation of the Recife classis and eventually the synod. Uniting a bunch of dis-jointed, scattered ministers and consistories, the classis was the best mission-ary tool available, a prerequisite to all others, for it was a powerful forum for cooperative planning and organization to complement the work of the Amsterdam and Walcheren classes on the other side of the ocean. The Recife classis ousted the troublesome Schagen as soon as it could, and it appointed Reverend Soler to the task that Schagen was supposed to have done before: the writing and publication of a multilingual tract that Soler began calling "A Short Explication of the Christian Religion." The classis also continued the discussion about Tupi villages and children, and it asked the High Council for assistance with slave conversions. Accordingly, the council issued a new law for slave owners in the Recife area, demanding that they rest their slaves on the Sabbath and send them to Soler's weekly Portuguese sermons.[43]

The missionary program that emerged in Brazil in the late 1630s was an adaptation of the program the Jesuits had used with the Tupi before. Wher-ever the company had not yet reached, wherever the WIC had not expelled the priests, the Tupi did it on their own, then asked for Protestant replace-ments.[44] Secular captains and lay preachers filled the vacuum early on, before the church established the classis system in Brazil. By January 1638 the direc-tors had sent a fresh cluster of clergy, and the classis finally had the manpower to "establish a minister [among the Tupi] . . . to preach the word of God, to administer the Holy Sacrament, and to practice church discipline." The first appointment was a young man from Holland named David á Doreslaer. Still working in cooperation with secular captains in each Tupi village, he traveled regularly from his new home in the main village of Mauritia to six or seven others.[45] His assistants, the Spaniard Dionisius Biscaretto and the Englishman Thomas Kemp, began their careers as schoolmasters and were later ordained to the ministry, serving about sixteen years as missionaries in both cases. En-couraged by the directors, full-time "village ministers" reached as many as five at once, and they were always assisted by lay preachers and teachers, includ-ing a few indigenous Brazilians.[46]

Missionaries reported gradual progress and endless difficulties in their work with African slaves and Native Americans. They catechized, baptized, and mar-ried among both groups regularly, though they seem to have favored the Tupi over the slaves. By 1640, just two years after his appointment, enough Tupi had become full members of the Dutch Reformed Church that Doreslaer was able to organize the first Communion service among them.[47] At the same time, many Tupi continued to drink more than the ministers liked, and they were slow to accept Dutch marriage and sexual mores. Ministers also complained about planters who still made their slaves labor on the Sabbath and didn't send

A Tupi man, woman, and child in Brazil. Originally printed in *Historia Naturalis Brasiliae*, by Willem Piso and Georg Marcgraf (1648). Courtesy of the Koninklijke Bibliotheek, The Hague.

the slaves to church. They complained about slaves drinking, stealing, committing adultery, and observing traditional African worship and funeral rites. So new were the Dutch in Brazil, communication was part of the problem. Yet the churches at home rejected Soler's solution, his "Short Explication," because they didn't want European and colonial Christians reading different publications. Instead they sent copies of the standard Heidelberg Catechism, translated into Spanish, which wasn't very useful in Brazil.[48]

The rejection of Soler's book was the first indication that the churches in the Netherlands might inadvertently become obstacles to the mission, sacrificing ease of instruction and ecclesiastical growth for the sake of unity and orthodoxy. What was usually a sluggish, transatlantic conversation and give-and-take about best missionary practices sometimes became a simple series of worried directives from Europe to America. For instance, when Doreslaer, at the behest of the Recife classis, undertook his own trilingual catechism, the churches at home once again tried to stop it. At least by 1641 he was writing in Tupi, and the directors agreed to publish his translation of the Heidelberg Catechism, as well as the formularies for baptism and Communion, which he was probably using in handwritten form anyway. The directors commended him for the progress he and other clergy were making with the Tupi. But the churches of the Netherlands, who had still not devised their own communication solution, reacted with horror. The questions in Doreslaer's catechism were too long and the answers too short, they said; and he had modified the formularies. One synod argued that colonial clergy should not do *anything* important without consent from home.[49]

In response to missionary complaints about the depth of Tupi conversion and the difficulties of working with adults, WIC directors decided in 1641 to ramp up their educational program and focus on children. They hired two schoolmasters who differed from their predecessors in that they had children of their own: Hendrik van Diever and Dirck van Lochem had lived exemplary lives, the church reported. More importantly, because they had families, and because their families would accompany them to Brazil, the Indians would now have good examples of "Christian housekeeping." Van Diever and Van Lochem would also teach slaves on nearby plantations, the directors wrote. A few months later they announced that they had hired nine more families for the same purpose, and over the course of the year the first of them arrived and received their assignments in the various villages.[50] The church and the High Council in Brazil appreciated the directors' intent, as well as the "great costs" involved in the undertaking, but they were less sanguine about the chances of success. Concerned that traditional Tupi culture would continue to inhibit serious reform, the council called a special meeting to discuss the problem with the clergy.[51]

The new strategy failed because the Tupi wanted nothing to do with it. To make Reformed teachings as efficacious as possible, the clergy proposed removing native children from their families and raising them with Dutch children in a special school outside the villages. The High Council liked the idea and suggested a few former Catholic cloisters. Amazingly, they didn't inform the Tupi about their plans until they had expended a great deal of energy and money. Company coffers can hardly bear it, the governor grumbled. Only after choosing a cloister and building barracks to house the soldiers who used to live in the cloister did they ask the church to meet with parents and draw up a list of potential students. Only then did they discover that the Tupi had no intention of relinquishing their children. The "civilization" of the Brazilian youth could not move forward without upsetting their elders, a despondent council reported to the directors. The timing was especially bad because Indians in the province of Siara had just rioted over a different issue. Not wanting to alienate their allies by "separating them from their children," the council resolved to have the ministers and schoolmasters continue their village and plantation work as before. The directors expressed their disappointment but agreed that it was probably best to abandon the cloister proposal.[52]

In the meantime, the Brazil church had to manage missionary progress in the company's other territories, especially after the 1641 Luanda conquest. The directors resolved not to put their African outposts directly under the Brazilian government, but the burgeoning slave trade helped maintain strong bonds between the continents, and Recife became an ecclesiastical clearinghouse of sorts. The classis sent books and personnel to Africa many times during the Johan Maurits years. The classis decided to split itself, creating a second classis and a synod in Brazil, because it wanted to regulate other conquests more effectively. As Doreslaer explained to the High Council, he and the other ministers could respond quickly to new problems and supervise religious affairs in Guinea and Luanda until "the churches there . . . could form their own proper gatherings."[53]

With help from the Amsterdam and Recife classes, the WIC revived its school in West Africa in the early 1640s, this time at Elmina. The main voice and influence behind the move was a *ziekentrooster*-turned-minister named Meindert Hendricks, who traveled from Elmina to Recife for his examination and ordination. The Amsterdam classis didn't like conceding control to Recife, and it demanded at first that Hendricks come all the way to Holland for the exams. The company insisted, however, that the Brazil nexus was faster and easier.[54] Corresponding now with both classes, Hendricks requested a schoolmaster and a large Bible of the latest translation, plus books and writing utensils to teach reading, writing, and religion to local youth. When exactly he began the school no one knows, but he described his hopes and his "good start" in the same 1642 letter in which he asked for educational supplies. Two years later the directors were still writing about their interest in the project and the importance of instructing black and mulatto children in "the Christian faith" and "the Dutch language." The children's new faith would save their souls; their new language skills, the directors didn't say, would facilitate communication and trade in Africa.[55]

Everyone had similar hopes for Luanda, which was even more clearly and directly supplied from Recife. Governor Johan Maurits employed hundreds of Tupi in the fleet that captured the Afro-Portuguese slave-trading town, and the classis appointed Fredericus Vittaeus as Luanda's first Reformed minister. WIC officers immediately assessed the population and called for more ministers and at least one schoolmaster. We must draw people to our religion, they said, in order to make them "faithful servants" of the new Dutch regime. They suggested that the WIC convert the king of Kongo and the Kongolese court for the same reason.[56] The Recife classis responded by calling Nicolaus Ketel and two *ziekentroosters* to work with Reverend Vittaeus, and the directors agreed to support two ministers, four *proponents*, and three teachers in Luanda and Kongo together. Soon Ketel was administering the Lord's Supper in Luanda, mostly to company soldiers, and he baptized a number of African children. He was uncomfortable performing the rite before any serious instruction had taken place. As he explained to his superiors, he only did so because the parents requested it, and the parents were Christians. He derided their religious knowledge and vowed that, in time, Protestant preachers and teachers would spread their own doctrines. Unfortunately, Vittaeus couldn't help him because the minister succumbed to a disease epidemic that began killing the Dutch right after their arrival.[57]

Reverend Ketel traveled from Luanda to the Kingdom of Kongo with the Dutch delegation that made an alliance with the Kongolese in 1642. The Dutch approached them with the same mind-set and expectations as they had the Tupi and so many Native Americans: despite their longtime Catholicism, the Kongolese had no affection for the Portuguese, the Dutch reassured themselves. They insisted that the Kongolese, like the Tupi, were suffering under the burdens of Portuguese tyranny, crying out for a Protestant savior. We could "extend their hearts to ours" by stationing a Calvinist minister at the king's court and teaching the Kongolese about our religion and government, wrote Pieter Mortamer, WIC commander in Luanda.[58] He soon found, though, that Kongo was not Brazil, and the Kongolese were not the Tupi. King Garcia II did agree to a military alliance with the WIC because he did want to drive the Portuguese from his lands, as the Dutch knew. But when it came to Reverend Ketel and the question of religion, Dutch predictions fell apart. King Garcia's letter to Johan Maurits is a remarkable specimen of careful diplomacy, condemning the Portuguese, on the one hand, for their selfish ambition and celebrating the new Dutch-Kongolese relationship, then refusing in the most courteous of terms to swap his priests for Protestant ministers. "I practice the true Catholic faith," the king explained.[59]

The first half of the 1640s was the zenith of Dutch power and missionary activity in the Atlantic world. In just a few years the WIC and its Calvinist clergy had established a substantial mission program among the Tupi and a less substantial, floundering but ongoing, experimental program among Brazil's black slaves. In Africa they had a new school at Elmina, a few clergy and schoolmasters in Luanda, and a foothold in the Kingdom of Kongo, where they continued to push their minister on King Garcia's court. The fact that all these relationships advanced the company's secular interests doesn't undermine the religious argument so much as it proves the intellectual union I'm trying to demonstrate. Most religious activities under the WIC were related in some way to secular goals. The Reformed Church and the company worked closely together to achieve material and spiritual ends that they didn't label as one or the other. With the Tupi, the directors went far beyond a simple alliance, spending money they didn't have to support schoolmaster families and implement the cloister plan.

That said, the Dutch Reformed mission was never very healthy, even at its height. Most leaders claimed the same basic purpose: to save the indigenous peoples of the Atlantic world by Christianizing and civilizing them, by altering their beliefs and culture. I have already shown how quickly the meaning of the word "save" changed and contracted with African slavery, and it soon began to contract for the Tupi, too. The Dutch paid Tupi fighters and laborers a wage, but their work reduced their time with the missionaries, as the directors learned after the Luanda voyage. They reproved Johan Maurits in that case because so many Tupi died. The directors had told him before not to use the Tupi except in great need, not to take them away from their farms nor interfere with their instruction. Their "upbringing" and salvation were very important, the directors wrote. They mattered as much as any "temporary profits."[60] In the same vein, clergy and Tupi complained regularly about abusive officers, Indians held on plantations against their will, and even occasional kidnappings and enslavement. Without a hint of irony, one Dutch officer said the WIC needed to force all rootless, unmonitored Tupi to return to their villages so the clergy, through their lessons in religion and manners, could preserve Tupi freedom and "remove all principles through which they or their children could be enslaved." In other words, he saw their history of enslavement to the Portuguese (and their ongoing troubles) as a product of Tupi culture and a reflection of ethnic, social weakness, with a dose of Dutch culture as the best possible cure.[61]

Ecclesiastical authorities couldn't address these issues nor resolve the tensions and contradictions in the Dutch mission as effectively as they otherwise might have done because of the disagreements and power struggles in their own ranks. After rejecting Soler's and Doreslaer's books, the churches of the Netherlands continued to create problems for the colonial clergy, raising questions about their judgment and commitment both because of the books and because they had apparently formed their second classis (and their synod) without consent. All the colonial clergy tried to distance themselves from Doreslaer, including the men who were on the classis when his catechism was approved and sent for publication. At first he tried to defend the work as a mere summary of the Heidelberg Catechism, for the Tupi language, he said, didn't have all the necessary words and ideas for a direct translation. He used "a more childish manner of instruction." So afraid was Doreslaer of the hubbub his book caused, so surprised at the controversy, he began to lose his enthusiasm for the mission, and he returned home early to defend his reputation and prove his orthodoxy.[62] Similarly, Reverend Kesseler left Brazil for Holland in early 1643 to save his own reputation and, rather disingenuously, deny his role in creating the synod. The church itself had robbed the colony of two important, gifted ministers exactly when it was struggling most to maintain sufficient numbers of them.[63]

The Dutch never enslaved Brazilian Indians for three reasons: First, the Tupi were valuable partners who resisted any loss of autonomy and expressed their desires and frustrations to the colonial council; second, the directors refused in this case to abandon the tyranny / savior myth so quickly; and third, the Dutch simply didn't have enough time in Brazil. The council did, however, contemplate and even promote Indian slavery, not for the Tupi, but for a people called the Tapuya. Johan Maurits described their cannibalism and other alien, unflattering traditions, then declared, "It does not appear that those persons have the understanding to use their freedom correctly, but that they require the command and direction of someone of greater judgment."[64] The directors rejected the governor's impassioned defense of Indian slavery and, after a group of Tupi traveled to Holland to make a personal appeal for their freedom in 1644, the company implemented a new system of Tupi self-government in the villages, discarding the secular officers who had overseen labor needs until then. The council had to assure the directors repeatedly in coming years that no, they didn't enslave Indians, Tapuya or Tupi.[65]

No one knows whether WIC directors could have resisted colonial pressures to control and enslave Indians forever because the experiment in Tupi self-government began just before the Portuguese uprising of 1645, which destroyed the Dutch Reformed mission in the entire South Atlantic. "Uprisings" (plural) might be a better word, for the Portuguese of Luanda never accepted the Dutch conquest there, either. Portuguese resistance in both places spoiled the dream of a prosperous Atlantic empire and redirected the company's limited attention and resources to defensive, military purposes. All the excitement about the Luanda mission was replaced by depressing descriptions of war, poverty, death, and the machinations of Catholic priests. Though Elmina wasn't directly involved in the rebellions, any chance of saving its school died because of them.[66] As for Brazil, the WIC and church decided after the uprising to leave the already floundering slave mission in the hands of individual consistories and focus what few resources they still could on their Tupi allies, who, for the most part, remained faithful. The Tupi leader Peter Potí wrote to Filipe Camarão, an Indian on the other side of the conflict, that "I am a Christian, and a better one than you," because Potí didn't practice idolatry. The Portuguese treated the Tupi "more as negros," he continued, but the Dutch let them live freely, "and so we want to live and die with them."[67]

Die with them they did, at least until the WIC was forced to abandon its allies and colonies in 1648 (Luanda) and 1654 (Brazil). Those losses make it easy to forget that the Dutch once had a considerable religious mission in the South Atlantic. The mission lived and died, succeeded and failed, only in part because of Dutch efforts and investments. Equally important were the needs and choices of the Tupi Indians, the Moureans and Elminans of the Gold Coast, and the Kongolese king Garcia II. Their interests and calculations about whether they should forge a relationship with the WIC and what that relationship required in terms of religious commitments could, in rare cases, fulfill the most hopeful Dutch predictions about their empire. More often, slaves, allies, and trading partners resisted change, and the Portuguese destroyed any chance to make headway among these groups in time.

Toward the Gospel of Subjection

The Calvinist missions in New Netherland and the Dutch Caribbean were negligible by comparison to Brazil's, both before and after the Portuguese revolt. New Netherland had an opportunity to create a significant mission because of the many Indian communities on the Hudson, Connecticut, and Delaware Rivers. The Dutch approached Native Americans there with some of the same promises of superior treatment and the same expectations about how their good example would draw people to Protestantism and the Dutch way of life. And the WIC was fairly careful about purchasing its lands. No one seemed to realize at first that, without Iberian enemies, Indians didn't have the same incentives as the Tupi to form strong cultural bonds with the newcomers. After Brazil, the churches at home were also less likely to allow the necessary flexibility and organizational tools to overcome these extra obstacles, leaving the colonial clergy too isolated for any extensive missionary project.[68]

The first minister in New Netherland, Jonas Michaelius, tried to teach Native Americans, but when they didn't respond as he wanted, his opinion of them quickly turned sour, and he even ruminated on the possibilities of seizing land from unfriendly, belligerent groups.[69] In his correspondence he rarely specified the tribal affiliations of his prospective neophytes. He wrote, "If we want to speak to them of God . . . we must do that, not under the name 'Menotto,' whom they know and serve (for that would be blasphemous), but as some great one, yea, the most almighty [chief]. . . . Hearing this, some of them begin to grimace and shake their heads, as if it were a simple fable, while others, to leave the oration in respect and friendship, will say 'Orith,' that is, 'good.'"[70] In a complaint that other ministers in New Netherland and the Wild

Coast would soon echo, Michaelius claimed that no Dutch actually knew Indian languages, only trade pidgins. When he and other colonists tried to learn more, Indians allegedly concealed their knowledge. Who was it, he wondered, who said that these people would be docile and predisposed to our religious principles? Rather than see Indian reticence for what it probably was—a protective measure—Michaelius decided that they were "stupid as garden poles." He promised to continue his linguistic studies and teaching efforts, though with little hope, for he didn't believe that he would see much fruit until the WIC separated Indian children from their parents.[71]

Slave baptisms in New Netherland were more common because the slaves saw several advantages to being Christian. Michaelius and his successor, Reverend Everardus Bogardus, had both served in West Africa before they came to America. Perhaps tainted by his earlier experience, Michaelius described the few slaves of his tenure as "thievish, lazy, and useless trash," and there's no evidence that he tried to teach them anything.[72] Bogardus was, at least in this respect, his opposite: there's no evidence that he taught Native Americans, but he did work with free blacks and slaves, whose numbers were growing by the 1640s. Of all the black baptisms and marriages in the New Netherland records, the large majority of them took place under Bogardus. He served personally as godfather to more than one black child and catechized and baptized a

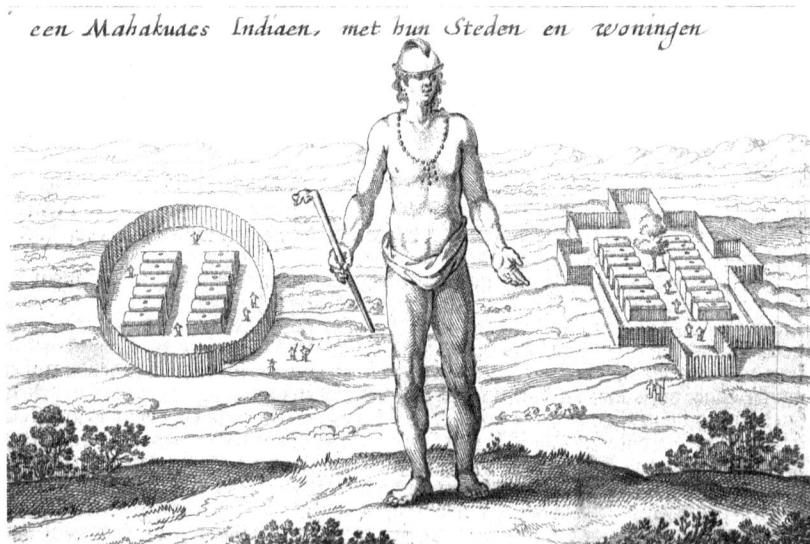

A Dutch depiction of a Mohawk Indian and his "cities and dwellings." Originally printed in *Beschrijvinghe van Virginia*, by Joost Hartgers (1651). Courtesy of the John Carter Brown Library, Providence, Rhode Island.

handful of black adults.[73] Most adult slaves didn't need baptism because they were, to use Ira Berlin's designation, "Atlantic creoles." They had lived and labored in Portuguese colonies and already knew European languages and institutions. Their willingness and ability to participate in the church in New Netherland is an indication that slavery was still young and undefined, that the slaves of that era still had prospects that slaves in other times and colonies wouldn't have. They sought baptism and Christian marriage because they didn't want to be outsiders; they wanted to participate in the emerging colonial society and give their children every possible opportunity.[74]

The creation of New Netherland's second clerical position in 1642 revived Dutch hopes and interest in the Indian mission. Reverend Johannes Megapolensis expressed his desire to "spread the Gospel of Jesus Christ among the blind heathens" before he ever left Holland, and the Amsterdam classis instructed him to "proclaim Christ to Christians and heathens."[75] But once again, isolation and native resistance wrecked his best efforts. Having two ministers in the colony didn't solve the isolation problem because they were too far apart for regular meetings and joint councils: Bogardus lived on Manhattan Island, Megapolensis on the upper Hudson. There at least the latter was better-positioned to interact with the Iroquois, who traveled for days to trade their furs with the Dutch at Fort Orange.

Megapolensis described meeting and walking with the Iroquois and other Indians deep in the woods, hours from any settlement. "They sleep by us, too, in our chambers before our beds. I have had eight at once lying and sleeping upon the floor near my bed, for it is their custom to sleep simply on the bare ground." The Indians attended the minister's regular prayers and sermons in groups as large as twelve, and he began compiling a vocabulary in the hopes of becoming "an Indian grammarian." Like Michaelius, though, Megapolensis could only report his frustration at the skepticism, disbelief, and obfuscation he encountered everywhere. "When we pray, they laugh at us," he wrote, and some of them "despise it entirely." Also like Michaelius, Megapolensis concluded that Indians were stupid because he couldn't convey his meaning in the broken trade pidgins the Dutch were still using in the 1640s. He slogged away at his vocabulary, but he made little progress. When he asked for the names of different objects, Indians either wouldn't tell him the names or gave him different answers for the same object, never letting him get too close. One longtime resident of Fort Orange told Megapolensis that the Iroquois must adopt a whole new language every few years.[76]

After Kieft's War, company directors began saying that it wasn't possible to convert adult Indians in New Netherland, and clergy continued to speculate about the value of force. An unnamed chieftain who lived briefly at New

Amsterdam in the early 1650s kept the missionary dream alive, so to speak, by accepting a Bible and attending school with European children. He learned to read and write in Dutch "tolerably well," and he could recite the Ten Commandments. Yet his religious knowledge was still thin, wrote Megapolensis. When he pawned his Bible and took up drinking, the clergy decided that he would not be the Christian emissary they had hoped. They said that they didn't expect much fruit from Indians "until they are brought under the government of Europeans." A few years later they wrote, "We can say little of the conversion of the heathens or Indians here, and see no way to accomplish it, until they are subdued by the numbers and power of our people, and reduced to some sort of civilization."[77]

Subjection was the easy, satisfying answer in an era of on-again, off-again Indian conflict. During the Peach and Esopus Wars of the 1650s and 1660s, Native Americans began to feature in Governor Petrus Stuyvesant's prayer day proclamations and other Dutch writings as an instrument of heaven's wrath, a tool for an angry God to punish the colonists for their drinking and Sabbath-breaking. Far from teaching Indians and bringing them to the true church, colonial rulers now had to organize Sunday patrols and appoint soldiers to protect white churchgoers as they made their way to and from services. And the deacons spent their limited funds to redeem Christian captives from indigenous enemies.[78] Reverend Hermanus Blom went furthest in drawing these lines between the Dutch and the natives, probably because he witnessed the Esopus attack at Wiltwijck firsthand. He depicted the village not with its true divisions and variety, but as "an inheritance of the Lord," a "feeble and infant congregation," an entire Church (capitalized in the original) planted in the New World. Regardless of whether all the Wiltwijck inhabitants really belonged to the church, they evidently became honorary members via their shared experience of violence and an all-too-literal baptism of fire. During the attack itself, some of the wounded "fled for refuge to my house," Blom recalled, and some people died in his arms. He described bloodied bodies and burnt corpses and how, for an entire month afterward, he went daily with his congregation to offer prayers "under the blue sky" atop each of the four corners of their small fort.[79]

Although Blom agreed with Stuyvesant that God was using the Indians to punish sinful colonists, his understanding of divine providence was flexible enough to believe at the same time that God had protected the survivors and would now avenge them. Blom prayed as the WIC prepared its counterattack that "the Lord our God will again bless our arms, and grant that the Foxes who have endeavoured to lay waste the vineyard of the Lord shall be destroyed."[80] Consciously or not, the minister was resurrecting the language of an earlier era, when the company's main purpose and pursuit was piracy and war. The strategy may have changed, as had the battlefield and enemy; the bloodshed continued.

Dutch Reformed clergy in New Netherland couldn't overcome Indian reticence and outright opposition to the Protestant religion because of their own history and leadership. Their forebears had established exacting, exclusionary standards of membership that made their work that much harder; and they didn't have the most effective tools at their disposal, largely for the same reason. No one ever seems to have considered *not* asking Indians to memorize the 129 questions and answers of the Heidelberg Catechism. Nor did the church in New Netherland create a classis or synod, which might have made a difference. It was no coincidence that the mission in Brazil only began with the formation of a classis. Because of translation, printing, travel costs, and other complications, missionary endeavors required intensive planning and coordination. New Netherland finally had enough clergy to consider a classis around the time of Brazil's collapse, but the churches at home, already sensitive about their control, resisted the idea of colonial councils because of scandalous ministers like Schagen and controversies like the one surrounding the Tupi catechism. When a former Brazil minister named Johannes Polhemus complained about communication in New Netherland and suggested a classis, the Amsterdam clergy just instructed him and his colleagues to write to each other more. When Reverend Megapolensis sent a manuscript for a simple catechism of his own creation, this one for the colonial youth, the same men tried to stop it. Though his effort was admirable, they wrote, it wouldn't be wise to use any book in the colonial churches—the "dependent churches"— that wasn't used in Holland. The accepted literature had been tested and found worthy, and anything else might lead to schism and confusion. In doctrine and liturgy, let us live in unity, the church repeated.[81]

Calvinist missionaries in the Dutch Caribbean and Wild Coast operated under similarly isolated, restrictive conditions. They did not at first have many potential proselytes in the islands, Indian or African, because a century and more of Spanish colonialism and slave raids had decimated the original Taíno and Carib populations. WIC commander Johannes van Walbeeck decided to deport most of the few hundred Native Americans on Curaçao. He didn't think the company could support them after the destruction of the invasion, and he didn't trust the Indians because, having lived so long under the Spanish, they were Catholic. He only let about eighteen families remain on the island on the promise that they would subject themselves to the Dutch.[82]

On paper, the church and company adopted benevolent, paternalistic rules and guidelines for Indians and slaves in Caribbean colonies: Indians must be paid for their work, not enslaved; blacks must be treated well; and both should be taught and attend church.[83] Clergy on Curaçao had limited success among the Indians who stayed there, possibly because they were already Christians and they were so few in number. They sometimes came to church, requested baptism for their children, and allowed their children to attend Dutch schools. The *ziekentrooster* Jan Walreven reported in 1649 that he and the local schoolmaster, Jan Galjaert, had been teaching European and Native American children together. Because their minister had just left for New Netherland, they didn't have anyone who could perform baptisms, but one of the WIC's French ministers stopped there during a tour of company islands and baptized fifteen children and twelve adult slaves. The latter had a fairly good Christian education, according to the minister, and they carried strong testimonials about their knowledge and conduct. Two passenger lists from 1660 suggest a kind of Dutch-native creolization by the second and third generations. Everyone listed as "Indians" had Dutch names.[84]

In every positive report, however, was a distrusting, doubtful, distancing attitude that only grew stronger in time. Reverend Johannes Backerus decried the "papist superstition" that still gripped the hearts of Indian churchgoers on Curaçao. Like Reverend Ketel at Luanda, he only baptized children because their parents were Christians. He didn't like doing so when the parents didn't really know Protestant doctrines, and he couldn't imagine "that they are included in God's covenant."[85] Reverend Adriaen Beaumont harbored the same misgivings in 1660 after performing a number of marriages and baptizing fifteen children, also on Curaçao. His superiors in Amsterdam responded to his explanations and justifications with a mild rebuke. Adult slaves and Indians must make a confession of faith before baptism, they said. He should not baptize any more children until their parents abandon "heathendom" and embrace the Christian lifestyle in its entirety, even if parents were previously baptized by Catholics. In his apology, Beaumont showed the same submissiveness and concern for his career that had driven some clergy home from Brazil. He confessed to acting too boldly in this case *because* of Brazil, probably meaning that the ease with which the Dutch had won Tupi converts caused misunderstandings about conversion and Native Americans in general. Now he promised to exercise even more caution in his work with non-Europeans.[86]

Inviting Africans and Native Americans to join the Christian community would have been problematic and impractical even without so many restrictive expectations because of the WIC's increasing dependence on slavery. Despite legal prohibitions, the Dutch even enslaved some Indians. The biggest culprits were the colonists and merchants of St. Eustatius, who kidnapped and sold Arawak Indians from the Essequibo colony and probably other places along the Wild Coast. During one three-year stretch, they absconded with eighty-one people from Essequibo alone. The commander there complained about the damage they were doing to the Dutch reputation and ability to interact with the Arawak, as did Stuyvesant. As joint governor of New Netherland and Curaçao, Stuyvesant issued instructions against Indian enslavement.[87] Yet he was willing to adopt the practice in limited circumstances. To punish the Esopus after the Esopus Wars, he claimed "all their land" and refused to return ten captives, shipping them instead to Curaçao "to be employed with the negros in the Company's service." Coincidentally, the ship that transported the Esopus was the *Nieuw Nederlantsche Indiaen.*[88]

By the 1660s, the Atlantic slave trade and black slavery in general were mature enough and valuable enough to destroy the cross-cultural, unifying religious opportunities of the past. After the war with Spain, islands like St. Eustatius and Curaçao had begun a slow transition from privateering bases and pitiable colonial laboratories to busy trade entrepôts, importing African slaves and manufactured European goods, then reexporting them to Spanish, French, and English colonies. The loss of Brazil expedited the transition because company employees and merchants scattered to other parts of the Dutch world, taking their numbers and knowledge with them. The WIC came to see the slave trade, which was one of its few remaining monopolies, as a way to restructure and unite its possessions. The other surviving remnant of the company's original designs was the hope that one or more of the small Wild Coast colonies might become a "new Brazil," centered on sugar and slave labor.[89]

These developments and changes in the slave system accompanied the erection of race-based walls in the Reformed Church. Where Dutch attitudes toward African slavery had begun with ambivalence and occasional discomfort and opposition, where "savagery" and cultural difference had always been more important than blackness, starting in the 1660s, Dutch writers and WIC directors embraced the so-called Hamitic myth, ascribing skin color and servitude to an ancient biblical curse.[90] The willingness of Reverend Bogardus to baptize and even serve as godfather to black children in New Netherland, cataloging white and black baptisms in the same record book, was, by the 1660s, a thing of the past. The slave trade to the WIC's North American colony hadn't been formalized and didn't start to flourish until New Netherland's final years, which transformed the small black population from "creole" to more clearly African and foreign. If the clergy of that era continued to baptize and marry slaves, the records are lost. Reverend Henricus Selyns demonstrated the new policy and mind-set in his outright refusal to baptize slaves in 1664. He preached to free blacks and slaves on the governor's farm, and he taught their children. But it had become "the custom among our colleagues," he wrote, to deny baptism to Africans "on account of their lack of knowledge and of faith, and partly because of the worldly and perverse aims on the part of said negroes." By "perverse," Selyns was referring to a parent's understandable, natural hope that his or her children might someday obtain freedom. Race-based slavery was changing everyone's understanding about what was natural and what was not.[91]

Slavery became a positive good for Calvinists insofar as it saved colonies that had struggled for years to find a purpose and grow beyond a few hundred inhabitants. The sugarcane at Essequibo gives us "new hope" and a newfound courage, wrote an enthusiastic colonist in the early 1660s. He praised God for the development and prayed for God's blessing on the crop.[92] According to Reverend Philippus Specht, many people who had formerly wandered from place to place were settling down at Curaçao, too. The loss of New Netherland to the English in 1664 probably had something to do with the island's newfound life and energy, but Specht gave the credit to the slave trade. "Because of the trade in negroes," the bay was full of ships, his congregation was growing, he was baptizing more than ever, and he was welcoming new members into the fold. Conversely, when the Dutch went to war again in 1672, the island—and by extension, Specht's church—were sleepy, sad places. The people who had begun their imperial experiment as violent aggressors and would-be saviors to slaves everywhere had reached a point where they could only thrive when their competitors agreed to leave them alone and let them traffic peacefully in human beings.[93]

Reverend Johannes Basseliers personified the new Dutch Atlantic and the spent, shrunken Calvinist mission of the WIC's last years. He was the first and, for a time, only Dutch Reformed minister in Suriname, which the company had exchanged for New Netherland at the end of the Second Anglo-Dutch War (1665–1667). In his isolation, Basseliers was like his predecessors, of course, because clergy of the Wild Coast, Caribbean, and New Netherland had often worked without companions (laymen excepted) and they had always worked without a local classis. He also knew the frustrations of predecessors in that his sincere, dedicated missionary efforts crumbled in the face of native independence and resistance. Like Michaelius and Megapolensis of New Netherland, he found that the Arawaks would never let him get close. They sometimes sat through a prayer or sermon, but they lived far away and refused further instruction. When Basseliers invited a native boy into his home, teaching him letters and prayers, the child's mother soon took him away. When he offered to build a residence next to his and invited Indians to live there and learn Dutch ways, they refused. Older Indians said they had never learned

European languages because their own mothers, when they were young, had not allowed it. And they wouldn't let Europeans live in their villages and learn their language with any real fluency.[94]

Basseliers personified the new Dutch Atlantic in that he lived and worked in the WIC's "new Brazil" and was himself a sugar planter and slave owner. He didn't just own one or two slaves as domestic servants, as company clergy often had. He owned several slaves and he supplemented his clerical income by participating in a burgeoning cash crop economy. Basseliers now shared in the widespread commitment to slavery and the subjection of peoples his predecessors had pledged to save, both physically and spiritually. Naïvety, indigenous disinterest, a too-controlling church, and the loss of so many colonies to rebellion and conquest destroyed the Dutch mission before anyone could develop effective programs and solutions to missionary challenges. The Dutch had resisted domination and subjection for a time. In purchasing their land in North America, accepting the Tupi decision not to participate in the boarding school, and acceding to their requests for self-government—even allowing the Iroquois and Arawaks the cultural space they wanted, essentially abandoning the mission—the Dutch showed that they could keep their first idealistic promises. Yet they did forsake those promises. Given the general trends of their colonial ideology and activities, subjection may have been the solution to missionary challenges even in a hypothetical Atlantic empire where they somehow managed to keep their earliest conquests and colonies.

CHAPTER 8

God and Mammon in the Dutch Atlantic World

Conflict over Religious Resources and Power

From 1662 to 1674, when the West India Company finally declared bankruptcy, individual company chambers bickered with their local Reformed churches over the question of clerical appointments: Should the church continue to recruit potential colonial clergy and introduce them to the company, or could the company act alone, finding its own favorite personnel before bringing them to the church for the exams? And who should issue the final, formal, written calling? Because clergy sometimes sided with the WIC's critics overseas, the directors were probably seeking greater loyalty and control. But the churches at home objected to all "innovations" and "novelties" in the decades-old hiring process. The Walcheren classis even announced that, if any change was made, it would stop participating altogether. Owing also to the WIC's financial trouble and declining church activity among third- and fourth-generation directors, church-company relations reached an all-time low.[1]

Disagreements between secular and religious authorities were common in early modern Europe. John Calvin had originally envisioned a civic-ecclesiastical system in which church and state cooperated peacefully to provide for the spiritual and temporal welfare of all people. The church would preach the Gospel, administer the sacraments, regulate relationships, and care for the poor; civic leaders would make godly laws, punish criminals in secular courts, and protect the church from heresy and schism. To borrow a term from

Diarmaid MacCulloch, Calvin intended the "hierarchy of authorities" and institutions on the one hand to parallel and complement the authorities and institutions on the other.[2] Famously, the ministers and magistrates of Calvin's Geneva quarreled almost as much as they cooperated. The city's longtime elites worried about losing their control, and they bristled when the ministers, most of whom, like Calvin, were foreigners, criticized them publicly and subjected them to humiliating discipline. Separate, complementary spheres of power easily became competitive and contentious when the line between them was so hazy and thin.

Similar tensions and problems existed wherever people adopted some version of Calvin's system, including the Netherlands and its joint-stock companies and colonies. Power-sharing arrangements in the Netherlands are difficult to pin down because compromises differed from province to province and town to town. Suffice it to say, rulers tended to resist a powerful church and clergy tended to guard their independence and control over membership and appointments, resulting in a long, sometimes-ugly tug-of-war. If anything, conditions in the WIC should have been worse because of the extra layers of authority. I have focused until now on concord and cooperation because they were also common, and historians have usually highlighted the conflict over the cooperation. However, I have addressed some of those conflicts. Examples include the Doornick affair in Brazil, the fight over Kieft's War and WIC governance in New Amsterdam, and regular allegations of disrespect, corruption, and connivance in the face of heresy and sin.

The difficulty for WIC leaders lay in running a business while simultaneously bearing the responsibilities of a huge, scattered state. Without any precedent, they couldn't know where their religious duties ended and their responsibilities to investors began, where to draw the boundary between God and Mammon in an organization that, by its very nature, served both.[3] In a comparable dilemma, colonial clergy were virtual servants of Mammon, a different breed of employee than colleagues paid by municipal or provincial governments in Europe. They worked for quasi-private companies whose success and failure had significant implications for their own livelihoods and the spread of their religion. In these organizations God and Mammon didn't just exist uncomfortably side by side; they were partners. Colonial clergy struggled to understand their relationship to this new kind of state, which was ostensibly subjected to the traditional state at home. They fluctuated between criticism and support, sometimes siding with WIC opponents to condemn alleged greed and neglect, sometimes praising it and tackling materialistic tasks on the company's behalf.

As the WIC exported the ideas and forms of the Protestant Reformation, it exported and refashioned the Reformation's internal tensions, as well. Whether any particular political or economic choice made one a "bad ruler" or a "bad minister" was usually open to interpretation and debate. No matter where it occurred, conflict between secular and ecclesiastical leaders had less to do with religion in a strict theological sense and more to do with the heightened clash of individual personalities in divided colonial settings. If we add to this potent, sensitive mix the seventeenth-century tendency to sacralize everything from warfare to commerce and governance, it's a wonder anyone ever got along. They did so more commonly in prosperous times. Again, money troubles and declining church activity among the directors heightened tensions in the WIC's later years. In addition, the company employed in that era a growing number of young clergy who, in part *because* of their youth, refused to restrain their righteous zeal in the interest of peace. With few local outlets to resolve grievances, colonial churches easily became alternate centers of power, natural hubs of opposition to unpopular policies and rulers.

The Real-World Costs of Religion

Clerical pay and funding for chapels, charity, and education were some of the company's greatest costs and potential sources of dispute. The WIC's strategy was to balance diverse expenses and find creative ways to spread or share them with legislative bodies like the States General and with the employees and colonists who benefited from public institutions. States General subsidies and colonial fines and taxes could only do so much, of course, because the States General wasn't a bottomless, magical well, and colonists had even fewer resources. The company's burden and dilemma was to found expensive communities and turn a profit before the new communities were well enough developed to pay for themselves, which did not bode well for said profits.

Deciding how much the WIC was willing to fund its religious mission in the Dutch Atlantic—putting a total price tag on religion, so to speak—is impossible now, but it wasn't cheap. The first items in the company's debit column would have come from its expenses at home: charitable activity in Europe and costs associated with training future colonial clergy. By way of reminder, the WIC gave one penny per thousand from all imported goods to Dutch-, French-, and English-speaking deaconries in the towns with company chambers. And most directors gave separate, individual contributions, too. They also paid or subsidized the educations of an unknown number of Calvinist refugees and other individuals from the 1620s through the 1640s, sometimes expecting repayment and sometimes acting in a more purely charitable fashion.

After alms and ecclesiastical training, the company's third and greatest expense involved salaries and other remuneration. Ministers and lay clergy contracted to work from one to four years, although they could extend afterward. Lay clergy earned between ƒ 8 and ƒ 40 per month. On the one extreme were the company's few indigenous clergy, on the other were experienced Europeans who had renewed their contracts and taken on extra duties, like teaching school. The average pay for white lay clergy was about ƒ 24 per month. They also enjoyed free food, lodging, and a seat at the governor's table with the other officers, which carried a social standing they might have lacked before. By contrast, sailors and soldiers earned between ƒ 8 and ƒ 14 per month.[4] Ministers usually earned ƒ 100 per month, with some exceptions: *proponents* (apprentice ministers) and non-Amsterdam clergy could earn as little as ƒ 40. When they arrived in America and began comparing their era's version of the pay stub, the men who were earning less weren't happy about the differences, and the directors were eventually forced to put all Brazilian ministers on the same footing. Like *ziekentroosters*, ministers received lodging, a place at the governor's table, or more often, in lieu of both, an added stipend called *kostgeld*, which started out in Brazil at about ƒ 24 per month. They also received a white servant or African slave.[5]

On the face of it, WIC compensation was strong, even greater than clerical pay in the Netherlands, where ministers also enjoyed benefits like housing but earned between ƒ 500 and ƒ 1,000 per year, depending on the location. The ƒ 1,200 that the company paid to so many ministers was, by comparison, competitive, and it was higher than the wages of most employees, placing clergy somewhere in the upper middle class. The fact that they worked in small, confined communities also gave them a greater prominence than ecclesiastical colleagues at home.[6]

Dutch taxpayers defrayed some of these salary costs via the five admiralties that oversaw customs and naval matters in most of the same towns and cities with WIC offices. The admiralties paid clerical salaries in some of the company's early military fleets, presumably because they had hired the personnel to whom the clergy preached.[7] The company also tried to cut ecclesiastical costs at one point by deducting a small percentage from the wages of sailors and soldiers. But it was a very unpopular policy, and it didn't last long. The Amsterdam chamber began the practice in October 1636 with all new hires. The first sign of trouble appeared about three years later, when men returned to the Netherlands and tried to collect their earnings. One *ziekentrooster* reported to the classis that he had heard lots of grumbling at the West

Indies House. Colonial ministers were soon writing about resentment among employees overseas, which undermined clerical standing and the work of the church in general. The deduction must have been a company-wide practice, because the Zeeland directors mentioned it in 1641, writing that it was in fact causing discontent and "contempt" for the ministers. The Amsterdam classis had been working with its own chamber about the policy, and the Nineteen Lords agreed in November to end it.[8]

High wages could be deceptive because of scarcity, inflation, and a lack of specie in the colonies, which inspired countless complaints and quarrels through the years.[9] So bad were some colonial economies, especially in times of war, the Walcheren classis asked that both companies be more generous with salaries. At first the WIC refused, and at one point it even tried to end the housing allowance in Brazil. But the idea died when clergy threatened to leave the colony en masse. Eventually the directors agreed to give an extra f 6 per month per child to ministers with children, and the company slowly raised everyone's *kostgeld* from f 24 to f 42 per month. A few men in Brazil received as much as f 100.[10]

Ministers were not unique in suffering from inflation and related financial difficulties, and again, they were among the more affluent members of society. Even in Brazil, which had the worst inflation, complaints centered on the food and housing allowance, not the salary. Salaries were usually credited to one's name in an ever-increasing total, collected sometimes overseas and sometimes in Europe by wives and children. More often the salary sat untouched for future use, more of a retirement fund than a salary per se. Reverends Thomas Kemp and Johannes Apricius both lived through the worst of Brazil and had a credit of greater than f 4,000 when they returned. Reverend Henricus Hermannius, a German minister who worked in Brazil at the same time, was owed f 8,000 after nine years, meaning that he had "borrowed" little more than a third of his salary. Perhaps using any of it was contrary to the WIC's promises, but it hardly meant poverty. When New Amsterdam colonists were asked to contribute to local defenses during the Anglo-Dutch Wars, Reverends Johannes Megapolensis and Samuel Drisius were two of the greatest donors at f 600 and f 500: an entire year's worth of earnings for rural clergy in Holland. With just f 1,000 one could purchase a small home in Holland, and unmarried Dutch laborers could meet their basic, indispensable needs on about f 80 per year.[11]

The WIC's fourth major expense involved church facilities. In Brazil the company didn't have to construct many new buildings because it could just commandeer them from the Portuguese. It did, however, build some, and it had to employ carpenters to make repairs. The WIC built or subsidized new chapels in Brazil at Mauritsstad, Cabo St. Agostinho, Goiana, and St. Antônio do Cabo, and in New Netherland at New Amsterdam, Rensselaerswijck, New Amersfoort, and Midwout. The company paid ƒ 4,000 for the Huguenot chapel in Mauritsstad, at least ƒ 1,000 and ƒ 2,000 for the buildings at St. Agostinho and St. Antônio, and an unknown amount for Goiana's. The High Council obtained another ƒ 4,000 for the Huguenot chapel from a Jewish merchant, fined for blasphemy. For the rest, the council imposed temporary duties on sugar exports and consumption taxes on items like wine and beer in areas with new churches. Any additional needs were raised locally through private subscription.[12] Likewise, the New Amsterdam chapel was partly funded by subscription and partly by the company. The patroon Kiliaen van Rensselaer paid for the chapel at Rensselaerswijck. Years later, his son Jan Baptist van Rensselaer spent ƒ 1,000 on a larger building, procuring an additional ƒ 1,500 in legal fines from the local court. The directors sometimes contributed the finishing touches, meaning pulpits and bells.[13]

The company incurred its fifth and sixth major expenses from institutions that weren't strictly ecclesiastical but still involved the church: poor relief and schools. As they did in the Netherlands, deacons cared for the poor, yet they had extra burdens in Brazil because the invasion and ongoing conflicts there left many widows and orphans and filled the hospital to overflowing. The typical means of obtaining alms in weekly services or door-to-door collections and boxes that hung throughout Recife were never enough. Redirected to the deacons, the lands and rents that used to support the Catholic priesthood were less productive than they had been before the invasion. The deaconry also received money from wills, legal fines, naval prizes, occasional taxes and tolls, and the directors and churches in the Netherlands. The High Council paid additional costs directly, just as governments at home subsidized their deacons. Already by 1644, before the Portuguese uprising made everything worse, the WIC had disbursed ƒ 60,000 for poor relief.[14]

New Netherland deacons had some similar expenses and similar sources of income. They had the same collections and scattered boxes, and they got money from legal fines and rare naval prizes. In a different, less aggressive version of the appropriated lands and rents in Brazil, the deacons in New Netherland also owned livestock and a farm on Long Island: the "poor farm," they called it.[15] One serious difference between poor relief in the two colonies was the relative financial health of the New Netherland deaconries. Where deacons in Brazil had to borrow money from the company, in North America it was the company and town governments that sometimes borrowed money from the deacons; and they gave loans to creditworthy colonists, too. In that sense they acted as a charitable institution and a bank: they lent money at interest in order to secure their financial future and ensure that they would always have the resources to satisfy their social charge.[16] While they weren't by any means wealthy, especially in their early years, they were successful enough in the long term to contribute ƒ 2,000, for example, for colonial defense. And when those defenses failed, they had the resources to redeem captives from Native American enemies.[17]

Company-affiliated schools existed in most Dutch territories, including West Africa and the Caribbean. The burden on the WIC in each case depended on the size of the local population and the ability and willingness of parents to defray educational costs. Schools were an ecclesiastical institution insofar as the church helped examine and appoint Calvinist schoolmasters, and the schoolmasters had to teach religious lessons from the Heidelberg Catechism. The WIC and the patroons paid salaries and provided Bibles, catechisms, psalm books, ABC books, paper and ink, and a space to teach. Again, parents helped defray these costs by contributing to the schoolmaster's salary, but they only had to do so if they (the parents) weren't on the company's payroll. The company bore the entire expense for any school in any place that didn't yet have a sizable colonial population. Only as the colonies grew could the WIC shift some costs to parents and taxpayers.[18]

In addition to the six categories listed here, the company had to make financial arrangements for the Tupi mission in Brazil and for all translation and printing needs. And there were countless smaller religious costs. At the request of the Recife classis, for instance, WIC directors hired a clerk to copy and send Holland's synodal minutes to the colony every year, providing an archive of the most recent Reformed decision making.[19] Other costs included horses for clergy in the army and regular cash disbursements to cover travel expenses when ministers had to go anywhere to organize a new consistory, check on existing churches, and preach and administer sacraments in towns with lay preachers.[20] Also expensive were the annual and biannual classis meetings in Brazil. They brought together every minister and at least one elder from every consistory in the colony, no matter how distant. Each person needed travel money, food, and lodging in Recife for about a week. The company sometimes paid the attendees cash and sometimes allowed them to eat with the High Council. In other years it utilized a combination of cash and WIC stores, even asking Reformed merchants to open their homes. With such high inflation, and with so many men, each of Brazil's twenty-three meetings cost thousands of guilders. One year the council had so little money and so few stores on hand, it canceled the synod altogether, which caused a minor scandal at home. Eventually it decided to cut costs by withholding the subsidy from the men who lived in Recife. The local clergy and elders were not happy, but this time the council stuck with its resolution.[21]

The price of religion in the Dutch Atlantic was steep. Given the number of clergy, salaries alone would have cost more than ƒ1,000,000 over the company's fifty-three years. And *kostgeld* would have added between 25 percent and 40 percent to that total.[22] Add up all the other religious costs and the WIC's civic purpose and functions start to overshadow its commercial ones, especially after it lost the fur and sugar monopolies. If it tried to save money and access alternate sources of funding, it was just balancing its corporate interests and financial well-being against its ecclesiastical responsibilities and oft-proclaimed goals of spreading the true religion. And the choices it made, like refusing to pay the Recife elders and ministers the same stipend as others for attending meetings *in* Recife, were not unreasonable. Not caring about costs would have meant an even shorter path to bankruptcy, a surer way to ruin whatever hopes the church had in America. Clergy who ignored the company's financial dilemmas in favor of their own dilemmas weren't being selfish either, because they endured real economic suffering. But most employees and colonial institutions shared in their troubles. The directors didn't neglect the church as much as they drove the WIC into the ground and took everything, including the church, with them.

Separating the Sheep and the Goats

Whether a conflict was about money or politics or anything else, the fight alone is insufficient evidence of inadequacy and incompetence on the part of secular and ecclesiastical opponents. Clergy might not like it when rulers meddled too much in religious affairs and rulers might decry too much politicking and materialism in their ministers, but the definition of "too much" could change from person to person and from council to council, growing especially muddled in Africa and America. The process of building and acquiring new colonies created unexpected burdens and pushed clergy into roles and activities they might have eschewed in Europe. Those decisions sometimes opened them up to criticism and accusations of impropriety. Only rarely, however, did they cross clear lines and garner enemies on both ends of the secular-ecclesiastical spectrum.

Complaints about lay preachers tended to come in spurts: first during the major fleet actions and hiring rush of the early 1630s, then again in the early 1640s. By that time the churches at home had established clear vetting

procedures, but the complaints started up again anyway. Upon investigation the church concluded that the fault didn't lie with its clergy, nor have
anything to do with their knowledge and skills. Rather, colonial ministers reported that the issue was one of respect and power. Some WIC captains, they
claimed, wouldn't give the *ziekentroosters* access to the captain's cabin and
table, as per their contracts. When the Amsterdam classis took these reports
to the company, the directors issued orders to set the officers straight, and
complaints about *ziekentroosters* dried up. Overall, their position was potentially contentious because, despite their public voice, they didn't fit clearly in
the WIC's hierarchy and command structure. On paper they belonged to the
officer corps, sometimes bearing the honorific *dominie* ("reverend"). Yet their
plebeian backgrounds and lack of formal training inspired extra resentment
among political and military peers who were sensitive to correction even
when it came from the learned, ordained ministers.[23]

Some *ziekentroosters* got in trouble with the church because of a similar am-
biguity regarding baptism and preaching. In general they weren't supposed to
do either, although the churches at home could and did make exceptions,
which were the probable source of confusion. They allowed lay baptism at
least once each in Africa and Asia before the WIC was founded, then did the
same in New Netherland and on the islands of Fernando de Noronha and
St. Martin afterward—places with small European populations and some pros-
pect of children or converts, approved in the Netherlands at the time of the
clergy's call.[24] The trouble came from *ziekentroosters* who performed baptisms
or preached extemporaneously without any approval. Their superiors might
feel strongly enough about the issue to label them "dissolute" and "ungodly."
And they even determined at one point that all lay baptisms were invalid.
But in more charitable moments those same superiors conceded that impro-
visation was necessary in isolated corners of the empire. Their sporadic
indignation was another manifestation of the church's general sensitivity to
questions of power and control, perhaps heightened in places like Brazil
because of the spiritual contest with Catholic priests.[25]

Rarely did a layman's secular work generate criticism. In fact, company directors appointed some *ziekentroosters* and schoolmasters jointly to positions
like factor and master's mate. If they didn't serve double duty from the start,
which wasn't common, many men did accept additional jobs overseas. After
his Latin school in Brazil failed to attract enough students, Bartholomeus Cole
became WIC clerk. Curaçao schoolmaster Jan Galjaert worked also as the
"overseer" of company goats. And Jan Huygen, an early New Netherland
ziekentrooster, was the WIC's storekeeper. Fellow *ziekentrooster* Bastiaen Jansz

Krol was very involved in the fur trade there, eventually rising to the position of commander at Fort Orange and even provisional governor.[26]

Secular labor was only a problem—sometimes a controversy—for ordained ministers. They didn't need the extra work because they earned so much more than lay preachers. But they could still serve the WIC in a secular sense, not fearing any blowback, in limited circumstances. If the company was the vehicle through which God established his work in America, as so many believed, who really could criticize clergy for advancing its interests? Who defined words like "secular" and "religious"?[27] Most simply, they reported regularly to colonial governors and the directors in Europe about the availability of lumber and fresh water in their new homes, the quality of local soil and its potential for livestock, sugar, manioc, and other agriculture, the existence of salt pans and mineral deposits, unfamiliar plant life and its possible uses, and the availability and need for supplies like medicine and gun powder. They shared their opinions on contentious issues like the company monopolies, and they acted as deputies from the colonies to the directors, the States General, and the prince of Orange on political and military matters. Sometimes acting in an official capacity and sometimes offering their views unsolicited, they were exceptional emissaries because of their education and frequent movement and contacts throughout the Atlantic world.[28]

Clergy wandered into questionable territory when some activity took them away from their church work. But even then they could justify their decisions and avoid trouble. The most obviously unacceptable labor or pursuit was for personal gain, as opposed to something that at least benefited the company and community. Reverend Daniel Schagen's is the best example: his plantation in Brazil profited no one but himself and kept him from his duties, including his Sabbath-day duties, so he was forced to return to Holland. On the other hand, Reverend Cornelius van der Poel once accepted a political commission to travel to the distant province of Maranhão to scout its condition and economic potential. He canoed "66 miles above the furthest plantation" on the Itapecuru River and later reported in Recife on the surrounding lands and unhealthy climate. Absent from his post for weeks, the Recife consistory complained to the High Council, but Van der Poel wasn't disciplined.[29]

Reverends Van der Poel, Stetten, and Kemp were all involved in the mining industry, which they celebrated as a godly enterprise because it could fund their anti-Catholic wars and the Indian mission. Stetten came closest to crossing the line of acceptable clerical behavior. In truth, had he identified a gold deposit, he probably would have left his vocation in the church. One of the earliest, longest-serving ministers in Brazil, the classis almost dismissed him during the reformation of 1636–1637 for unknown reasons, and he turned to mining during the brief period before his reinstatement. He had some experience with the work already, boasting the necessary education and a knowledge of minerals, possibly because he was a German refugee and some of Europe's important mining centers were in the Holy Roman Empire. When he requested books, he knew specific titles, and he asked for equipment from "Duytslandt" (Germany).[30] As a refugee, his relationship with the directors was unique. They were not just his employers but his patrons, and he groveled before them, connecting the WIC's work with God's work even more than most men. He had "nothing left in the world" and must "begin here anew," he wrote. He was an unworthy, humble, "faithful servant," always prepared to demonstrate his gratitude. He prayed for the directors' health and happiness, thanked God for their success, and vowed to serve them until his death. In the perfect illustration of the partnership between piety and trade, betraying none of the usual Protestant anxieties about church décor and idolatry, Stetten affixed a large WIC logo to the new chapel at Cabo St. Agostinho. In doing so, he explained, he intended to honor the company and proclaim the directors' first church in that region.[31]

The same partnership was apparent in Stetten's work at the mine. Seven years after his reinstatement, the WIC's finances growing worse daily, the High Council asked him (or agreed to his request) to return to the place where he had previously searched for gold. The council handed him the perfect opportunity: he could serve his family, the company, and the "fatherland" at the same time. With a group of soldiers, miners, Tupi Indians, and African slaves, he traveled to his old site and, after calling on God with "folded hands" and "bowed knees," began to dig, sending occasional samples of ore to the council, which shipped them to the Netherlands. Later recounting his prayer to the directors, he asked that "God would . . . animate me with the Holy Spirit and lead me in this work: to begin, arrange, and execute it for the praise and honor of the Holy Trinity, for you and your posterity's benefit and profit, that the congregation of Jesus Christ be assisted here and in all lands and the enemies of God and his word be destroyed." Stetten hoped to provide great riches, he continued. After his miners had cleared one promising vein, "I went with everyone into the mountain and exhorted them to thank God Almighty with me, from their hearts, that he would continue to bless us with these gifts." He also asked his motley crew to sing a "hymn of praise" before setting them to work on a new vein. Since many of them probably couldn't speak or read Dutch, theirs could not have been a very rousing refrain.[32]

In light of Schagen's plantation and the complaints about Van der Poel's assignment, Stetten's mining, which occupied him for about five months, pro-

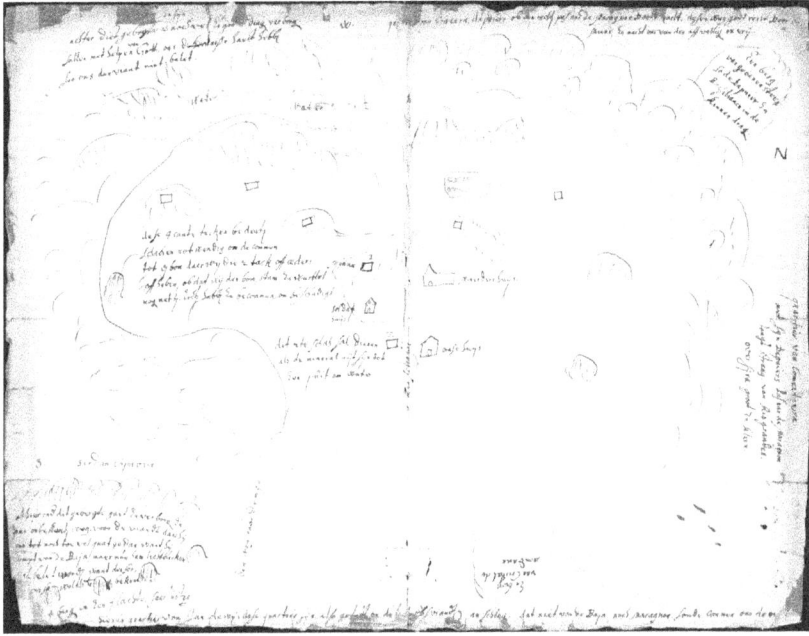

Rev. Jodocus à Stetten's map of his Brazilian mine. In the Old West India Company Collection at the Nationaal Archief, The Hague.

voked surprisingly little controversy. There must have been some grumbling, for in his letters he mentioned people who wondered "if it is lawful for a minister to do such things." Yet the church covered for him by adding his old post to the route of the traveling ministers, visited every other week, and his colleagues didn't talk about his mining adventure at either of the classes before or afterward. He responded to critics with another speech on the godly uses of gold and silver: "I say it is lawful for any man to provide the means of waging a righteous war against the unbelieving enemies of God and his Holy Word, for the protection of the congregation of Christ." Precious metals supplied physical nourishment, sustained the true religion and congregation of God, and again, enabled the WIC to wage its "righteous war against our enemies and God's."[33] Stetten grew more personally involved in the war during the Portuguese revolt, when the council asked him to accompany a group of Tapuya Indians against the rebels in Rio Grande. He said he was "entirely willing" to accept the assignment and "whatever else the company's service might require."[34]

Reverend Kemp's mining experience was less dubious than Stetten's, yet almost as confused in its objectives and still very different from clerical work in the Netherlands. Also a foreigner (an Englishman), Kemp was asked to travel to the province of Ceará four years after Stetten's failed experiment. Kemp did not go as the head of his expedition, but accompanied an elder in the Recife consistory, Matthias Beck, as assistant and translator. With soldiers, miners, slaves, and Indians, they sought to reclaim the province for the Dutch and pursue rumors of precious metals. Kemp also baptized and enlisted Indians, which legitimized his involvement. Yet he wasn't just a missionary. Besides preaching, baptizing, and performing marriages, he questioned Indians about local conditions, delivered gifts and messages from Beck, and pressured native leaders to locate old, forgotten mines. He also accompanied Beck to inspect them, once located, and the main Indian town served as a meeting place to collect minerals. When Kemp was away from the fort in pursuit of converts, Beck appointed a lay preacher to offer the evening prayers and ask for a divine blessing on their project. Once again proving the ability to make any endeavor godly, Beck said that the mine was really for the Indians: "This work . . . will be for their preservation and prosperity," he told Kemp. Although they now go "naked and bare, without clothing," the mine would supply an "abundance" of every necessity. They could labor in it and provide other useful services to the Dutch, who would reward them fairly, Beck asserted.[35]

Comparable examples in New Netherland include Reverends Megapolensis and Drisius. The former signed a contract in which he promised his new boss, the onetime WIC director and patroon Kiliaen van Rensselaer, that he would "befriend and serve the Patroon in all things," as long as Megapolensis could do so "without interfering with or impending his [ecclesiastical] duties." Over the next years, the minister was a long-distance advisor and agent for Van Rensselaer, who remained in Europe. Megapolensis arbitrated among Van Rensselaer's other officers and agents when they didn't get along. He witnessed deeds, dabbled in matters of farming and labor, passed on messages from the patroon, and, in a sense, spied for him. Similarly, the colonial council appointed Megapolensis as an arbiter during the Kieft-Bogardus quarrels of the 1640s. After Kieft and Bogardus drowned in the *Princess Amelia* shipwreck, Megapolensis reported, "I attempted several times to smooth the differences which had arisen here, but all in vain."[36]

Moving from Rensselaerswijck to New Amsterdam in 1648, Megapolensis didn't have all the same diverse responsibilities, probably because the capital was more developed and had more clergy than his original American home. But he did still advise WIC rulers, and there is some evidence that he was a friend and guest in their homes. He was also the likely author of a prayer recorded in the inaugural minutes of the New Amsterdam court in 1653. Not quite as jolting as Stetten's prayers about gold and mining, the Megapolensis prayer communicated the same reverence for secular power and callings. However unworthy, men owed their position to God, he wrote; and God's word would guide the court's decisions and make it "a terror to evil-doers." The prayer's other possible author, the English-speaking Reverend Drisius, agreed the same year to serve his governor and the WIC by traveling to Virginia to negotiate a peace treaty and commercial pact with that colony.[37]

Both ministers had skills and knowledge that were rare enough and valuable enough to ignore church policies regarding superfluous clerical labor, especially when their labors benefited the company and community more than the individual. Calvinist theologians and influential church councils tried to hold ministers to a high standard of plain living and keep them focused on their main duties, just as they taught austerity and social, religious responsibility to merchants. The concept and language of secular-ecclesiastical separation had existed in Christianity for centuries: "Render therefore unto Caesar the things which are Caesar's; and unto God the things that are God's," and most famously, "Ye cannot serve God and mammon."[38] When they tried, however, Christians had never really known how to satisfy those charges. In an era when church and state were still conjoined, when so many believers saw their every undertaking through the lens of faith, they couldn't easily determine where God's work ended and the service of Mammon began. Life under a large company in a foreign land added whole new layers of complexity and possibility, creating new so-called religious responsibilities and new ways to serve a state that was so much more than a state.

Megapolensis's stepson is one example of someone who did finally cross lines and earn the ire of fellow ministers, not for extra labors or squabbling with the WIC, but for a combination of marital discord and defying church authority. His name was Reverend Wilhelmus Grasmeer, and he replaced Megapolensis in Rensselaerswijck after Megapolensis moved to New Amsterdam. The problem was that, because of the ongoing, unresolved situation with his wife, he had left the Netherlands without the proper dismissals, testimonials, and permissions. In other words, he used his family connections to skirt the usual hiring process.[39]

So egregious did they find his choices, Grasmeer's old Alkmaar classis worked with the Amsterdam classis first to stop him and then, when they learned of his departure and appointment, make him return to Europe. In the next months they held a slew of meetings and sent numerous letters and warnings about the "scandalous" minister. Do not let him officiate in any office, they instructed their American counterparts.[40] More than once they wrote to

Governor Petrus Stuyvesant, the New Amsterdam consistory, and even the people of Rensselaerswijck, imploring them to end their new relationship with Grasmeer and deport him. Four European supporters defended him at North Holland's next synod, blaming the whole fiasco on his allegedly querulous, violent wife, but the synod maintained a united front. Finally, almost two years after leaving Holland, Grasmeer succumbed to pressure and gave up his post. With ten months of additional meetings, apologies, a reunion with his wife, and on the strength of strong testimonials from colonists, he cleared his name. By that point, though, the Dutch Republic was at war with England, and fearing for his safety, he chose not to risk a third crossing.[41]

The Grasmeer episode was just one of several similar episodes in the mid-seventeenth-century Dutch Atlantic, all of them demonstrating the church's serious concern regarding the quality of colonial ministers and the lengths it would go to guard and control colonial religion. Although Grasmeer had the support of his old consistory in the Netherlands, although his new American congregation was happy with his appointment, none of it was enough. The division between him and his wife and classis—and his evading the usual channels of authority—were violations of such magnitude that the church couldn't ignore them. No matter one's talents and no matter the distance, it wouldn't tolerate men who flouted hiring policies and escaped the vetting process.[42]

In the end, many disputes and allegations of clerical misconduct boiled down to questions of power and the perceived violation of extremely hazy religio-political and economic boundaries. From the lowly lay preachers who claimed a moral charge over higher-ranking officers to the ordained ministers who took on nonessential secular duties; from the laymen who exercised vital but unsanctioned spiritual powers to the independent Grasmeers of the Dutch Empire, operating for a time outside the church hierarchy: in their various wanderings it was easy to step on someone else's toes and threaten someone else's authority. The number of truly bad clergy—meaning those who lacked the necessary skills, refused to do their jobs, or flouted Calvinist morality—was relatively small. Perhaps 25 of 360 known ministers and laymen belong in that category. Examples include the *ziekentrooster* Christoffel Cornelisz, who fathered an illegitimate child with his own slave, sold them both, then established a tavern, and Reverend Gilbertus de Vaux, who fought with other ministers and WIC officers everywhere he went. The governor of Brazil said that his conduct ranged from "bad to worse," and he speculated that De Vaux was insane. Men like him generated a disproportionate amount of controversy and had a disproportionate impact on the reputation of clergy in general.[43]

The Company's Protracted Decline

According to the Gospel of Matthew, Jesus Christ once said that "all they that take the sword shall perish with the sword."[44] Few if any Calvinist clergy seem to have shared that message with WIC directors, neither before nor after they began their work in the Atlantic world. Nevertheless, it was still fitting that the WIC, born in a war that so many supporters called holy, died in the Portuguese revolt of 1645–1654. Obviously the directors didn't think their company was dead at that point. They continued to resuscitate its bloodied, spoilt carcass for decades before finally giving up and accepting bankruptcy in 1674. So dependent was the church on the WIC, the church's mission and relationship with the company suffered most during the latter's interminable death throes.

As the costs of conquest piled up and the directors failed year after year to recoup the WIC's losses, the lesser company chambers increasingly shirked their ecclesiastical commitments and the Zeeland and Amsterdam chambers were left holding the bag. They filled their own quotas and sometimes more, but they also sometimes turned the church away empty-handed, arguing that the other chambers needed to contribute personnel too. The church pressured the lesser chambers, and the Nineteen Lords issued directives in 1645 and 1647 about how many clergy each of them would hire in the future.[45] At least one former colonial minister, Nicolaus Ketel, suggested that the church address the problem by letting American consistories and classes examine and call their own clergy from among the local colonists, which probably would have accomplished more than any other proposal. But the Amsterdam classis always cared more about quality and control than it did simple numbers. The States General helped out by sending two ministers to Brazil in 1647 and funding additional personnel with money from a much larger subsidy bestowed on the WIC in 1653.[46]

Clerical recruitment and retention suffered when rumors began to spread that the WIC wouldn't be able to satisfy all its debts. *Ziekentrooster* Jan Walreven wrote from Curaçao in 1649 that, according to his contacts, the longest-serving ministers had the most trouble getting their pay. "Therefore," he continued, "I am requesting of their honors that when I have served my time, they will be pleased to release me."[47] And the rumors proved true: as clergy came home from Africa and America in the late 1640s and 1650s with thousands of guilders credited to their accounts, the directors couldn't and didn't pay them in a timely manner. The Dutch States General went so far as to order a formal freeze on all salaries as it tried to help the company sort through the increasing financial morass. Even with regular intervention and advocacy from Reformed classes and synods, some men had to wait years for their money, and even then compensation could take the form of low-interest bonds. Not surprisingly, more and more potential ministers wanted to serve the East India Company, not the West India Company.[48]

In many respects the relationship between church and company did not change. They continued to cooperate as they always had; their burden was just greater after the Portuguese revolt and their resources more scarce. Solutions to challenges like Tupi poverty and increased numbers of widows and orphans in Brazil usually involved raising funds through Protestant charitable networks, then shipping linens and other necessities to colonial deaconries on the next available WIC vessel. Donors during the years-long Tupi collection included the States of Zeeland, the prince of Orange, and at least six Dutch Reformed classes in Holland and Zeeland.[49] When these efforts fell short, the deaconries in Brazil actually started returning poor European women and orphans to the Netherlands, no longer able to support them. The orphans were divided among the different WIC chambers, and each chamber conferred them in turn on local municipal authorities. For the children in the Amsterdam orphanage, the directors gave coins and other gold and silver paraphernalia worth f 1,304. The Zeeland deacons at first received no support for their colonial orphans, but the company eventually donated an unspecified amount of West African gold.[50]

The WIC had to pay clerical widows whatever it still owed their husbands at the time of death, plus an extra three or four months' salary and *kostgeld*.[51] But these widows didn't obtain their funds any more promptly than anyone else. Combined with all the other mounting payment problems, their experiences contributed as much as anything to the company's bad reputation and new accusations of greed and neglect. Probably the longest, most frustrating story was that of Rachel à Stetten, whose case was unusually complicated because her sometimes-miner, sometimes-minister husband, Jodocus à Stetten, didn't die but was taken captive during his military expedition with the Tapuya Indians. Things probably would have been better for Rachel if he had died, for she never saw him again anyway, and his confused ecclesiastical, military functions and years-long absence allowed each layer of the hierarchical company and federalist Dutch state to dismiss her claims to his salary or pass her along as someone else's responsibility. Her greatest advocates were the different bodies of the Reformed Church, which represented her repeatedly before the High Council in Brazil and the directors and States General in the Netherlands, winning minor concessions like *kostgeld*. After her husband died in captivity, the Amsterdam and Walcheren classes helped her obtain f 100 from the Zeeland directors and, one year later, f 118 in cash and a f 500 bond. For her other needs, she lived the last six years of her life on church alms.[52]

Rachel à Stetten pleaded her own case in a 1652 letter to the Amsterdam classis. Although she never got what she wanted, the letter is worth quoting at length because there is so little other surviving correspondence from the wives of company clergy. More importantly, it reveals her sense of mistreatment and the WIC's reluctance after the Portuguese revolt to pay anything more than it had to pay. "Overwhelming need requires that I, with this missive, implore Your Honors for help," Rachel began.

> It was about five years ago that the government asked my husband, Jodocus à Stetten, a minister, to serve in the army in Rio Grande, which he accepted on certain conditions: to wit, that I, for the support of myself and my children, would enjoy in his absence his monthly *kostgeld* and lodging, and in case he was captured, that I would continue to receive both his salary and his *kostgeld*. . . . Their honors fulfilled their promise to me in part, until June 24, 1650, at which time they denied me any additional lodging and *kostgeld*, saying that my husband would soon return from Bahia and they would not pay my expenses any longer. So I had to relocate and have lived in poverty ever since. Afterward I tried to buy something on my husband's account in order to undertake something new, and so to live, but that was also denied me, so I have nothing now to live on. And knowing that Your Honors are advocates for widows and orphans . . . I humbly request that you assist me in this matter with the Nineteen Lords, that I might enjoy some support from the salary earned by my husband or, if their honors do not permit that, that I might enjoy what is owed him according to past agreements and promises.

Rachel went on to specify what she thought the WIC owed: ƒ 150 per month for the sixty-six months of her husband's confinement or, in the very least, ƒ 48 per month for the months since the company stopped her *kostgeld*. In a wry postscript she warned that WIC rulers in Brazil "do not part with money gladly."[53]

Moving from Brazil to New Netherland after Brazil fell to the rebels in 1654, Reverend Johannes Polhemus found that money was also scarce on the Hudson River. There, however, the company wasn't quite as reluctant to part with its resources. Polhemus and his wife and children were somehow separated in Brazil's final days, and his family ended up in Holland, not knowing if he was alive or dead. His wife Catarina received several small disbursements from the church and company in Holland, and then, learning where Johannes was, she and the children joined him in 1656.[54] In exchange for certain taxes and fees, the WIC had recently shifted some social costs to the New Amsterdam court. But the costs were always greater than public receipts, and small communities like the ones on Long Island, where the Polhemus family ended up, had even fewer means than the capital. So the WIC still sometimes had to step in and help. Governor Stuyvesant intervened, for example, when Polhemus informed him in December 1656 that his new residence wasn't finished, and that "my house remains open . . . and I with my wife and children must live and sleep on the bare ground and in the cold." The governor contributed planks to finish the house, and he pressured the Midwout magistrates and other nearby towns to devise a plan to pay the minister. When they fell short, Stuyvesant made up the difference, paying the majority of Polhemus's salary for his first eighteen months of service (about ƒ942). Ministers in other small towns actually had to sue the inhabitants to obtain their earnings.[55]

The company found a potential solution to the personnel shortages and pay problems of its last years—but not the squabbles of that period—by loosening the restrictions on secular work in some colonies and hiring more *proponents* than ever before. The WIC offered Wild Coast ministers a combination of salary, land, and slaves, so that someone like Johannes Basseliers, just like Reverend Schagen before him, could operate a sugar plantation, but without the same controversy and punishment.[56] A kind of on-call, transitory, apprentice minister, a *proponent* was a cheaper option than the ordained minister because the *proponent* had only just graduated from the university and was still looking for a first full-time post. There hadn't been as many *proponents* available to the WIC at its founding because employment needs in the Netherlands were still so great. By midcentury that calculation had begun to change, for Dutch universities had churned out a lot of young men for the ministry, and there was finally an excess at home. When the classes needed colonial ministers after that point, they looked first to their own *proponents*, which increased the number of young, inexperienced clergy overseas and contributed to secular-ecclesiastical tensions. The availability of *proponents* also explains the end of the WIC's targeted university support.[57]

Most scholars of the Dutch Atlantic would probably name a conflict from an earlier era, that of Willem Kieft and Everardus Bogardus in New Netherland, as the worst of the seventeenth century. After all, their rivalry and power struggles involved years of criticism, the obstruction of church services, and even an alleged assassin. They proved, among other things, that contention wasn't limited to the WIC's last decades.

But contention could grow worse, and in the case of Cornelis Goliath and Johannes Urselius, it could get even more dramatic than the Kieft-Bogardus fiasco. Reverend Urselius traveled to the Wild Coast in 1659 and was immediately assigned to company headquarters on the Essequibo River, about sixty miles from another Dutch settlement on the Pomeroon River. He was not encouraged by what he found. Of the 1,600 colonists who had migrated in recent years, only between 300 and 400 had stayed or survived, and they were spread out over many miles. For the most part they were sick, hungry, and unhappy. According to the Reformed consistory, the commissary on the Essequibo, the aforementioned Goliath, was a tyrant. He tried to force himself on the consistory as one of its members, and when they refused him, he forbade them to meet at all. So "unbearable" was his administration, the consistory asserted, the colonial council finally removed him from his position.[58]

The councilors reported the same events very differently. They conceded that people were unhappy with Goliath and, under pressure, they probably did remove him. But they accused Reverend Urselius of outright revolt. Describing him as a "grasping wolf," they detailed a supposed plot to seize Goliath, commandeer two yachts, and sail to the Caribbean with local slaves. Had they been successful, the rebels would have sold the slaves and kept the proceeds for themselves, the council maintained. It went on to explain that Urselius made his plans in the consistory and riled up church members in their homes during his regular visits, using his sermons, prayers, and "daily conversations" for the same purpose. The uprising was scheduled for an important holiday, when Reformed members came together from throughout the colony to worship and celebrate the Lord's Supper. In normal circumstances it was held a few times per year. In this case, because Urselius had just arrived, it was probably the first in the colony's history. As he and his accomplices went from house to house to question church members on their faith and conduct, preparing them for the gathering, they also made secret assignments for the mutiny. However, the council learned of their plans, and on the day in question, with help from the "good inhabitants," the rebels were caught and sent to the Caribbean.[59]

Urselius's real purpose had more to do with righting perceived wrongs and alleviating misery than with the selfish, malevolent motives the council ascribed to him and his followers. Complicating the situation even further, he arrived in Essequibo with explicit instructions from his classis at home to deal with Cornelis Goliath on a separate, unrelated matter. The commissary was a full member of the Dutch Reformed Church, suspended from Communion in his home town of Oostkapelle four years before for the "terrible sin" of manslaughter. Goliath had appealed the decision to the Walcheren classis, who reviewed the case after he departed for America and determined that his consistory had acted appropriately. The classis also transferred authority over Goliath from Oostkapelle to the new Essequibo consistory. In other words, in a period of great difficulty, anger, and division, when colonists were dying or leaving the Wild Coast, the classis granted Urselius the power to sit in judgment of the very man whom many people blamed for their problems. No wonder Goliath intruded in the consistory; no wonder he tried to halt its meetings. If the council's descriptions of the failed rebellion were accurate, he had reason to fear.[60]

Separated by fifteen years and hundreds of miles, the Kieft-Bogardus and Goliath-Urselius stories bear striking similarities. In both cases the minister posed a threat to the authority of an unpopular ruler, and both ministers became critics and opposition leaders, using the pulpit and consistory to attack enemies. They both exploited their visitation privileges to communicate with Reformed allies, as well. Just as Kieft and his supporters refused to attend sermons, making the church the ultimate marker of New Netherland's political divisions, resistance to Goliath and the council in Essequibo was centered in the church. In settings where WIC officers exercised total political and military control, where civic government was just beginning to emerge, discontent naturally gravitated toward *the* alternate source of authority, the only institution with an accepted and authoritative role in society and the only person—the Reformed minister—who could claim some kind of right or power outside the company, for he was just as much an independent servant of the church as an "employee." That Urselius was simply filling a role that some people considered legitimate, that his actions were not beyond the pale, is suggested by his later career. Though he had to go before the Zeeland directors and apologize for what he called his "imprudence," stating that he was just "a young minister," they released him from his contract. His classis accepted his explanation, gave him his testimonials, and allowed him to preach. By 1662 he had a permanent post at the village of Cadzand in southwest Zeeland.[61]

Warfare and scarcity were common culprits behind the discontent and bickering that sometimes divided church and company. But Reverend Philippus Specht discovered a few years after the Urselius incident that stability and prosperity were no guarantor of peaceful relations, which also depended upon the religio-political compatibility of secular and ecclesiastical leaders. Although Specht's run-ins with two governors on Curaçao weren't as dramatic as those of his colleagues in New Netherland and Essequibo, they provide yet another example of contention in the WIC's last years. Specht got along fine with Governor Mathias Beck in the 1660s. Then everything changed in the next decade under Governors Dirck Otterinck and Jan Doncker. Curaçao was becoming a thriving commercial entrepôt, and Specht was very happy about it; but success also caused problems for him. "Wherever God's church grows, especially

in places of trade and prosperity, numerous nations and evil people flow there."
More and more, he went on, "unrighteousness gets the upper hand, and we
must, therefore, urge the practice of godliness continually and be vigilant
against the shocking, serious sins of drunkenness, whoredom, and adultery."
To that end, Specht's consistory complained to Otterinck about single men
and women living together. After various "requests and remonstrations," the
governor agreed to deport "four adulterous whores."[62]

The church's complaints and Reverend Specht's efforts to eradicate the behavior that he found so objectionable soon began to rub people the wrong
way. Specht claimed that Otterinck resented him and undermined his work
from the start, forcing Specht to back down from his reform project. Serious
trouble began when Otterinck's wife arrived and the minister asked to see her
testimonials, which all church members had to show when they came to a new
place. Otterinck took offense and refused, claiming that, as governor, he had
authority over the church. When the consistory continued to protest against
adultery and other behaviors, he allegedly told one elder, "Where there is trade,
there must be whores." Like Bogardus, Urselius, and other clergy, Specht took
the fight to the pulpit, preaching a sermon from the Old Testament about
Israel's improper relations with "the daughters of Moab," the wrath of God,
and (in the Bible story) the execution of two offenders. Specht decried the "aw-
fulness of the sins of whoredom and adultery" and warned about inviting the
"terrible judgments of God" on Curaçao. Coming on the heels of the dispute
with the governor's wife, the sermon didn't go over well among Specht's opponents. They called him a firebrand and troublemaker, and the church's relations with the company continued to deteriorate.[63]

After Otterinck died, Specht said that Governor Doncker also refused to
listen to him, "even if it meant preventing enormous sins." Basically their dispute centered on the question of power. Otterinck and Doncker didn't want
people to think that Specht controlled them, nor would they let him undermine the colonial regime; yet Specht could not, in good conscience, remain
silent about conduct he detested, appealing at least once to his instructions
and authority from the Amsterdam classis, which was not subject to the WIC.
He went "with tears to the pulpit, knowing well that chastising sins . . . would
not be pleasant for some, and they would hate me." "In these heathen and dissolute lands," he wrote, vigilance was critical; only "repentance" would deflect God's wrath and protect them from disaster. "As God is my witness, if it
were possible, if I could have held the entire community in my heart, and with
my arms carried them into heaven, I would have done it." Unfortunately for
Specht, the governor did not want the minister to hold him or carry him anywhere. Doncker heard each sermon as a denunciation of his government, and

he finally banned Specht from the pulpit altogether. In 1676, more than eight years after leaving the Netherlands and just two years after the first WIC went bankrupt, Specht sailed home and took up a post in the army. As a warning to others, Doncker allegedly burned his Curaçao property to the ground.[64]

Specht shared one characteristic with all the "trouble" ministers described above: their youth. He, Bogardus, and Urselius went straight from school to the company. Except briefly as *proponents*, none had experience in the Netherlands before, which may help explain their zeal. Time spent working in a busy, diverse city like Amsterdam could teach clergy the value of restraint. Even the Amsterdam classis—often so strident and unbending—said as much to another of its younger colonial ministers, Bartholomeus IJsebout, who spent four months on Curaçao and witnessed Specht's clash with Otterinck. IJsebout had lived for a few years on the Gold Coast before Curaçao and in one letter he described the relations of WIC employees and African women. But the classis obliterated the offending lines and chided him for being too frank, explaining that a good minister had to mix his ardor with "understanding." IJsebout needed to "moderate" himself with caution so he didn't give offense or cause a scandal. In a gentler version of Otterinck's "Where there is trade, there must be whores," the classis argued that "the considerations of trade and government . . . cannot always be reconciled with the views of a minister of tender conscience." Instead, IJsebout had to "take comfort in the witness of [his] conscience." If young clergy were deficient in some meaningful way it was mostly in the sense that inexperience heightened their combativeness.[65]

Each of the clergy in question had supporters at home and overseas, and none of them suffered lasting consequences for their choices. Except for Urselius's apology regarding the near-insurrection in Essequibo and his explanation that he was a "young minister," each of them defended his ground until the end. In IJsebout's case the Amsterdam ministers scolded him not so much for condemning sexual misconduct but for naming names. Otherwise his peers commended him and he continued to report his "ardent exhortations and reprimands," his fight against "unzealous religion." God will "spew lukewarm people from his mouth," IJsebout wrote.[66] Likewise, the Amsterdam classis defended Bogardus and Specht, praising Specht for trying to deport "foul" women and taking his side against the governor in the matter of the testimonials.[67] Ministers who used the power of their office to change society in direct, heavy-handed ways didn't engage in prohibited behavior. However much some rulers resented it, they were playing the established role of the Calvinist reformer in Dutch society.

The same problems and disagreements between secular and ecclesiastical authority that existed in Africa and America had existed in the Netherlands for a long time; their extension simply demonstrates that the Dutch success-fully exported the public church—and all the baggage that accompanied it—as they spread throughout the world. If contention in America was sometimes worse, it was because individual rulers and clergy had a louder voice in small, developing, and oftentimes endangered societies where their particular reli-gious leanings and personalities mattered more and their decisions were potentially more impactful and divisive. Similarly, prostitution, illicit worship, and other phenomena of social growth could not hide as easily as they did in larger towns and cities, posing an embarrassing challenge even to clergy who, in other circumstances, might have preferred silence to confrontation. Those who opposed an indulgent ruler or sided with colonists against the WIC on other matters could do so because their association with the churches of the Neth-erlands and their callings and instructions from Reformed councils there con-ferred a measure of autonomy and separation from government that was unique to colonial clergy. They were in the best position to voice the righteous indignation of malcontents who, more often than not, confused their own feel-ings and their own wrath with the wrath of God.

Conclusion

The Dutch Joint-Stock Companies and
the Catholic Powers in Comparative Perspective

On December 15, 1652, a comet appeared in the sky over Brazil, remaining visible to the naked eye, presumably only at night, until the last sighting on December 25. The event was remarkable enough that at least two Dutch colonial officers recorded the comet's attributes and progress in their journals: Hendrik Haecx, WIC political councilor in Brazil, and Jan van Riebeeck, commander of the VOC's South African colony, almost four thousand miles away. Van Riebeeck sometimes gets credit for discovering what astronomers now call C/1652 Y1, even though it wasn't visible from South Africa and didn't appear in his journal until two days after Haecx first started writing about it.[1] Both men wondered about the possible otherworldly significance of the comet. "We pray to the good God, who knows the meaning of this appearance best, that he will look with mercy on all those who love and await his appearances," wrote Haecx. Van Riebeeck scribbled more succinctly, "The Lord knows the meaning of it." Printed in Amsterdam the next year, an anonymous etching of the same comet included a similar short appeal: "God grant the outcome in our favor."[2]

In combining their physical, technical descriptions with their concerns about heavenly signs, Haecx and Van Riebeeck showed again the comfortable coexistence of material and spiritual matters that lie at the heart of this book's purpose and argument. Their brief ruminations in this case strayed from clear religious belief—meaning a widely accepted institutional creed—to what most

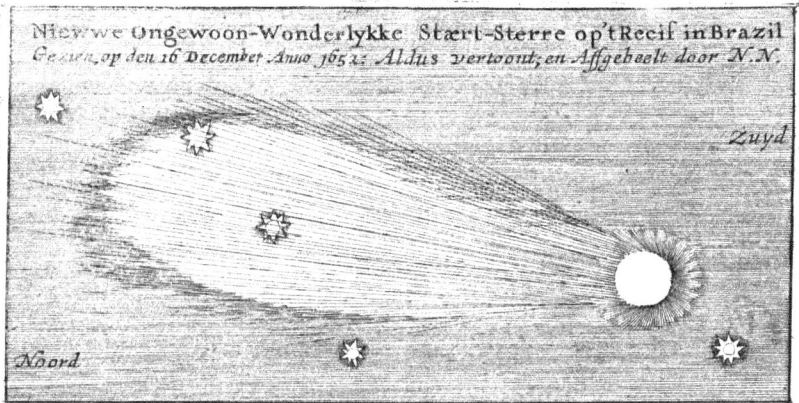

The comet described by Hendrik Haecx and Jan van Riebeeck: *Niewwe Ongewoon-Wonderlykke Staert-Sterre* (1653). Courtesy of the Koninklijke Bibliotheek, The Hague.

people today would label "superstition," which was, even by seventeenth-century Dutch standards, a negative thing. The word *superstitie* appears endlessly in Dutch sources, but usually about others, and usually to criticize and belittle an enemy or outsider: Catholics and the indigenous peoples of Africa and America, all of whom were too "idolatrous" for Dutch tastes. In religious affairs, the Dutch liked to think they were different.[3]

In a sense, they were right—not as they implied, that theirs was the only rational, legitimate form of worship; but the Reformation had certainly created space between the beliefs and rites of Catholics and Protestants, the latter becoming less ceremonial and less accepting of tangible devotional objects. In a different but related vein, modern scholars have also found that the Dutch parted from contemporaries, whether Catholic or Protestant, in their reactions to magic and witch beliefs. There was less intensity of feeling regarding witchcraft in the early modern Netherlands, fewer executions, and a winding down of witch trials and executions altogether about one generation before the same practices stopped in neighboring states. The change occurred when university professors and lawyers began to question the reliability of torture-induced confessions and other flawed evidence. The professionalization of Dutch courts, religious pluralism, and economic stability all helped eradicate witch scares and witch deaths in the Netherlands.[4]

The gradual professionalization or secularization of the legal system couldn't end magical, mystical thinking among the general populace. No one has studied these issues in Dutch colonies, but the Haecx-Van Riebeeck reactions to the 1652 comet reveal a certain level of mysticism even in the commercial and ruling classes. And I have provided several other examples: prophecies about the WIC's first Grand Design, signs and visions surrounding the Nassau and Brouwer fleets, suspicions regarding the use of "the devilish arts" when a voyage didn't go as planned, and Dutch concerns about Devil worship among Africans and Native Americans. Caspar Barlaeus captured the tug-of-war in Dutch culture between reason and superstition when, in his book on Brazil, he wrote that "a belief in miracles and omens has almost died out among our people, and our most rational thinkers would hesitate to interpret a chance happening as a token of God's purpose." Yet even Barlaeus went on to describe "two omens that could not be wholly ignored," referring to the recent, unexpected, unexplainable behavior of a few fish and birds. "These incidents," he continued, "were interpreted as positive signs promising a favorable journey at sea or on land. And perhaps a benign deity . . . used these tokens as portents of what was to come." Barlaeus wrote later in the same book about how some colonists interpreted an eclipse as a sign of "the fall and extinction of Spain's glory in these regions."[5]

Neither the eclipse nor the comet signified anything positive—at least not for the WIC. Dutch Brazil fell to the enemy less than two years after the passage of C/1652 Y1, and with the loss of New Netherland a decade later, a once-impressive Atlantic empire became a much-reduced handful of forts, small colonies, and trade entrepôts, more commercial than colonial in nature. With a better-tuned prophetic vision, Haecx and Van Riebeeck might have written instead that the comet proved God's anger toward the Dutch or maybe announced the rise of their neighbors and new enemies across the English Channel.

I have argued that a deep religious sensibility and social, institutional commitment to the Dutch Reformed Church and its politics permeated the WIC and influenced its plans and activities. To cast the company or Dutch imperialism in general as simplified, stripped-down commercial phenomena is to engage in a kind of reverse prophecy—also known as anachronism—by working backward from what we know the company and Dutch Atlantic became by the late seventeenth and eighteenth centuries. And the "vision" isn't quite right even then. The WIC was founded in the wake of serious religious controversy and Calvinist ascendance after the Synod of Dordrecht, born in a new era of hostility and warfare with Catholic Spain. Even in another context it would have had to work with the church because the early modern joint-stock company, as much as it traded, was also an administrator and civic arm of the state that created it. In this case the WIC became a tool for extending the Protestant Reformation and the Reformation's wars to other continents. United also through their overlapping functionaries and power holders in the Dutch Republic, the company and church could easily collaborate in hiring and supervising orthodox ministers and spiritual spokespersons overseas: hundreds of men from Calvinist Europe who used their skills and scriptures to sanctify the WIC and promote a broad, contested concept of reformation. Conversely, I have also argued that warfare, the divisions of reform, and ecclesiastical sensitivity and control were sometimes costly and damaging to Dutch imperial interests.

Many of these beliefs, traits, and relationships were true of the Dutch East India Company, too. For pragmatic reasons I opted not to include the VOC in this study. But I have mentioned it from time to time, usually when it shared something with the WIC: the influence of southern Netherlanders, ministers who worked in both hemispheres during their careers, the church's identical hopes and attempted oversight of both companies, and so on. Taking some space in these final pages for a more focused comparison will help clarify the differences and identify broad patterns in how the Dutch (not just the WIC) approached religious issues in their empire. I have regularly used the term "Dutch" for convenience' sake, and I have tried to be sensitive to its shortcomings when, after all, so many clergy and other employees and colonists were not Dutch, strictly speaking. It's ironic that, because of the opportunity to find broad patterns, the global view is the best tool for giving meaning to these narrow, national, ethnic terms that are otherwise so problematic in studying huge empires.

The most glaring difference between the VOC and WIC was related to distance and the difficulty of controlling underlings on the other side of the globe, which was a boon to the Calvinist mission in Asia. The VOC was created almost twenty years before the WIC, never really as a peaceable entity, but also not so clearly and publicly a means of conquest. The Dutch were at war with Spain and Portugal even then, so they could and did end up seizing territory and attacking the enemy in Asia. And to secure a monopoly in spices, they used force against some English and Asians. Yet the VOC's aggression toward nonenemies was an on-the-ground development, and it made the directors and investors at home quite nervous.[6] Likewise, the great distances didn't allow as much meddling and interference in ecclesiastical affairs from Dutch Reformed authorities in the Netherlands. They still called the majority of the VOC's hundreds of clergy—more than 900 ordained ministers and at least 800 lay clergy in the seventeenth and eighteenth centuries combined—and the churches at home still worried about orthodoxy and sent regular instructions. But again, the church in Asia, based in Batavia, enjoyed more independence than the American churches. The Batavian church called itself a synod and, as the name suggests, it became what Recife had only briefly been for the Dutch Atlantic: a decision-making and distribution center for ecclesiastical supplies and clerical assignments for locally trained men and newly arrived ministers from Europe.[7]

The religious makeup and strength of the mission in each locale depended on Dutch power there, not simply, as I have argued, on Dutch desires and efforts. As was true of the WIC in West Africa, the VOC could not found churches and missions where it was weakest: China and Japan. The company shot itself in the foot when it approached China with the same belligerence it used elsewhere, trying to force its way into Chinese markets and thereby ensuring that the Chinese, who quickly came to despise these uncouth "barbarians," would never grant the VOC a permanent foothold on the mainland.[8] The Dutch had better luck in Japan because they arrived just as the Japanese were expelling the Portuguese and hunting down Christian converts. Still seeking a European trade partner, the Japanese granted the VOC the rights to operate from the small island of Deshima in Nagasaki Harbor. But they restricted Dutch movement and influence to that one place. When the Dutch had to go ashore to pay tribute to Japanese rulers and renew their trading rights, any papers and books were inspected and confiscated. Officers on Deshima sometimes even forbade employees from changing their clothes on Sunday, for fear of how it might look.[9]

With joint support from the Netherlands and Batavia, the VOC was able to promote the Dutch Reformed Church and operate extensive missions especially in island cultures where indigenous power wasn't as great and where, like the WIC in Brazil, the company inherited a large, preexisting Christian population. Ceylon (now Sri Lanka) is the best Brazil-like example. The VOC united with the Kingdom of Kandy to fight the Portuguese there in 1640, only subduing them after many years of conflict. And there the Dutch had to provide worship services and school for the 250,000 Catholics already living on the island. Starting with just one minister, three *ziekentroosters*, and two schoolmasters, by the end of the century the church had thirteen ordained ministers on Ceylon, and those ministers oversaw teaching in 119 schools with 38,000 children. Suggesting that the Portuguese in Dutch Brazil did in fact have reason to worry about their religious rights, the Dutch on Ceylon banned all Catholic and Buddhist priests and founded two seminaries for training schoolmasters and Dutch-indigenous intermediaries. For instructional purposes they also created a simplified catechism of the type that Reverends Soler and Doreslaer tried to make for the Brazil mission and Reverend Megapolensis for New Netherland. But the Ceylon ministers didn't have to worry about the same interference from the Amsterdam classis. Because they had their own synod, and because the VOC had a printing press in Batavia, their catechism didn't have to go to the Netherlands for approval and printing.[10]

It would be easy to look at the situation in Brazil, Ceylon, and other colonies and towns with Catholics and conclude that the Dutch were only interested in missions when they had to be, when preexisting populations required a strong religious presence. However, the VOC invested a great amount of time and money to create a loyal Protestant population even where there were no Christians before. The benefit to the company, to be cynical about it, was precisely that: the same local commanders who devised the VOC's hyperviolent policies in the 1610s and 1620s had also decided that the company would be better off if they could build Christian communities that would, they hoped, be loyal Dutch allies, should the need arise. They toyed with European immigration, but fearing for the company's trade monopoly, they decided instead to create community by encouraging employees to marry local women and converting other indigenous people. In the Spice Islands the VOC utilized heavy-handed tactics associated more often today with Spanish colonialism in America, subjecting and moving whole villages, destroying native places of worship, and founding their own schools and churches in their place. By the end of the century the VOC had fifty-four schools with over 4,700 children and an unknown number of converts on Ambon and other Maluku Islands, while Batavia boasted about 5,000 members, plus *liefhebbers*: people who attended church but didn't accept full membership.[11]

Scholarship on the VOC has identified some of the same disagreements between church and company in Asia that I have explored in this book: allegations of corruption, complaints about sin and non-Reformed worship, and so on. Like the WIC's sphere of influence, the outcome in each case ranged from cooperation and an intolerant enforcement of Calvinist dogma to discord and permissiveness. One could find examples all over that spectrum depending (again) on the power of the company in each locale, the size and economic importance of the controversial population, the political, religious proclivities of colonial rulers, and the clergy's inclination to engage. When relations turned sour, distance and independence gave VOC officers the option to move clergy from one location to another against their will, which comes up repeatedly in the VOC literature. I found no examples of the same practice in the Dutch Atlantic.

The most intensive VOC mission in a colony without any prior European influence was on Formosa (now Taiwan). After failing to win the China trade, the Dutch built a fort on Formosa in 1624 as the next-best alternative. From there they knew they could still trade with visiting Chinese merchants and smugglers for the silk and porcelain that attracted the VOC to the area in the first place. The island was already inhabited by a tribal, deer-hunting (and head-hunting) Austronesian people who shared almost nothing culturally or politically with the Chinese on the nearby mainland. Yet the company, hoping to turn the island into a breadbasket for its other possessions, soon began encouraging Chinese immigration by offering land, assistance in getting started, and years of tax-free farming. Historian Tonio Andrade calls this fascinating phenomenon "co-colonization," meaning the encouragement of non-European immigration within Asia as a means to expand the VOC's influence and territory. Eventually numbering in the tens of thousands, the newcomers hunted deer and grew sugar and rice for local consumption and export. Taxes and tolls became heavy enough at one point to incite a rebellion, put down at the cost of 4,000 Chinese lives.[12]

The Dutch Reformed mission on Formosa was not to the Chinese, but the aborigines, who actually assisted the Dutch in quelling the Chinese revolt. Their religion was detestable to Calvinists because of unique features like a female-only priesthood and regular abortions, performed by priestesses called Inibs. The first Reformed minister to settle in an indigenous village (Sinkan) did so with permission, which wasn't unusual, for Chinese fur traders sometimes did the same. At first Georgius Candidius had trouble getting anyone in Sinkan to listen to him; but the Dutch governor soon came with gifts and urged the Sinkans to hear and obey the man. Candidius started performing baptisms in 1631, and by 1634 the whole village had converted.[13] A more substantial flood of conversions began when the VOC fought and subjected Mattau, the dominant village in the region, because other villages immediately came seeking an alliance with their powerful new neighbor. Afterward, the governor sent a minister named Robertus Junius to inform them of their duties as subjects of the company. Junius encouraged them to accept the Protestant religion, and as a symbol of their oath, he convinced them to destroy what he called their "idols."

Over the next few years, Junius and his colleagues founded schools and hired schoolmasters for several villages. By 1643 they had baptized 5,400 people in six of them. They held the first Communion around the same time, and at Sinkan they even organized a consistory with indigenous elders. Ultimately the church spread to other villages in the same way. As the VOC's power and the Chinese population grew, less forceful methods of conversion like gift-

The Voluntary Sacrifice of Reverend Hambroeck on Formosa, 1662, by Jan Willem Pieneman (1810). Courtesy of the Rijksmuseum, Amsterdam.

giving and divide-and-conquer gave way to greater coercion, similar to trends that I detected in the Dutch Atlantic. The company banished 250 Inibs and used corporal punishment to root out native practices. Conversion came to mean the acceptance of Christian sexual and marriage norms and the adoption of plows and European-style clothing. However, like so many things Dutch, the experiment came to a swift and bloody end in 1661 when a Chinese ruler named Zheng Chenggong invaded Formosa from the mainland, attacking and driving the company out. As the Japanese were then doing to Catholic priests in Japan, he crucified Calvinist ministers who refused to leave their neophytes without a Christian shepherd.[14]

Dutch religious endeavors can seem quite substantial when they are collected from different colonies and compiled in one narrative, especially when I cheat and include stories that don't belong in my more narrow study. Those who study other empires will also know that, even with the VOC thrown in, Calvinist ministers and missions appear less substantial next to Catholic missions in the same period. The Dutch Reformed Church used maybe as many as 1,200 ordained clergy outside Europe in the seventeenth and eighteenth centuries, and most of them were not "missionaries" in a strict sense.[15] Compare those numbers with the 802 regular clergy in Mexico in 1559, the 559 Jesuits in the Portuguese Empire in 1607, and the 1,300 priests in Lima, Peru, in 1630—1,300 priests not in the whole colony, just in the capital. And Lima had 1,366 nuns at the same time! The city also claimed more chapels in 1630 (twenty-five) than the WIC built in all of its colonies between 1621 and 1674. In any given year there were probably more Catholic priests in either Iberian empire than there were ministers in the entirety of the Dutch Empire in the early modern period.[16]

What to make of these differences? Must I conclude after all that the Dutch were too pragmatic and commercial to compete with Catholic counterparts in religious matters? Max Weber might explain clerical scarcity as a by-product of the multiplicity of options: if Calvinists could promote God's glory in any earthly calling and find signs of God's favor even in their professional successes, the most devoted Calvinists wouldn't necessarily believe that the priestly life was the most holy, nor end up in the ministry. And in keeping with Weber, I have emphasized the Dutch tendency and ability to exalt secular work and seek evidence of, on the one hand, divine support, or, on the other, divine displeasure and wrath.[17] But I would not argue that this ability was uniquely Calvinist. Mercantile work probably grew in respect and esteem in Holland and England first because they went further faster in diminishing feudal, noble, monarchical influences, creating space for alternative economic models and ideals. If there was a religious component to the increasingly positive attitudes about trade, the more likely cause was the Protestant "priesthood of all believers," which allowed wealthy men from all occupations to participate in ecclesiastical councils and influence long-term church positions and policies. The priesthood of all believers isn't unrelated to Weber's treatment of "the calling," but I'm dealing less with psychology and more with tangible matters like access and a merchant's potential impact in the church.[18]

Regardless of one's views on Weber, making simple comparisons between Catholics and Protestants can quickly cause an apples and oranges problem. Most obviously, on the question of numbers I was comparing the work and missionaries of an internationally connected but local, national institution in a rather small country, a church and country which, before the 1590s, had no history or tradition of global expansion and evangelism, with the international, long-established, long-organized, and well-supported Catholic Church. And the VOC and WIC had many millions fewer people living under their control. If I continue to compare oranges with oranges—or better yet, Orangists with

Orangists—an entirely different picture emerges. If, for example, I compare WIC numbers and ratios of ministers-to-population with related numbers and ratios in the Netherlands, the company does well: Amsterdam had about 200,000 residents, yet between the years 1621 and 1674, the same years of the first WIC, the city only employed seventy different *proponents* and ministers, averaging 18.4 ministers per year or one minister for every 10,870 people.[19] In 1650, the country as a whole had about 1,500 ministerial positions in a population of 1,850,000—or in that case one minister for every 1,233 people. Amsterdam could get by with far fewer ministers per person because its population was so densely settled.[20]

Ratios in Brazil and New Netherland were much closer to the favorable numbers of the Dutch Republic (1:1,233) than they were to Amsterdam's lopsided ratio (1:10,870). Racial, ethnic diversity and unstable borders make it harder to know the population for every year the company was in Brazil, but there are some figures for the early to mid-1640s, when Dutch-controlled territory had almost 45,000 people, including men and women of European descent, Tupi Indians, and African slaves. Ordained clergy (not counting Catholic priests) also reached a high of twenty-one men in the same period, for a total of one minister for every 1,762 white colonists and one for every 2,142 people overall. Here I'm comparing long-term averages in Europe with the high point in Brazil, which is almost as dubious as comparing Catholics and Protestants. But it's better than nothing, and it shows that for a time at least the company was no more stingy in its use of ministers than Dutch cities at home.[21] Before the English conquest, New Netherland had six ministers and between 7,000 and 10,000 people of European descent, plus an unknown number of Native Americans. Excluding the Indians, the colony had one minister for every 1,166 to 1,666 people—almost identical to the Netherlands. And with any of these places, both at home and in America, one must remember that no one had to (and a majority of people did not) belong to the Reformed Church. Yet the population numbers and ratios include everyone.

Implied in the term "priesthood of all believers," the Dutch also maximized their ordained ministers with elders, deacons, *ziekentroosters*, and other lay clergy. Amsterdam could get by with relatively few clergy both because it was urban and because ecclesiastical responsibilities were spread among the many members of the consistory and classis. Dutch colonies didn't have as many councils and layers of councils, but the WIC compensated with an increased use of lay clergy. *Ziekentroosters* usually preceded the ordained minister to a new colony and often outnumbered him afterward, which wasn't the case at home. With its average 18.4 ministers, Amsterdam had only three *ziekentroosters* in 1603 and eight of them by 1664. To make a one-to-one comparison between Catholic priests and Protestant ministers is thus to ignore the dis-proportionate work and contributions of laymen in the Dutch world, creat-ing yet another apples and oranges problem.[22]

Aside from questions about numbers, Catholics had many advantages over Protestants in spreading their faith, beginning with flexibility. Among the above-mentioned preexisting support and useful traditions were two separate orders of the priesthood, one for local parish work (the secular priesthood) and one with more mobility and a completely different command structure (the regular priesthood): Franciscans, Jesuits, etc. The various orders of the regular priesthood were critical for global missionary work because they didn't have to stay in one town with one congregation, as did the secular priests and Calvinist ministers. *All* Catholic priests were more flexible in the sense that they took vows of celibacy and didn't have wives, children, and the time com-mitments and financial duties of husbands and fathers. To be sure, lay clergy offered some benefits to Calvinists, comparable to Catholicism's multilayered priesthood. But the Dutch damaged Calvinism's other sources of flexibility—its portable structure and localist impulses—with their post-Arminius, post-Dordrecht rigidity and control. By contrast, Franciscans are famous for nominal instruction prior to mass baptisms, Jesuits for finding success by adapting them-selves to local cultures and focusing their energy on key Christian beliefs and sacraments. Ironically, the rigidity of the anti-hierarchical Calvinists wouldn't begin to characterize and dampen Catholic missions until the Chinese Rites Controversy ended in the eighteenth century with a top-down decision against the preferred Jesuit way.[23]

Catholics also enjoyed advantages of doctrine and ritual. As they extended their power around the world, Europeans found people in most places who believed in multiple spirits and deities, and most of them had traditions, cer-emonies, and devotional objects to connect with and influence their deities. These features were at least somewhat true of belief systems as disparate as Aztec religion in Mexico and Buddhist practice in Asia. With its veneration of saints and its acceptance and use of images, relics, and objects like rosaries, Catholicism was more familiar and attractive to potential converts. Protestant worship was much more focused on preaching and reading "the word" in plain, stripped-down chapels and, in Dutch colonies, even mills and political, mili-tary spaces. The WIC didn't construct as many chapels because it simply didn't have to: Protestants tended not to care as much about having a grand house of worship. Exploring these differences between Catholics and Protestants in Brazil, Barlaeus wrote that "the Dutch . . . consider any place equally suitable for a sacred service."[24] Overall, Protestantism was less ritualistic, with no im-ages or objects to take the place of indigenous ones, and no saints who could replace or merge with indigenous deities. Given the added issues of corporate sponsorship and the heightened instructional requirements of Calvinist membership, perhaps the key question isn't about why the Dutch had fewer clergy and smaller missions than Catholics in the early modern era, but how they managed to convert anyone.

Consider how Reverend Henricus Selyns saw and interpreted these global developments by the late seventeenth century. Born in Holland, he served the WIC in New Amsterdam from 1660 to 1664, then traveled to America again in 1682 to work with Dutch congregations in New York City. In a 1697 poem for his friend Cotton Mather, the famous Puritan minister and supporter of the Salem witch trials, Selyns celebrated the advent of European law and Christian religion in North America. But he singled out the English and their diverse subjects in an oddly possessive way, describing "Our royal charters," "our courts," and the science and wisdom of Harvard College. God had blessed "Our Boston and the Churches of the West," he asserted. Selyns also denounced witchcraft and "the devil's arts," and he praised the growth of Christianity among Native Americans. Then he concluded by contrasting the bloody divisions and religious conflicts of Europe with the peaceful New World.[25]

At first glance, the Selyns poem is full of jarring imprecision and inaccuracy. Why would a Dutchman praise one of the architects of Salem and lay claim to English accomplishments? Why would a Dutchman worry about witchcraft and celebrate Indian missions in North America, ignoring the failures of his own Dutch Reformed colleagues in New Netherland and the long and in his case personal history of colonial wars and conquests? If he could answer those questions himself, Selyns would probably remind us that a friendly commemorative work isn't the place for tragedy and misery. However, he might not understand our confusion about missionaries, witchcraft, and the English themes in the poem because, as I have tried to show, the seventeenth-century Dutch and English were not always so different in religious matters. In fact, the stanza about missions may not have been a reference to Puritans at all. The Mohawk had grown receptive to Protestantism in recent years because of disagreements among them over their relationship with the French and the conversion and movement of some Mohawk to the Canadian border. To stop the hemorrhage and bind themselves to the English, other Mohawk requested missionaries from New York, and it was the Dutch clergy of the colony who undertook the project, building a Protestant Mohawk community around the time that Selyns was writing.[26]

On the topic of England, he was right at home, for Dutch Calvinists had had close relations with English Puritans for a long time. Selyns had worked in Holland and had seen its many foreign churches, then he lived and worked in Dutch and English colonies, making him in the 1690s "at home" with England in a more literal sense, as well. During his original experience in New Amsterdam he would have known many English, and in New York City he interacted with many Dutch. Even now, more than thirty years after the conquest, he was reporting to the Dutch Reformed Church in Amsterdam, which was still controlling American affairs and preventing the creation of a local classis.[27] Selyns had spent his entire career in an international community that allowed him, when it was convenient, to ignore ethnic, national differences and the affairs of state. Empire and religion—especially monotheistic religion—are fairly borderless subjects anyway. With or without a large Dutch footprint in the Atlantic world, with or without many obvious Dutch achievements, he could at least include himself in a story of successful, enduring Protestant expansion.

Notes

Abbreviations Used in Notes

AAC   Archief van de Admiraliteitscolleges
Aanw.   Aanwisten van de voormalige Eerste Afdeling van het Algemeen
         Rijksarchief
ACA   Archief van de Classis Amsterdam
ACALK   Archief van de Classis Alkmaar
ACD   Archief van de Classis Dordrecht
ACE   Archief van de Classis Edam
ACU   Archief van de Classis Utrecht
ACW   Archief van de Classis Walcheren
ACZ   Archief van de Classis Zierikzee
ADA   Archief van de Diaconie Amsterdam
AEKA   Archief van de Engelse Kerk te Amsterdam
AKA   Archief van de Hervormde Kerkenraad te Amsterdam
AKD   Archief van de Hervormde Kerkenraad te Dordrecht
AKH   Archief van de Hervormde Kerk te Rotterdam
AKHA   Archief van de Hervormde Kerk te Haarlem
AKL   Archief van de Hervormde Kerkenraad te Leiden
AKV   Archief van de Hervormde Kerk te Vlissingen
ASG   Archief van de Staten Generaal
ASNH   Archief van de Synode te Noord Holland
ASU   Archief van de Synode te Utrecht
ASV   Archief van de Stad Veere
ERSNY   E. T. Corwin, ed., *Ecclesiastical Records of the State of New York*, 7
         vols. (Albany, NY: J. B. Lyon, 1901–1916)
f./ff.   folio(s)
GAR   Gemeentearchief Rotterdam
GASD   Gemeentearchief Schouwen-Duiveland
GAV   Gemeentearchief Vlissingen
HV   Handschriften Verzameling

HWF   Archief van het Staten van Holland en West-Friesland
inv. nr.   inventarisnummer
KB   Koninklijke Bibliotheek (The Hague)
KJV   King James Bible
MSS   manuscripts
NA   Nationaal Archief
NHA   Noord-Hollands Archief
NNBW   P. J. Blok and P. C. Molhuysen, eds., *Nieuw Nederlandsch Biografisch
            Woordenboek*, 10 vols. (Leiden, 1911–1937)
Not. Arch. Notarieel Archief
NYCM   New York Colonial Manuscripts
OSA   Oud Synodaal Archief
OWIC   Oude Westindische Compagnie
RAL   Regionaal Archief Leiden
SAA   Stadsarchief Amsterdam
SADOR   Stadsarchief Dordrecht
SV   Stadsbestuur Vlissingen
UA   Utrechts Archief
VS   Verspreide West-Indische Stukken
WD   Van Wassenaer van Duvenvoorde Archief
WFA   Westfries Archief
ZA   Zeeuwsarchief

Introduction

1. Charles Boxer, *The Dutch Seaborne Empire, 1600–1800* (London: Penguin, 1990),
128. Boxer only quotes the first half of the king's remark (and in French; the translation is my own). The other half is from E. Wrangel, *De Betrekkingen Tusschen Zweden
en de Nederlanden* (Leiden: Brill, 1901), 9.

2. Boxer, *Dutch Seaborne Empire*, 126; George L. Smith, *Religion and Trade in New
Netherland: Dutch Origins and American Development* (Ithaca, NY: Cornell University
Press, 1973), intro.; C. H. Firth, "Secretary Thurloe on the Relations of England and
Holland," *English Historical Review* 21 (1906): 319–327. See also "Speech XVI," in *Oliver
Cromwell's Letters and Speeches*, ed. Thomas Carlyle (New York: William Colyer, 1846),
313. The Cromwell line is sometimes rendered as "gain" and "godliness."

3. This quotation is a favorite among Dutch historians, cited in Pieter Emmer, *The
Dutch in the Atlantic Economy, 1580–1800* (Brookfield, VT: Ashgate, 1998), 101; Cornelis
Goslinga, *The Dutch in the Caribbean and on the Wild Coast, 1580–1680* (Gainesville: Uni-
versity of Florida Press, 1971), 369; J. H. J. Hamelberg, *De Nederlanders op de West-Indische
Eilanden* (J. H. de Bussy, 1901), 96; G. V. Scammel, *The World Encompassed: The First
European Maritime Empires, c. 800–1650* (New York: Methuen, 1981), 414.

4. Boxer, *Dutch Seaborne Empire*, chaps. 1–2; Julia Adams, *The Familial State: Ruling
Families and Merchant Capitalism in Early Modern Europe* (Ithaca, NY: Cornell University

Press, 2005); Marjolein C. 't Hart, *The Making of a Bourgeois State: War, Politics, and Finance during the Dutch Revolt* (New York: Manchester University Press, 1993), pt. 1. Recent general histories of the Dutch Republic include Willem Frijhoff and Marijke Spies, *Dutch Culture in a European Perspective: 1650, Hard-Won Unity* (New York: Palgrave Macmillan, 2005), and Maarten Prak, *The Dutch Republic in the Seventeenth Century*, trans. Diane Webb (New York: Cambridge University Press, 2009).

5. Immanuel Wallerstein, "Dutch Hegemony in the Seventeenth-Century World Economy," in *Dutch Capitalism and World Capitalism: Capitalisme hollandais et capitalisme mondial*, ed. M. Aymard (Cambridge: Cambridge University Press/Editions de la Maison des Sciences de l'Homme, 1982), 95; Jan de Vries and Ad van der Woude, *The First Modern Economy: Success, Failure, and Perseverance of the Dutch Economy, 1500–1815* (Cambridge: Cambridge University Press, 1997). See also Jan de Vries, "On the Modernity of the Dutch Republic," *Journal of Economic History* 33, no. 1 (March 1973): 191–202.

6. For this and the next paragraph, see Wallerstein, "Dutch Hegemony," as well as Jan de Vries, *The Dutch Rural Economy in the Golden Age, 1500–1700* (New Haven, CT: Yale University Press, 1974); Jonathan Israel, *Dutch Primacy in World Trade, 1585–1740* (Oxford: Clarendon Press, 1989); Marius van Nieuwkerk, *Hollands Gouden Glorie: De Financiele Kracht van Nederland door de Eeuwen Heen* (Haarlem: Becht, 2005); Cle Lesger, *The Rise of the Amsterdam Market and Information Exchange: Merchants, Commercial Expansion, and Change in the Spatial Economy of the Low Countries, c. 1550–1630* (Burlington, VT: Ashgate, 2006).

7. Henk den Heijer, *De Geoctrooieerde Compagnie: de VOC en de WIC als voorlopers van de naamloze vennootschap* (Deventer: Stichting tot Bevordering der Notariele Wetenschap Amsterdam, 2005). For the exchange bank and stock exchange, see also Simon Schama, *The Embarrassment of Riches: An Interpretation of Dutch Culture in the Golden Age* (New York: Vintage, 1987), 343–371.

8. Anon., *The Dutch-mens pedigree or A relation, shewing how they were first bred, and descended from a horse-turd, which was enclosed in a butter-box* (London, 1653). Pepys is cited in Schama, *Embarrassment*, 234.

9. For a different but related discussion about the relationship between business and "virtue" (and the declining reputation of businessmen among intellectuals), see Deirdre McCloskey, "Bourgeois Virtue and the History of P & S," *Journal of Economic History* 58, no. 2 (June 1998): 297–317.

10. Philip J. Stern, *The Company-State: Corporate Sovereignty and the Early Modern Foundations of the British Empire in India* (New York: Oxford, 2011). For modern business methods and joint-stock companies as imperial instruments, see also Robin Blackburn, *The Making of New World Slavery: From the Baroque to the Modern, 1492–1800* (New York: Verso, 1997), 9, 129, 187; S. van Brakel, *De Hollandsche Handelscompagnieen der Zeventiende Eeuw: hun Ontstaan, hunne Inrichting* (The Hague: Martinus Nijhoff, 1908); Den Heijer, *Geoctrooieerde Compagnie*; Niel Steensgaard, "The Dutch East India Company as Institutional Innovation," in Aymard, *Dutch Capitalism*, 235–257.

11. Max Weber, *The Protestant Ethic and the Spirit of Capitalism*, trans. Talcott Parsons (New York: Charles Scribner's Sons, 1958). See also R. H. Tawney, *Religion and the Rise of Capitalism* (Harcourt, Brace, 1926). Weber and Tawney both wrote about English/American Protestantism, not Dutch. For an overview of the theory and its supporters and critics, see Hartmut Lehmann, ed., *Weber's Protestant Ethic: Origins,*

Evidence, Contexts (New York: Cambridge University Press, 1993), 305–325. See also Robert Wuthnow and Tracy L. Scott, "Protestants and Economic Behavior," in *New Directions in American Religious History*, ed. D. G. Hart and Harry S. Stout (New York: Oxford University Press, 1997).

12. Albert Hyma, "Calvinism and Capitalism in the Netherlands, 1555–1700," *Journal of Modern History* 10, no. 3 (September 1938): 321–343; W. F. Wertheim, "Religion, Bureaucracy, and Economic Growth," in *The Protestant Ethic and Modernization*, ed. S. N. Eisenstadt (New York: Basic Books, 1968), 259–270; J. H. van Stuijvenberg, "The Weber Thesis: An Attempt at Interpretation," *Acta Historiae Neerlandicae* 8 (1975): 50–66; Schama, *Embarrassment*, 124, 298, 322–340; De Vries, *First Modern Economy*, 165–172. For a related argument about Weber and science, see Harold Cook, *Matters of Exchange: Commerce, Medicine, and Science in the Dutch Golden Age* (New Haven, CT: Yale University Press, 2007). Heinz Schilling offers a nonpsychological, anti-Weberian explanation of Calvinist success in "Innovation through Migration: The Settlements of Calvinistic Netherlanders in Sixteenth- and Seventeenth-Century Central and Western Europe," *Histoire sociale—Social History* 16, no. 31 (May 1983): 7–33.

13. On changing attitudes, see Weber, *Protestant Ethic*, and Tawney, *Religion*. For a more recent study, see Deirdre McCloskey, *Bourgeois Dignity: Why Economics Can't Explain the Modern World* (Chicago: University of Chicago Press, 2010).

14. Jelle C. Riemersma, *Religious Factors in Early Dutch Capitalism* (The Hague: Mouton, 1967), 6, 25–33.

15. Charles H. Lippy, Robert Choquette, and Stafford Poole, *Christianity Comes to the Americas, 1492–1776* (New York: Paragon House, 1992), 306; Paul van Dyke, "How and Why the Dutch East India Company Became Competitive in Intra-Asian Trade in East Asia in the 1630s," *Itinerario* 21, no. 3 (1997): 41–56. For the WIC as trading company, see also J. G. van Dillen, "De West-Indische Compagnie, het Calvinisme en de Politiek," *Tijdschrift voor Geschiedenis* 74 (1961): 145–171; Thomas J. Condon, *New York Beginnings: The Commercial Origins of New Netherland* (New York University Press, 1968); Smith, *Religion and Trade*; Ernst van den Boogaart, "De Nederlandse expansie in het Atlantisch Gebied," *Algemene geschiedenis der Nederlanden*, ed. D. P. Blok et al. (Haarlem: W. de Haan, 1977–1983), 7:220–254; Wim Klooster, "The Place of New Netherland in the West India Company's Grand Scheme," in *Revisiting New Netherland: Perspectives on Early Dutch America*, ed. Joyce D. Goodfriend (Leiden: Brill, 2005), 57–70. An alternative view is available in Benjamin Schmidt, *Innocence Abroad: The Dutch Imagination and the New World, 1570–1670* (Cambridge: Cambridge University Press, 2001), esp. 178.

16. Donna Merwick, *The Shame and the Sorrow: Dutch-Amerindian Encounters in New Netherland* (Philadelphia: University of Pennsylvania Press, 2006), 3, 264, 267; Patricia Seed, *Ceremonies of Possession in Europe's Conquest of the New World, 1492–1640* (New York: Cambridge University Press, 1995), chap. 5. See also Donna Merwick, *Possessing Albany, 1630–1710: The Dutch and English Experience* (New York: Cambridge University Press, 1990); Matthew Dennis, *Cultivating a Landscape of Peace: Iroquois-European Encounters in Seventeenth-Century America* (Ithaca, NY: Cornell University Press, 1995); Anthony Pagden, *Lords of All the World: Ideologies of Empire in Spain, Britain, and France, c. 1500–1800* (New Haven, CT: Yale University Press, 1995), 4. Pagden doesn't write about Dutch ideology, he says, because theirs was a seaborne empire. Except as foils for

others, they are also left out of the story in the more recent book *Empires of God: Religious Encounters in the Early Modern Atlantic*, ed. Linda Gregerson and Susan Juster (Philadelphia: University of Pennsylvania Press, 2011). The first New Netherland historian, Washington Irving, called the Dutch an "amphibious animal." For similar language, see Irving, *A History of New York, from the Beginning of the World to the End of the Dutch Dynasty*, in *Washington Irving: History, Tales and Sketches*, ed. James W. Tuttleton (New York: Library of America, 1983), 478, 628; John Romeyn Brodhead, *History of the State of New York* (New York: Harper and Brothers, 1853), 20; J. A. Doyle, *The Middle Colonies* (New York: Longmans, Green, 1907), 3–4; David M. Ellis, James Frost, Harold Syrett, and Harry Carman, *A Short History of New York State* (Ithaca, NY: Cornell University Press, 1957), 19, 28; David M. Ellis, *New York: State and City* (Ithaca, NY: Cornell University Press, 1979).

17. On experimentation/adaption in the English world, see Alison Games, "Beyond the Atlantic: English Globetrotters and Transoceanic Connections," *William and Mary Quarterly* 63, no. 4 (October 2006): 675–692. See also Pagden, *Lords*, who makes a case that the Spanish, French, and English (not Dutch) observed each other and borrowed rhetoric and ideas.

18. Claims about disinterest and neglect are ubiquitous. See Brodhead, *History*, 224; Johan E. Elias, *Het Voorspel van den Eersten Engelschen Oorlog* ('s-Gravenhage: Martinus Nijhoff, 1920), 122; Van Dillen, "West-Indische Compagnie"; Smith, *Religion and Trade*; George L. Smith, "Guilders and Godliness: The Dutch Colonial Contribution to American Religious Pluralism," *Journal of Presbyterian History* 47 (March 1969): 1–30; Condon, *New York*, 116–143; S. G. Nissenson, *The Patroon's Domain* (New York: Octagon Books, 1973), 156–160; Henri and Barbara van der Zee, *A Sweet and Alien Land: The Story of Dutch New York* (New York: Viking Press, 1978), 9, 40–41, 494; Oliver Rink, *Holland on the Hudson: An Economic and Social History of Dutch New York* (Ithaca, NY: Cornell University Press, 1986), 77, 92, 228–229; Rink, "Private Interest and Godly Gain: The West India Company and the Dutch Reformed Church in New Netherland, 1624–1664," *New York History* 75, no. 3 (July 1994): 245–264. For "institutions," see, for example, Lippy et al., *Christianity*, 306–307; Scammel, *World Encompassed*, 373–393; Doyle, *Middle Colonies*; Milton Klein and Jacob Cooke, "Editor's Introduction," in Michael Kammen, *Colonial New York: A History* (New York: Charles Scribner's Sons, 1975).

19. One of the most problematic overviews of colonial clergy is in Jean Gelman Taylor, *The Social World of Batavia: European and Eurasian in Dutch Asia* (Madison: University of Wisconsin Press, 1983), 21–24. See also Goslinga, *Dutch in the Caribbean*, 368 ("laziness and inefficiency"); Scammel, *World Encompassed*, 414–415 ("of the poorest quality"); Ellis et al., *Short History*, 27 (quarrelsome; did not care for communicants); Hamelberg, *Nederlanders*, 96 (on one minister, Rev. Philippus Specht, whom I deal with in chapters 6 and 8); Rink, *Holland on the Hudson*, 229 ("not among the best qualified, and in some cases . . . clearly incompetent"); Van der Zee and Van der Zee, *Sweet and Alien Land*, 282 ("uneducated," "illiterate").

20. J. A. van Houtte, *Economische en Sociale Geschiedenis van de Lage Landen* (Zeist: W. de Haan N. V., 1964), 151–152; Anthony Reid, "Early Southeast Asian categorizations of Europeans," in *Implicit Understandings: Observing, Reporting, and Reflecting on the Encounters between Europeans and Other Peoples in the Early Modern Era*, ed. Stuart B. Schwartz (Cambridge: Cambridge University Press, 1994), 287–292. See also Scammel,

World Encompassed; Lippy et al., *Christianity*; Ellis et al., *Short History*; Van der Zee and Van der Zee, *Sweet and Alien Land*; Jean Gelman Taylor, *Social World of Batavia*; as well as Riemersma, *Religious Factors*; Van Dyke, "How and Why," 42, 48; Michel Doortmont and Jinna Smit, *Sources for the Mutual History of Ghana and the Netherlands* (Leiden: Brill, 2007), 285–286; Ineke van Kessel, ed., *Merchants, Missionaries, and Migrants: 300 Years of Dutch-Ghanaian Relations* (Amsterdam: KIT Publishers, 2002), 11–15, 26. Though writing about one location, some of these authors make broad generalizations about the Dutch and the Dutch Empire. In that regard see also, for example, Alan Taylor, *American Colonies: The Settling of North America* (New York: Penguin, 2001), 253. Taylor writes an excellent overview of the Netherlands and Dutch expansion. Yet he mistakes the New Netherland experience for the rest of it when he compares the Dutch with the French, Spanish, and "Puritan English," writing that the Dutch had no interest in missions because they were "fundamentally commercial in outlook."

21. W. J. van Hoboken, "The Dutch West India Company, the Political Background of Its Rise and Decline," in *Britain and the Netherlands: Papers Delivered to the Oxford-Netherlands Historical Conference* [1959], ed. J. S. Bromley and E. H. Kossmann (London: Chatto and Windus, 1960), 41–61. See also Goslinga, *Dutch in the Caribbean*, 89–115; Charles Boxer, *The Dutch in Brazil* (Hamden, CT: Archon Books, 1973), 11.

22. Van Dillen, "West-Indische Compagnie"; Van Dillen, *Van Rijkdom en Regenten: Handboek tot de Economische en Sociale Geschiedenis van Nederland Tijdens de Republiek* ('s-Gravenhage: Martinus Nijhoff, 1970), 151. See also Van Hoboken, "Een wederwoord inzake de West-Indische Compagnie," *Tijdschrift voor Geschiedenis* 75 (1962): 49–53, and Van Dillen's reply in the same issue, 53–56.

23. Smith, *Religion and Trade*, intro., p. 86, chaps. 7–8, 15. Along the same lines, see Pieter Emmer, "The West India Company, 1621–1791: Dutch or Atlantic?" in *The Dutch in the Atlantic Economy*, 65–90. Smith wasn't just responding to Van Hoboken, but to Frederick J. Zwierlein, *Religion in New Netherland, 1623–1664* (New York: Da Capo Press, 1971). First published in 1910, Zwierlein's book challenged the notion that the Dutch were tolerant. For the continued use of tolerance after Zwierlein, see the following paragraph and note, as well as Ellis Raesly, *Portrait of New Netherland* (Port Washington, NY: Ira J. Friedman, 1945), 2–7, 77, 235–238; Ellis et al., *Short History*, 18, 27–28; Ellis, *New York*, 56; Kammen, *Colonial New York*, 18, 62; Alice Kenney, *Stubborn for Liberty: The Dutch in New York* (Syracuse, NY: Syracuse University Press, 1975), 257–267; Bruce Bliven Jr., *New York: A Bicentennial History* (New York: W. W. Norton, 1981), 18–19; Mary K. Geiter and W. A. Speck, *Colonial America: From Jamestown to Yorktown* (New York: Palgrave Macmillan, 2002), 89. For tolerance in Brazil, see Smith, *Religion and Trade*, 123–125; Frans Schalkwijk, *The Reformed Church in Dutch Brazil, 1630–1654* (Zoetermeer: Boekencentrum, 1998), chaps. 12–14; Jonathan Israel and Stuart B. Schwartz, *The Expansion of Tolerance: Religion in Dutch Brazil (1624–1654)* (Amsterdam: Amsterdam University Press, 2007); Evan Haefeli, "Breaking the Christian Atlantic," in *The Legacy of Dutch Brazil*, ed. Michiel van Groesen (New York: Cambridge University Press, 2014), 124–145.

24. On the tolerance theme, see also Russell Shorto, *The Island at the Center of the World: The Epic Story of Dutch Manhattan and the Forgotten Colony that Shaped America* (New York: Vintage, 2005), 85, 96–97, 274–277, 301–311; Mak Geert and Russell Shorto, *1609: The Forgotten History of Hudson, Amsterdam and New York* (New York: Henry

Hudson 400 Foundation, 2009). Probably taking their cues from Shorto, journalists and others associated with the quadricentennial adopted the same storyline. See Sam Roberts, "Henry Hudson's View of New York: When Trees Tipped the Sky," *New York Times*, January 25, 2009, A29, http://www.nytimes.com/2009/01/25/nyregion/25manhattan.html (accessed December 2010); Kenneth T. Jackson, "A Colony with a Conscience," *New York Times*, December 27, 2007, http://www.nytimes.com/2007/12/27/opinion/27jackson.html (accessed December 2010); Joep de Koning, "Governor's Island: A Place Where New York Began," *Newsday*, May 24, 2001, city edition.

25. For the New Netherland Project, now called the New Netherland Research Center, see Joyce D. Goodfriend, "Writing/Righting Dutch Colonial History," *New York History* 80 (January 1999): 5–28; Charles T. Gehring, "A Survey of Manuscripts relating to the History of New Netherland," in Goodfriend, *Revisiting*, 287–307.

26. Jaap Jacobs, *The Colony of New Netherland: A Dutch Settlement in Seventeenth-Century America* (Ithaca, NY: Cornell University Press, 2009); Janny Venema, *Beverwyck: A Dutch Village on the American Frontier, 1652–1664* (Albany: State University of New York Press, 2003). See also Martha Shattuck, "'For the Peace and Welfare of the Community': Maintaining a Civil Society in New Netherland," *De Halve Maen* 72, no. 2 (Summer 1999): 27–32; Adriana E. van Zwieten, "The Orphan Chamber of New Amsterdam," *William and Mary Quarterly* 53, no. 2 (April 1996): 319–340; Simon Middleton, "Order and Authority in New Netherland: The 1653 Remonstrance and Early Settlement Politics," *William and Mary Quarterly* 67, no. 1 (January 2010): 31–68; Evan Haefeli, *New Netherland and the Dutch Origins of American Religious Liberty* (Philadelphia: University of Pennsylvania Press, 2012).

27. Willem Frijhoff, "The West India Company and the Reformed Church: Neglect or Concern?" *De Halve Maen* 70 (1997): 59–68; Frijhoff, *Wegen van Evert Willemsz. Een Hollands weeskind op zoek naar zichzelf, 1607–1647* (Nijmegen: SUN, 1995); translated as *Fulfilling God's Mission: The Two Worlds of Dominie Everardus Bogardus, 1607–1647* (Leiden: Brill, 2007).

28. Schalkwijk, *Reformed Church*.

29. Benjamin Schmidt, "Exotic Allies: The Dutch-Chilean Encounter and the (Failed) Conquest of America," *Renaissance Quarterly* 52, no. 2 (Summer 1999): 440–473; Schmidt, *Innocence Abroad*. In the same vein, Mark Meuwese argues in *Brothers in Arms, Partners in Trade: Dutch-Indigenous Alliances in the Atlantic World, 1595–1674* (Leiden: Brill, 2011) that the attachments between the Dutch and their indigenous allies were genuine and impactful. Other recent social and religious histories include L. J. Joosse, *"Scoone Dingen Sijn Swaere Dingen": Een onderzoek naar de motieven en activiteiten in de Nederlanden tot verbreiding van de gereformeerde religie gedurende de eerste helft van de zeventiende eeuw* (Leiden: J. S. Groen en Zoon, 1992); L. J. Joosse, *Geloof in de Nieuwe Wereld: ontmoeting met Afrikanen en Indianen, 1600–1700* (Kampen: Kok, 2008); Deborah Hamer, "Creating an Orderly Society: The Regulation of Marriage and Sex in the Dutch Atlantic World, 1621–1674" (PhD diss., Columbia University, 2014); Stephen Staggs, "'Gentiles by Nature': Indian-Dutch Relations in New Netherland/New York, 1524–1750" (PhD diss., Western Michigan University, 2014).

30. For "neglected," see Benjamin Schmidt, "The Dutch Atlantic: From Provincialism to Globalism," in *Atlantic History: A Critical Appraisal*, ed. Jack P. Greene and Philip D. Morgan (Oxford: Oxford University Press, 2009), 163–190; and Johannes

Postma and Victor Enthoven, eds., *Riches from Atlantic Commerce: Dutch Transatlantic Trade and Shipping, 1585–1817* (Leiden: Brill, 2003).

31. For Atlantic history, see David Armitage, "Three Concepts of Atlantic History," in *The British Atlantic World, 1500–1800*, ed. David Armitage and Michael J. Braddick (New York: Palgrave, 2002); Bernard Bailyn, *Atlantic History: Concepts and Contours* (Cambridge, MA: Harvard University Press, 2005); Alison Games, "Atlantic History: Definitions, Challenges, and Opportunities," *American Historical Review* 111, no. 3 (June 2006): 741–757.

32. Dutch scholars were for a long time hesitant to embrace the field of Atlantic history. See Pieter Emmer and Wim Klooster, "The Dutch Atlantic, 1600–1800: Expansion without Empire," *Itinerario* 23, no. 2 (1999): 48–49; Schmidt, "Dutch Atlantic." For other critics, see the other essays in Greene and Morgan, *Atlantic History*, as well as the articles in the forum, "Beyond the Atlantic," *William and Mary Quarterly* 63, no. 4 (October 2006): 675–742.

33. On the complexity of the word "Dutch," see Willem Frijhoff, "Dutchness in Fact and Fiction," in *Going Dutch: The Dutch Presence in America 1609–2009*, ed. Joyce D. Goodfriend, Benjamin Schmidt, Annette Stott (Leiden: Brill, 2008), 327–358.

34. Goslinga, *Dutch in the Caribbean*, 299–302.

35. Wim Klooster, *The Dutch Moment: War, Trade, and Settlement in the Seventeenth-Century Atlantic World* (Ithaca, NY: Cornell University Press, 2016), 2.

36. See, for example, Christine Leigh Heyrman, *Commerce and Culture: The Maritime Communities of Colonial Massachusetts, 1690–1750* (New York: W. W. Norton, 1984); Stephen Innes, *Creating the Commonwealth: The Economic Culture of Puritan New England* (New York: W. W. Norton, 1995); Mark Valeri, *Heavenly Merchandize: How Religion Shaped Commerce in Puritan America* (Princeton, NJ: Princeton University Press, 2010).

1. The Dutch Reformed Church and the World

1. J. E. Abrahamse, *De grote uitleg van Amsterdam: Stadsontwikkeling in de zeventiende eeuw* (Bussum: Thoth, 2011).

2. L. M. Helmus, "Schilderen in opdracht: Noord-Nederlandse contracten voor altaarstukken, 1485–1570" (PhD diss., University of Amsterdam, 2010), chap. 5.

3. Cle Lesger, *The Rise of the Amsterdam Market and Information Exchange: Merchants, Commercial Expansion, and Change in the Spatial Economy of the Low Countries, c. 1550–1630* (Burlington, VT: Ashgate, 2006), 222, 245.

4. J. Keuning, *Petrus Plancius: Theoloog en Geograaf, 1552–1622* (Amsterdam: P.N. van Kampen and Zoon, 1946).

5. Keuning, 68. See also Kees Zandvliet, *Mapping for Money: Maps, Plans, and Topographic Paintings and Their Role in Dutch Overseas Expansion during the 16th and 17th Centuries* (Amsterdam: Batavian Lion International, 1998), 33–49. Keuning wrote in Dutch; the translation is my own. Unless otherwise noted, all translations from MSS and other Dutch texts are mine.

6. The term "true Reformed religion" (or some variant) is ubiquitous in Dutch sources. See, for example, *Copie van Requesten van de goede gehoorsame Burgeren ende Gemeente deser Stede Amstelredamme, wenschende onse E.E. Heeren Burgemeesteren, 36 Raden, geluck, heyl en saligheyd* (Amsterdam, 1628), B2.

7. General histories consulted for this chapter include Jonathan Israel, *The Dutch Republic: Its Rise, Greatness, and Fall, 1477–1806* (Oxford: Clarendon, 1995); J. C. H. Blom and E. Lamberts, eds., *History of the Low Countries* (New York: Berghahn Books, 1999); Willem Frijhoff and Marijke Spies, *Dutch Culture in a European Perspective: 1650, Hard-Won Unity* (New York: Palgrave Macmillan, 2005); and Maarten Prak, *The Dutch Republic in the Seventeenth Century*, trans. Diane Webb (New York: Cambridge University Press, 2009).

8. Diarmaid MacCulloch, *The Reformation: A History* (New York: Viking, 2004), chaps. 3–4.

9. Alastair Duke, *Reformation and Revolt in the Low Countries* (London: Hambledon Press, 1990).

10. Duke.

11. For the Dutch Reformed Church, see also A. Th. van Deursen, *Bavianen en Slijkgeuzen: Kerk en kerkvolk ten tijde van Maurits en Oldenbarnevelt* (Assen: Van Gorcum, 1974), as well as note 15 below. For the church's role in the revolt, see Guido Marnef, "The Dynamics of Reformed Religious Militancy: The Netherlands, 1566–1585," in *Reformation, Revolt, and Civil War in France and the Netherlands, 1555–1585*, ed. Philip Benedict, Guido Marnef, Henk van Nierop, and Marc Venard (Amsterdam: Royal Netherlands Academy of Arts and Sciences, 1999); Philip Benedict, *Christ's Churches Purely Reformed: A Social History of Calvinism* (New Haven, CT: Yale University Press, 2002), 173–201.

12. Marjolein C. 't Hart, *The Making of a Bourgeois State: War, Politics, and Finance during the Dutch Revolt* (New York: Manchester University Press, 1993).

13. H. A. Enno van Gelder, "Nederland geprotestantiseerd?" *Tijdschrift voor Geschiedenis* 81 (1968): 445–464.

14. Duke, *Reformation*, 269; Benedict et al., *Reformation*, 199; Jaap Jacobs, *New Netherland: A Dutch Colony in Seventeenth-Century America* (Leiden: Brill, 2005), 263–325.

15. On the complicated arrangements between Dutch rulers and nonconformers in the Netherlands, see R. Po-Chia Hsia and Henk van Nierop, eds., *Calvinism and Religious Toleration in the Dutch Golden Age* (Cambridge: Cambridge University Press, 2004); Christine Kooi, *Calvinists and Catholics during Holland's Golden Age: Heretics and Idolaters* (Cambridge: Cambridge University Press, 2012); Evan Haefeli, *New Netherland and the Dutch Origins of American Religious Liberty* (Philadelphia: University of Pennsylvania Press, 2012), chap. 2.

16. Van Deursen, *Bavianen*, 227–274; R. B. Evenhuis, *Ook Dat Was Amsterdam: De kerk der hervorming in de gouden eeuw*, vol. 1 (Amsterdam: W. Ten Have N. V., 1965), 216–250; Carl Bangs, "Dutch Theology, Trade, and War, 1590–1610," *Church History* 39, no. 4 (December 1970): 470–482.

17. Ties among European Calvinists are explored in Ole Peter Grell, *Brethren in Christ: A Calvinist Network in Reformation Europe* (New York: Cambridge University Press, 2011); Graeme Murdock, *Beyond Calvin: The Intellectual, Political, and Cultural World of Europe's Reformed Churches, c. 1540–1620* (New York: Palgrave Macmillan, 2004), 31–53; Robert M. Kingdon, "International Calvinism," in *Handbook of European History, 1400–1600: Late Middle Ages, Renaissance, and Reformation*, 2 vols., ed. Thomas A. Brady Jr., Heiko A. Oberman, and James D. Tracy (Grand Rapids, MI: Eerdmans, 1995), 2:229–247; Keith Sprunger, *Trumpets from the Tower: English Puritan Printing in the Netherlands,*

1600–1640 (New York: Brill, 1994); Sprunger, *Dutch Puritanism: A History of English and Scottish Churches of the Netherlands in the Sixteenth and Seventeenth Centuries* (Leiden: Brill, 1982); Andrew Pettegree, *Emden and the Dutch Revolt: Exile and the Development of Reformed Protestantism* (New York: Oxford University Press, 1992); Pettegree, *Foreign Protestant Communities in Sixteenth-Century London* (New York: Oxford University Press, 1986); J. F. Bosher, "Huguenot Merchants and the Protestant International in the Seventeenth Century," *William and Mary Quarterly* 52, no. 1 (January 1995): 77–102; W. J. op 't Hof, "Piety in the Wake of Trade: The North Sea as an Intermediary of Reformed Piety up to 1700," in *The North Sea and Culture, 1550–1800*, ed. J. Roding and L. Heerma van Voss (Hilversum: Verloren, 1996), 248–265.

18. Stadsarchief Amsterdam, toegangsnr. 376, Archief van de Hervormde Kerkenraad te Amsterdam, inv. nr. 3, f. 22 (hereafter cited as SAA AKA).

19. For company organization, see Henk den Heijer, *De geschiedenis van de WIC* (Zutphen: Walburg Pers, 1994); Den Heijer, *De Geoctrooieerde Compagnie: de VOC en de WIC als voorlopers van de naamloze vennootschap* (Deventer: Stichting tot Bevordering der Notariele Wetenschap Amsterdam, 2005); Wim Klooster, *The Dutch in the Americas, 1600–1800* (Providence, RI: John Carter Brown Library, 1997).

20. For "exhorter" and "respect," see Nationaal Archief, toegangsnr. 1.01.46, Archief van de Admiraliteitscolleges, inv. nr. 1358, April 5 and July 5, 1612 (hereafter cited as NA AAC). For the rest, see NA AAC 1357–1358, August 31, 1611, May 5, 1612; SAA AKA 4:18–19; SAA, toegangsnr. 379, Archief van de Classis Amsterdam, inv. nr. 2, f. 77 (hereafter cited as SAA ACA). See also SAA ACA 19:17.

21. SAA AKA 4:151, 179.

22. For "atheist," see SAA ACA 2:124–125. For "prison" and "peace," see SAA AKA 4:284–285. For the rest, see SAA AKA 4:290, 312–314; SAA ACA 2:125–126; NA AAC 1358 (November 15, 1618) and 1541 (November 24, 1618). See also Samuel Brun, "Samuel Brun's Voyages of 1611 to 1620," in *German Sources for West African History, 1559–1669*, ed. and trans. Adam Jones (Wiesbaden: Franz Steiner Verlag GMBH, 1983), 80.

23. SAA AKA 5:126–136; NA, toegangsnr. 1.05.01.01, Oude Westindische Compagnie, inv. nr. 1, ff. 5–17 (hereafter cited as NA OWIC); Noord-Hollands Archief, toegangsnr. 119, Archief van de Synode te Noord Holland, inv. nr. 3, August 8, 1623 (hereafter cited as NHA ASNH).

24. Nicolaes van Wassenaer, *Historisch verhael*, 21 vols. (Amsterdam: 1622–1635), 7:46–48. For Ziegler, see Ron Heisler, "Philip Ziegler: The Rosicrucian King of Jerusalem," originally published in the *Hermetic Journal* (1990); now available at http://www.levity.com/alchemy/h_zeiglr.html (accessed March 2017).

25. Van Wassenaer, *Historisch verhael*, 7:46–48, as well as Dan. 5, KJV; all subsequent biblical references are to the KJV.

26. For Amsterdam, see SAA ACA 2:128, 133; 4:33, 77; 157:29, 32–33; 163:1. For Walcheren, see Zeeuwsarchief, togangsnr. 28.1, Archief van de Classis Walcheren, inv. nr. 2, ff. 10–12, and inv. nr. 65, f. 1 (hereafter cited as ZA ACW); Gemeentearchief Vlissingen, toegangsnr. 357, Archief van de Hervormde Kerk te Vlissingen, inv. nr. 363, August 1, 1646 (hereafter GAV AKV). See also Evenhuis, *Ook Dat Was Amsterdam*, 1:182–185; L. J. Joosse, *"Scoone Dingen Sijn Swaere Dingen": Een onderzoek naar de motieven en activiteiten in de Nederlanden tot verbreiding van de gereformeerde religie gedurende de eerste helft van de zeventiende eeuw* (Leiden: J. S. Groen en Zoon, 1992).

27. See, for example, ZA ACW 73, Walcheren classis to Amsterdam consistory, November 1624; SAA ACA 157:101, 106–109; ZA ACW 3:43; GAV AKV 363 (April 8, 1643).

28. SAA ACA 4:111; Gemeentearchief Schouwen-Duiveland, toegangsnr. 424, Archief van de Classis Zierikzee, inv. nrs. 20–24, Dapper to Schouwen classis and Udemans, March 20, 1637 (hereafter cited as GASD ACZ). See also GASD ACZ 2:36–37.

29. NHA ASNH 3 (August 8, 1623); NA, togangsnr. 3.18.63.01, Archief van de Classis Dordrecht, inv. nr. 81, f. 194, and inv. nr. 83, July 1–August 3, 1641, art. 13 (hereafter cited as NA ACD).

30. SAA ACA 3:37, 48.

31. Utrechts Archief, toegangsnr. 24-1, Archief van de Classis Utrecht, inv. nr. 346, August 31–September 3, 1624 (hereafter cited as UA ACU); NA ACD 81:242–243.

32. NHA ASNH 3 (August 12, 1625); 4 (August 21, 1640); UA ACU 346 (September 6, 1636); 347 (September 1–4, 1641); NA ACD 83 (July 5–23, 1639, art. 14; July 3–August 3, 1640, art. 9); E. T. Corwin, ed., *Ecclesiastical Records of the State of New York*, 7 vols. (Albany, NY: J. B. Lyon, 1901–1916), 1:123–126, 130–134 (hereafter cited as *ERSNY*); UA, toegangsnr. 1401, Oud Synodaal Archief, inv. nr. 321, ff. 29–40 (hereafter cited as UA OSA). See also UA OSA 151:197; and the materials from late 1641 to early 1642 in UA OSA 321:17–27, 45–48.

33. J. A. B. Jongeneel, "The Missiology of Gisbertus Voetius," *Calvin Theological Journal* 26 (1991), 51. See also W. van 't Spijker, "Gisbertus Voetius," in *De Nadere Reformatie: Beschrijving van haar Voornaamste Vertegenwoordigers*, ed. T. Brienen et al. ('s-Gravenhage: Uitgeverij Boekcentrum B. V., 1986), 49–84; *Biografisch Lexicon voor de Geschiedenis van het Nederlandse Protestantisme*, 6 vols. (Kampen: J. H. Kok, 1978–2006), 2:442–449.

34. Jongeneel, "The Missiology."

35. ZA ACW 3:33; NHA ASNH 4 (August 12, 1642); GAV AKV 363 (July 10 and October 2, 1642); GASD ACZ 20–24 (July 29 and August 5, 1642); NA OWIC 25:33.

36. NA OWIC 24:48.

37. For "great costs," see UA, toegangsnr. 24-2, Archief van de Classis Amersfoort, inv. nr. 2, f. 140. For the rest, see the minutes of every relevant synod between about 1642 and 1650, but esp. NHA ASNH and UA ACU. See also NA, toegangsnr. 1.01.03, Archief van de Staten Generaal, deel 1, inv. nr. 4845, October 7, 1642 (hereafter cited as NA ASG).

38. For the original plan, see NHA ASNH 4 (August 12, 1642).

39. Colonial reports from the Amsterdam classis can be found in the minutes of most synods in most years from the 1640s onward. For Walcheren, see GAV AKV 363 (September 24, 1643).

40. NA OWIC 59:40.

41. For a different overview of colonial clergy (but just in New Netherland/New York), see Dirk Mouw, "Dutch Clergy in Colonial America," in *Transatlantic Pieties: Dutch Clergy in Colonial America*, ed. Leon van den Broeke, Hans Krabbendam, and Dirk Mouw (Grand Rapids, MI: Eerdmans, 2012), 1–33.

42. NA OWIC 8:6–7; SAA AKA 243:38.

43. Numerous appearances are found in SAA AKA 3–7; SAA ACA 3–7: 157–158, 163–165.

44. For Kesseler, Soler, and Megapolensis, see SAA ACA 4:82, 86; *ERSNY* 1:146; NHA, toegangsnr. 122, Archief van de Classis Alkmaar, inv. nr. 3, f. 42 (hereafter cited as NHA ACALK). Megapolensis's longer explanation ("prayer" and "spread") is not in *ERSNY*.

45. SAA ACA 224:24–25.

46. SAA ACA 157:32–34, 68, 81.

47. See a similar overview of former occupations for VOC *ziekentroosters* in C. A. L. van Troostenburg de Bruyn, *De Hervormde Kerk in Nederlandsch Oost Indie onder de Oost-Indische Compagnie, 1602–1795* (Arnhem, 1884), 335–376.

48. F. van Lieburg, *Profeten en hun vaderland: De geografische herkomst van de gereformeerde predikanten in Nederland van 1572 tot 1816* (Zoetermeer: Boekencentrum, 1997); for Germany, see chap. 5.

49. NA ACD 81:269–270; 82:26–27, 82–86.

50. Kesseler appears many times in SAA AKA and SAA ACA between 1626 and 1636. See also NA OWIC 14:182. For Polhemus and "persecution," see SAA ACA 4:66; *Biografisch Lexicon* 6:232–233.

51. I give more examples of foreign clergy in my dissertation: D. L. Noorlander, "Serving God and Mammon: The Reformed Church and the Dutch West India Company in the Atlantic World, 1621–1674" (PhD diss., Georgetown University, 2011), chap. 3.

52. Sprunger, *Dutch Puritanism*, 91.

53. *Biografisch Lexicon* 3:28. See also NA OWIC 21:174. For the English military presence in Holland, see Charles Wilson, *Queen Elizabeth and the Revolt of the Netherlands* (London: Macmillan, 1970), chaps. 4–5. See also Sprunger, *Dutch Puritanism*, 183; Sprunger, *Trumpets from the Tower*, chaps. 2–4.

54. For Hartsteen, Hendrix, and Schoon, see SAA ACA 157 (August 5 and October 4, 1639; August 13, 1640; August 6 and October 8, 1641; February 25 and August 19, 1642; April 5 and October 30, 1645).

55. For "reversed," see Adolphus Empenius in SAA ACA 157 (March 9–September 28, 1648). "Great lengths" refers to Wilhelmus Grasmeer, whose case I describe in chapter 8.

56. Dirck Pietersz. Drijstrang is an early example. See SAA AKA 4:290, 335, 375–377. For Backerus, see SAA ACA 4 (May 6, July 1, September 2, October 7, and November 18, 1641); 157:36, 41–45, 52, 58; *ERSNY* 1:136–142; NHA ACALK 3:23. Quotations and translations are all from *ERSNY*.

57. SAA ACA 19 (September 9, 1632). For the *formulierboek*, see SAA ACA 32. See the Walcheren book in ZA ACW 45—though Walcheren didn't ask Indies ministers to sign until the 1650s. The synod of North Holland thought even *ziekentroosters* should sign: *ERSNY* 1:79–81; and the church in Rotterdam did make them sign. See Gemeentearchief Rotterdam, toegangsnr. 23.01, Archief van de Hervormde Kerk te Rotterdam, inv. nrs. 1a and 1d (at the back of the book). Enkhuizen might have done the same: SAA ACA 3:120.

58. SAA AKA 243:25. "Jacoby Hermanus" is Jacob Harmensz, the birth name of Jacobus Arminius.

59. Westfries Archief, toegangsnr. 0656, Archief van de Hervormde Kerk te Hoorn, inv. nr. 584, May 3, 1629 (hereafter cited as WFA AKH).

60. Jongeneel, "Missiology," 69.

61. *Levendich Discovrs vant ghemeyne Lants welvaert, voor desen de Oost, ende nu oock de West-Indische generale Compaignie aenghevanghen, seer notabel om lesen. Door een Lief-Hebber des Vaderlandts* (1622), esp. C2–C3.

2. Faith and Worship in a Merchant Community

1. There is no biography of Johannes de Laet. See Jaap Jacobs, "Johannes de Laet en de Nieuwe Wereld," *Jaarboek van het Centraal Bureau voor Genealogie* 50 (1996): 109–130; and the forum in the special issue of *Lias*, "Johannes de Laet (1581–1649): A Leiden Polymath," 25, no. 2 (1998): 135–229. De Laet's wives were Jacobmijntje van Loor and Maria Boudewijns van Berlicum. See Rolf H. Bremmer Jr., "The Correspondence of Johannes de Laet (1581–1649) as a Mirror of His Life," *Lias* 25, no. 2 (1998): 139–164. For Van Berlicum's birth in Hamburg, see De Laet's family at the *Verre Verwanten* TV/radio program website, http://www.20eeuwennederland.nl (under the Afleveringen, serie 3 tab) (accessed June 2010).

2. Jacobs, "Johannes de Laet." For Dordrecht, see Henk Florijn, "Johannes de Laet (1581–1649) and the Synod of Dort, 1618–1619," *Lias* 25, no. 2 (1998): 165–176. For De Laet's consistory, classis, and synod service, see the elder/deacon elections and selection of classis deputies every December and January at the Regionaal Archief Leiden, toegangsnr. 511, Archief van de Hervormde Kerkenraad te Leiden, inv. nrs. 2–4 (hereafter cited as RAL AKL); NA ACD 81:27; 84 (July 1648).

3. Johannes de Laet, *Historie ofte jaerlijck verhael van de verrichtinghen der geoctroyeerde West-Indische Compagnie, zedert haer begin tot het eynde van 't jaer sesthien-hondert ses-en-dertich* (Leiden, 1644), 3–4. For thanks, sin, and God's will, see, for example, 41, 54, 68, 70, 89, 143, 170, 222, 289, 290, 297, 387, 425, 461, 482.

4. E. Stols, "De Zuidelijke Nederlanden en de oprichting van de Oost- en Westindische Compagnieen," in *Economische ontwikkeling en sociale emancipatie*, vol. 1, ed. P. A. M. Geurts and F. A. M. Messing (Den Haag: Martinus Nijhoff, 1977), 130.

5. W. J. van Hoboken, "The Dutch West India Company, the Political Background of Its Rise and Decline," in *Britain and the Netherlands: Papers Delivered to the Oxford-Netherlands Historical Conference* [1959], ed. J. S. Bromley and E. H. Kossmann (London: Chatto and Windus, 1960), 41–61.

6. By "directors," I mean approximately 192 men I identified for this study, mostly from the Amsterdam and Zeeland chambers. Sources for names include De Laet, *Historie*; WIC minutes and correspondence in NA OWIC and NA ASG, deel 2 (bijlagen); and Stadsarchief Amsterdam, toegangsnr. 5075, Notarieel Archief (hereafter cited as Not. Arch.).

7. Donald K. McKim, ed., *The Westminster Handbook to Reformed Theology* (London: John Knox Press, 2001), 53, 66–67, 173–175, 182. For "the body of Christ," see also 1 Cor. 12. On the consistory, see Van Deursen, *Bavianen*, chap. 5.

8. I determined consistory activity by searching consistory minutes from towns that sent directors to the Amsterdam chamber: Amsterdam, Haarlem, Leiden, Utrecht, Gouda, and Deventer. Zeeland records are spotty, but ZA has consistory minutes for Middelburg's English consistory and Veere's consistory. Lists of elders and deacons also exist in the two "synodalia" collections there (toegangsnr. 33.1, inv. nrs. 231, 235). For

Vlissingen, see the list of elders and deacons (1615–1718) at GAV (only recently discovered and still uninventoried at the time of my visit). I found Tholen consistory information at the Gemeentearchief Tholen, Archief van het Stadsbestuur, inv. nrs. 1–2, 17. Finally, I found a few Walloon elders/deacons in *Livre Synodal contenant les articles resolus dans les Synodes des Eglises wallonnes des Pays-Bas, 1563–1685* (La Haye: Martinus Nijhoff, 1896). Between 45 percent and 55 percent of Zeeland directors are known to have served on their consistories. With all the gaps in the records, the total was likely greater than 55 percent.

9. The same analysis is not possible for the Zeeland chamber because of missing records.

10. A. Th. van Deursen, *Bavianen en Slijkgeuzen: Kerk en kerkvolk ten tijde van Maurits en Oldenbarnevelt* (Assen: Van Gorcum, 1974), chap. 6; Philip Benedict, *Christ's Churches Purely Reformed: A Social History of Calvinism* (New Haven, CT: Yale University Press, 2002), 454–455; Charles Parker, *The Reformation of Community: Social Welfare and Calvinist Charity in Holland, 1572–1620* (Cambridge: Cambridge University Press, 1998).

11. Van Deursen, *Bavianen*, chap. 5. For the visitation list, see SAA AKA 736. The seven directors were Rombout Jacobsen, Hendrick Broen, Samuel Becker, Kiliaen van Rensselaer, Willem Bruyn, Jacob Quina, and Marcus van Valkenburch.

12. NA OWIC 34:29, 131. For Duvelaer, see the nominations of 1666 in the same minutes, as well as P. J. Blok and P. C. Molhuysen, eds., *Nieuw Nederlandsch Biografisch Woordenboek*, 10 vols. (Leiden, 1911–1937), 8:447 (hereafter cited as *NNBW*); M. P. de Bruin and P. J. van der Feen, eds., *Encyclopedie van Zeeland*, 3 vols. (Middelburg: Koninklijk Zeeuwsch Genootschap der Wetenschappen, 1982–1984), 1:374. The symbols *f* and fl. signify "guilder" (the florin/florijn guilder).

13. NA OWIC 34:32, 56, 62, 106; 37:31–33, 92–93; 38:5, 13; GAV, toegangsnr. 100, Stadsbestuur Vlissingen, inv. nr. 193, ff. 80–97 (hereafter cited as GAV SV).

14. The directors at Dort were Symon Schotte, Johannes de Laet, Johan van Hemert, and (maybe) Everhard Becker. See J. H. Donner and S. A. van der Hoorn, eds., *Acta of Handelingen der Nationale Synode* (Leiden, 1883–1886), 6–7, 43, 263.

15. SAA ACA 2–3. Classis rules and order of business are found at the start of each volume.

16. See, for example, Kiliaen van Rensselaer, Nicolaas van Damme, and Jacob Velthuysen at SAA, toegangsnr. 318, Archief van de Engelse Kerk te Amsterdam, inv. nr. 27, September 8, 1639 (hereafter cited as SAA AEKA); NHA, toegangsnr. 1551, Archief van de Hervormde Kerk te Haarlem, inv. nr. 22, November 22, 1639 (hereafter cited as NHA AKHA); NA ACD 83 (July 5–23, 1639, art. 14).

17. R. B. Evenhuis, *Ook Dat Was Amsterdam: De kerk der hervorming in de gouden eeuw*, vol. 1 (Amsterdam: W. Ten Have N. V., 1965), 216–250; Carl Bangs, "Dutch Theology, Trade, and War, 1590–1610," *Church History* 39, no. 4 (December 1970): 470–482; S. A. C. Dudok van Heel, *Van Amsterdamse burgers tot Europese aristocraten* ('s-Gravenhage: Koninklijk Nederandsch Genootschap voor Geslacht- en Wapenkunde, 2008), chap. 5. See also Van Deursen, *Bavianen*, 91; Johan E. Elias, *Geschiedenis van het Amsterdamsche Regentenpatriciaat* (The Hague: Martinus Nijhoff, 1923).

18. The other four were Jacob Geritsz Hoyngh, *burgemeester* in 1618 and 1620; Jan Gysbertsz de Vries and Jacob Pieterss Hoochcamer, who joined the *vroedschap* in 1611

and 1618, respectively; and Jonas Witsen, *burgemeester* in 1619 and 1623–1624—all before the Libertine takeover of the 1620s.

19. Evenhuis, *Ook Dat Was Amsterdam*, 1:304–305; Jonathan Israel, *The Dutch Republic: Its Rise, Greatness, and Fall, 1477–1806* (Oxford: Clarendon, 1995), 494–495; George L. Smith, *Religion and Trade in New Netherland: Dutch Origins and American Development* (Ithaca, NY: Cornell University Press, 1973), 121–122.

20. *Copie van Requesten van de goede gehoorsame Burgeren ende Gemeente deser Stede Amstelredamme, wenschende onse E.E. Heeren Burgemeesteren, 36 Raden, geluck, heyl en saligheyd* (Amsterdam, 1628), B2–B3.

21. Johannes Baers, *Olinda* (Amsterdam, 1630), 4. See also Israel, *Dutch Republic*, 507; Wim Klooster, "The Place of New Netherland in the West India Company's Grand Scheme," in *Revisiting New Netherland: Perspectives on Early Dutch America*, ed. Joyce D. Goodfriend (Leiden: Brill, 2005), 66.

22. Van Hoboken, "Dutch West India Company"; Smith, *Religion and Trade*, 122.

23. *Copie van Requesten*, B2. On patriots / patriotism, see also, for example, *De Vruchten van 't Monster van den Treves* (1630).

24. For selecting directors, see Henk den Heijer, *De Geoctrooieerde Compagnie: de VOC en de WIC als voorlopers van de naamloze vennootschap* (Deventer: Stichting tot Bevordering der Notariele Wetenschap Amsterdam, 2005), 109–145. For "complained," see SAA, toegangsnr. 5025, Archief van de Amsterdam Vroedschap, inv. nr. 14, f. 145; inv. nr. 15, f. 98 and (for "foreigners") f. 115.

25. These and other examples of individual politics come from Evenhuis, *Ook Dat was Amsterdam*; Van Heel, *Van Amsterdamse Burgers*; and Elias, *Geschiedenis*. None of the authors identify the individuals in question as directors.

26. I checked marriage and baptismal data at SAA, toegangsnr. 5001, Archief van de Burgerlijke Stand. Baptismal records are available at the SAA's website (www .amsterdam.nl / stadsarchief). Smith (*Religion and Trade*, 138) lists the directors with Arminian or Lutheran sympathies: Hans Bontemantel, Albert Bas, Albert Pater, Cornelis Cloeck, Jean and Henry Gras, Abraham de Visscher, and Paulus Timmerman. However, only Bontemantel appears in the Arminian baptismal registers. Most of the rest appear in the Dutch Reformed registers and none as elders and deacons in the Arminian / Lutheran consistory records at SAA. The Jan van Erpecum and Nicolaas van Damme who served as Lutheran elders were not the WIC directors of the same names.

27. The title of this section is from Ps. 116:14, cited by Willem Teellinck, *Davids Danckbaerheyt voor Gods weldadicheyt* (Middelburg, 1624).

28. Willem Usselincx, *Korte Onderrichtinghe ende vermaeninge aen alle liefhebbers des Vaderlandts om liberalijcken te teeckenen inde West-Indische Compagnie* (Leiden, 1622), Cii; Usselincx, *Voortganck vande West-Indische Compagnie* (Amsterdam, 1623), 8.

29. *Consideratien ende Redenen der E. Heeren Bewind-hebberen vande Geoctroieerde West-Indische Compagnie inde Vergaederinghe vande Ed. Hoog-Moghende Heren Staten Generael deser Vereenigde Vrye Nederlanden overgelevert nopende de teghenwordige deliberatie over den Treves met den Coning van Hispanjen* (Haerlem, 1629), 4, 11.

30. Den Heijer, *Geoctrooieerde Compagnie*, 73.

31. Teellinck, *Davids Danckbaerheyt*, 58; Dionysium Spranckhuysen, *Trivmphe van weghen de geluckighe ende over-rijcke victorie* (Delft, 1629), 20; Godefridus Udemans, *'t*

Geestelick Roer van 't Coopmans Schip, 3rd ed. (Dordrecht, 1655), 38–42 (and 92–319, specifically addressed to the WIC and VOC). For Udemans's book in the Atlantic, see NA OWIC 23:128, 180, and the booklist at NA OWIC 60:80. For Asia, see WFA AKH (November 6 and 13, 1642).

32. For "celebrate," see Spranckhuysen's prayer of thanks, where he praises God for making the Dutch rich: *Trivmphe*, 49–54. On the topic of wealth and discomfort, see Simon Schama, *The Embarrassment of Riches: An Interpretation of Dutch Culture in the Golden Age* (New York: Vintage, 1987), chap. 5; Benjamin Schmidt, *Innocence Abroad: The Dutch Imagination and the New World, 1570–1670* (Cambridge: Cambridge University Press, 2001), chaps. 4–5.

33. Schama, *Embarrassment*, 312–314.

34. SAA, Not. Arch. 694B, omslag 59, 384–405. See also Not. Arch. 178:39–41; 126:3; 739:144–145.

35. Schama, *Embarrassment*, 314.

36. SAA, toegangsnr. 377, Archief van de Diaconie Amsterdam, inv. nr. 64, ff. 17–20, 144–148; inv. nr. 65, ff. 225–235 (hereafter cited as SAA ADA). No totals from WIC boxes are possible because deacons often lumped boxes together in the records. For the financial needs of the average family, see A. Th. van Deursen, *Plain Lives in a Golden Age: Popular Culture, Religion, and Society in Seventeenth-Century Holland* (Cambridge: Cambridge University Press, 1991), pt. 1.

37. SAA ADA 64. See November 2, 1652 (Specx); February 21, 1640 (Broen); March 4, 1649 (Bartringh); August 5, 1653 (Le Thor); February 25, 1648 (Van Geel); January 3, 1630 (Loten); February 29, 1644 ("wives"). For Le Thor and Northoppinghen, see his inventory at SAA, Not. Arch. 1303:213–229; 954:206.

38. NA OWIC 22:46; 24:129; 25:147, 50.

39. For Amsterdam, see SAA ADA 64:182, 184, 192, 198, 210, 219, 233; SAA ADA 1:11. For Zeeland, see NA OWIC 20:102, 106; 21:54, 80, 90; 27:91. See also NA, toegangsnr. 1.11.01.01, Aanwisten van de voormalige Eerste Afdeling van het Algemeen Rijksarchief, inv. nr. 992, December 4, 1651 (hereafter cited as NA Aanw.).

40. The company paid poor monies as late as 1669. See NA OWIC 15:140. For WIC bonds, see SAA ADA 64:44; 65:31; 1:94.

41. For a fine, see NA OWIC 20:71–72. See also SAA ADA 64:181, 184–185, 188–189; NA OWIC 15:141–143; 27:98, 105, 118.

42. Various wills are mentioned in SAA ADA 64. For "French poor," see NA OWIC 20:102. See also NA OWIC 9:229; 52:59; 53:3; 61:57.

43. WIC wages are listed in Charles Boxer, *The Dutch Seaborne Empire, 1600–1800* (London: Penguin, 1990), app. 2. For "ƒ24" and "ƒ93," see SAA ADA 64:198, 246. Other examples are found on SAA ADA 64:197, 201, 212–213, 228.

44. NA OWIC 20:14, 128; 24:72; 25:10.

45. For WIC employment needs, see Pieter Emmer and Wim Klooster, "The Dutch Atlantic, 1600–1800: Expansion without Empire," *Itinerario* 23, no. 2 (1999): 48–69; Victor Enthoven, "Dutch Crossings: Migration between the Netherlands and the New World, 1600–1800," *Atlantic Studies* 2, no. 2 (October 2005): 153–176.

46. Ole Peter Grell, *Brethren in Christ: A Calvinist Network in Reformation Europe* (New York: Cambridge University Press, 2011), chap. 5; Graeme Murdock, *Beyond Calvin: The Intellectual, Political, and Cultural World of Europe's Reformed Churches, c.*

1540–1620 (New York: Palgrave Macmillan, 2004), chap. 2; Evenhuis, *Ook Dat was Amsterdam*, 1:185–189.

47. The phrase "brethren in Christ" comes from Grell, *Brethren in Christ*. For De Bra (and the Blommaert family), see 245–247. For other refugees / migrants in Germany, see Heinz Schilling, "Innovation through Migration: The Settlements of Calvinistic Netherlanders in Sixteenth- and Seventeenth-Century Central and Western Europe," *Histoire sociale—Social History* 16, no. 31 (May 1983): 7–33.

48. Grell, *Brethren in Christ*, 237–238, 240–241.

49. Though it only begins in 1638, the names of various directors appear in SAA AKA 149. For the prince of Anhalt, see NA OWIC 18*.

50. SAA ACA 4:300; SAA, Not. Arch. 848:807; *ERSNY* 1:169–183 ("love"). For the English circle (Loten, Cave, and Man), see SAA, Not. Arch. 1114:247; SAA AEKA 84–94. Elders and deacons are listed on the inside covers.

51. NA OWIC 34:18.

52. NA OWIC 1:9–10, 98, 183–184; 2 (n.p.: May 30, 1631).

53. NA OWIC 1:104; 2 (n.p.: August 30, 1630); 22:1; 23:1; 24 (n.p.: January 2, 1640); 14:1; 17:2–3.

54. On Teellinck and Udemans, see the previous section (as well as chapter 1).

55. NA OWIC 1:5, 43; 6:1.

56. NA OWIC 17:23, 26, 38, 41; 20:10, 56; 27:23; 32:1; 34:12, 46; GAV SV 193:10.

57. NA OWIC 21:175, 278; 22:13, 52; 24 (n.p.: January 9, 1640); 25:44; 30:79–80.

58. NA OWIC 22:119; 25:64. For "principal," see NA OWIC 24:104; 35:10.

59. SAA AKA 6:265–267.

60. NA OWIC 22:122; SAA ACA 157: 28, 38, 111–112.

61. SAA ACA 4:124.

62. See, for example, ZA ACW 73 (October 18, 1624); UA, toegangsnr. 24-3, Archief van de Classis Rhenenwijk, inv. nr. 1, f. 171; UA ACU 1:285; 2:112, 122, 186, 226.

63. *ERSNY* 1:244–245, 248–249.

64. SAA AKA 5:126, 129; NA OWIC 1:16, 98, 111; 34:18; ZA ACW 65:18–19.

65. For Germans, see NA OWIC 20:85, 97–98, 103, 110–111, 119–120; 21:51, 53, 58, 126–127; SAA ACA 4:259, 263, 268, 291; 157:77, 81, 94–95, 102. For Loosvelt, see NA OWIC 21:38a (August 8, 1630). For Plante and the unnamed individual, see *Album Studiosorum Academiae Groninganae* (Groningen: Het Historisch Genootschap te Groningen, 1915), 25; NA OWIC 14:145. See also NA OWIC 14:14; 21:38a; 24:120; 25:135–136, 154, 162–164; 26:47, 59.

66. NA OWIC 22:95.

67. For Walcheren, see ZA ACW 2:242; ZA, toegangsnr. 33.1, Handschriften Verzameling, inv. nr. 237, f. 262 (hereafter cited as ZA HV). For the Rotterdam directors, see NA ACD 83 (July 5–23, 1639, art. 14). For "fruit," see SAA ACA 157:95. Other WIC-supported students include, for example, Bartholomeus Cole, Florentius Strerarius, and Johannes Stuperus. Like Loosvelt, Cole and Strerarius were both disappointments.

68. NA Aanw. 644, Hendrik Haecx diary, June 29–July 6, 1645. For his church service in Brazil, see NA OWIC 69 (September 2, 1642).

69. NA Aanw. 644, Hendrik Haecx diary, September 1645–May 1646. For his return, see November 1647–January 1648. He visited with the clergy on December 4, 1647.

3. Baptized by Water and Fire

1. NA OWIC 23:50; 49:17.

2. Joel 3:10. The opposite ("swords into plowshares") is from Isa. 2:4 and Mic. 4:3.

3. *Consideratien ende Redenen der E. Heeren Bewind-hebberen vande Geoctroieerde West-Indische Compagnie inde Vergaederinghe vande Ed. Hoog-Moghende Heren Staten Generael deser Vereenigde Vrye Nederlanden overgelevert nopende de teghenwordige deliberatie over den Treves met den Coning van Hispanjen* (Haerlem, 1629), 13–22. See also *Derde Discovrs* (1622); *De Vruchten van 't Monster van den Treves* (1630); and the September 13, 1630, Michaelius letter in Albert Eekhof, *Jonas Michaelius, Founder of the Church in New Netherland* (Leiden: A. W. Sijthoff, 1926), 67. For "righteous war," see, for example, NA OWIC 2:11–19; 59:93.

4. *Fin de la Guerre* (Amsterdam, n.d.), 43.

5. Godefridus Udemans, *'t Geestelick Roer van 't Coopmans Schip*, 3rd ed. (Dordrecht, 1655), bk. 6.

6. Udemans, *Geestelick Roer*. See also Dionysium Spranckhuysen, *Trivmphe van weghen de geluckighe ende over-rijcke victorie* (Delft, 1629); Samuel Ampzing, *West-Indische Trivmph Basvyne* (Haarlem, 1629). The two scriptural examples are from Ampzing (Deut. 20:14; 2 Chron. 20:24–29). For the Israel analogy among other Calvinists, see Ole Peter Grell, *Brethren in Christ: A Calvinist Network in Reformation Europe* (New York: Cambridge University Press, 2011), chap. 3; G. Groenhuis, *De Predikanten: De Sociale Positie van de Gereformeerde Predikanten in de Republiek der Verenigde Nederlanden voor 1700* (Groningen: Wolters-Noordhoff, 1977), 77–107; Graeme Murdock, *Beyond Calvin: The Intellectual, Political, and Cultural World of Europe's Reformed Churches, c. 1540–1620* (New York: Palgrave Macmillan, 2004), 118–124.

7. For foreign investment, see NA OWIC 18*. J. Franklin Jameson writes about Frederick's ambassador in *Willem Usselinx: Founder of the Dutch and Swedish West India Companies* (New York: Putnam's Sons, 1887), 66. Versions of the "helping allies" and "distracting the Spaniards elsewhere" arguments appear in *Fin de la Guerre*, title page, A4, 41; *Consideratien ende Redenen*, 19, 23–24, 29–32; *De Vruchten van 't Monster*, A3.

8. Benjamin Schmidt covers the Native American theme in *Innocence Abroad: The Dutch Imagination and the New World, 1570–1670* (Cambridge: Cambridge University Press, 2001). For the southern Netherlands, see Jan Moerbeeck, *Redenen waeromme de West-Indische Compagnie dient te trachten het Landt van Brasilia den Coninck van Spangien to ontmachtigen* (Amsterdam, 1624), 15; and *De Vruchten van 't Monster*, A4.

9. Willem Usselincx, "Corte aenwysinge van de voornaemste verschillen tusschen 't concept van octroy op West Indien dat by de Hoog Mogende Heeren Mynheeren de Staten Generael in de maent van Februario anno 1619 aen de respective Provincien is gesonden ende tgene daerna by de Gecommitteerde uit de groote zeesteeden van Hollandt ende West-Vrieslandt is beraemt," in *Geschiedenis der Staathuishoudkunde in Nederland tot het einde der Achtiende Eeuw*, by O. van Rees (Utrecht: Kemink en Zoon, 1868), 408–432. See also Jameson, *Willem Usselinx*, chap. 4; Oliver Rink, *Holland on the Hudson: An Economic and Social History of Dutch New York* (Ithaca, NY: Cornell University Press, 1986), chap. 2; Schmidt, *Innocence*, 176–184, 193; Henk den Heijer, *De geschiedenis van de WIC* (Zutphen: Walburg Pers, 1994), 21–28; Jaap Jacobs, *New Netherland: A Dutch Colony in Seventeenth-Century America* (Leiden: Brill, 2005), chap. 1.

10. For resistance theory, see Philip Benedict, *Christ's Churches Purely Reformed: A Social History of Calvinism* (New Haven, CT: Yale University Press, 2002), 46, 88–89, 147, 158–159, 187–188; Murdock, *Beyond Calvin*, chap. 3.

11. Jacob Steendam, *Den Distelvink*, 3 vols. (Amsterdam, 1649–1650), 2:176–178.

12. Spranckhuysen, *Trivmphe*, 56.

13. For "shipwreck," see Steendam, *Distelvink*, 1:176–178. For captains appointing readers, see, for example, Arent Jansen Bloemendael and Abraham Caspersz in SAA ACA 4:271; 157:39; and Rocus Cluisen in NA OWIC 20:56.

14. Herman Ketting, *Leven, werk en rebellie aan boord van Oost-Indiëvaarders (1595–1650)* (Amsterdam: Aksant, 2002), 185–186; Nicolaas Witsen, *Aeloude en hedendaegsche scheepsbouw en bestier* (Amsterdam, 1690), 516.

15. For instructions regarding prayers, see NA ASG, deel 2, 5755 (December 12, 1635); 5759:209–236; SAA ACA 163:13–16; 212:170–176; *Groot Placaet Boeck, vervattende de Placaeten, Ordonnantien ende Edicten van de Doorluchtige, Hoogh Mog. Heeren Staten Generael der Vereenighde Nederlanden* (The Hague, 1658), 626–654. For Havermans, see the booklist in ZA ACW 73; Johan Havermans, *Christelijcke Gebeden en Danck-seggingen* (Amsterdam, 1634).

16. Willem Teellinck, *Ecce Homo ofte Ooghen-Salve voor Die noch sitten in blintheydt des ghemoedts* (Middelburg, 1622), 4–12. The Cunyngham journal is in NA OWIC 43. See entries for June 18, 1625, and March 24, 1626.

17. NA OWIC 43 (June 16, 1625); ZA HV 182 (July 26, 1629). See also Havermans, *Christelicke Gebeden*, 315–319.

18. Steendam, *Distelvink*, 3:63–67. For the book lists, see Klaas Ratelband, *Vijf Dagregisters van het Kasteel Sao Jorge da Mina* (The Hague: Martinus Nijhoff, 1953), 367–369; ZA ACW 73 (1624 list); NA OWIC 60:80.

19. For De Vries, see *Korte historiael ende journaels aenteyckeninge van verscheyden voyagiens in de vier deelen des wereldts-ronde* (Hoorn, 1655), 17–18. For Selyns, see *ERSNY* 1:487–489. See also Spranckhuysen, *Trivmphe*, 56; Teellinck, *Ecce Homo*, 4–12.

20. Bullinger and Schultetus both appear on the book lists cited above. Bullinger's *Huys-boeck* was used in the Dutch Atlantic even before the WIC was founded: NA AAC 1541 (November 24, 1618). Examples of sermons are all taken from Bullinger.

21. Udemans, *Geestelick Roer*, 62–91.

22. On WIC ships, see Remmelt Daalder and E. K. Spits, eds., *Schepen van de Gouden Eeuw* (Zutphen: Walburg Pers, 2005), 91–98.

23. NA OWIC 43 (May 26, 1625); 45 (August 2, 1632); 56:264; ZA HV 182 (February 16, 1630).

24. De Laet, *Historie*, 78. De Laet mentions prayer days and days of thanks many times in the same book. For other examples of going ashore to worship, see Jan D. Lam, *Expeditie naar de Goudkust* (Zutphen: Walburg Pers, 2006), 118; NA OWIC 55:51.

25. Cornelis van Hille, *De Ziekentroost: een korte onderwijzing in het ware geloof en in de weg der zaligheid, om gewillig te sterven* [1571] (Barendrecht: Lectori Salutem, 1998). For prayers, see Havermans, *Christelijcke Gebeden*, 144–147, 319–323, 354–363. See also Johannes de Niet, *Ziekentroosters op de pastorale markt, 1550–1880* (Rotterdam: Erasmus Publishing, 2006).

26. NA Aanw. 644 (September 12, 1647).

27. NA ASG, deel 2, 5759, 209–224; *Groot Placaet Boeck*, 626–654. For the *provoost*, see Ketting, *Leven*, 103–106, 188.

28. NA OWIC 1:183–184; 11 (February 1, 1646); 49:38. See also George L. Smith, *Religion and Trade in New Netherland: Dutch Origins and American Development* (Ithaca, NY: Cornell University Press, 1973), 23–39.

29. NA ASG, deel 2, 5755 (December 12, 1635); SAA ACA 212:170–176; NA OWIC 14:99; SAA ACA 185:86.

30. Charles Boxer, *The Dutch Seaborne Empire, 1600–1800* (London: Penguin, 1990), 128.

31. SAA ACA 4:242; 157:46, 61–62. For Claesz, see the Stadsarchief Dordrecht, toegangsnr. 27, Archief van de Hervormde Kerkeraad te Dordrecht, inv. nr. 4, ff. 76–77 (hereafter cited as SADOR AKD). For Dincklagen, see NA OWIC 21:188–189. See also Rev. Michaelius's complaints about the captain of his ship: *ERSNY* 1:50–51.

32. De Laet, *Historie*, 39–40 (a cross atop a hill in Africa), 58–59 (Puerto Rico), 184–185 (Recife), 190–191 (Olinda), 229 (Cape Verdes), 309 (St. Francisco de Campeche), 352–354 (Trucillo), 432–436 (Curaçao). See also the descriptions in ZA HV 182.

33. Spranckhuysen, *Trivmphe*, 57, 71; NA OWIC 52:15; 54:164. See also Johannes Baers, *Olinda, ghelegen int landt van Brasil, inde capitania van Phernambuco, met mannelijcke dapperheyt ende groote couragie inghenomen, ende verovert op den 16. Februarij A. 1630* (Amsterdam, 1630), 37.

34. NA OWIC 2:11–19; 57:121; 58:266. For "earshot," see De Laet, *Historie*, 504. See other examples on pp. 62, 175, 185, 249, and 503; as well as NA ASG, deel 2, 5753 (April 1632); NA OWIC 68 (March 9, 1638); Charles T. Gehring and J. A. Schiltkamp, eds. and trans., *Curaçao Papers, 1640–1665* (Interlaken, NY: Heart of the Lakes Publishing, 1987), 31.

35. NA OWIC 50:18; 68 (February 2, 1637); Udemans, *Geestelijck Roer*, bk. 6 (esp. the prayer at the end).

36. De Laet, *Historie*, 503–505.

37. Gedeon Moris, *Copye van 't Journael gehouden by Gedeon Moris, koopman op het Schip van de West Indische Compagnie genaemt de Princesse* (Amsterdam, 1640).

38. Udemans, *Geestelijck Roer*, bk. 6.

39. Baers, *Olinda*, 1–12. See Baers and his father in *NNBW* 1:223–224. His father's book was *Een geestelijcke, schriftmatige voorbereydinge totten heyligen, hoochweerdighen sacramente des avontmaels* (Franeker, 1597).

40. Baers, *Olinda*, 12–23.

41. Baers, 7, 13–20.

42. De Laet, *Historie*, 243, 322.

43. De Laet, 221–222, 416–424. For Pater's and Du Busson's deaths, see Charles Boxer, *The Dutch in Brazil* (Hamden, CT: Archon Books, 1973), 47–48, 184.

44. Boxer, *Dutch in Brazil*, 47.

45. *Een cort ende warachtich Verhael vande vermaerde See-strid en loffelijcke Victorie die Godt Almachtich verleent heeft de Generale West-Indische Compagnie onder 't beleyt vanden Manhasten Admirael Generael Adriaen Janssen Pater* (Middelburgh, 1631), A4.

46. Steendam, *Distelvink*, 2:115–128.

47. For Waerdenburch, see Frans Schalkwijk, *The Reformed Church in Dutch Brazil, 1630–1654* (Zoetermeer: Boekencentrum, 1998), 38–39n6, 240; NA OWIC 49:17. For Ruychaver, see SAA ACA 157: 63, 78–79; NA OWIC 9:159–161; 11 (January 19, 1645).

48. On the Dutch "cult of naval heroes," which served provincial and nationalistic purposes, see Michiel van Groesen, ed., *The Legacy of Dutch Brazil* (New York: Cambridge University Press, 2014), chap. 10.

49. NA OWIC 2 (December 16, 1634); De Laet, *Historie*, 348; see also p. 343, when the Dutch broke open a church during Mass and took the priest prisoner.

50. NA OWIC 2:11–19. See also Jacque Osiel's and Elias Herckman's reports in NA OWIC 46; NA ASG, deel 5, 12564.12 (April 15, 1643); De Laet, *Historie*, 16, 51, 53, 60, 187, 190, 193, 196, 202, 290, 356, 412, 438, 478.

51. De Laet, *Historie*, 468–469 (numbered incorrectly as 478–479); 472–477. See also Boxer, *Dutch in Brazil*, 58–63.

52. NA OWIC 1:32, 126–128; 57:84 (peace a prerequisite to profits); 58:266 (when the soldiers in Angola ignored orders and plundered). See also Udemans, *Geestelijck Roer*, bk. 6; Bullinger, *Huys-boeck*, 64–68.

53. NA OWIC 2 (August 30, 1630); De Laet, *Historie*, 296–298.

54. NA OWIC 52:127; De Laet, *Historie*, 331, 335, 454, 464.

55. Spranckhuysen, *Trivmphe*, 71–72.

56. NA OWIC 51:31; 63:15. For French defectors, see De Laet, *Historie*, 198, 200. See also p. 486 and, for French defectors on Curaçao, NA ASG, deel 2, 5758 (March 1673). See also NA OWIC 60:1, "Pamflet in het Frans." For Soler, see B. N. Teensma, ed. and trans., *Vincent Joachim Soler's Seventeen Letters, 1636–1643* (Rio de Janeiro: Editora Index, 1999), 57–60.

57. Lam, *Expeditie*, 111. See also 95, 110, 125; NA OWIC 43 (October 24, 1625); De Laet, *Historie*, 54, 68.

58. De Laet, *Historie*, 507.

59. NA OWIC 68 (May 11, 1639); NA ASG, deel 2, 5755, c. 1022–1030 (February 28, 1640); NA OWIC 55:1. For other days of thanks, see De Laet, *Historie*, 189–190, 335, 369, 424; Baers, *Olinda*, 23–28; Spranckhuysen, *Trivmphe*, 72; NA OWIC 50:18, 91; 52:14; 57:121.

60. Thomas Weller, "Trading Goods—Trading Faith? Religious Conflict and Commercial Interests in Early Modern Spain," in *Forgetting Faith? Negotiating Confessional Conflict in Early Modern Europe*, ed. Isabel Karremann, Cornel Zwierlein, and Inga Mai Groote (Berlin: De Gruyter, 2012), 221–239.

61. Ibid. See also *NNBW* 1:201; Joan Aventroot, *Sendbrief van Joan Aventroot tot den Grootmachtichsten Coninck van Spaengien* (Amsterdam, 1615).

62. Aventroot, *Sendt-Brief* (1630), 4–9.

63. Aventroot, 4–9.

64. Original sources on the Nassau Fleet are in W. Voorbeijtel Cannenburg, *Reis om de wereld van de Nassausche vloot, 1623–1626* ('s-Gravenhage: Martinus Nijhoff, 1964); for the comment about Aventroot, see p. 108. Schmidt writes about the Nassau and Brouwer fleets in *Innocence*, which I used as a source for what follows.

65. Voorbeijtel Cannenburg, *Reis*, lviii–lix, 117.

66. Cannenburg, 31–32.

67. Cannenburg, 27–30.

68. *Verhael van 't ghene Den Admirael l'Hermite in zyne reyse naer de Custen van Peru verricht, ende oock wat Schepen hy ghenomen ende verbrandt heeft, inde Haven van Callao, tot den 1 Julij 1624 toe* (Amsterdam, 1625), A2. For "premonition," see Voorbeijtel Cannenburg, *Reis*, 29–30n5.

69. Voorbeijtel Cannenburg, *Reis*, 65–75.

70. Cannenburg, lxxxv; *Waerachtigh verhael van het succes van de Vlote onder den Admirael Iaqves l'Hermite in de Zuyt-zee, op de Custen van Peru, en de Stadt Lima* (1625), B.

71. Voorbeijtel Cannenburg, *Reis*, 84–104.

72. Aventroot, *Sendt-Brief*, 7–8.

73. Aventroot, esp. 8, 13, 27–29.

74. Schmidt, *Innocence*, 204–206; Cannenburg, *Reis*, 55, 78–79.

75. NA ASG, deel 5, 12564.11 (October 4, 1642); NA OWIC 17 (1651).

76. *Journael ende Historis verhael van de Reyse gedaen by Oosten de Straet le Maire, naer de Custen van Chili, onder het beleyt van den Heer Generael Hendrick Brouwer* (Amsterdam, 1646); Caspar van Baerle, *The History of Brazil under the Governorship of Count Johan Maurits of Nassau, 1636–1644*, trans. Blanche T. van Berckel-Ebeling Koning (Gainesville, FL: University Press of Florida, 2011), chap. 13. See also Schmidt, *Innocence*, 206–209.

77. Weller, "Trading Goods," 232.

4. Planting the Lord's Vineyard in Foreign Soil

1. SAA AKA 5:231; also published as "Copie-Boek van den Kerkeraad van Amsterdam, 1589–1635," app. A of Albert Eekhof, *Bastiaen Jansz. Krol: Krankenbezoeker, Kommies en Kommandeur van Niew-Nederland, 1595–1645* ('s-Gravenhage: Martinus Nijhoff, 1910), xxiii.

2. Wim Klooster, "The Place of New Netherland in the West India Company's Grand Scheme," in *Revisiting New Netherland: Perspectives on Early Dutch America*, ed. Joyce D. Goodfriend (Leiden: Brill, 2005), 57–70.

3. *Octroy, By de Hooghe Moghende Heeren Staten Generael, verleent aende West-Indische Compagnie* (The Hague, 1621), sect. 2.

4. Nicolaes van Wassenaer wrote about Jews, Greeks, and Romans in his *Historisch verhael*, 21 vols. (Amsterdam: 1622–1635), 7:10. For examples of pamphlets that are primarily about trade and war but cover colonization, too, see *Derde Discovrs* (1622); *Levendich Discovrs vant ghemeyne Lants welvaert, voor desen de Oost, ende nu oock de West-Indische generale Compaignie aenghevanghen, seer notabel om lesen. Door een Lief-Hebber des Vaderlandts* (1622); *Fin de la Guerre* (Amsterdam, n.d.). For the alternative point of view (that the Dutch were traders), see *Reden van dat die West-Indische Compagnie* (1636).

5. For Reformed beliefs about when the church was established, compare clerical instructions in SAA ACA 19. Only a minister could organize a church. To do so he had to call a consistory and exercise discipline.

6. For *ziekentroosters* and the "pastoral care" they provided in the Netherlands, see Johannes de Niet, *Ziekentroosters op de pastorale markt, 1550–1880* (Rotterdam: Erasmus Publishing, 2006), chap. 1.

7. By "Caribbean" or "Greater Caribbean," I'm referring to the Caribbean islands and the northern coast of South America, including the Guyanas, which don't technically border the Caribbean Sea.

8. Cornelis Goslinga, *The Dutch in the Caribbean and on the Wild Coast, 1580–1680* (Gainesville: University of Florida Press, 1971), 52. For early Dutch activity in the Caribbean, see ibid., chaps. 3–4; Henk den Heijer, *De geschiedenis van de WIC* (Zutphen: Walburg Pers, 1994), chap. 5; Wim Klooster, *Illicit Riches: Dutch Trade in the Caribbean, 1648–1795* (Leiden: KITLV Press, 1998), chaps. 1–2.

9. Henk den Heijer gives an overview of Dutch settlements on the Wild Coast (though he downplays the role of religion) in "'Over warme en koude landen': Mislukte Nederlandse volksplantinge op de Wilde Kust in de zeventiende eeuw," *De Zeventiende Eeuw* 21, no. 1 (2005): 79–90.

10. "Memorial to the Dutch States-General on the Colonization of Guiana" [1603], in *Report of the Special Commission Appointed by the President, January 4, 1896, to Examine and Report upon the True Divisional Line between the Republic of Venezuela and British Guiana*, vol. 2 (Washington, DC: Government Printing Office, 1898), 27–36.

11. Founded in 1616 at Fort Kijkoveral, the colony was called Essequibo. See Goslinga, *Dutch in the Caribbean*, 412.

12. Frank Lestringant and Ann Blair provide background on French-speaking Protestants in America in "Geneva and America in the Renaissance: The Dream of the Huguenot Refuge, 1555–1600," *Sixteenth Century Journal* 26, no. 2 (Summer 1995): 285–295.

13. John Peters, "Volunteers for the Wilderness: The Walloon Petitioners of 1621 and the Voyage of the *Nieu Nederlandt* to the Hudson River in 1624," *Proceedings of the Huguenot Society of Great Britain and Ireland* 24, no. 5 (1987), 423. For the rest of this paragraph, see pp. 421–433; and Mrs. Robert W. de Forest, *A Walloon Family in America: Lockwood de Forest and His Forbears, 1500–1840* (New York: Houghton Mifflin, 1914).

14. Mrs. de Forest, *Walloon Family*, 21.

15. "Voyage to Guyana," in ibid., 233–239. The whole account is on pp. 169–279.

16. Ibid., 245, 247, 251.

17. For Berbice, see Goslinga, *Dutch in the Caribbean*, chap. 16; Den Heijer, *De geschiedenis*, chap. 5.

18. For Tobago, see Goslinga, *Dutch in the Caribbean*, chap. 16.

19. NA OWIC 42:35, 42, "Conditien ende Articulen."

20. NA OWIC 37:58; *ERSNY* 1:75, 78–79. See also NA, toegangsnr. 3.20.87, Van Wassenaer van Duvenvoorde Archief, inv. nr. 2052, "Extract uyt het Register der Resolutien vande E. Ed: heeren Bewinthebberen vande Westindische Comp. ter vergaderinge vande XIX" (March 10, 1628) (hereafter cited as NA WD).

21. ZA HV 182. For an English translation and transcription, see Martin van Wallenburg, Alistair Bright, Lodewijk Hulsman, and Martijn van den Bel, trans., "The Voyage of Gelein van Stapels to the Amazon River, the Guianas and the Caribbean, 1629–1630," *Journal of the Hakluyt Society* (January 2015), 29–30.

22. "Pretty bad" is from Van Wallenburg et al., "Voyage," 31; and "prayers" is my own translation from the original: ZA HV 182.

23. NA OWIC 50:80. For Van Walbeeck as elder, see NA OWIC 63:4.

24. NA OWIC 50:80.

25. NA OWIC 14:24. See also NA OWIC 14:9. On the schism in the English-speaking church, see Keith Sprunger, *Dutch Puritanism: A History of English and Scottish Churches*

of the Netherlands in the Sixteenth and Seventeenth Centuries (Leiden: Brill, 1982), 116–118. That the two Fletchers are the same is suggested by the timing of events and the appearance of a second common name (William Watson) in the WIC's records and Sprunger's account of the English controversy. One of the men the Fletcher/Watson faction tried to appoint in Amsterdam was John Davenport, future Puritan leader in New England.

26. NA OWIC 50:28. See also NA OWIC 14:9, 20, 25–26.

27. Willem Frijhoff, "A Misunderstood Calvinist: The Religious Choices of Bastiaen Jansz Krol, New Netherland's First Church Servant," *Journal of Early American History* 1, no. 1 (2011), 64. The essay was published in a different form in Leon van den Broeke, Hans Krabbendam, and Dirk Mouw, eds., *Transatlantic Pieties: Dutch Clergy in Colonial America* (Grand Rapids, MI: Eerdmans, 2012), 37–57.

28. Frijhoff, "Misunderstood Calvinist," as well as SAA ACA 19 (December 7, 1623; January 25, 1624).

29. "Provisional Regulations for the Colonists," in *Documents relating to New Netherland, 1624–1626, in the Henry E. Huntington Library* (San Marino, CA: Huntington Library, 1924), 2–18.

30. For Krol's French, see Frijhoff, "Misunderstood." For the rest, see Peters, "Volunteers." P. Gantois appears in Peters's appendix.

31. Jaap Jacobs, *The Colony of New Netherland: A Dutch Settlement in Seventeenth-Century America* (Ithaca, NY: Cornell University Press, 2009), 30; Oliver Rink, *Holland on the Hudson: An Economic and Social History of Dutch New York* (Ithaca, NY: Cornell University Press, 1986), 69–81.

32. "Instructions," in *Documents relating to New Netherland*, 48. For the WIC ships and settlers of 1625–1626, see Rink, *Holland*, 81–83; Van Wassenaer, *Historisch verhael*, 9:40–44.

33. "Instructions," in *Documents relating to New Netherland*, 36, 72; and in the same book, "Special Instructions for Cryn Fredericksz," 143, 148/E9, 164/E17.

34. "Special Instructions," 160–163/E15–16. Most translations in this paragraph are Van Laer's. Only the last one is my own.

35. Jeroen van den Hurk, "Plan versus Execution: The 'Ideal City' of New Amsterdam. Seventeenth-Century Netherlandic Town Planning in North America," *New York History* 96, nos. 3–4 (Fall–Winter 2015): 265–283; Charles Gehring, "New Netherland: The Formative Years, 1609–1632," in *Four Centuries of Dutch-American Relations*, ed. Hans Krabbendam, Cornelis A. van Minnen, and Giles Scott-Smith (Albany: State University of New York Press, 2009), 79.

36. "Peter Schagen Letter," New Netherland Institute, https://www.newnetherlandinstitute.org/history-and-heritage/additional-resources/dutch-treats/peter-schagen-letter (accessed January 2015).

37. Nicolaes van Wassenaer, "Historisch Verhael," in *Narratives of New Netherland*, ed. J. Franklin Jameson (New York: Charles Scribner's Sons, 1909), 83–84.

38. Russell Shorto, *The Island at the Center of the World: The Epic Story of Dutch Manhattan and the Forgotten Colony that Shaped America* (New York: Vintage, 2005), 48.

39. *ERSNY* 1:43–44; Gerald F. de Jong, *The Dutch Reformed Church in the American Colonies* (Grand Rapids, MI: Eerdmans, 1978), 13; SAA AKA 5:336.

40. *Biografisch Lexicon voor de Geschiedenis van het Nederlandse Protestantisme*, 6 vols. (Kampen: J. H. Kok, 1978–2006), 1:182–183. See also the documents at the back of Albert Eekhof, *Jonas Michaelius, Founder of the Church in New Netherland* (Leiden: A. W. Sijthoff, 1926), esp. 86–88 (for Leiden University) and 94–95 (for Germany).

41. Michaelius described these experiences in two letters. See the letter of August 8, 1628, in Eekhof, *Jonas Michaelius*, 99–114 (the English translation begins on 107); and the August 11 letter in *ERSNY* 1:49–68. In both cases I'm relying on the printed translations, not my own.

42. Ibid. (both letters). See also the Van Foreest exchange in Eekhof, *Jonas Michaelius*, 57–70. All translations are from Eekhof except one: he used "fecundity" instead of "fertility." I changed it for clarity's sake.

43. Shorto, *Island*, 64.

44. Eekhof, *Jonas Michaelius*, 111; *ERSNY* 1:51, 67.

45. Eekhof, *Jonas Michaelius*, 111.

46. *ERSNY* 1:52. Michaelius's description of the early church runs from pp. 52–55. See p. 54 for Krol as another elder.

47. Diarmaid MacCulloch, *The Reformation: A History* (New York: Viking, 2004), 581–583.

48. MacCulloch, 581–583. See also A. Th. van Deursen, *Bavianen en Slijkgeuzen: Kerk en kerkvolk ten tijde van Maurits en Oldenbarnevelt* (Assen: Van Gorcum, 1974), 196–200; R. B. Evenhuis, *Ook Dat Was Amsterdam: De kerk der hervorming in de gouden eeuw*, vol. 1 (Amsterdam: W. Ten Have N. V., 1965), 17–18.

49. *ERSNY* 1:53–54.

50. *ERSNY*, 1:45–48, 53; Eekhof, *Bastiaen Jansz. Krol*; "Letter of Isaack de Rasiere," *Documents relating to New Netherland*, 176.

51. Michaelius to Van Foreest, September 13, 1630, in Eekhof, *Jonas Michaelius*, 67–69. For Michaelius's commitment to remain aloof and his misgivings about trade, see *ERSNY* 1:55, 63.

52. For more on the Minuit-Michaelius fight, see Jacobs, *Colony*, 149–150; Shorto, *Island*, 65.

53. A. J. F. van Laer, ed., *Van Rensselaer Bowier Manuscripts: Being the Letters of Kiliaen van Rensselaer, 1630–1643* (Albany: University of the State of New York, 1908), 208. For the settlers, see Janny Venema, *Kiliaen van Rensselaer (1586–1643): Designing a New World* (Hilversum: Verloren, 2010), 246–247, 250–256.

54. SAA ACA 4:22; SAA AKA 6:327; *ERSNY* 1:83, 119, 163–164, 216. *ERSNY* says that the schoolmaster, Adam Rolands/Roelandsen, arrived in 1633 with Bogardus and Van Twiller, but I think that's a mistake. He probably didn't arrive until late 1637 or 1638. See SAA ACA 157:1 (August 4, 1637).

55. Jameson, *Narratives*, 83–84.

56. The classic work on disease in America is Alfred Crosby, *The Columbian Exchange: Biological and Cultural Consequences of 1492* (Westport, CT: Greenwood Press, 1972). See also Noble David Cook, *Born to Die: Disease and New World Conquest, 1492–1650* (New York: Cambridge University Press, 1998). For Africa, see Philip Curtin, "Epidemiology and the Slave Trade," *Political Science Quarterly* 83, no. 2 (June 1968): 190–216. See also Klaas Ratelband, *Nederlanders in West Afrika, 1600–1650: Angola, Kongo en São Tomé* (Zutphen: Walburg Pers, 2000).

254 NOTES TO PAGES 103-106

57. For the necessity of a minister, see NA AAC 1367; 1369 (July 24, 1621; July 28, August 1 and 9, November 9, 1623; August 15, 1624); SAA AKA 5:107, 129; NA OWIC 1:16.

58. See the Drijstrang and Tiaeus instructions at SAA ACA 19 (December 3, 1619; September 1, 1625).

59. NA ASG, deel 5, 12564.42 (August 25, 1659). For worship in general, see SAA AKA 243:25; and the many references in Klaas Ratelband, *Vijf Dagregisters van het Kasteel Sao Jorge da Mina* (The Hague: Martinus Nijhoff, 1953): 2, 4, 25, 27, 44, 45, 50, etc. See also Willem Frijhoff, *Wegen van Evert Willemsz. Een Hollands weeskind op zoek naar zichzelf, 1607–1647* (Nijmegen: SUN, 1995), chap. 13.

60. "Michael Hemmersam's Description of the Gold Coast, 1639–1645," in *German Sources for West African History, 1559–1669*, trans. and ed. Adam Jones (Wiesbaden: Franz Steiner Verlag GMBH, 1983), 127, 130. On WIC forts and churches, see A. W. Lawrence, *Trade Castles and Forts of West Africa* (Stanford, CA: Stanford University Press, 1964), pt. 2, chap. 3; pt. 4, chaps. 1–2.

61. "Michael Hemmersam's Description," 130–131. See also Frijhoff, *Wegen*, chap. 13.

62. For Hendricks, see SAA ACA 4:378; NA OWIC 11 (January 19, 1645).

63. SAA ACA 210:214–217; 158:92. The next minister confirmed the number of members: SAA ACA 210:221–222. See also Rev. Nicolaus Ketel's report of thirty-six members in Luanda in the 1640s: UA, toegangsnr. 52-1, Archief van de Synode te Utrecht, inv. nr. 279, September 15, 1642 (hereafter cited as UA ASU).

64. Donald R. Hopkins, "Dracunculiasis," *Cambridge World History of Human Disease*, ed. Kenneth Kipple (Cambridge: Cambridge University Press, 1993), 687–689. See also the dead *ziekentroosters* in NA OWIC 58:207. Ministers who died in Africa include Fredericus Vittaeus (1642), Johannes van Steenlandt (1655), Martinus Westerwyck (1656 or 1657), Joannes Schulperoort (1659), Henricus Benningh (1666), and Abraham Oudewater (1672).

65. SAA AKA 243:25; NA OWIC 11 (February 3, 1634). For "discouraged," see SAA ACA 5:37; 210:217, 221–222.

66. Ratelband, *Vijf Dagregisters*, 174–175; for his other ailments, see 89, 133, 146–147.

67. Ratelband, *Vijf Dagregisters*, 174–175.

68. Evenhuis, *Ook Dat Was Amsterdam*, 1:71–73; MacCulloch, *Reformation*, 557–560; A. Th. van Deursen, *Plain Lives in a Golden Age: Popular Culture, Religion, and Society in Seventeenth-Century Holland* (Cambridge: Cambridge University Press, 1991), 244–246, 263.

69. Ratelband, *Vijf Dagregisters* is full of funerals; see 5, 22n1, 42, 63, 71, 183, 278, etc.

70. For mockery, see also the Hermanss experience in SAA ACA 2:124–125; "Samuel Brun's Voyages of 1611–1620," in Jones, *German Sources*, 80. For IJsebout, see SAA ACA 210:215.

71. NA OWIC 11 (February 3, 1634). For officers on the consistory, see SAA ACA 210:215, 217; 7:39.

72. For alcohol problems, see NA ASG, deel 5, 12564.12, 22; Ratelband, *Vijf Dagregisters*, 225, 228, 247, and (for a disruptive incident involving sex) 265–266.

73. For missing prayer, see Ratelband, *Vijf Dagregisters*, 53. Punishments are meted out numerous times in the registers. For an example of whipping, see 153; thrown in a pit, 247; the wooden horse, 248, 298, 354. Sylvia R. Frey writes about the wooden horse in "Courts and Cats: British Military Justice in the Eighteenth Century," *Military Affairs* 43, no. 1 (February 1979): 5–11. See also John S. Hare, "Military Punishments in the War of 1812," *Journal of the American Military Institute* 4, no. 4 (Winter 1940): 225–239.

74. Ratelband, *Vijf Dagregisters*, 45, 90, 266. For rulers and Reformed theologians, see the sermon (used by the WIC) in Heinrich Bullinger, *Huys-boeck* (1582), 64b–68b.

75. NA OWIC 11 (Reynier Doeckens account; March 18–November 18, 1647, esp. May 2); UA ASU 279 (September 15, 1642). For marriages at Elmina, see Ratelband, *Vijf Dagregisters*, 14, 216, 256–257, 263. For complaints about fornication/adultery, see NA AAC 1364 (November 15, 1618); NHA, toegangsnr. 123, Archief van de Classis Edam, inv. nr. 3, f. 411 (hereafter cited as NHA ACE); and any of IJsebout's letters in SAA ACA 210:214–217.

76. SAA ACA 210:214–217, 221–222.

77. Van Wassenaer, *Historisch Verhael*, 17:58–60.

78. Van Wassenaer, 17:58–60.

79. Van Wassenaer, 17:58–60.

80. Jacob Steendam, *Den Distelvink*, 3 vols. (Amsterdam, 1649–1650), 1:72–76, 98–101; 2:139, 176–178; 3:71–73, 84–85.

81. Steendam, 1:76–79, 2:99–103, 129, 132.

82. SAA AKA 245:66; SAA ACA 210:217.

5. Reformers in the Land of the Holy Cross

1. Charles Boxer, *The Dutch in Brazil* (Hamden, CT: Archon Books, 1973), 32–158. For problems in the church, see NA OWIC, 8:153–154, 175–176; 22:154–155; NA, toegangsnr. 3.01.04.01, Archief van het Staten van Holland en West-Friesland, inv. nr. 1358C, "Rapport . . . van Brazil" (1636) (hereafter cited as NA HWF); NA ACD 82:583–584; SAA ACA 4:80–84.

2. T. Brienen et al., eds., *De Nadere Reformatie: Beschrijving van haar Voornaamste Vertegenwoordigers* ('s-Gravenhage: Uitgeverij Boekcentrum B. V., 1986).

3. For the meanings of religious tolerance and the negative connotations of that term, see Evan Haefeli, *New Netherland and the Dutch Origins of American Religious Liberty* (Philadelphia: University of Pennsylvania Press, 2012), ix–xi, 1–19.

4. Stuart Schwartz, *Sugar Plantations in the Formation of Brazilian Society: Bahia, 1550–1835* (New York: Cambridge University Press, 1985), 1–72; John Hemmings, *Red Gold: The Conquest of the Brazilian Indians* (Cambridge, MA: Harvard University Press, 1978); C. R. Boxer, *The Portuguese Seaborne Empire, 1415–1825* (New York: Knopf, 1969), chap. 5; Boxer, *Dutch in Brazil*, 17–20.

5. B. N. Teensma, ed. and trans., *Vincent Joachim Soler's Seventeen Letters, 1636–1643* (Rio de Janeiro: Editora Index, 1999), 11–12; ZA ACW 73 (May 18, 1636); NA OWIC 56:125; 60:164. For the Dutch population, see Victor Enthoven, "Dutch Crossings: Migration between the Netherlands and the New World, 1600–1800," *Atlantic Studies* 2, no. 2 (October 2005): 153–176.

6. For tolerance in Brazil, see George L. Smith, *Religion and Trade in New Nether-land: Dutch Origins and American Development* (Ithaca, NY: Cornell University Press, 1973), 123–125; Frans Schalkwijk, *The Reformed Church in Dutch Brazil, 1630–1654* (Zoe-termeer: Boekencentrum, 1998), 231–300; Jonathan Israel and Stuart B. Schwartz, *The Expansion of Tolerance: Religion in Dutch Brazil (1624–1654)* (Amsterdam: Amsterdam University Press, 2007); Boxer, *Dutch in Brazil*, 117, 123–124; Evan Haefeli, "Breaking the Christian Atlantic," in *The Legacy of Dutch Brazil*, ed. Michiel van Groesen (New York: Cambridge University Press, 2014), 124–145.

7. NA OWIC 51:25. See also the report of July 2, 1636, in NA ASG, deel 2, 5754. For "military church" (in the section title), see Schalkwijk, *Reformed Church*, 67, 82.

8. NA OWIC 50:124; 51:117; 53:116. Stetten's "Jurnael der Kercken in Paraíba" is at NA, toegangsnr. 1.05.06, Verspreide West-Indische Stukken, inv. nr. 1408 (hereafter cited as NA VS). Stetten blamed negative rumors about his own conduct on a man and woman who tried to tarnish his name because he criticized their adulterous relationship.

9. NA OWIC 8:153–154, 175–176. For other bad reports see note 1 above and NA HWF 1358C, "Rapport . . . van Brazil" (1636); Caspar van Baerle, *The History of Brazil under the Governorship of Count Johan Maurits of Nassau, 1636–1644*, trans. Blanche T. van Berckel-Ebeling Koning (Gainesville, FL: University Press of Florida, 2011), 49.

10. *Album studiosorum Academiae Lugduno Batavae MDLXXV–MDCCCLXXV* (Den Haag: Martinus Nijhoff, 1925), 124; SAA ACA 4:34, 66; NA OWIC 52:99. The three men were Daniel Neveux, Johannes Harmann Osterdag van Appellen, and Samuel Fol-kerius. Neveux was a *ziekentrooster*: NA OWIC 8:153–154. See also NA OWIC 22:154–155; Schalkwijk, *Reformed Church*, 130–131.

11. SAA ACA 4:82, 84; GASD ACZ 2:22; NA ACD 82:583–584.

12. J. A. G. de Mello, *Nederlanders in Brazilie, 1624–1654* (Zutphen: Walburg, 2001), 35–135.

13. For Dapper, see GASD ACZ 20–24 (March 20, 1637).

14. Schalkwijk, *Reformed Church*, 88–92. For the Dutch classis system, see A. Th. van Deursen, *Bavianen en Slijkgeuzen: Kerk en kerkvolk ten tijde van Maurits en Oldenbarnevelt* (Assen: Van Gorcum, 1974), 5–7; Leon van den Broeke, *Een geschiedenis van de classis* (Kampen: Kok, 2005).

15. UA ASU 212:5–16.

16. UA ASU 212: 5–16. The minister who left before the reformation began was Neveux. The one without skills was Folkerius. For the investment scam (Oosterdag), see NA OWIC 68 (March 16 and 26, 1639); UA ASU 212:33–36. For Schagen, see NA OWIC 52:14, 99 (also in ZA ACW 73); SAA ACA 163:28.

17. NA OWIC 68 (March 9 and 17, April 9 and 20, 1637); 52:87.

18. Boxer, *Dutch in Brazil*, 67. See also (esp. for the German connection) Van Baerle, *History*, 31–33. For more on Johan Maurits, see Wim Klooster, *The Dutch in the Ameri-cas, 1600–1800* (Providence, RI: John Carter Brown Library, 1997), chap. 3; E. van den Boogaart, ed., *Johan Maurits van Nassau-Siegen, 1604–1679: A Humanist Prince in Europe and Brazil* (The Hague: Johan Maurits van Nassau Stichting, 1979).

19. Teensma, *Vincent Joachim Soler*, 11–12, 17–18, 39–40, 51–53.

20. On the reformation, see GASD ACZ 20–24 (March 20, 1637); 2:70; NA OWIC 52:70; 53:4; 53:46.

21. Teensma, *Vincent Joachim Soler*, 11–12.

22. For the number of ministers in any given year, see Schalkwijk, *Reformed Church*, 109. For "thirteen" and "almost thirty," see NA OWIC 70 (February 15, 1645); 57:38.

23. Schalkwijk, *Reformed Church*, 70–74, 88–94.

24. NA ASG, deel 2, 5753 (April 4, 1634); 5759, 209–224; *Groot Placaet Boeck, vervattende de Placaeten, Ordonnantien ende Edicten van de Doorluchtige, Hoogh Mog. Heeren Staten Generael der Vereenighde Nederlanden* (The Hague, 1658), 622; NA OWIC 2 (August 9, 1636).

25. For "church of the conquerors," see note 7 above.

26. Johannes Baers, *Olinda, ghelegen int landt van Brasil, inde capitania van Phernambuco, met mannelijcke dapperheyt ende groote couragie inghenomen, ende verovert op den 16. Februarij A. 1630* (Amsterdam, 1630), 33; NA OWIC 71 (September 13, 1645); NA Aanw. 644, 50–52 (August 12–16, 1646).

27. NA OWIC 51:25; 68 (July 27, 1636); 70–71 (July 1, 1644; February 13, 1647); 73 (December 5 and 25, 1649).

28. For officers in the consistory, see Schalkwijk, *Reformed Church*, 117–122, 239–240; and the Brazil classis minutes at NA, UA, and ZA. For an example of elders / deacons before the council, see NA OWIC 68 (February 13, 1637).

29. UA ASU 212:5–16; NA OWIC 68 (March 19, 1637).

30. NA OWIC 53:4; 68–69 (April 16 and November 7, 1637; October 17, 1640; March 14, 1643).

31. NA OWIC 61:7; 70–72 (June 4, 1643; February 23, 1646; June 5, 1648).

32. NA OWIC 51:25, 85, 117. The other seven ministers were Johannes Apricius, Dionisius Biscaretto, David à Doreslaer, Johannes Eduardus, Thomas Kemp, Johannes Osterdag, and Vincent de Vaux.

33. Schalkwijk, *Reformed Church*, 152–167.

34. Schalkwijk, 152–167. See also NA OWIC 53:22; 46 (April 4, 1640); 68 (May 16, 1639). On Portuguese obstinacy, see Van Baerle, *History*, 130. Soler once claimed that some were becoming receptive in *Cort and sonderlingh Verhael* (Amsterdam, 1639), 7.

35. Merry E. Wiesner-Hanks, *Christianity and Sexuality in the Early Modern World: Regulating Desire, Reforming Practice* (New York: Routledge, 2000); Diarmaid MacCulloch, *The Reformation: A History* (New York: Viking, 2004), chap. 16. For marriage regulation under the WIC, see Deborah Hamer, "Creating an Orderly Society: The Regulation of Marriage and Sex in the Dutch Atlantic World, 1621–1674" (PhD diss., Columbia University, 2014).

36. UA ASU 212:5–16, 37–42; NA OWIC 8:359, 366–367; 53:4, 55:116, 59:43, 61:7; 68–69 (September 11, 1638; January 18, 1641; May 20 and July 23, 1642); ZA ACW 73 (October 17, 1641). See also NA OWIC 3:102, 108; 14:26, 136; SAA ACA 5:108–110; 163:56–58.

37. NA OWIC 71 (February 15, 1646).

38. NA OWIC 70 (September 13, 1644); 9:226, 229; 61:57. See also NA OWIC 68 (February 23, June 25, and September 11, 1638). Schalkwijk (*Reformed Church*, 284) claims incorrectly that the church got what it wanted.

39. NA OWIC 53:4; 59:40.

40. NA OWIC 53:4; UA ASU 212:25–32, 37–42.

41. NA OWIC 68 (November 9, 1638).

42. UA ASU 212:37–42; NA OWIC 55:116; 69 (January 18, 1641).

43. See, for example, UA ASU 212:1–16, 25–32; NA OWIC 68 (March 11 and 19, December 28, 1637; January 15, November 22, 1638); 52:99; 53:4.

44. For "very bad," see NA OWIC 69 (December 11, 1642). For the rest, see NA OWIC 69 (September 15, 1637; February 23, 1638; December 8, 1642; June 4, 1643); NHA AKHA 22 (October 8, 1638); NA OWIC 61:7.

45. For other examples of deportations (sometimes only to other provinces), see NA OWIC 68–71 (April 19, 1638; August 1 and 24, 1639; December 9, 1640; January 3, August 21, and September 8, 1641; March 14 and August 5, 1643; September 13, 1644; February 15, 1646); 57:139.

46. NA OWIC 70 (June 4, 1643).

47. NA OWIC 68 (September 11, 1638; October 17, 1640). For other complaints, usually about low-ranking officers, see also NA OWIC 69 (March 27, 1641; October 27, 1642); 56:125, 59:40; ZA ACW 73 (November 4, 1641); SAA ACA 4:312; 157:128.

48. NA OWIC 71 (February 3 and 15, 1646). See also NA OWIC 69–70 (January 18, 1641; February 27, 1645).

49. NA OWIC 69 (May 20, 1642).

50. NA OWIC 68–70 (December 7, 1639; October 17, 1642; June 30, 1645).

51. NA OWIC 60:10.

52. NA OWIC 56:125. For a consistory destroyed when elders were transferred, see the case of Itamaraca (Rev. Polhemus) at UA ASU 212:37–42. See also NA OWIC 68–72 (November 2, 1640, January 17, March 27, April 12, June 7, December 5, 1641; August 19, 1648); 55:116.

53. For power sharing and Portuguese orphan masters/*schepenen*, see NA OWIC 69–70 (June 4, 1641; October 7, 1642; June 30, 1644). See also NA OWIC 48 (August 23, 1636); 9:39–41; 57:32; 58:268. The operation of sugar mills on Sunday was a regular problem. See ZA ACW 73 (October 17, 1641); NA OWIC 68–69 (November 22, 1638; May 20, 1642).

54. NA OWIC 57:50.

55. NA OWIC 69 (September 29, October 9 and 15, and November 25–26, 1642; January 2, 1643); SAA ACA 157:116.

56. On the 1634 Paraíba treaty, the provisions of which were eventually extended elsewhere, see Schalkwijk, *Reformed Church*, 274. See also NA OWIC 8:160–172; 53:22; 55:118; 69 (June 11, 1641); NA ASG, deel 2, 5756, 204–213.

57. NA OWIC 68–70 (February 13, April 16, 1637; January 15, 1638; July 22, August 6, 1641; July 23, 1642, October 29, December 11, 1643); 8:359, 366–367; 53:4; UA ASU 212:25–32.

58. NA OWIC 68–70 (January 15, September 11, November 22, 1638; May 6 and 16, 1639; November 7, 1640; June 23 and 27, July 1, 1644); UA ASU 212:25–32. For a similar quarrel about facilities in Igaraçu, see NA OWIC 68–70 (May 6, 1639; November 2, 1640; February 5, June 23, 1643).

59. NA OWIC 68 (May 20, 1639). For Jesuit property, see NA OWIC 8:160–172.

60. NA OWIC 2:11–19; 8:160–172; 51:25; 53:22; 46 (April 4, 1640); 68 (May 4, 1637). For lands/tithes, see also Schalkwijk, *Reformed Church*, 278–279.

61. NA OWIC 8:160–172; 53:22; 68 (May 4, 1637). See also Schalkwijk, *Reformed Church*, 268–300.

62. NA OWIC 51:25; 52:42; 55:1, 25; 48 (August 23, 1636); 69–70 (January 17, 1639; December 7, 1643); 8:222–223, 313, 317–318, 330.

63. NA OWIC 25:20; 56:197, 259; ZA ACW 73 (October 17, 1641); SAA ACA 4:258.

64. NA OWIC 53:4; 55:116; 59:43; UA ASU 212:25–32, 37–42; NA OWIC 68–70 (January 15, November 22, 1638; June 5, 1641; January 27, 1642, March 3, 1643; March 6, 1645); 8:359, 366–367. See other examples of the council's response in NA OWIC 68–69 (September 14, 1638; September 9, 1641).

65. NA OWIC 69 (June 11, 1641); ZA ACW 73 (October 17, 1641); NA OWIC 25:20; 60:10.

66. NA OWIC 69 (January 27, 1642). For the murder, see Schalkwijk, *Reformed Church*, 294.

67. NA OWIC 69 (September 8–9, 1641).

68. NA OWIC 68–69 (July 2, 1637; September 1, 1640); NA OWIC 56:283.

69. NA OWIC 22:87; 51:25, 42; 56:157. For what the colony could bear, see UA ASU 212:37–42; NA OWIC 69 (January 18, 1641).

70. NA ASG, deel 2, 5756, 244–249.

71. For "at first," see NA OWIC 56:303. For plantations, see NA OWIC 68 (September 1 and October 3, 1640); 8:359, 366–367.

72. NA OWIC 57:32. See also NA OWIC 8:368; 9:1–25; SAA ACA 157:63, 67, 75–76; 163:96–99.

73. NA OWIC 59:131. See also the Hamel, Van Bullestrate, and Bas report at the Koninklijke Bibliotheek (The Hague), Special Collections, 76 A 16 (hereafter cited as KB).

74. Van Baerle, *History*, 47, 285.

75. NA OWIC 24:104; 35:6–7, 10. See also NA OWIC 9:1–25, where the directors mention the 26th article of the treaty. For the latter, see Carlos Calvo, ed., *Colección Completa de los Tratados: Convenciones, Capitulaciones, Armisticios y Otros Actos Diplomáticos* (Paris, 1862), 63–64. See also Van Baerle, *History*, 220–222; and for Dutch-Portuguese diplomacy, Cornelis van de Haar, *De diplomatieke betrekkingen tussen de Republiek en Portugal, 1640–1661* (Groningen: Wolters, 1961).

76. Schalkwijk, *Reformed Church*, 275.

77. SAA ACA 157:75–76.

78. NA OWIC 70–71 (April 10, 1645; February 15, 1646); 9:261; 60:79.

79. NA OWIC 9:261; 60:10. See also NA OWIC 70 (December 7, 1643; April 10, 24, and 25, May 1, 1645); 59:40; 60:79.

80. For details on the planning and events of the rebellion, see Boxer, *Dutch in Brazil*, chaps. 5 and 6.

81. NA OWIC 60:131; ZA, toegangsnr. 2000, Archief van de Stad Veere, inv. nr. 1784, December 14, 1645, "Remonstrantie" (hereafter cited as ZA ASV). See also Schalkwijk, *Reformed Church*, 298–299.

82. *Manifest Door d'Inwoonders van Parnambuco uytgegeven tot hun verantwoordinge op't aennemen der wapenen tegens de West-Indische Compagnie* (Antwerp, 1646), 2, 9. For the Dutch response, see *Korte Antwoort Tegens 'T Manifest ende Remonstrantie* (1647).

83. For the poison affair, see SAA, Not. Arch. 1290:60; *Extract ende Copye van verscheyde Brieven en Schriften, Belangende de Rebellie der Paepsche Portugesen van desen Staet in Brasilien* (1646), 25. For the cryptic note, see NA OWIC 62:119.

84. NA OWIC 61:7; 63:4; 64:27; SAA ACA 212:188–190. See also SAA ACA 4:312.

6. Turmoil in the Garden of Eden

1. Nina Baym, ed., *The Norton Anthology of American Literature*, 6th ed., vol. A: *Literature to 1820* (New York: W. W. Norton, 2003), 276–284. The idea that Africa impacted Steendam's view of New Netherland is not original to this book. See Willem Frijhoff, *Wegen van Evert Willemsz. Een Hollands weeskind op zoek naar zichzelf, 1607–1647* (Nijmegen: SUN, 1995), chap. 13.

2. Steendam knew about these troubles because he wrote about them in "The Complaint of New Amsterdam." See Henry Murphy, ed., *Jacob Steendam, Noch Vaster* (The Hague, 1861), 36–43.

3. NA WD 2052, April 16, 1638, "Extract uyt het Register." See the WIC's response in NA WD 2048.

4. The WIC's free trade debates are covered in Jaap Jacobs, *New Netherland: A Dutch Colony in Seventeenth-Century America* (Leiden: Brill, 2005), chap. 3; Oliver Rink, *Holland on the Hudson: An Economic and Social History of Dutch New York* (Ithaca, NY: Cornell University Press, 1986), chaps. 4–5; Cornelis Goslinga, *The Dutch in the Caribbean and on the Wild Coast, 1580–1680* (Gainesville: University of Florida Press, 1971), chap. 12; Charles Boxer, *The Dutch in Brazil* (Hamden, CT: Archon Books, 1973), 75–82. For 100,000, see Henk den Heijer, *De geschiedenis van de WIC* (Zutphen: Walburg Pers, 1994), 83. For "half a million," see E. B. O'Callaghan, *History of New Netherland; or, New York Under the Dutch*, vol. 1 (New York: D. Appleton, 1846), 350; John Romeyn Brodhead, *History of the State of New York* (New York: Harper and Brothers, 1853), 405; Edwin G. Burrows and Mike Wallace, *Gotham: A History of New York City to 1898* (New York: Oxford University Press, 1999), 40.

5. For New Netherland's relative isolation, see Wim Klooster, "The Place of New Netherland in the West India Company's Grand Scheme," in *Revisiting New Netherland: Perspectives on Early Dutch America*, ed. Joyce Goodfriend (Leiden: Brill, 2005), 57–70.

6. Dutch colonial success has been a topic since the 1980s. For commercial success, see Rink, *Holland*. For social institutions, see Jaap Jacobs, *The Colony of New Netherland: A Dutch Settlement in Seventeenth-Century America* (Ithaca, NY: Cornell University Press, 2009); Janny Venema, *Beverwyck: A Dutch Village on the American Frontier, 1652–1664* (Albany: State University of New York Press, 2003).

7. Rink, *Holland*, 134–138; Jacobs, *Colony*, 76. In *Religion and Trade in New Netherland: Dutch Origins and American Development* (Ithaca, NY: Cornell University Press, 1973), chap. 11, Smith writes incorrectly, in my opinion, that 1647 was the point at which the directors began to think of the colony in a new way.

8. *ERSNY* 1:53, 120–121. On ministers and patroonships, see ibid., 1:75.

9. Morton Wagman, "Liberty in New Amsterdam: A Sailor's Life in Early New York," *New York History* 64, no. 2 (April 1983): 101–119; Scott Christianson, "Criminal Punishment in New Netherland," in *A Beautiful and Fruitful Place: Selected Rensselaer-*

swijck Seminar Papers, ed. Nancy Anne McClure Zeller (Albany, NY: New Netherland Publishing, 1991), 83–90. For the baptismal register, see *ERSNY* 1:123.

10. David de Vries, *Korte historiael ende journaels aenteyckeninge van verscheyden voyagiens in de vier deelen des wereldts-ronde* (Hoorn, 1655), 163–164; *ERSNY* 1:85–86, 119, 163–166, 216, 254–260, 266–267.

11. *ERSNY* 1:156–157, 168–169. For the settlers, see S. G. Nissenson, *The Patroon's Domain* (New York: Octagon Books, 1973), chap. 3, and Janny Venema, *Kiliaen van Rensselaer (1586–1643): Designing a New World* (Hilversum: Verloren, 2010), 257.

12. Jacobs, *Colony*, 76–81. See also Russell Shorto, *The Island at the Center of the World: The Epic Story of Dutch Manhattan and the Forgotten Colony that Shaped America* (New York: Vintage, 2005). For the Indian wars, see Donna Merwick, *The Shame and the Sorrow: Dutch-Amerindian Encounters in New Netherland* (Philadelphia: University of Pennsylvania Press, 2006), 133–180; Rink, *Holland*, 216–221; Allen W. Trelease, *Indian Affairs in Colonial New York: The Seventeenth Century* (Ithaca, NY: Cornell University Press, 1960), chap. 3.

13. For tyranny, see Benjamin Schmidt, *Innocence Abroad: The Dutch Imagination and the New World, 1570–1670* (Cambridge: Cambridge University Press, 2001), 179–181.

14. I'm referring to Bogardus's disagreements with Van Twiller and others. See Frijhoff, *Wegen*, chap. 16.

15. Frijhoff, *Wegen*, chap. 17; Jacobs, *Colony*, 151–152; Smith, *Religion and Trade*, 169–173. See also *ERSNY* 1:196–200. For Kieft and his officers on one side of the division and Bogardus/community on the other, see *ERSNY* 1:230.

16. Frijhoff, *Wegen*, esp. chap. 20.

17. *ERSNY* 1:233–237. For the reorganization, see Charles T. Gehring and J. A. Schiltkamp, eds. and trans., *Curaçao Papers, 1640–1665* (Interlaken, NY: Heart of the Lakes Publishing, 1987), xiv–xv; Jacobs, *Colony*, 63–64.

18. *ERSNY* 1:252; Jacobs, *Colony*, 80–83, 152–154.

19. *ERSNY* 1:257.

20. *ERSNY*, 1:254–260.

21. *ERSNY*, 1:266–268, 275–276.

22. For Van der Donck, see Shorto, *Island*.

23. *ERSNY* 1:278.

24. Dennis J. Maika, "Securing the Burgher Right in New Amsterdam: The Struggle for Municipal Citizenship in the Seventeenth-Century Atlantic World," in *Revisiting New Netherland*, ed. Goodfriend, 93–128.

25. "Flirted with colonization" refers to the settlers of the 1620s and the patroonship plan.

26. For Dutch congregations, see Gerald F. de Jong, *The Dutch Reformed Church in the American Colonies* (Grand Rapids, MI: Eerdmans, 1978), chaps. 2–3; Charles E. Corwin, *A Manual of the Reformed Church in America, 1628–1922*, 5th ed. (New York, 1922), 17.

27. *ERSNY* 1:348–351, 382–386, 393–400, 457–458, 487–489, 534–535, 547–550; SAA ACA 6:158, 157:190, 357, 421.

28. For the hesitation about Curaçao, see NA OWIC 22:157; SAA ACA 157:92. Klooster describes its function as a military outpost in *Illicit Riches: Dutch Trade in the Caribbean, 1648–1795* (Leiden: KITLV Press, 1998), chap. 3.

29. SAA ACA 4:159, 169; 157:21–23; NA OWIC 54:197.

30. SAA ACA 224:1–2.

31. SAA ACA 224: 4–5.

32. Jaap Jacobs, "Like Father, Like Son? The Early Years of Petrus Stuyvesant," in Goodfriend, *Revisiting New Netherland*, 205–242; Donna Merwick, *Stuyvesant Bound: An Essay on Loss across Time* (Philadelphia: University of Pennsylvania Press, 2013), chap. 1.

33. For "benefactor" and Selyns, see *ERSNY* 1:296, 363–364, 477. For the rest, see Smith, *Religion and Trade*, 187–188; Burrows and Wallace, *Gotham*, 43–59. See also Joyce D. Goodfriend, "The Struggle over the Sabbath in Peter Stuyvesant's New Amsterdam," in *Power and the City in the Netherlandic World*, ed. Wayne te Brake and Wim Klooster (Leiden: Brill, 2006), 205–224.

34. Cited in Burrows and Wallace, *Gotham*, 58, and Christianson, "Criminal Punishment," 86.

35. Though I differ from her on religious topics, on the law and courts, see Martha Shattuck, "A Civil Society: Court and Community in Beverwijck, New Netherland, 1652–1664" (PhD diss., Boston University, 1993); Shattuck, "'For the Peace and Welfare of the Community': Maintaining a Civil Society in New Netherland," *De Halve Maen* 72, no. 2 (Summer 1999): 27–32. See also Dennis Sullivan, *The Punishment of Crime in Colonial New York: The Dutch Experience in Albany during the Seventeenth Century* (New York: Peter Lang, 1997).

36. E. B. O'Callaghan, *Laws and Ordinances of New Netherland, 1638–1674* (Albany, NY: Weed, Parsons, and Co., 1868), 60–61, 93–94, 98–99.

37. O'Callaghan, 258–259, 310. See also Goodfriend, "Struggle."

38. O'Callaghan, 60–61, 98–99 (emphasis added).

39. O'Callaghan (and 93–94).

40. For specific examples, see A. J. F. van Laer, trans., *Minutes of the Court of Rensselaerswyck, 1648–1652* (Albany, NY: 1922), 85; Charles T. Gehring, ed. and trans., *Council Minutes, 1652–1654* (Baltimore: Genealogical Publishing, 1983), 120–122; Charles T. Gehring, ed. and trans., *Fort Orange Court Minutes, 1652–1660* (Syracuse, NY: Syracuse University Press, 1990), 248–249. For the church and WIC working together to regulate marriage banns and force couples to marry, see also Gehring, *Fort Orange Court Minutes*, 162–164; and the colonial council minutes of August 9, 1660, at the New York State Archives, New York Colonial Manuscripts (hereafter cited as NYCM), 9:356.

41. Gehring, *Council Minutes, 1652–1654*, 120–122, 171, 183–184.

42. In "Creating an Orderly Society: The Regulation of Marriage and Sex in the Dutch Atlantic World, 1621–1674" (PhD diss., Columbia University, 2014), Deborah Hamer writes more about order and company authority than Calvinism per se, but the dissertation is relevant to this discussion.

43. Linda Biemer, "Criminal Law and Women in New Amsterdam and Early New York," in Zeller, *Beautiful and Fruitful Place*, 73–82.

44. A. J. F. van Laer, ed., *Council Minutes, 1638–1649* (Baltimore: Genealogical Publishing, 1974), 46–47; Berthold Fernow, ed., *The Records of New Amsterdam from 1653 to 1674*, 7 vols. (New York, 1897), 3:23. Other court records consulted for Dutch colonial crime include Van Laer, *Minutes of the Court of Rensselaerswyck*; Gehring, *Fort Orange Court Minutes*; Peter R. Christoph, Kenneth Scott, and Kenn Stryker-Rodda, eds., and

Dingman Versteeg, trans., *Kingston Papers*, vol. 1 (Baltimore: Genealogical Publishing, 1976); Gehring, *Council Minutes, 1652–1654*; Charles T. Gehring, ed. and trans., *Council Minutes, 1655–1656* (Syracuse, NY: Syracuse University Press, 1995); and the still-to-be-published records (NYCM) at the New York State Archives.

45. NYCM 8:1049–1057.

46. New Amsterdam's consistory records are in A. P. G. Jos van der Linde, ed., *Old First Dutch Church of Brooklyn, New York: First Book of Records, 1660–1752* (Baltimore, MD: Genealogical Publishing, 1983).

47. Van Laer, *Minutes of the Court of Rennselaerwyck*, 111–112.

48. Van Laer, *Council Minutes, 1638–1649*, 46–47; Fernow, *Records*, 3:23.

49. Hamer, "Creating an Orderly Society," 128–129. For examples of warnings and a case that didn't stick, see Gehring, *Council Minutes, 1652–1654*, 137; Fernow, *Records*, 1:299–300.

50. Fernow, *Records*, 1:317; Gehring, *Minutes, 1655–1656*, 69; NYCM 9:681.

51. Van Laer, *Council Minutes*, 271; Fernow, *Records*, 3:328, 5:272. For the family, see Fernow, *Records*, 3:102–114 and NYCM 9:29–35.

52. Shorto, *Island*, 187–189.

53. Van Laer, *Council Minutes*, 326–328; NYCM 9:294–298. Only the translations from the latter are my own.

54. The proclamations are interpreted differently in Merwick, *Stuyvesant Bound*, chap. 7, and in Jaap Jacobs, "'Hot Pestilential and Unheard-Of Fevers, Illnesses, and Torments': Days of Fasting and Prayer in New Netherland," *New York History* 96, nos. 3–4 (Summer–Fall 2015): 284–300. My own view is closer to Merwick's on this issue, though I used Jacobs (esp. p. 288) for some information in this paragraph and the next two.

55. Van Laer, *Council Minutes*, 506–510.

56. Van Laer, 506–510.

57. Gehring, *Council Minutes, 1655–1656*, 207–209. See also Gehring, *Council Minutes, 1652–1654*, 159; NYCM 15:122; Jacobs, "Hot Pestilential," 297.

58. Gehring, *Council Minutes, 1655–1656*, 207–209. See also Van der Linde, *Old First*, 33–35, 69–73.

59. NYCM 10/2:292–294; NYCM 10/3:119; Goodfriend, "Struggle."

60. For "communication," see Volckering's letter in Gehring and Schiltkamp, *Curaçao Papers*, 229–230. See also the flow of colonial news in SAA ACA 157:408–410; 168:67. Klooster gives Curaçao's population in *Illicit Riches*, 59.

61. Gehring and Schiltkamp, *Curaçao Papers*, 216–217, 221–222. The baptismal register is at SAA ACA 224:27–34. An alternative view, that the Dutch Atlantic was never integrated after Brazil, is found in Pieter Emmer and Wim Klooster, "The Dutch Atlantic, 1600–1800: Expansion without Empire," *Itinerario* 23, no. 2 (1999): 48–69; Pieter Emmer, "The West India Company, 1621–1791: Dutch or Atlantic?," in *The Dutch in the Atlantic Economy, 1580–1800* (Brookfield, VT: Ashgate, 1998), 65–90.

62. SAA ACA 224:11–13, 17–21; 157:415, 425; NHA ASNH 5 (August 9, 1661).

63. SAA ACA 224:35. See also 24–25.

64. SAA ACA 158:92; 168:51; 224:39.

65. David Steven Cohen, "How Dutch Were the Dutch of New Netherland?" *New York History* 62, no. 1 (January 1981): 43–60.

66. Frederick J. Zwierlein, *Religion in New Netherland, 1623–1664* (New York: Da Capo Press, 1971), 144. For foreign language needs and foreign clergy, see D. L. Noorlander, "Serving God and Mammon: The Reformed Church and the Dutch West India Company in the Atlantic World, 1621–1674" (PhD diss., Georgetown University, 2011), 105–117.

67. *ERSNY* 1:319, 511, 519. I changed one spelling: "points" instead of "poincts."

68. For examples of Puritans and "independents" lumped in among other dissenters, see ibid., 1:335, 396–397.

69. Gehring, *Council Minutes, 1652–1654*, 13.

70. The treatment of religious dissenters in New Netherland is covered most thoroughly (though at times problematically) in Zwierlein, *Religion*, chaps. 6–8. Zwierlein uses some questionable sources. See also Smith, *Religion and Trade*, 190–211; De Jong, *Reformed Church*, 35–38; Rink, *Holland*, 230–233; Jacobs, *Colony*, chap. 5; Evan Haefeli, *New Netherland and the Dutch Origins of American Religious Liberty* (Philadelphia: University of Pennsylvania Press, 2012), chaps. 2–7 (and p. 105 for the deportation of Lutheran ministers from the Delaware).

71. *ERSNY* 1:361–362. The two men were English, not Lutherans, and Stuyvesant rescinded one of the banishments. *ERSNY* calls them Baptists, but I find no evidence of that in the sources. See also Gehring, *Fort Orange Court Minutes*, 216, 220.

72. *ERSNY* 1:408–409.

73. O'Callaghan, *Laws*, 211.

74. *ERSNY* 1:317–318.

75. *ERSNY*, 1:387, 449, 483.

76. Smith, *Religion and Trade*, chap. 15.

77. Jonathan Israel, *The Dutch Republic: Its Rise, Greatness, and Fall, 1477–1806* (Oxford: Clarendon, 1995), chap. 30; Herbert Rowen, *John de Witt: Statesman of the "True Freedom"* (Cambridge: Cambridge University Press, 2003). For De la Court's writings on tolerance, see his *Interest van Holland often Gronden van Hollands welvaren* (Amsterdam, 1662); or, in English, *The True Interest and Political Maxims of the Republic of Holland* (London, 1746).

78. NA OWIC 17:79–144. De la Court appeared first on October 19, 1667, and continued to attend until the 1672 French invasion. His name appears on the lists of attendees again in 1674.

79. On Amsterdam's Delaware interests, see Haefeli, *New Netherland*, 233–234.

80. *ERSNY* 1:320–322, 324, 423; see also 515–516.

81. *ERSNY*, 1:352, 354–355, 374–375, 378–381, 409–411.

82. *ERSNY*, 1:423, 425, 431.

83. *ERSNY*, 1:440, 471, 476–477, 485–486, 505–506.

84. *ERSNY*, 1:423, 425, 460.

85. Charles T. Gehring, ed. and trans., *Correspondence, 1647–1653* (Syracuse, NY: Syracuse University Press, 2000), 154.

86. NA OWIC 18 (July 18, 1669). For "1658 and 1659," see David Nassi's "Freedoms and Exemptions" in NA ASG, deel 5, 12564.42 (September 12, 1659). Zwierlein (*Religion*, 249n2) thinks the Nassi concessions were modeled on a Zeeland charter from the previous year.

87. *ERSNY* 1:335; Fernow, *Records* 1:290–291.

88. Gehring, *Council Minutes, 1655–1656*, 128. The rest comes from Jacobs, *Colony*, 198–202.

89. *ERSNY* 1:352.

90. Jacobs, "Hot Pestilential," 293.

91. *ERSNY* 1:414.

92. In *New Netherland*, 166, Haefeli calls Stuyvesant's Quaker policy "quite mild" (comparatively speaking). That said, Haefeli's overview of these events is one of the best.

93. *ERSNY* 1:410. For three additional possible deportations during the troubles of 1657–1658, see NYCM 8:991. I didn't count them in my totals because their origins and situation are unclear.

94. Smith, *Religion and Trade*, 224–227; Jacobs, *Colony*, 167–171; Haefeli, *New Netherland*, chap. 6.

95. Haefeli and Jacobs say we don't know what happened next. However, Zwierlein (*Religion*, 234) claims that the six men left for Oyster Bay, "beyond the jurisdiction of the Dutch government."

96. *ERSNY* 1:530 (emphasis added).

97. As of May 2016, the Bowne House Historical Society was describing this incident inaccurately. See the John Bowne biography on their website: http://www .bownehouse.org.

98. *ERSNY* 1:530.

99. *ERSNY*, 1:349, 470.

7. The Harvest Was Great, the Laborers Few

1. The title of this chapter comes from Luke 10:2. The most thorough overview of Dutch missionary theology is L. J. Joosse, *"Scoone Dingen Sijn Swaere Dingen": Een onderzoek naar de motieven en activiteiten in de Nederlanden tot verbreiding van de gereformeerde religie gedurende de eerste helft van de zeventiende eeuw* (Leiden: J. S. Groen en Zoon, 1992). English-only readers will find a useful summary of the book on pp. 591–600. See also L. J. Joosse, *Geloof in de Nieuwe Wereld: ontmoeting met Afrikanen en Indianen, 1600–1700* (Kampen: Kok, 2008), chap. 1; J. A. B. Jongeneel, "The Missiology of Gisbertus Voetius," *Calvin Theological Journal* 26 (1991): 47–79.

2. See Benjamin Schmidt, *Innocence Abroad: The Dutch Imagination and the New World, 1570–1670* (Cambridge: Cambridge University Press, 2001) for the tyranny/savior dynamic in Dutch expansion.

3. The idea that the Dutch weren't interested in ministering to Africans and Native Americans, that they were "indifferent," is ubiquitous. I cited some examples in the introduction. See also Allison Blakely, *Blacks in the Dutch World: The Evolution of Racial Imagery in a Modern Society* (Bloomington: Indiana University Press, 1993), 210; Leon van den Broeke, Hans Krabbendam, and Dirk Mouw, eds., *Transatlantic Pieties: Dutch Clergy in Colonial America* (Grand Rapids, MI: Eerdmans, 2012), 28; Frederick J. Zwierlein, *Religion in New Netherland, 1623–1664* (New York: Da Capo Press, 1971), chap. 9.

4. SAA ACA 163:3–4 (also in *ERSNY* 1:92–94); NA ASG, deel 2, 5755 (December 12, 1635) (reissued later and recorded in SAA ACA 212:170–176). Other instructions are found in SAA ACA 19 (December 3, 1619; September 9, 1632).

5. ZA ACW 2:10.

6. Some of the challenges listed in this and the next paragraph are discussed in Gerald de Jong, "The Dutch Reformed Church and Negro Slavery in Colonial America," *Church History* 40, no. 4 (December 1971): 423–436; Willem Frijhoff, "Jesuits, Calvinists, and Natives: Attitudes, Agency, and Encounters in the Early Christian Missions in the North," *De Halve Maen* 81, no. 3 (Fall 2008): 47–54; Jaap Jacobs, *New Netherland: A Dutch Colony in Seventeenth-Century America* (Leiden: Brill, 2005), 322; Mark Meuwese, "'For the Peace and Well-being of the Country': Intercultural Mediators and Dutch-Indian Relations in New Netherland and Dutch Brazil, 1600–1664" (PhD diss., Notre Dame, 2003); Mark Meuwese, "Dutch Calvinism and Native Americans: A Comparative Study of the Motivations for Protestant Conversion among the Tupis in Northeastern Brazil (1630–1654) and the Mohawks in Central New York (1690–1710)," in *The Spiritual Conversion of the Americas*, ed. James Muldoon (Gainseville: University Press of Florida, 2004), 118–141.

7. Cited in Dienke Hondius, "Afrikanen in Zeeland, Moren in Middelburg," *Zeeland, Tijdschrift van het Koninklijk Zeeuwsch Genootschap der Wetenschappen* 14 (2005), 16. The translation is mine.

8. Blakely, *Blacks*, chap. 1; Pieter Emmer, *The Dutch Slave Trade, 1500–1850*, trans. Chris Emery (New York: Berghahn Books, 2006), chap. 1.

9. Hondius, "Afrikanen," 13–24.

10. Emmer, *Dutch Slave Trade*, chap. 1. For "human nature" and disease, see Ellert de Jonghe, *Waerachtig Verhael vande machtige scheeps armade, toegherust byde moghende E. heeren Staten Generael . . . onder het ghebiet en gheleyde van joncker Pieter vander Does* (Amsterdam, 1600), esp. the conclusion; Ernst van den Boogaart, "Colour Prejudice and the Yardstick of Civility: The Initial Dutch Confrontation with Black Africans, 1590–1635," *Racism and Colonialism: Essays on Ideology and Social Structure*, ed. Robert Ross (Leiden: Leiden University Press, 1982), 33–54.

11. Ernst van den Boogaart and Pieter Emmer, "The Dutch Participation in the Atlantic Slave Trade, 1596–1650," in *The Uncommon Market: Essays in the Economic History of the Atlantic Slave Trade*, ed. Henry A. Gemery and Jan S. Hogendorn (New York: Academic Press, 1979), 353–375; Engel Sluiter, "New Light on the '20 and Odd Negroes' Arriving in Virginia, August 1619," *William and Mary Quarterly* 54, no. 2 (April 1997): 395–398.

12. *Levendich Discovrs vant ghemeyne Lants welvaert, voor desen de Oost, ende nu oock de West-Indische generale Compaignie aenghevanghen, seer notabel om lesen. Door een Lief-Hebber des Vaderlandts* (1622), B3. On the superiority of free labor, see also Willem Usselincx, *Octroy ofte Privilegie, Soo by den Alderdoorluchtigsten Grootmachtigen Vorst ende Heer, Heer Gustaeff Adolph / Der Sweden* ('s-Gravenhage, 1627), 3–5.

13. NA OWIC 1:1–2, 8 (July 24, August 3–4, 1623).

14. The 1624 agenda is in NA OWIC 1:98 (September 10, 1624). I wrote about these themes in chapters 2 and 3. On freeing the Portuguese (and Portuguese Jews), see also Jan Moerbeeck, *Redenen waeromme de West-Indische Compagnie dient te trachten het Landt van Brasilia den Coninck van Spangien to ontmachtigen* (Amsterdam, 1624).

15. *Waerachtigh verhael van het succes van de Vlote onder den Admirael Iaqves l'Hermite in de Zuyt-zee, op de Custen van Peru, en de Stadt Lima* (1625), backside of A3. For the *encomenderos*, see the proposed alliance of the States General with the Lords of Peru

in Joan Aventroot, *Sendbrief van Joan Aventroot tot den Grootmachtichsten Coninck van Spaengien* (Amsterdam, 1615).

16. Van den Boogaart and Emmer, "Dutch Participation."

17. SAA ACA 6:160.

18. NA OWIC 68 (May 25, 1637); Caspar van Baerle, *The History of Brazil under the Governorship of Count Johan Maurits of Nassau, 1636–1644*, trans. Blanche T. van Berckel-Ebeling Koning (Gainesville, FL: University Press of Florida, 2011), 124. The "necessity" argument is also found in NA OWIC 8:151–152; 53:22; NA ASG, deel 2, 5756, 53–54, 70a (June 1, 1641).

19. NA OWIC 8:160–172; NA OWIC 68 (May 4 and 25, 1637); Van Baerle, *History*, 51.

20. NA ASG, deel 2, 5753 (April 4, 1634); *Groot Placaet Boeck, vervattende de Placaeten, Ordonnantien ende Edicten van de Doorluchtige, Hoogh Mog. Heeren Staten Generael der Vereenighde Nederlanden* (The Hague, 1658), 622; NA OWIC 48, instruction 85–86 (August 23, 1636).

21. Godefridus Udemans, *'t Geestelick Roer van 't Coopmans Schip*, 3rd ed. (Dordrecht, 1655), 313–319.

22. Udemans, 313–319; NA OWIC 8:151–152.

23. NA OWIC 64:27.

24. Slave lists appear as "Verkooprekening van negros" or "Recueil van de verkochte negros," all in NA OWIC 52–60. The first one is NA OWIC 52:47 (October 24, 1636) and the last one is NA OWIC 60:52 (April 5, 1645). For slaves acquired from the council, see, for example, NA OWIC 69 (October 26, 1641).

25. NA OWIC 57:39. For "domestic," see also the October 26 citation in the last note and NA OWIC 60:15 (December 7, 1644).

26. NA OWIC 68 (May 16, 1639); 71 (January 24, 1647).

27. NA OWIC 58:344 (November 7, 1642); 60:10 (February 13, 1645).

28. NA OWIC 52:48 (January 23, 1637); 56:311 (September 11, 1641).

29. NA OWIC 51:25 (June 11, 1636). References to the deacons and hospitals appear throughout WIC records. See, for example, NA OWIC 68 (August 6, 1635; February 1, 1636); 70 (January 16, 1645); 71 (March 22, 1646), and the Hamel report at KB, Special Collections, 76 A 16.

30. Johannes de Mey, *Schriftmattige Oeffeninghen over Bysondere vraegh-stucken ende gevallen der gewisse, rakende de Christelicke bescheydentheyt* (Middelburg, 1659), 31–41; Georgius de Raad, *Bedenckinghen over den Guineeschen Slaefhandel der Gereformeerden met de Papisten* (Vlissingen, 1665), 29 (for "Christian freedom"). Rev. Jacobus Dapper of Brazil was also worried about selling slaves to Catholics: GASD ACZ 2:37.

31. De Mey addresses this issue in *Schriftmattige*, 40.

32. Charles Boxer, *The Dutch in Brazil* (Hamden, CT: Archon Books, 1973), 83–84; Pierre Moreau, *Klare en Waarachtige Beschryving van de leste Beroerten en Afval der Portugezen in Brasil* (Amsterdam, 1652), 16–17.

33. Jacobus Hondius, *Swart Register van duysent Sonden* (Amsterdam, 1679), 363–364.

34. Early descriptions are found in Pieter de Marees, *Description and Historical Account of the Gold Kingdom of Guinea (1602)*, ed. and trans. Albert van Dantzig and Adam Jones (New York: Oxford University Press, 1987), 67–72; "Samuel Brun's Voyages" and "Michael Hemmersam's Description," in *German Sources for West African History,*

1559–1669, trans. and ed. Adam Jones (Wiesbaden: Franz Steiner Verlag GMBH, 1983), 86, 117–119; Nicolaes van Wassenaer, *Historisch verhael*, 21 vols. (Amsterdam: 1622–1635), 6:67–68, 7:88, 8:26–28; Johannes de Laet, "From 'The New World,'" in *Narratives of New Netherland*, ed. J. Franklin Jameson (New York: Charles Scribner's Sons, 1909), 36–60. For "the Devil," see also Gerrit Gerbrantsz Hulck, *Een Korte Beschrijvinge vande Staponjers in Brasiel* (Alkmaar, 1635).

35. The directors wrote about good examples in NA OWIC 1:126–128; 8:153–154, 175–176. For similar expectations in New Netherland, see *Documents relating to New Netherland, 1624–1626, in the Henry E. Huntington Library* (San Marino, CA: Huntington Library, 1924), 2–4, 72–75.

36. NA OWIC 8:135; 11 (February 3, 1634); SAA AKA 243:25.

37. Meuwese, "'For the Peace,'" chaps. 1–2; Meuwese, "Dutch Calvinism." See also J. A. G. de Mello, *Nederlanders in Brazilie, 1624–1654* (Zutphen: Walburg, 2001), chap. 4.

38. NA OWIC 49:135. See also NA OWIC 59:142.

39. NA OWIC 1:126–128; 8:19, 160–172. On the Tupi and Portuguese, see *Extract uyt den Brief vande Politijcque Raeden in Brasil* ('s-Gravenhage, 1635); Michiel van Groesen, ed., *The Legacy of Dutch Brazil* (New York: Cambridge University Press, 2014), 61.

40. NA VS 1408 (October 20, 1635); NA OWIC 50:124; 68 (July 2, 1636).

41. NA OWIC 68 (July 2, 1636).

42. SAA ACA 4:65; NA OWIC 8:189–190. See also NA OWIC 51:23.

43. UA ASU 212:5–16; NA OWIC 68 (April 16, 1637).

44. NA OWIC 53:22.

45. NA OWIC 53:4; 68 (January 9, 1638); B. N. Teensma, ed. and trans., *Vincent Joachim Soler's Seventeen Letters, 1636–1643* (Rio de Janeiro: Editora Index, 1999), 51–53. In *Brothers in Arms, Partners in Trade: Dutch-Indigenous Alliances in the Atlantic World, 1595–1674* (Leiden: Brill, 2011), chap. 3, Meuwese writes about secular captains and other aspects of the Dutch-Tupi relationship.

46. Vincentius Soler, *Cort and sonderlingh Verhael* (Amsterdam, 1639); UA ASU 212:25–32 (Kemp); NA OWIC 68–70 (May 16, 1639; November 26, 1640; July 30, 1644); 56:303. For the directors, see NA OWIC 8:359, 366–368.

47. Soler, *Cort and sonderlingh Verhael*; UA ASU 212:25–32, 37–42; NA OWIC 55:116.

48. Soler, *Cort and sonderlingh Verhael*; UA ASU 212:25–32, 37–42; NA OWIC 55:116; 53:4; SAA ACA 163:28.

49. Frans Schalkwijk, *The Reformed Church in Dutch Brazil, 1630–1654* (Zoetermeer: Boekencentrum, 1998), 218–227. I explore the catechism affair (and the reaction at home) in D. L. Noorlander, "The Reformed Church and the Regulation of Religious Literature in the Early Dutch Atlantic World," *Itinerario* 42, no. 3 (December 2018): 375–402.

50. SAA ACA 163:96–99; NA OWIC 9:1–25; 69 (May 12, July 6, and August 1, 1642).

51. NA OWIC 69 (June 11 and July 11, 1642); 57:8. De Mello writes about educational plans in *Nederlanders*, chap. 4.

52. NA OWIC 59:142. For the rest, see NA OWIC 9:39–41, 180, 187; 52:32; 57:8; 123; 58:268; 59:142; 60:10; 69–70 (February 5, June 11, and July 11, 1642; February 4 and October 5, 1643).

53. ZA ACW 73 (October 17, 1641); NA OWIC 69 (October 23, 1641). For the integration of the Dutch Atlantic in the Johan Maurits years, see Pieter Emmer and Wim Klooster, "The Dutch Atlantic, 1600–1800: Expansion without Empire," *Itinerario* 23, no. 2 (1999): 48–69. For Brazil and Africa, see Klaas Ratelband, *Nederlanders in West Afrika, 1600–1650: Angola, Kongo en São Tomé* (Zutphen: Walburg Pers, 2000), chap. 8; Schalkwijk, *Reformed Church*, 98–99. See also the letters between the regions in NA OWIC 49–67.

54. SAA ACA 157:23; 4:195–198.

55. The Recife classis mentioned its correspondence with Hendricks in ZA ACW 73 (October 17, 1641). For the rest, see SAA ACA 157:63, 78–79; NA OWIC 9:159–161.

56. ZA ACW 73 (October 17, 1641); NA OWIC 56:272; NA, toegangsnr. 1.10.69, Collectie Radermacher, inv. nr. 545, suggestions 10–11 (February 12, 1642). See also NA ASG, deel 2, 5756, 167–176, instructions 11–13. The most thorough overview of the Luanda conquest is Ratelband, *Nederlanders.*

57. SAA ACA 157:75; NA ASG, deel 2, 5756, 145–147 (February 18, March 4, 1642); SAA ACA 4:246. The Ketel letter is in UA ASU 279 (September 15, 1642).

58. F. Capelle, "Beschriving van Angola," NA OWIC 46 (n.d.); 58:266 (October 14, 1642). See also NA OWIC 58:211; NA ASG, deel 5, 12564.12, f. 23, May 21, 1643.

59. NA OWIC 58:242; NA ASG, deel 2, 5760, 670–671 (March 28, 1642); UA, toegangsnr. 76, Archief van het Huis Zuilen, inv. nr. 922, f. 41, March 28, 1642.

60. NA OWIC 9:1–25.

61. NA OWIC 69 (August 28, 1642). On the question of regulation, see also UA ASU 212:25–32, 37–42; NA OWIC 55:116. Rev. Kemp drew the same link between weakness and slavery in NA OWIC 75 (March 24, 1651).

62. SAA ACA 157:79, 90–92; 4:268. For Doreslaer's return, see NA OWIC 69 (November 26, 1642); NA ACD 83 (July 6–25, 1643), art. 12; Schalkwijk, *Reformed Church*, 221–223.

63. SAA ACA 4:312; NA OWIC 69 (February 2, 1643); 58:268. Johan Maurits said he could have persuaded Kesseler to stay in Brazil if not for the controversy.

64. NA OWIC 57:153.

65. Meuwese, *Brothers*, chap. 3. For "assure," see NA OWIC 58:268 and the Hamel report, 25–27.

66. NA OWIC 63:10; Ratelband, *Nederlanders.* Elmina's school struggled for the same reasons as its predecessor: communication issues, African indifference, etc. See "Michael Hemmersam's Description," in Jones, *German Sources*, 118.

67. NA OWIC 61:59; 62:57a. For the fate of the slave mission, see NA OWIC 71 (September 28, 1645); 61:7.

68. Early WIC expectations regarding Indian treatment are laid out in *Documents relating to New Netherland*, 2–4, 72–75. See also Donna Merwick, *The Shame and the Sorrow: Dutch-Amerindian Encounters in New Netherland* (Philadelphia: University of Pennsylvania Press, 2006), 33–86. Jeroen Dewulf argues that Dutch attitudes and policies toward slaves changed after Brazil in "Emulating a Portuguese Model: The Slave Policy of the West India Company and the Dutch Reformed Church in Dutch Brazil (1630–1654) and New Netherland (1614–1664) in Comparative Perspective," *Journal of Early American History* 4 (2014): 3–36.

69. Michaelius to Van Foreest in Albert Eekhof, *Jonas Michaelius, Founder of the Church in New Netherland* (Leiden: A. W. Sijthoff, 1926), 110.

70. *ERSNY* 1:58. I tweaked the *ERSNY* translation. I also added quotation marks to three words for the sake of clarity.

71. *ERSNY*, 1:56–62. Meuwese argues that the Indians purposefully kept ministers like Michaelius at arm's length in "For the Peace," 123–124.

72. *ERSNY* 1:62.

73. Willem Frijhoff, *Wegen van Evert Willemsz. Een Hollands weeskind op zoek naar zichzelf, 1607–1647* (Nijmegen: SUN, 1995), chap. 18.

74. Ira Berlin, *Many Thousands Gone: The First Two Centuries of Slavery in North America* (Cambridge, MA: Harvard University Press, 1998), intro. and chap. 2. See also Joyce Goodfriend, "Black Families in New Netherland," *Journal of the Afro-American Historical and Genealogical Society* 5, nos. 3–4 (Fall–Winter 1984): 94–107; Joyce Goodfriend, "The Souls of New Amsterdam's African American Children," in *Opening Statements: Law, Jurisprudence, and the Legacy of Dutch New York*, ed. Albert M. Rosenblatt and Julia C. Rosenblatt (Albany: State University of New York Press, 2013), chap. 2; Patricia Bonomi, "'Swarms of Negroes Comeing about My Door': Black Christianity in Early Dutch and English North America," *Journal of American History* 103, no. 1 (June 2016): 34–58; Chris Moore, "A World of Possibilities: Slavery and Freedom in Dutch New Amsterdam," in *Slavery in New York*, ed. Ira Berlin and Leslie M. Harris (New York: New Press, 2005), 29–56.

75. NHA ACALK 3:42; *ERSNY* 1:147.

76. "A Short Account of the Mohawk Indians, by Reverend Johannes Megapolensis, Jr., 1644," in Jameson, *Narratives*, 172–178.

77. *ERSNY* 1:267–268, 322–323, 326–327, 398.

78. Charles T. Gehring, ed. and trans., *Council Minutes, 1655–1656* (Syracuse, NY: Syracuse University Press, 1995), 132–136, 207–209, 257, 299; *ERSNY* 1:451–453.

79. *ERSNY* 1:534–535, 545–546. See also A. P. G. Jos van der Linde, ed., *Old First Dutch Church of Brooklyn, New York: First Book of Records, 1660–1752* (Baltimore, MD: Genealogical, 1983), 69, 71, 73; Peter R. Christoph, Kenneth Scott, and Kenn Stryker-Rodda, eds., and Dingman Versteeg, trans., *Kingston Papers*, vol. 1 (Baltimore: Genealogical Publishing, 1976), 126–127.

80. *ERSNY* 1:534–535, 545–546.

81. SAA ACA 6:336; *ERSNY* 1:525–526, 533–534; SAA ACA 158:14–15. See also Gerald F. de Jong, *The Dutch Reformed Church in the American Colonies* (Grand Rapids, MI: Eerdmans, 1978), chap. 11.

82. NA OWIC 50:26, 80.

83. Charles T. Gehring and J. A. Schiltkamp, eds. and trans., *Curaçao Papers, 1640–1665* (Interlaken, NY: Heart of the Lakes Publishing, 1987), 5, 74–75; *Livre Synodal contenant les articles resolus dans les Synodes des Eglises wallonnes des Pays-Bas, 1563–1685* (La Haye: Martinus Nijhoff, 1896), April 25–27, 1657, art. 4.

84. NA OWIC 54:197; 224:4–5; SAA ACA 157:249–250; 224:6, 8–10. For the passenger lists, see Gehring and Schiltkamp, *Curaçao Papers*, 171.

85. NA OWIC 24:4–5; SAA ACA 4:335. Calvinist restrictions on baptism and marriage weren't new: see SAA AKA 4:309; Gehring and Schiltkamp, *Curaçao Papers*, 5; *Livre Synodal*, September 13, 1656, art. 19.

86. SAA ACA 157:415, 425, 432–433; 224:11–13, 17–21; 6:229.

87. NA OWIC 25:106, 26:61, 73; Gehring and Schiltkamp, *Curaçao Papers*, 74. See also Rev. de Mey's eyewitness account of kidnapping and enslavement in *Schriftmattige*, 33.

88. NYCM 13:117.

89. These transitions are covered in Wim Klooster, *Illicit Riches: Dutch Trade in the Caribbean, 1648–1795* (Leiden: KITLV Press, 1998), chap. 3; Cornelis Goslinga, *The Dutch in the Caribbean and on the Wild Coast, 1580–1680* (Gainesville: University of Florida Press, 1971), chaps. 12–13, 16. See also Stuart Schwartz, "Looking for a New Brazil," in Van Groesen, *Legacy*, 41–58.

90. The biggest Dutch proponent of the Hamitic myth was the theologian Johannes Picardt, *Korte beschrijvinge van eenige Vergetene en Verborgene Antiquiteiten der Provintien en Landen Gelegen tusschen de Noord-Zee, de Yssel, Emse en Lippe* (Amsterdam, 1660). Van den Boogaart argues in "Colour Prejudice" that the myth was never as important to the Dutch as it was to others. On its becoming important in the later seventeenth century, see Joosse, *Geloof*, chap. 9, and Joosse, "Zeeuwse predikanten en hun visie op slavernij en slavenhandel, 1640–1740," *Archief: Mededelingen van hen Koninklijk Zeeuwsch Genootschap der Wetenschappen* (2005): 77–98.

91. *ERSNY* 1:548–549. On the slave trade in New Netherland, including changing attitudes and new racial walls, see Joyce D. Goodfriend, "Burghers and Blacks: The Evolution of a Slave Society at New Amsterdam," *New York History* 59 (April 1978): 125–144; Frijhoff, *Wegen*, chap. 18; Jaap Jacobs, *The Colony of New Netherland: A Dutch Settlement in Seventeenth-Century America* (Ithaca, NY: Cornell University Press, 2009), 172–176; Dewulf, "Emulating"; Bonomi, "Swarms."

92. ZA ASV 1784 (January 2, 1660).

93. SAA ACA 224:35, 39, 44–49 (esp. the postscript).

94. Basseliers's letters are in the back of J. M. van der Linde, *Surinaamse Suikerheren en Hun Kerk: Plantagecolonie en handelskerk ten tijde van Johannes Basseliers, predikant en planter in Suriname, 1667–1689* (Wageningen: H. Veenman en Zonen N. V., 1966); see esp. 198–202.

8. God and Mammon in the Dutch Atlantic World

1. For Amsterdam, see SAA ACA 6:446, 448; 157:437; 158:57; 165:105; NA OWIC 15:3, 252. For Zeeland, see GAV AKV 364 (April 11, 1663; November 20, 1670); ZA ACW 5:152–155, 165, 204; 6:235. I wrote about declining church activity in chapter 2.

2. Diarmaid MacCulloch, *The Reformation: A History* (New York: Viking, 2004), 230–240. See also George L. Smith, *Religion and Trade in New Netherland: Dutch Origins and American Development* (Ithaca, NY: Cornell University Press, 1973), chap. 2.

3. For Christian concerns about wealth, see Simon Schama, *The Embarrassment of Riches: An Interpretation of Dutch Culture in the Golden Age* (New York: Vintage, 1987).

4. In *The Dutch Seaborne Empire, 1600–1800* (London: Penguin, 1990), app. 2, Charles Boxer lists pay rates at ƒ30–36 (lay clergy) and ƒ80–100 (ministers). My numbers come from a variety of sources. Because of the pay differences outlined above, I would put the averages at about ƒ24 and ƒ80, respectively. For low indigenous pay, see NA OWIC 69 (July 12, 1642).

5. For the equal pay controversy, see NA OWIC 24:79; 25:51.

6. G. Groenhuis discusses clerical pay and social standing (at home) in *De Predikanten: De Sociale Positie van de Gereformeerde Predikanten in de Republiek der Verenigde Nederlanden voor 1700* (Groningen: Wolters-Noordhoof, 1977). In *Wegen van Evert Willemsz. Een Hollands weeskind op zoek naar zichzelf, 1607–1647* (Nijmegen: SUN, 1995), chap. 13, Willem Frijhoff suggests that confined spaces gave clergy extra power.

7. L. J. Joosse, *Geloof in de Nieuwe Wereld: ontmoeting met Afrikanen en Indianen, 1600–1700* (Kampen: Kok, 2008), 115–119.

8. NA OWIC 14:196; 24:79; SAA ACA 4:242; 157:28, 33, 59, 61–63. See the report from Brazil that the problem was fixed: SAA ACA 157:114–115.

9. For cost-of-living complaints, see NA OWIC 23:123; 26:92. J. A. G. de Mello also deals with high costs in *Nederlanders in Brazilie, 1624–1654* (Zutphen: Walburg, 2001), chap. 2.

10. The housing controversy reached its peak in 1642. See NA OWIC 69 (August 20, 1642); 57:227. For the *f* 6 raise, see NA OWIC 8:313, 317–318, 330; and 56:1, when clergy thanked the directors. Examples of differing (and rising) *kostgeld* are found in NA OWIC 68 (March 2 and May 6, 1637); 75 (June 1, 1651).

11. For Kemp and Apricius, see NA ASG, deel 5, 12564.42 (September 1659). For Hermannius, see SAA ACA 6:78. For Megapolensis and Drisius, see *ERSNY* 1:541. I wrote about the costs of a house and the basic needs of laborers in Holland in chap. 2.

12. NA OWIC 68–70 (July 28, 1636; September 11, 1638; May 21, 1639; April 5, August 6, and November 2, 1641; February 6, March 18, April 5 and 16, May 20, September 1, and October 9, 1642; January 2 and February 5, 1643; June 23, 1644); 55:132. For the Jewish fine and the Huguenot chapel, see Frans Schalkwijk, *The Reformed Church in Dutch Brazil, 1630–1654* (Zoetermeer: Boekencentrum, 1998), 262–263.

13. See chapter 6, as well as *ERSNY* 1:157, 169, 344, 372–373, 495; Gerald F. de Jong, *The Dutch Reformed Church in the American Colonies* (Grand Rapids, MI: Eerdmans, 1978), 28–34.

14. Schalkwijk, *Reformed*, 121–128. For the deacons in charge of the hospital, which was abnormal, see NA OWIC 68 (February 1, 1636); 51:25. For fines, prizes, and money from the directors or churches of the Netherlands, see, for example, NA OWIC 68–69 (May 11, 1637; March 22, 1638; January 27, 1642; April 20, 1652); 14:163–164; SAA AKA 149:102.

15. Charles T. Gehring, ed. and trans., *Council Minutes, 1655–1656* (Syracuse, NY: Syracuse University Press, 1995), 53. The deacons got *f* 500 in prize money in 1648: see A. J. F. van Laer, ed., *Council Minutes, 1638–1649* (Baltimore: Genealogical Publishing, 1974), 567. See also Janny Venema, "Poverty and Charity in Seventeenth-Century Beverwijck/Albany, 1652–1700," *New York History* 80, no. 4 (October 1999): 369–390.

16. Harm Zwarts, "Reformed Deaconries as Providers of Credit in Dutch Settlements, 1650–1700," *New York History* 96, nos. 3–4 (Fall 2015): 301–317. For WIC/government loans, see *ERSNY* 1:267–268; A. P. G. Jos van der Linde, ed., *Old First Dutch Church of Brooklyn, New York: First Book of Records, 1660–1752* (Baltimore, MD: Genealogical, 1983), 15, 175.

17. Gehring, *Council Minutes, 1655–1656*, 299; *ERSNY* 1:541.

18. I wrote about the African schools in chapter 7. For Curaçao, see, for example, SAA ACA 157:249–250, 415; and for Brazil, where employees didn't have to contribute, NA OWIC 68 (March 11, 1637). According to NA OWIC 57:38, there were five Dutch schoolmasters in Brazil in 1642. For New Netherland, see Charles T. Gehring and Nancy A. Kelley, eds., *Education in New Netherland and the Middle Colonies: Papers of the 7th Rensselaerswyck Seminar of the New Netherland Project* (Albany, NY: New Netherland Project, 1985).

19. SAA ACA 157:74; 163:30–32, 96–99; 164:24–38.

20. The cost of a one-month visit to towns south of Recife by two ministers in 1643 was ƒ 330. At other times the High Council paid clergy an extra ƒ 72 per year for services to a nearby fort or set up a monthly fund of ƒ 100 to reimburse circuit preachers. See NA OWIC 68–75 (March 19, 1637; November 26, 1640; June 8 and October 31, 1641; February 11, 1642; February 27, March 2, May 1, and June 11, 1643; July 1 and 25, 1644; April 12, 1645; March 18, 1650; June 12, 1651).

21. NA OWIC (February 2, 1637; April 22, 1639; October 2, 1641; February 2 and 10, July 30, 1644; February 23, 1645; July 11 and 13, November 30, and December 19, 1645); 58:268; 59:40; 60:10. For the classis/synod meeting twenty-three times, see Schalkwijk, *Reformed*, 86.

22. I estimate clerical wages by multiplying the number of clergy (roughly 360 men) by their average wages (ƒ 80 for ministers, ƒ 24 for lay clergy) and average time served (about 66 months), for a total of ƒ 1,013,760. I used a figure of ƒ 80 instead of ƒ 100 for ministers because of *proponent* pay and other differences I saw from time to time and colony to colony. It's only a rough estimate, but a conservative one because there were certainly more clergy than the men I identified.

23. The cabin comes up in SAA ACA 4:242; 157:46, 61–62. See also "Instructions," NA ASG, deel 2, 5755 (December 12, 1635).

24. SAA ACA 2:77; 19:35–36; SAA AKA 4:124, 154, 187. See also the Krol experience at the start of chapter 6.

25. "Dissolute" and "ungodly" are in SAA ACA 5:48; 157:181; 163:174–176. For examples of the rest, see UA ASU 212:25–32; SAA ACA 4:295; 163:148–151.

26. For the double appointments, see NA OWIC 20:65, 77; 21:109, 151; 24:59, 86; 26:66, 117. For Cole, see NA OWIC 69 (November 28, 1642). For Galjaert, see Charles T. Gehring and J. A. Schiltkamp, eds. and trans., *Curaçao Papers, 1640–1665* (Interlaken, NY: Heart of the Lakes Publishing, 1987), 80. For Huygen and Krol, see *ERSNY* 1:45–48, 53.

27. NA OWIC 53:4.

28. For Brazil, see Stadsarchief Deventer, toegangsnr. 703, inv. nr. 50; B. N. Teensma, ed. and trans., *Vincent Joachim Soler's Seventeen Letters, 1636–1643* (Rio de Janeiro: Editora Index, 1999), 53; NA OWIC 53:116; 54:132; 70 (May 15, 1643). For Africa, see NA ASG, deel 5, 12564.12, "Extract" (July 10, 1643); 12564.15, Ketel letter (June 10, 1643); NA OWIC 9:196.

29. NA OWIC 70 (May 15 and 20, 1643).

30. NA OWIC 59:93; 60:75–76. For Stetten's mining during his period of limbo, see NA OWIC 68 (December 7, 1637). In various letters he also mentions having been to the mine seven years before. For his giving up the clerical vocation, see his letter of

June 24, 1645, when he asked the directors to grant him permanent charge over the mine. He would make it his "office and work," he wrote.

31. NA OWIC 50:124, 150; 51:85; 53:116; 55:132.

32. NA OWIC 60:75–76, 86. For his involvement with the mine, see also NA OWIC 9:236–238; 60:10; 70 (January 28, 1644; February 3–8 and 21, April 5–6, and May 12, 1645).

33. NA OWIC 69:93. For the church covering his post, see NA OWIC 70 (July 25, 1644; February 27, 1645).

34. NA OWIC 70 (July 11 and 25, 1645). See also NA OWIC 60:130, 210.

35. NA OWIC 65:77, 106. For "designs" and other quotations, see April 14, 1649. See also Charles Boxer, *The Dutch in Brazil* (Hamden, CT: Archon Books, 1973), 220.

36. *ERSNY* 1:145, 200, 238; A. J. F. van Laer, ed., *Van Rensselaer Bowier Manuscripts: Being the Letters of Kiliaen van Rensselaer, 1630–1643* (Albany: University of the State of New York, 1908), 604–606, 645–655; Gerald de Jong, "Dominie Johannes Megapolensis: Minister to New Netherland," *New York Historical Quarterly* 52, no. 1 (January 1968): 6–47; Janny Venema, *Kiliaen van Rensselaer (1586–1643): Designing a New World* (Hilversum: Verloren, 2010), 263.

37. *ERSNY* 1:314–315, 319–321. For Megapolensis as guest, see A. J. F. van Laer, trans., *Minutes of the Court of Rensselaerswyck, 1648–1652* (Albany, NY: 1922), 41, 43. He also reported to Stuyvesant on the Esopus massacre, and more famously, he advised the governor on surrendering to the English (1664). See *ERSNY* 1:446; De Jong, "Dominie."

38. Matt. 6:24 and 22:21.

39. The story unfolded in the Alkmaar classis: NHA ACALK 4 (November 27, 1647–April 16, 1652). See also NHA ACALK 20 (November 23, 1649).

40. SAA ACA 164:93–94. For this and what follows, see also SAA ACA 5:151, 198; 157:134; 164:64–65, 97–98, 99–101, 102–104; NHA ASNH 4 (August 16, 1650; August 15, 1651; August 12, 1652); WFA, toegangsnr. 1608, Archief van de Classis Enkhuizen, inv. nr. 2, July 28, 1652.

41. Some of these sources are also available in *ERSNY*; see 1:272–273, 284, 288–295, 307.

42. Two other examples include Machiel Zyperus and Petrus Wachtendorp, both of whom were investigated and kept from colonial callings. For Zyperus, see SAA ACA 157:415, 425, 432–433; 224:11–13, 17–21. For Wachtendorp, see SAA ACA 213 (1661); 6:265, 268, 301–302, 345, 371; 157:435; 158:4–5. See also the Doreslaer and Kesseler stories in chapter 7.

43. For Cornelisz, see SAA ACA 157:228. For De Vaux, see esp. NA OWIC 58:268, as well as Schalkwijk, *Reformed*.

44. Matt. 26:52.

45. NA OWIC 25:169; SAA ACA 5:54–56; 157: 139–140, 209–210; 163:148–151; *ERSNY* 1:191, 193–194.

46. For Ketel, see SAA ACA 4:347–349. The two ministers sent to Brazil with the States General fleet in 1647 were Brassicanus and Cammius. For the States General in 1653, see GAV AKV 363 (February 13, 1653); SAA ACA 5:283, 287; 164:138; NA ASG, deel 1, 4846 (March 20, 1653). Schoolmaster Jan Engelaer was sent with this subsidy.

Whether other clergy were sent with the same money before the loss of Brazil is unknown.

47. SAA ACA 224:8–10.

48. For the States General, see SAA ACA 164:172. For clergy who had trouble collecting their wages, see Groninger Archief, toegangsnr. 692, inv. nr. 53, September 11, 1654; SAA ACA 6:78; NA ASG, deel 5, 12564.42, minutes of the Nineteen Lords (September 1659); NA OWIC 6:45, 54. For "bonds," see NA OWIC 28:2. See also SAA ACA 6:483; NA OWIC 15:129, 132; 16:64.

49. SAA ACA 5:6, 10, 48, 100; 157:160–167, 185, 192, 208, 214, 244; 163:146, 148–151, 174–177; 164:24–28; 212:188–190; NHA ACE 4:385; GAV AKV 363 (August 22 and September 4 and 26, 1647); NA OWIC 64:27; 73 (May 1, 1649). See also Schalkwijk, *Reformed*, 208–210.

50. NA ASG, deel 1, 4846 (October 29, 1654); SAA ADA 65:32; NA OWIC 27:57, 91–98, 105.

51. See the Doornick contract in NA OWIC 24:42–44.

52. For Stetten's capture, see NA OWIC 63:35–36; Pierre Moreau, *Klare en Waarachtige Beschryving van de leste Beroerten en Afval der Portugezen in Brasil* (Amsterdam, 1652), 64–66. At first the High Council didn't want to pay Rachel *kostgeld*, but in the end they did (for about three years). See SAA ACA 212:177, 208, 210. Company payments in the Netherlands are mentioned in NA OWIC 27:12, 40. For an example of "alms," see SAA ACA 6:285.

53. SAA ACA 212:167–168. See also her shorter 1650 letter: SAA ACA 212:212.

54. NA OWIC 75 (February 24, 1654); NHA ASNH 4 (August 18, 1654); SAA ACA 5:367, 371; 157:357.

55. ERSNY 1:362, 416–417; Gehring, *Council Minutes, 1655–1656*, 285–286. Stuyvesant also had to intervene for Selyns: ERSNY 1:477. For "sue," see the Blom experience in Peter R. Christoph, Kenneth Scott, and Kenn Stryker-Rodda, eds., and Dingman Versteeg, trans., *Kingston Papers*, vol. 1 (Baltimore: Genealogical Publishing, 1976), 117–120.

56. SAA ACA 6:196; 157:412. For Basseliers, his pay troubles, and his slaves and plantation, see the letters at the back of J. M. van der Linde, *Surinaamse Suikerheren en Hun Kerk: Plantagecolonie en handelskerk ten tijde van Johannes Basseliers, predikant en planter in Suriname, 1667–1689* (Wageningen: H. Veenman en Zonen N. V., 1966).

57. For the post-1650 excess, see F. van Lieburg, *Profeten en hun vaderland: De geografische herkomst van de gereformeerde predikanten in Nederland van 1572 tot 1816* (Zoetermeer: Boekencentrum, 1997), chap. 2.

58. ZA ACW 4:152. See also Cornelis Goslinga, *The Dutch in the Caribbean and on the Wild Coast, 1580–1680* (Gainesville: University of Florida Press, 1971), 422–423.

59. ZA ASV 1784 (October 5, 1660).

60. ZA, toegangsnr. 703, inv. nr. 1:47. See also March 31, 1657; January 1658 (p. 52); April 7 and October 5, 1658; GAV AKV 364 (November 14, 1658). The classis first gave power to deal with Goliath to Pieter Lodewycks. Lodewycks died, however, and Urselius went instead.

61. ZA ACW 4:158–159, 163–164; 45 (January 19, 1662); GAV AKV 364 (February 24 and June 23, 1661); NA OWIC 33:31.

62. SAA ACA 224:39.

63. SAA ACA 224:41–42; NA OWIC 16:121. For "daughters," see Num. 25:1.

64. SAA ACA 224:44–49; 158:162; GAR HV 1463a–b.

65. SAA ACA 158:60; 168:34–35; 210:215.

66. SAA ACA 210:217.

67. For Bogardus, see, for example, ERSNY 1:142, 149–151. For Specht, see SAA ACA 168:75. See also SAA ACA 7:64; 224:43.

Conclusion

1. NA Aanw. 644 (December 15–26, 1652). The Van Riebeeck journal is quoted in Monthly Notes of the Astronomical Society of South Africa 7, no. 1 (January 1948): 10.

2. Niewwe Ongewoon-Wonderlykke Staert-Sterre op 't Recife in Brazil Gezien (Amsterdam, 1653).

3. See, for example, NA OWIC 51:23 (February 20, 1636); ZA ACW 73 (November 4, 1641).

4. Marijke Gijswijt-Hofstra, "Six Centuries of Witchcraft in the Netherlands," in Witchcraft in the Netherlands from the Fourteenth to the Twentieth Century, ed. Marijke Gijswijt-Hofstra and Willem Frijhoff (Rotterdam: Universitaire Pers Rotterdam, 1991), 1–36; Herman Belien, "Judicial Views on the Crime of Witchcraft," in Gijswijt-Hofstra and Willem Frijhoff, Witchcraft, 53–65; Hans de Waardt, "Witchcraft and Wealth: The Case of the Netherlands," in The Oxford Handbook of Witchcraft in Early Modern Europe and Colonial America, ed. Brian P. Levack (Oxford: Oxford University Press, 2013), 232–248.

5. Caspar van Baerle, The History of Brazil under the Governorship of Count Johan Maurits of Nassau, 1636–1644, trans. Blanche T. van Berckel-Ebeling Koning (Gainesville, FL: University Press of Florida, 2011), 33–34, 190. Related astrological examples and prophecy (African prophecies that some Dutch believed in) are found in Nicolaes van Wassenaer, Historisch verhael, 21 vols. (Amsterdam: 1622–1635), 6:67–68, 7:88b. See also the comet interpretation in Charles T. Gehring and J. A. Schiltkamp, eds. and trans., Curaçao Papers, 1640–1665 (Interlaken, NY: Heart of the Lakes Publishing, 1987), 211.

6. General VOC histories include Charles Boxer, Jan Compagnie in War and Peace, 1602–1799: A Short History of the Dutch East-India Company (Hong Kong: Heinemann Asia, 1979); F. S. Gaastra, The Dutch East India Company: Expansion and Decline (Zutphen: Walburg Pers, 2003). For the use of force against nonenemies, see Peter Borschberg, "Hugo Grotius, East India Trade and the King of Johor," Journal of Southeast Asian Studies 30, no. 2 (September 1999): 225–248; Vincent C. Loth, "Armed Incidents and Unpaid Bills: Anglo-Dutch Rivalry in the Banda Islands in the Seventeenth Century," Modern Asian Studies 29, no. 4 (October 1995): 705–740.

7. C. A. L. van Troostenburg de Bruyn, De Hervormde Kerk in Nederlandsch Oost-Indie onder de Oost-Indische Compagnie, 1602–1795 (Arnhem: H.A. Tjeenk Willink, 1884). Other books consulted for this paragraph and for what follows on religion under the VOC include G. M. J. M. Koolen, Een Seer Bequaem Middel: Onderwijs en Kerk onder de 17e-Eeuwse VOC (Kampen: J. H. Kok, 1993); J. J. A. M. Kuepers, The Dutch Reformed Church in Formosa, 1627–1662: Mission in a Colonial Context (Switzerland: Nouvelle Revue de science missionnaire, 1978); Hendrik Niemeijer, Batavia: Een Koloniale Samenleving in de 17de Eeuw (Amsterdam: Balans, 2005). For missions, see also L. J. Joosse, "Scoone

Dingen Sijn Swaere Dingen": Een onderzoek naar de motieven en activiteiten in de Nederlanden tot verbreiding van de gereformeerde religie gedurende de eerste helft van de zeventiende eeuw (Leiden: J. S. Groen en Zoon, 1992). They aren't strictly about religion, but one also gets a sense of Dutch mission in Tonio Andrade, *How Taiwan Became Chinese: Dutch, Spanish, and Han Colonization in the Seventeenth Century* (New York: Columbia University Press, 2008), and G. J. Knaap, *Kruidnagelen en Christenen: De Verenigde Oost-Indische Compagnie en de Bevolking van Ambon, 1656–1696* (Leiden: KITLV, 2004). For Dutch institutions and the church in South Africa, see Ad Biewenga, *De Kaap de Goede Hoop: Een Nederlandse vestigingskolonie, 1680–1730* (Amsterdam: Prometheus, 1999).

8. John E. Wills, *Pepper, Guns and Parleys: The Dutch East India Company and China, 1662–1682* (Cambridge, MA: Harvard University Press, 1974), esp. chap. 1. See also Tonio Andrade, "The Company's Chinese Pirates: How the Dutch East India Company Tried to Lead a Coalition of Pirates to War against China, 1621–1662," *Journal of World History* 15, no. 4 (December 2004): 415–444.

9. Catharina Blomberg, "Jammaboos and Mechanical Apples: Religion in Olof Eriksson Willman's Travel Diary from Japan, 1651–1652," *Itinerario* 22, no. 2 (1998): 85–102.

10. Koolen, *Seer Bequaem Middel*, 186, 192–200; Sinnappah Arasaratnam, *Dutch Power in Ceylon, 1658–1687* (Amsterdam: Djambatan, 1958), chap. 10. For Batavia's publishing history, see Adrienne Zuiderweg, "Nieuwsgaring in Batavia tijdens de VOC," *Tijdschrift voor tijdschriftstudies* 28 (2010): 108–126.

11. Koolen, *Seer Bequaem Middel*, chap. 4; Knaap, *Kruidnagelen*; and (for 5,000) Niemeijer, *Batavia*, pt. 5.

12. Andrade, *How Taiwan Became Chinese*. See also Andrade, "Pirates, Pelts, and Promises: The Sino-Dutch Colony of Seventeenth-Century Taiwan and the Aboriginal Village of Favorolang," *Journal of Asian Studies* 64, no. 2 (May 2005): 295–321.

13. Kuepers, *Dutch Reformed Church*.

14. Kuepers.

15. I get 1,200 by adding my numbers (120) with Van Troostenburg de Bruyn's (900), then using a best educated guess to fill gaps for missing records and years without studies (1674–1800 in the Atlantic world).

16. Robert Ricard, *The Spiritual Conquest of Mexico: An Essay on the Apostolate and Evangelizing Methods of the Mendicant Orders in New Spain, 1523–1572* (Berkeley: University of California Press, 1966), chap. 1; Dauril Alden, *The Making of an Enterprise: The Society of Jesus in Portugal, Its Empire, and Beyond, 1540–1750* (Stanford, CA: Stanford University Press, 1996), pt. 1; "Pedro de León Portocarrero's Description of Lima, Peru," in *Colonial Latin America: A Documentary History*, ed. Kenneth Mills, William B. Taylor, and Sandra Lauderdale Graham (New York: SR Books, 2004), 188.

17. For the literature on Weber, see my introduction.

18. For the priesthood of all believers, see the introduction and chapter 2.

19. Amsterdam ministers are listed in R. B. Evenhuis, *Ook Dat Was Amsterdam: De kerk der hervorming in de gouden eeuw* (Amsterdam: W. Ten Have N. V., 1965–1971), 2:390–391, and 3:362–363.

20. For 1,500 positions, see Willem Frijhoff and Marijke Spies, *Dutch Culture in a European Perspective: 1650, Hard-Won Unity* (New York: Palgrave Macmillan, 2005), 360. Population figures are from Jan de Vries and Ad van der Woude, *The First Modern*

Economy: Success, Failure, and Perseverance of the Dutch Economy, 1500–1815 (Cambridge: Cambridge University Press, 1997), 50.

21. In "Dutch Crossings: Migration between the Netherlands and the New World, 1600–1800," *Atlantic Studies* 2, no. 2 (October 2005): 153–176, Victor Enthoven only gives the Dutch, Indian, and slave figures. For the 30,000 Portuguese and twenty-one ministers, see chapter 5.

22. Johannes de Niet, *Ziekentroosters op de pastorale markt, 1550–1880* (Rotterdam: Erasmus Publishing, 2006), chap. 2.

23. For Jesuit flexibility and the Chinese Rites Controversy, see Liam Matthew Brockey, *Journey to the East: The Jesuit Mission to China, 1579–1724* (Cambridge, MA: Harvard University Press, 2007). See also the Jesuit "flying missions" in James Axtell, *The Invasion Within: The Contest of Cultures in Colonial North America* (New York: Oxford University Press, 1985).

24. Van Baerle, *History*, 144.

25. Charles E. Corwin, *A Manual of the Reformed Church in America, 1628–1922*, 4th ed. (New York, 1902), 735–740.

26. Mark Meuwese, "Dutch Calvinism and Native Americans: A Comparative Study of the Motivations for Protestant Conversion among the Tupis in Northeastern Brazil (1630–1654) and the Mohawks in Central New York (1690–1710)," in *The Spiritual Conversion of the Americas*, ed. James Muldoon (Gainseville: University Press of Florida, 2004), 118–141.

27. Gerald F. de Jong, *The Dutch Reformed Church in the American Colonies* (Grand Rapids, MI: Eerdmans, 1978), esp. chap. 11.

INDEX

admiralties, 22, 50, 195
Adriaensz, Joris, 168
aelmoeseniers, 49
Aertss, Cornelis, 31
Aertss, Jonas, 147
Africa. *See specific region or fort*
alms. *See* deacons; directors (WIC): charitable activity
Alrichs, Jacobs, 155
Alva, Fernando Alvarez de Toledo, duke of, 141
Amazon River, 22, 87
Ambon, 221
America. *See specific fort, colony, or region*
Amsterdam: *burgemeesters*, 42–43, 52, 159–160, 242n18; burghers, 42; Calvinist years, 19, 42, 242n18; Calvinist-Libertine quarrels, 42–45, 111; the Dam, 115; docks, 14, 94; German congregation, 31, 115; growth, 11–14; the Lord's Supper, 100; Lutheran church, 157; map, 40; New Amstel colony, 158, 160; *Nieuwe Kerk*, 39, 44; *Nieuwezijds Kapel*, 54; orphanage, 47, 50; *Oude Kerk*, 11–12, 39, 44, 86; population, 225; religious center, 14, 51, 146; total clergy, 225; trade entrepôt, 2, 51; upper class, 46; *vroedschap*, 42–43, 50; WIC facilities, 47–48, 51, 195–196; *wisselbank*, 2, 47. *See also* classis: of Amsterdam; connivance; consistory: of Amsterdam; West India Company: Amsterdam chamber
Amsterdam (ship), 81
Anabaptism, 34, 156
ancient Israel, 9, 60–61, 66–67, 72–76, 78, 109, 136, 149, 153, 213. *See also* Bible: Old Testament
Andrade, Tonio, 222
Andries, Dirck, 50
Andriesz, Claes, 151
Anglicanism, 32

Angola, 167
Anhalt-Bernburg, 52
Annobón, 81
anti-Catholicism, 14, 60, 89; Brazil, 122, 130–135; Curaçao, 92, 188; Nassau Fleet, 81–82; the slave trade, 172; WIC ideology, 9, 37–38, 60, 71, 85; WIC propaganda, 35. *See also* Catholicism
Antwerp, 37, 134
Appellen, Johannes Harmann Osterdag van, 256n10, 257n32
Apricius, Johannes, 196, 257n32
Arentss, Jan, 22
Arminian controversy, 19–21, 26, 30, 33–34, 36–38, 42–44, 60, 165, 243n26
Arminius, Jacobus, 19, 21, 226, 240n58
Articles and Conditions, 139
Aruba, 91, 142
Asia. *See* East Indies (Dutch)
Assuerus, Meynert, 22, 103
Atlantic history, 7–8
Austria, 15
Aventroot, Joan, 79–85, 168
Axim, 59
Aztecs, 226

Bachiler, Samuel, 32
Backerus, Johannes, 33, 142, 147, 188
Baers, Johannes, 73–75
Baers, Paschasius, 74
Bahia, 23–24, 75, 129, 131, 134, 209
Baldivia, 84
Banckert, Joost, 69–70
banishment: Brazil, 123–124, 127, 129, 131–134; Curaçao, 92, 187, 213–214; Formosa, 223; New Netherland, 151–152, 155–157, 160–162, 206
baptism, 200; Brazil, 175–177, 204; Curaçao, 188; Formosa, 222; Luanda, 180; New Netherland, 86, 95, 139, 147, 154, 159–160, 184–185, 189–190, 200

Barlaeus, Caspar, 133, 169, 218
Bartolotti, Guillelmo, 46–47, 52, 168
Bartringh, Jan, 48
Bas, Albert, 243n26
Bas, Pieter, 125
Basseliers, Johannes, 190–191, 210
Batavia, 220–221
Beaumont, Adriaen, 155, 188
Beck, Artus, 50
Beck, Helena, 50
Beck, Mathias, 119, 155, 204, 212
Becker, Everhard, 242n14
Becker, Samuel, 242n11
Beeck, Isaac van, 52, 150
beeldenstorm. See iconoclasm
Belgic Confession, 33–34
Benderius, Laurentius, 105, 174
Benedictines, 129
Benguela, 72
Benningh, Henricus, 254n64
Berbice, 90–92, 94
Berlin, Ira, 185
Beverwijck, 146
bewindhebbers. See directors (WIC)
Beza, Theodore, 15–16
Bible: Amalekites, 74; in colonies, 97, 99–101, 122, 144, 150–151, 153, 179, 186, 198; on conquest, 60–61; Daniel, 23; David, 61, 67, 75–76; on drawing lots, 80; Elisha, 73; Garden of Eden, 136; Godyn library, 47; Goliath, 61; Gospel of Luke, 45; Joel, 59; Jericho, 61; Joshua, 61; Lamentations, 153; Mary, 16; Matthew, 207; on mission, 164; Moses, 74–75; New Testament, 59, 76; Old Testament, 9, 59–61, 73, 75, 87, 152, 171, 213; Paul, 150; Protestant reformers, 16; Psalms, 53, 67, 69, 74; Revelation, 79; at sea, 65, 67–69; on slavery, 171–172; Sodom and Gomorrah, 152; WIC admirals, 71; WIC propaganda, 45. *See also* ancient Israel; Jesus Christ
Bicker, Andries, 44
Bicker, Cornelis, 44
Biemer, Linda, 150
Bijma, Balthasar van, 77
Biscaretto, Dionisius, 176, 257n32
Blijhooft, Z., 172
Blom, Hermanus, 186
Blommaert, Samuel, 168
Bogaert, Harmen Meyndertsz van den, 152
Bogardus, Everardus, 6, 101–102, 140–142, 184–185, 189, 204, 210, 212–214
Bonaire, 87, 91, 142

Bontemantel, Hans, 243n26
books: Asia, 220–221; Brazil, 122, 175–179, 181, 202, 221; Curaçao, 147; New Netherland, 144, 187, 221; provision of, 22–23, 144, 179, 198; at sea, 65, 67, 73–74; Udemans, 169–170; West Africa, 179
Boston, 227
Bowne, John, 162–163
Boxer, Charles, 71, 75
Bra, Abraham de, 51
Brabant, 97
Brassicanus, Theodorus, 274n46
Brazil: Catholic priests, 127–134, 157, 197, 200; conquest, 23–24, 44, 59, 61, 72–80, 110, 113, 168–169; favored colony, 25, 30, 135; French soldiers, 78; High Council, 57, 78, 110, 117–134, 155, 169–170, 175–179, 182, 197–198, 201–202, 208; links with other colonies, 84, 93, 118, 138, 142, 173, 179–180, 209; map, 112; negotiations with Portugal, 54, 133; population, 111, 225; Portuguese-Dutch relations, 77–78, 110, 113–114, 120–123, 127–135, 196, 220; Portuguese revolt, 114, 134–135, 144, 160, 170, 182–183, 203, 207–209; reformation, 111–120, 146; *schepenen*, 119–120, 124, 127; scholarship on, 6. *See also* church-company relations: Brazil; classis: of Recife; classis: of Paraíba; consistory: of Recife; synod: of Brazil
Broen, Hendrick, 48, 52, 242n11
Broen, Marcus, 52
Brosterhuyzen, Jan van, 104
Brouwer, Hendrick, 83–84
Brouwer Fleet, 79, 83–84, 218
Brussels, 12
Bruyn, Willem, 242n11
Buddhism, 226
Buenos Aires, 83–84
Bullinger, Heinrich, 67–68
Burgh, Albert, 44
Burgundians, 15
Busson, Philbert du, 75

Caanan, 61
Cabo St. Agostinho, 197, 202
Cadzand, 212
Calvin, John, 15–17, 19–20, 47, 97, 192–193
Calvinism. *See* clergy; Dutch Reformed Church
Camarão, Filipe, 182
Cammius, Wilhelmus, 274n46
Canary Islands, 79

www.ingramcontent.com/pod-product-compliance
Lightning Source LLC
Chambersburg PA
CBHW020840270326
41928CB00006B/494